KT-226-773

Acknowledgments

Thanks to Nancy Stevenson, acquisitions editor, for the chance to revise the fifth edition of this incredible reference tool. All credit goes to Bryan Pfaffenberger for creating a dictionary that answers to the how and why things work rather than just what the words mean. If revisions of existing definitions resulted in errors, they are mine. Product developer Steve Shafer, production editor Susan Dunn, and technical editor Chris Pichereau asked penetrating questions and even found ways to improve definitions that have withstood four previous scrubbings. When it became necessary to turn to vendors for information, a few cheerfully sent extensive product literature and patiently answered question after question: Advanced Micro Products, Cyrix, Insight, Lotus Corporation, Intel Corporation, Iomega, and NEC. Finally, special thanks to a great resource, felow Que author Ed Tiley.

—J.P.

Trademarks

Preface

Take a look at any personal computer magazine, and you're likely to come away perplexed. What is *page mode RAM*? What on earth do they mean by *object linking and embedding*? Is my monitor *interlaced* or not, and should I care?

Dealing with obscure computer terminology isn't much fun, but it's an unfortunate fact of modern life. Computer people aren't slowing down the production of new terms—far from it.

What's worse, you really need to deal with many new terms to get the most out of your personal computer system. When you buy a computer, for instance, you'd be wise to learn what a local bus video system can do for you—especially if you want to run Microsoft Windows.

This dictionary is for you, the personal computer user. It's designed to serve as a tool for personal computer users using today's personal computer systems.

That's one reason this dictionary is updated so frequently—five times, in fact, since its first publication in 1990! Computer people keep inventing new terms, so users need an up-to-date dictionary. For you, a dictionary written in the mid 1980s just isn't going to do. In terms of fast-moving computer technology, the mid 1980s is roughly equivalent to the Jurassic, when large lizards roamed the Earth.

The terms you'll find in this dictionary are those that you will encounter as you buy, use, expand, and upgrade your system. Use this dictionary to help you navigate your way through terminological trials such as the following:

- **Buying your computer system.** Do I need *cache memory* or will a *hardware cache* do? What in the heck does it mean that this monitor has .28 dot pitch?

- **Understanding application program capabilities.** Huh? This has *drag-and-drop editing*, you say, but can only serve as a *client* for *OLE*?

- **Reading computer manuals.** What do they mean by "run it in the *background*"?

- **Using computer networks.** You say I shouldn't *lurk* in this *newsgroup*, and that I should *post* a message instead?

This dictionary is easy to use. Each term is listed alphabetically, in boldface type. Any pronunciation guides appear in italic after the term being defined.

If you're baffled by words you've never heard before, they may be acronyms, such as *DIP* or *OLE* or *EISA*. You can turn to the acronym itself to find out what the term stands for (such as *document image processing* for *DIP*), and the spelled-out entry defines the concept in full. You'll find lots of cross-references, too, that help you find related terms and concepts.

A dictionary for users should include tips and cautions as well as definitions and explanations. After all, if you go to all the trouble of looking up *industry-standard bus* and *local bus*, you deserve to be tipped off that a *local bus system* is a lot better! This is a unique feature of this dictionary that you won't find elsewhere.

Using This Dictionary to Learn Computer Concepts

If you're new to personal computing, you can use this dictionary to learn the fundamental concepts of user computing. Disregarding specific brands and products, the following list is a quick overview of some of the more important conceptual entries, broken down by subject category:

- *Adapters and buses:* adapter, address bus, bus, expanded memory, expansion slot, Extended Industry Standard Architecture (EISA), Micro Channel Bus, network interface card, open architecture, open bus system, and video adapter

- *Applications:* communications program, computer-aided design (CAD), database management, database management program, desktop publishing (DTP), draw program, paint program, presentation graphics, spreadsheet program, and word processing program

- *Artificial intelligence and expert systems:* expert system, knowledge base, and knowledge representation

- *Communications:* asynchronous communication, communications program, electronic mail, modem, and terminal emulation

- *Database management:* database, database design, database management, database management program, database management system (DBMS), database structure, data field, data independence, data integrity, data manipulation, data record, record-oriented database management program, relational database management, relational database management program, and table-oriented database management program

- *Desktop publishing:* page description language (PDL), page layout program, and PostScript

- *Disks, disk drives, and secondary storage:* CD-ROM, disk drive, floppy disk, floptical disk, hard disk, optical disk, and secondary storage

- *Display adapters and monitors:* analog monitor, Color Graphics Adapter (CGA), color monitor, digital monitor, Enhanced Graphics Adapter (EGA), Hercules Graphics Adapter, monitor, monochrome display adapter (MDA), monochrome monitor, and Video Graphics Array (VGA)

- *Files and file formats:* binary file, file, file format, file name, graphics file format, and text file

- *Fonts and typography:* bit-mapped font, body type, dingbat, display type, font, font family, outline font, printer font, screen font, and typeface

- *Graphics:* analytical graphics, animation, bit-mapped graphic, draw program, multimedia, paint program, presentation graphics program, raster graphics, and vector graphics

- *Keyboards, mice, and other input devices:* character, cursor-movement keys, extended character set, input, keyboard, keyboard layout, mouse, and trackball

- *Macintosh:* desktop, Finder, graphical user interface (GUI), icon, and System

- *Measurements:* access time, benchmark, dots per inch (dpi), kilobyte, megabyte, megahertz (MHz), pica, point, response time, and transfer rate

- *Memory:* base memory, bit, byte, cache memory, dynamic random-access memory (DRAM), expanded memory, extended memory, firmware, memory, primary storage, random access, random-access memory (RAM), read-only memory (ROM), secondary storage, sequential access, storage, and virtual memory

- *Microprocessors:* 8-bit computer, 16-bit computer, 32-bit computer, central processing unit (CPU), chip, digital, digital computer, instruction cycle, instruction set, integrated circuit, microprocessor, numeric coprocessor, protected mode, real mode, and wait state

- *Microsoft Windows:* application program interface (API), graphical user interface (GUI), Microsoft Windows, TrueType, and windowing environment

- *Multimedia:* base-level synthesizer, CD-ROM, extended-level synthesizer, General MIDI (GM), Multimedia Personal Computer (MPC), Musical Instrument Digital Interface (MIDI), and synthesizer

- *Networks:* baseband, broadband, bus network, connectivity, connectivity platform, contention, distributed processing system, electronic mail (e-mail), file server, local area network (LAN), multiplexing, network architecture, network interface card, network operating system, peer-to-peer network, platform independence, ring network, star network, token-ring network, workgroup, and workstation

- *On-line communications:* archie, cyberspace, FTP, FYI, Gopher, Mosaic, netiquette, netnews, newsgroups, PMJI, uudecode, and uuencode

- *Operating systems and utilities:* argument, argument separator, background, backup, backup utility, basic input/output system (BIOS), batch file, boot, cold boot, command-line operating system, command processor, context switching, crash, current directory, current drive, delimiter, extension, file name, graphical user interface (GUI), hard disk backup program, interactive processing, load, multitasking, system disk, system file, system prompt, system software, tree structure, warm boot, and wild card

- *Ports and interfaces:* interface, parallel port, port, RS-232C, and serial port

- *Printers:* built-in font, cartridge, continuous paper, daisy-wheel printer, dot-matrix printer, downloadable font, friction feed, imagesetter, laser printer, letter-quality printer, non-impact printer, page description language (PDL), parallel printer, plotter, PostScript, PostScript laser printer, print engine, printer driver, printer font, resolution, serial printer, thermal printer, toner, and tractor feed

- *Programming:* algorithm, assembly language, branch control structure, case branch, control structure, conventional programming, debugging, DO/WHILE loop, extensible, FOR/NEXT loop, high-level programming language, IF/THEN/ELSE, instruction, interpreter, loop, loop control structure, low-level programming language, machine language, macro, modular programming, nested structure, object code, object-oriented programming language, procedural language, program, sequence control structure, software command language, source code, structured programming, subroutine, and variable

- *Programming languages:* BASIC, bundled software, C, character-based program, command-driven program, copy protection, default setting, documentation, freeware, graphics-based program, groupware, integrated program, menu-driven program, Pascal, public domain software, run-time version, shareware, SmallTalk, software, and vaporware, and Visual Basic

- *Spreadsheets:* absolute cell reference, active cell, automatic recalculation, built-in function, cell, cell address, cell pointer, cell protection, constant, edit mode, entry line, forecasting, formula, key variable, label, macro, mixed cell reference, model, range, range expression, range name, recalculation method, relative cell reference, spreadsheet program, value, what-if analysis, worksheet, and worksheet window

- *Systems and system vendors:* clone, closed bus system, compatibility, desktop computer, hardware, hardware platform, high end, home computer, laptop computer, low end, mainframe, microcomputer, minicomputer, multiuser system, open architecture, open bus system, personal computer, portable computer, and professional workstation

- *User interface and windowing systems:* application program interface, graphical user interface (GUI), mouse, pull-down menu, scroll bar/scroll box, user interface, window, and windowing environment

- *Word processing:* attribute, base font, block, block move, boilerplate, document base font, document format, embedded formatting command, emphasis, forced page break, format, hanging indent, hard space, hidden codes, indentation, initial base font, insert mode, justification, leading, mail merge, off-screen formatting, on-screen formatting, overtype mode, proportional spacing, scroll, selection, soft page break, soft return, style sheet, what-you-see-is-what-you-get (WYSIWYG), word processing, word processing program, and word wrap

3-D graph   See *three-dimensional graph*.

3-D spreadsheet program   See *three-dimensional spreadsheet*.

3 1/2-inch disk   A floppy disk, originally developed by Sony Corporation, used for magnetically storing data. The disk is enclosed in a hard plastic case with a sliding metal access door.

Beginning with MS-DOS 3.2, 3 1/2-inch disk drives offered storage capacities of 720K (double density). Support of 1.44M (high density) disks began with MS-DOS 3.3. MS-DOS 5.0 includes support for 2.88M disks. Macintosh computers format 3 1/2-inch disks with a storage capacity of 800K (double density) or 1.4M (high density).

Increasingly, software publishers distribute their products on 3 1/2-inch disks, but 5 1/4-inch disks are sometimes supplied; be sure you buy or order the correct size.

The 2.88M disk requires a drive and controller card manufactured to support this type of drive. Now, it's one of several high-capacity removable disks. See *floppy disk*.

5 1/4-inch disk   A floppy disk enclosed in a flexible plastic case. The most widely used floppy disk before 1987, 5 1/4-inch disks are still used for commercial software distribution. They're an inexpensive (albeit less convenient) storage medium for backups of your data. See *floppy disk*.

8-bit computer   A computer that uses a central processing unit (CPU) with an 8-bit data bus and that processes one byte (8 bits) of information at a time.

The first microprocessors used in personal computers, such as the MOS Technology 6502, Intel 8080, and Zilog Z-80, were installed in 8-bit computers such as the Apple II, the MSAI 8080, and the Commodore 64. Millions of these computers are still in use for educational and home-computing applications, but the popular business and professional software is available only for 16-bit and 32-bit personal computers such as the IBM Personal Computer and the Apple Macintosh. See *central processing unit (CPU), CP/M (Control Program for Microprocessors), data bus,* and *microprocessor.*

8-bit video adapter   A color video adapter that can display 256 colors simultaneously. See *video adapter.*

16-bit computer   A computer that uses a central processing unit (CPU) with a 16-bit data bus and processes two bytes (16 bits) of information at a time.

Many computers, such as the original IBM Personal Computer and IBM Personal Computer XT and compatibles, use the Intel 8088, which can process two bytes at a time internally but has an external data bus only eight bits wide, rather than the little-used Intel 8086, which has a full 16-bit data bus. IBM chose to use the Intel 8088 to take advantage of the many inexpensive, off-the-shelf peripherals developed for 8-bit computers. The IBM Personal Computer AT, introduced in 1984, uses a microprocessor with a true 16-bit structure; the data bus that extends beyond the microprocessor is also 16 bits wide. To run Microsoft Windows and some DOS applications such as WordPerfect 6.0, you must have a computer with an Intel 80286 microprocessor; acceptable performance requires an Intel 80386 (or more recent) microprocessor. See *data bus, Intel 8086, Intel 8088, Intel 80286, Intel 80386DX, Intel 80386SX, microprocessor,* and *peripheral.*

24-bit video adapter   A Macintosh color video adapter that can display more than 16 million colors simultaneously. With a 24-bit video card and monitor, a Macintosh can display beautiful, photographic-quality images. This video card and full-color monitor, however, can add as much as $1,800 to the cost of a Macintosh system.

32-bit computer   A computer that uses a central processing unit (CPU) with a 32-bit data bus and processes four bytes (32 bits) of information at a time.

A
B
C

Personal computers advertised as 32-bit machines—such as Macintosh Plus, Macintosh SE, and IBM PC compatibles based on the 80386SX microprocessor—aren't true 32-bit computers. These computers use microprocessors (such as the Motorola 68000 and Intel 80386SX) that can process four bytes at a time internally, but the external data bus is only 16 bits wide. 32-bit microprocessors, such as the Intel 80386DX and the Motorola 68030, use a true 32-bit data bus and 32-bit peripherals. See *data bus, Intel 80386DX, Intel 80386SX, Intel 80486DX, Intel 80486SX, Motorola 68000, Motorola 68020, Motorola 68030, Motorola 68040,* and *microprocessor.*

100% column graph   See *one hundred percent (100%) column graph.*

286   See *Intel 80286.*

386DX   See *Intel 80386DX.*

386 Enhanced mode   An operating mode of Microsoft Windows that takes full advantage of advanced technical capabilities such as multitasking, virtual memory, and protected mode. To use 386 Enhanced mode, your computer must have an 80386 or higher microprocessor and at least 2M of random-access memory (RAM).

The Intel 8088 and 8086 microprocessors, used in the earliest IBM PCs and compatibles, run DOS programs using *real mode.* Real mode causes problems when you try to run more than one program at a time because nothing prevents a poorly designed program from invading another program's memory space, resulting in a system crash and lost work. Also, the 1M RAM limit of these chips, along with the DOS 640K limit on the amount of RAM accessible to programs, has proved insufficient.

The Intel 80386 microprocessor introduced several technical improvements. For compatibility, an 80386 can run in real mode, but also offers *protected mode.* In protected mode, the 80386 can address up to 4 gigabytes of RAM, far more than you can install in any PC. The chip also can simulate more than one 8086 "machine" in the available RAM. These machines, called *virtual machines*, are protected from one another, preventing memory conflicts.

Running a DOS program in the protected mode of an 80386 computer requires software to manage the memory. Like a traffic cop, this software—called a *memory-management program*—channels DOS programs into their own 640K virtual machines, where they execute happily without interfering with other programs. Many memory-management programs are available for 80386 and 80486 computers, but by far the most popular is Microsoft Windows. Windows is much more than a memory-management program; it's a complete application program interface for personal computing.

In 386 Enhanced mode, Windows also takes advantage of the 80386 microprocessor's virtual memory capabilities. *Virtual memory* is a way of extending RAM by using part of the hard disk as though it were RAM. Most DOS applications swap program instructions and data back and forth from disk rather than keep them in memory. The 80386 implements virtual memory at the operating system level, rather than lets each program worry about virtual memory individually. This means that memory-management software sees an almost unlimited amount of RAM in which to run programs. Disks are significantly slower than RAM, however, so if you frequently run more than one program with Windows, you should have more than the minimum 2M of RAM (at least 4M and preferably 8M) to take full advantage of multitasking. See *extended memory, memory-management program, Microsoft Windows, multiple program loading, multitasking, protected mode, random-access memory (RAM), real mode,* and *virtual memory.*

386SX   See *Intel 80386SX.*

486DX   See *Intel 80486DX.*

486DX2   See *Intel 80486DX2.*

486DX4   See *Intel 80486DX4.*

486SX   See *Intel 80486SX.*

586   See *Intel Pentium.*

8086   See *Intel 8086.*

8088   See *Intel 8088.*

8514/A   See *IBM 8514/A display adapter.*

68000   See *Motorola 68000.*

68020   See *Motorola 68020.*

68030   See *Motorola 68030.*

68040   See *Motorola 68040.*

@function   See *built-in function.*

^   See *caret.*

A
B
C

A-B roll editing   In multimedia, a method for creating a master edited videotape by directing selected portions of video signals from two video sources (VCRs or camcorders) to a destination recording device, usually a VCR.

abandon   To clear a document, spreadsheet, or other work from the screen—and therefore from the computer's memory—without saving it to disk. The work is irretrievably lost.

abort   To cancel a program, command, or procedure while it's in progress. You can abort the procedure, or aborting can occur because of a bug in the program, power failure, or other unexpected cause.

absolute address   In a program, specifying a memory location by its address instead of using an expression to calculate the address.

absolute cell reference   A spreadsheet cell reference that doesn't adjust when you copy a formula. An absolute cell reference includes the $ symbol before both the column letter and the row number (A6). Use absolute cell references when you refer to cells containing key variables, such as the Social Security rate or a standard discount. See *key variable*, *low-level format*, and *relative cell reference*.

absolute value   The positive value of a number, regardless of its sign (positive or negative). The absolute value of –357, for example, is 357. In Lotus 1-2-3 and other spreadsheet programs, the @ABS built-in function returns the absolute value of a number.

accelerator board   A circuit board containing a faster or more advanced microprocessor than a slower microprocessor in your computer. If, for example, you have an IBM PC-compatible computer based on the Intel 8088 microprocessor, you can install an accelerator board containing the faster 80286 or 80386 micro-processor. See *hard disk*.

CAUTION: *Don't expect more of an accelerator board than it can deliver. An accelerator board can speed the tasks carried out within the microprocessor, such as sorting or calculating, but does little to improve the speed of disk operations, such as retrieving a file.*

accent   A mark that forms one of the accented characters of many languages. The following accents are used frequently:

´ Acute	˘ Breve	ç Cedilla
^ Circumflex	¨ Diaeresis	` Grave
‾ Macron	~ Tilde	¨ Umlaut

Accented characters are included in most font sets, and some application programs include commands or keystrokes that insert accented characters for you. See *compose sequence* and *extended character set*.

access   To retrieve data or program instructions from a disk drive or another computer connected to your computer by a network or a modem.

access arm   See *head arm*.

access code   An identification number or password you use to gain access to a computer system.

access hole   See *head slot*.

access privileges   On a network, the capability to open and modify directories, files, and programs located on other computers in the network. See *local area network (LAN)*.

access time   The amount of time that lapses between a request for information from memory and the delivery of the information; usually stated in nanoseconds (ns). This type of access time is known as memory access time.

When accessing data from a disk, access time includes only the time the disk heads take to move to the correct track (*seek time*); the time the heads take to settle down after reaching the correct track (*settle time*); and the time required for the correct sector to move under the head (*latency*). Disk access time is usually measured in microseconds (ms). Typical disk access times range between 9 ms (fast) and 100 ms (slow). See *hard disk* and *operating system*.

➜ **TIP:** *If you're using an IBM PC-compatible computer based on an 80286, 80386, or 80486 microprocessor, recently manufactured hard disks large enough to hold several 20M-30M applications all have acceptable access times. Invest any extra dollars in more RAM and use a software disk cache for best performance.*

accounting package   A set of personal computer programs intended to help a small-business owner automate a firm's accounting functions. Drawbacks to using accounting packages are that most small-business owners don't have the accounting knowledge required by many available programs, and using these programs without a point-of-sale system that automatically posts receipts to the ledgers means that you must enter the information for each sale daily. Check out the features in the available packages and show it to your accountant before making a purchase. See *integrated accounting package* and *modular accounting package*.

accumulator   A register, or storage location, in a central processing unit that holds values to be used later in a computation. Computer multiplication, for example, frequently is done by a series of additions; the accumulator holds the intermediate values until the process is completed. See *central processing unit (CPU)*.

accuracy   A statement of how correct a measurement is; unlike *precision*, which is the number of decimal places to which the measurement is computed. A computer-based statistical analysis

a

may report, for instance, that a device likely will run for 8,025 hours without failure, with an error margin of plus or minus 25 hours.

acoustic coupler   A modem with cups that fit around the earpiece and mouthpiece of a standard (not cellular) telephone headset. The cups contain a microphone and a speaker that convert the computer's digital signals into sound, and vice versa. With the increasing use of modular telephone connections, direct-connect modems have supplanted acoustic modems in general use. See *direct-connect modem* and *modem.*

acoustical sound enclosure   An insulated cabinet for noisy impact printers that reduces the noise such printers make. See *impact printer.*

acronym   A word formed from the first letters (and sometimes other letters) of a series of words, such as BASIC (Beginner's All-Purpose Symbolic Instruction Code) and WYSIWYG (what-you-see-is-what-you-get).

active area   In a Lotus 1-2-3 worksheet, the area bounded by cell A1 and the lowest rightmost cell containing data.

active cell   In a spreadsheet, the cell in which the cell pointer is now located. Synonymous with *current cell.*

active database   In database management, the database file now in use and present in random-access memory (RAM).

active file   The worksheet on-screen when you're working with Lotus 1-2-3 Release 3.

active index   In database management programs, the index file now being used to determine the order in which data records are displayed. See *index.*

active matrix display   In notebook computers, a full-color liquid-crystal display (LCD) in which each of the screen's pixels is controlled by its own transistor. Active matrix displays offer higher resolution and contrast than cheaper passive matrix displays. See *passive matrix display.*

active sensing   In multimedia, a MIDI message that tells a device to monitor its channels to determine whether messages occur on the channels within a predetermined maximum time (called a *time window*). See *Musical Instrument Digital Interface (MIDI).*

active window   In a program or operating system that displays multiple windows, the window in which the cursor or highlight is located and where text appears if you type (see fig. A.1). See *windowing environment.*

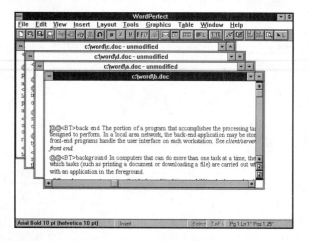

Fig. A.1   *An active document window superimposed on other document windows in WordPerfect 6.0 for Windows.*

TIP: *The color of the active window's title bar is usually different from the other windows' title bars.*

activity light   On the front panel of a computer, a small colored light that flickers when a disk drive is reading or writing data.

actuator   `ak-chew-a-ter   See *head actuator.*

Ada   A high-level programming language developed by the U.S. Department of Defense and required by the DOD for all military programming applications.

Ada was written to answer the military's need for a single computer language capable of real-time process control (the operation of a highly complex device such as a missile). Ada was named for Lady Augusta Ada Byron, Countess Lovelace, considered to be the world's first female computer scientist. Ada uses the principles of structured programming, including the use of program modules that can be compiled separately. Ada programs are designed to be highly readable so that they're easier to maintain. See *compiler, high-level programming language, Modula-2, Pascal, real time,* and *structured programming.*

CAUTION: *Ada is now available for personal computers, but if you decide to learn the language, make sure that you choose a compiler certified by the DOD.*

adapter   A circuit board that plugs into an expansion slot in a computer, giving the computer additional capabilities. Synonymous with *card.* Popular adapters for personal computers include display adapters that produce video output; memory expansion boards; boards that provide serial ports, parallel ports, and game ports; internal modems; and clock/calendar boards. See *circuit board, clock/calendar board, expansion bus, internal modem, motherboard, open bus system, parallel port, serial port,* and *video adapter.*

adapter segment   See *upper memory area.*

Adaptive Differential Pulse Code Modulation (ADPCM)   In multimedia, a method of digital waveform compression where the difference between successive samples rather than their actual values is encoded. Using ADPCM, the quantity of audio information that can be stored on a single compact disk increases from 1 hour to about 16 hours, while maintaining or improving fidelity. ADPCM is the storage technique used by CD-ROM XA and CD-I disks. See *CD-ROM eXtended*

Architecture (CD-ROM XA), Compact Disk-Interactive (CD-I), and *pulse code modulation (PCM).*

ADB See *Apple Desktop Bus (ADB).*

add-in program An accessory or utility program designed to work with and extend the capabilities of an application program. Add-in programs can be created by other software developers, such as Allways by Funk Software, or included with the application, such as the auditors, file viewers, and "what-if" programs included in many spreadsheet programs.

address A precise location in a computer system that's identified by a name, number, or code label. The user or a program can specify the address. See *memory address.*

address bus An internal electronic channel from the microprocessor to random-access memory (RAM), along which the addresses of memory storage locations are transmitted. Like a post office box, each memory location has a distinct number or address; the address bus provides the means by which the microprocessor can access every location in memory.

The width (or number of wires) of the address bus determines the maximum number of possible memory locations and, therefore, the maximum amount of memory the processor can address. Early IBM personal computers used address buses 20 bits wide (20 wires); these computers could identify and use a maximum of 220 memory locations (1M of RAM). Using an address bus width of 32 bits, more recent IBM PC-compatible computers can address a maximum of 4 gigabits of RAM. See *binary numbers, bus, expanded memory (EMS), extended memory, Microsoft Windows,* and *Operating System/2 (OS/2).*

ADI See *Apple Desktop Interface (ADI).*

Adobe PostScript See *PostScript.*

ADPCM See *Adaptive Differential Pulse Code Modulation (ADPCM).*

a

ADSL   See *asynchronous digital subscriber loop (ADSL)*.

Advanced Interactive eXecutive (AIX)   An IBM version
of the UNIX operating system. AIX runs on PS/2 computers
equipped with the Intel 80386 microprocessor, IBM workstations,
minicomputers, and mainframes.

Advanced Micro Devices (AMD)   A manufacturer of,
among other things, microprocessor chips. AMD manufactures
the following chips:

Chip	Description
Am386DX	An 80386DX-type microprocessor chip released in March 1991. The chip is available in 25, 33, and 40 MHz speeds, the only 386/40 available today. The 40 MHz chip is the same price as the Intel 386/33, but delivers a 20 percent increase in speed.
Am386SX	An 80386SX-type microprocessor chip released in July 1991. The main differences between this and the Am386DX are the 16-bit data path and the fact that the chip uses up to 35 percent less power. The speed and decreased power demands of the Am386SX/40 have made it popular in entry-level laptop and notebook computers.
Am486DX	A competitively priced clone of the Intel 486DX microprocessor chip. The chip is available in 33 and 40 MHz speeds.
Am486DX2	A competitively priced clone of the Intel 486DX2 clock-doubling microprocessor chip. The chip is available in clock speeds of 50 and 66 MHz.

See *Intel 80386DX, Intel 80386SX, Intel 80486DX, Intel
80486DX2,* and *reverse engineering*.

Advanced Run-Length Limited (ARLL)   A method of
storing and retrieving information on a hard disk that increases
the density of Run-Length Limited (RLL) storage by more than

25 percent and offers a faster data-transfer rate (9 megabits per second). See *data-encoding scheme* and *Run-Length Limited (RLL)*.

aftermarket   The market for software and peripherals created by the sale of large numbers of a specific brand of computer or software packages such as Lotus 1-2-3 and WordPerfect. See *add-in program*.

agate   A 5.5-point type size still used in newspaper classified advertising but too small for most other uses.

aggregate function   In database management programs, a command that performs arithmetic operations on the values in a specific field in all the records within a database, or in one view of the database. dBASE, for example, performs the following aggregate functions:

Function	Description
Average	Computes the arithmetic mean of the values
Sum	Adds all the values
Minimum	Finds the smallest value
Maximum	Finds the largest value
Count	Counts the number of records that meet the specified criteria

aggregate operator   In a database management program, a command that tells the program to perform an aggregate function.

Suppose that you own a videotape rental store and want to know how many tapes are more than two weeks late. Because the date is May 19, you want to know how many rentals were due on or before May 5 (less than 05/06/94). The following dBASE expression finds the information:

```
COUNT FOR due_date <05/06/94
```

You see a response such as the following:

```
2 records
```

See *aggregate function.*

AI   See *artificial intelligence (AI).*

AIX   See *Advanced Interactive eXecutive (AIX).*

alert box   In a graphical user interface, a dialog box that appears on-screen to warn you that the command you've given may
result in lost work or other errors, or that explains why an action
can't be completed. Alert boxes remain on-screen until you take
some action to remove the box or cancel the operation.

algorithm   A mathematical or logical procedure for solving a
problem. An algorithm is a recipe for finding the right answer to a
difficult problem by breaking down the problem into a specific
number of simple steps. The steps must be well-defined so that
you can perform them successfully even though you don't fully
understand what you're doing. You use algorithms every day,
when mowing the lawn, placing long-distance telephone calls, or
packing grocery bags.

The British logician Alan Turing proved that the algorithmic
approach can solve any mathematical or logical problem that has a
solution. The computer programs you use every day include one
or more algorithms.

Algorithms also are used to improve the performance of your
computer. Algorithms are used, for example, in caches to determine what data is replaced by incoming data.

alias   A secondary or symbolic name for a file or computer
device. In a spreadsheet, a range name, such as Income, is an alias
for a range, such as A3..K3. In computer networks, group aliases
provide a handy way to send a message to two or more people
simultaneously.

With the Macintosh System 7 software, you can create aliases for commonly accessed program and document icons. If you drag an alias to the Apple Menu Items folder within the System Folder, the alias appears on the Apple pull-down menu, allowing fast access to this item.

aliasing   In computer graphics, the undesirable jagged or stair-stepped appearance of diagonal lines in computer-generated graphic images. A low-resolution display causes this appearance. Synonymous with the *jaggies*. See *antialiasing*.

alignment   In personal computing, the accurate placement of the read/write heads over the tracks they must read and write.

> **CAUTION:** *Because a jolt can knock a floppy disk drive out of alignment, be careful not to drop or knock your computer around when moving the machine. A drive slightly out of alignment may have trouble reading floppy disks, especially those formatted by a different computer. If your machine can't read an important floppy disk, don't assume that the disk is bad. Try reading the disk on another computer.*

In desktop publishing, synonymous with *justification*.

allocate   To reserve memory that's sufficient for a program's application. In Microsoft Windows, use the PIF Editor to set a minimum, desired, and maximum amount of memory to ensure the best performance from DOS applications running in Windows. Macintosh users can use the Finder to find out the suggested memory size and the current memory allocation for each program.

all points addressable (APA) graphic   See *bit-mapped graphic*.

alphanumeric characters   Characters available on a keyboard, including upper- and lowercase letters A through Z, numbers 0 through 9, punctuation marks, and special keyboard symbols. See *data type*.

alpha test   The first stage in the testing of computer products before the product is released for public use. Alpha tests usually are conducted by the hardware manufacturer or software publisher. Later tests, called *beta tests*, are conducted by users. See *beta test*.

Alt key   On IBM PC-compatible keyboards, a key used in combination with other keys to select commands from the menu or as shortcut keys to execute commands. In WordPerfect, for example, pressing Alt+F2 begins a search-and-replace operation. See *Control (Ctrl) key* and *Shift key*.

ALU   See *arithmetic-logic unit (ALU)*.

Am386DX, Am386SX, Am486DX, and Am486DX2
See *Advanced Micro Devices (AMD)*.

America Online   A full-service, Windows-based on-line computer service providing e-mail, forums, software downloads, news, weather, sports, financial information, conferences, on-line gaming, an encyclopedia, and other standard features, available to its subscribers for a monthly fee.

In the America Online Computing & Software menu is the Industry Connection, where you'll find forums sponsored by all major hardware manufacturers and software publishers. When you want to leave a message for *InCider* magazine or the WordPerfect Support Center, you'll find it here.

With almost 1 million subscribers, America Online is the third largest on-line service, after CompuServe and Prodigy. America Online has lacked the shopping capabilities of its rivals, a deficiency it remedied by purchasing Redgate Communications Company in April 1994. Another recent addition is its access to the Internet for e-mail, newsgroups, Gopher, Wide Area Information Service databases, and FTP. See *Internet*.

American National Standards Institute (ANSI)   A non-profit organization devoted to the development of voluntary standards designed to improve the productivity and international competitiveness of American industrial enterprises. ANSI committees have developed recommendations for computer languages such as COBOL, C, and FORTRAN and the DOS device driver ANSI.SYS.

American Standard Code for Information Interchange   See *ASCII*.

Amiga   A personal computer developed by Commodore International, based on the Motorola 68000 microprocessor and used for home computing applications. Because of the Amiga's outstanding color graphics and multichannel stereo sound, some consider it to be the computer of choice for playing computer games and composing music. The machine has found little acceptance as a business computer, however, because of the lack of business software for the machine. See *Musical Instrument Digital Interface (MIDI)*.

ampersand   A character (&) sometimes used in place of the English word *and*; originally a ligature of *et*, which is Latin for *and*. The ampersand is used as an operator in spreadsheet programs to include text in a formula.

analog   A representation of the changing values of a property using an indicator that can vary continuously.

A speedometer is an analog device that shows changes in speed using a needle indicator that can move over an infinite range of speeds up to the maximum limit of the vehicle. A thermometer is another example of an analog device, the mercury being the indicator of temperature. Analog techniques also are used for the reproduction of music in standard LP records and audio cassettes. See *digital*.

analog computer   A computer used to measure conditions that change constantly, such as temperature, heartbeat, or atmospheric pressure. Analog computation is used widely in laboratory settings to monitor ongoing, continuous changes and to record these changes in charts or graphs. See *digital computer.*

analog device A computer peripheral that handles information in continuously variable quantities rather than digitize the information into discrete, digital representations. An analog monitor, for example, can display thousands of colors with smooth, continuous gradations.

analog monitor A monitor that accepts a continuously varied video input signal and consequently can display a continuous range and infinite number of colors. In contrast, a digital monitor can display only a finite number of colors. EGA monitors are digital; VGA monitors are analog. Most analog monitors are designed to accept input signals at a precise frequency; however, higher frequencies are required to carry higher-resolution images to the monitor. For this reason, multiscanning monitors have been developed that automatically adjust themselves to the incoming frequency. See *digital monitor, Enhanced Graphics Adapter (EGA), multiscanning monitor,* and *Video Graphics Array (VGA).*

analog transmission A communications scheme that uses a continuous signal varied by amplification. See *broadband* and *digital transmission.*

analog-to-digital converter An adapter that allows a digital computer (such as an IBM Personal Computer) to accept analog input from laboratory instruments. Analog-to-digital converters are frequently used when monitoring temperature, movement, and other conditions that vary continuously. A sound board is an analog-to-digital converter. See *analog, digital,* and *real time.*

analogical reasoning A form of analysis in which the dynamics of something in the real world—such as the aerodynamics of a proposed airplane—are understood by building a model and exploring its behavior. One of the computer's greatest contributions has been to lower the cost (and increase the convenience) of analogical reasoning.

Analogical reasoning predates the computer; the use of airplane models in wind tunnels is a well-known example. Computers, however, have made it possible to develop models of highly complex and even chaotic systems—the human immune system, human societies, ecologies, world weather, even the cosmos—that can't be understood through any means other than analogical reasoning.

analysis   A method of discovery in which a situation is broken down to its component parts, and the parts are studied to try to understand how they affect one another. In personal computing, a common form of analysis is sensitivity testing, or "what-if" analysis, using a spreadsheet program. In sensitivity testing, you alter the variables in a formula to see how changing each variable affects the outcome of the calculation.

analytical graphics   The preparation of charts and graphs to help in the understanding and interpretation of data.

The graphs available with spreadsheet programs fall into this category: they're useful for clarifying trends in worksheet numbers. The newest versions of popular spreadsheet programs include fonts, figures, colors, and other features you can use to improve the printed appearance of these graphs, but presentation graphics packages still have the edge in creating stunning charts. See *presentation graphics*.

anchor cell   In Lotus 1-2-3 and Quattro Pro, the cell in a range in which the cell pointer is located. See *range*.

anchored graphic   A graph or picture fixed in an absolute position on the page rather than attached to specific text. See *floating graphic* and *wrap-around type*.

animation   Creating the illusion of movement in a computer program by saving a series of images that show slight changes in the position of the displayed objects, and then displaying these images back fast enough that the eye perceives smooth movement. See *cell animation*.

annotation   An explanatory note or comment inserted into a document such as a business report or analytical worksheet.

a

With some applications, you can insert an annotation as an icon that, when clicked by the person who reads the document, opens a separate window containing the note. Users of personal computers equipped with digital sound and microphones can add voice annotations to their documents.

> **TIP:** *Windows 3.1 users can use the Annotate command on the Help Edit menu to add comments to Help topics. A paper clip to the left of the topic title indicates an annotation.*

anonymous FTP   In systems linked to the Internet, the use of the FTP program to contact a distant computer system to which you have no access rights, log on to its public directories, and transfer files from that computer to your own disk storage area. If that system supports anonymous FTP, when you log on and are asked to type a password, you type **anonymous**.

For help in finding files to access via anonymous FTP or other means, you can use archie, Gopher, WAIS, and the World-Wide Web. See *archie, file transfer protocol (FTP), Gopher, Internet, UNIX, Wide Area Information Server (WAIS)*, and *World-Wide Web (WWW)*.

ANSI   See *American National Standards Institute (ANSI)*.

ANSI screen control   A set of standards developed by the American National Standards Institute (ANSI) to control the display of information on computer screens. See *ANSI.SYS*.

ANSI.SYS   *an-see-sis*   In MS-DOS, a configuration file containing instructions needed to display graphics and to control cursor location, line wrapping, and the behavior of the keyboard, following the recommendations of the American National Standards Institute.

Some programs require that you include the instruction DEVICE=ANSI.SYS in the CONFIG.SYS file so that the program screens display properly. See *CONFIG.SYS*.

answer mode   See *auto-dial/auto-answer modem.*

answer/originate   In data communications, the capability of a communications device to receive (answer) and send (originate) messages.

antialiasing   The automatic removal or reduction of stair-step distortions in a computer-generated graphic image. This is accomplished by filling the jagged edges with gray or color to make the jaggies less noticeable. Unfortunately, the result is a fuzzy display, an effect some users find unpleasant or uncomfortable. See *aliasing.*

antistatic mat   A mat or pad placed on or near a computer device. The mat absorbs static electricity, which can damage semiconductor devices if the devices aren't properly grounded.

antivirus program   A utility designed to check for and remove computer viruses from memory and data storage disks.

An antivirus program detects a virus by searching for *virus signatures,* programming code recognized as that of one of the 1,500+ viruses known to afflict many computer systems. An antivirus program can also be used to create a checksum for vulnerable files on your disk, save the checksums in a special file, and then use the checksums to determine whether files have been modified, perhaps by a new virus. Special memory-resident programs can check for unusual attempts to access vital disk areas and system files, and check files you copy into memory to be sure they aren't infected. See *checksum, Trojan horse, vaccine, virus,* and *worm.*

APA graphic   See *bit-mapped graphic.*

API   See *application program interface (API).*

APL (A Programming Language)   A high-level programming language well suited for scientific and mathematical applications. APL uses Greek letters and requires a display device that can display these letters. Used on IBM mainframes, the language is now available for IBM PC-compatible computers. See *high-level programming language.*

a

append To add data at the end of a file or a database. In data-base management, for example, to append a record is to add a new record after all existing records.

Apple Desktop Bus (ADB) An interface for connecting keyboards, mice, trackballs, and other input devices to Macintosh computers. These computers come with an ADB serial port capable of a maximum data transfer rate of 4.5 kilobits per second. You can connect up to 16 devices to one ADB port, with each additional device daisy-chained to the previous device. See *asynchronous communication* and *daisy chain*.

Apple Desktop Interface (ADI) A set of user-interface guidelines, developed by Apple Computer and published by Addison-Wesley, intended to ensure that the appearance and operation of all Macintosh applications are similar. See *user interface*.

Apple File Exchange A utility program provided with each Macintosh computer that allows Macs equipped with suitable disk drives to exchange data with IBM PC-compatible computers.

AppleShare A network operating system developed by Apple Computer, Inc., for the Macintosh computer. To use the network, each user installs the AppleShare driver and at least one computer is configured as the server. Users then choose a server and begin working. The Macintosh being used as the server can't be used for other applications; that computer becomes a "slave" of the net-work. See *AppleTalk*, *local area network (LAN)*, *LocalTalk*, and *virtual device*.

AppleShare file server In an AppleTalk local area network, a Macintosh computer running AppleShare file server software so that all network users can share the programs and data stored on the Macintosh. See *local area network (LAN)*.

applet A small application that performs a specific task, such as the Cardfile and Calculator available in Microsoft Windows.

An applet can be designed to be accessible only from within a program, such as Microsoft Graph packaged with Word for

Windows and Excel. The work that you create with this kind of applet becomes an embedded object within the document you are creating. See *embedded object*, *object*, and *object linking and embedding (OLE)*.

AppleTalk   A local area network standard developed by Apple Computer, Inc. AppleTalk can link as many as 32 Macintosh computers, IBM PC-compatible computers, and peripherals such as laser printers. Every Macintosh computer has an AppleTalk port through which you can quickly and easily connect the machine to an AppleTalk network. The only hardware required for an AppleTalk network is connectors and ordinary telephone wire for cables (called *twisted-pair cable*).

IBM PC-compatible computers can be attached to the network using special adapters that provide AppleTalk ports for IBM PC-compatibles. AppleTalk networks are slow, however—capable of transmitting only up to 230 kilobits per second compared to EtherTalk, which is capable of speeds of up to 10 million bits per second. AppleTalk's simplicity and low cost, however, make it an attractive option for networks of modest size and use.

application   The use of a computer for a specific purpose, such as writing a novel, printing payroll checks, or laying out the text and graphics of a newsletter.

The term *application* also is frequently used instead of *application software* or *application program*. See *application software*, *program*, and *system software*.

application control menu   In Microsoft Windows and Windows applications, a menu displayed by selecting the control button on the far left of the title bar. You can use this menu with the keyboard to minimize, maximize, and restore the application window; to move and resize the application window; to switch to other active Windows applications; and to close the application in the window. An abbreviated control menu is available in some DOS programs such as PC Tools.

application development system   A coordinated set of program development tools, typically including a full-screen

a

editor; a programming language with a compiler, linker, and debugger; and an extensive library of ready-to-use program modules. The use of an application development system lets experienced users develop a stand-alone application more easily than writing a program using a language such as C++ or COBOL.

application heap   In a Macintosh computer, the area of memory set aside for user programs. Synonymous with *base memory*.

application icon   In Microsoft Windows, an on-screen graphic representation of a minimized program. The icon appears at the bottom of the screen on the Program Manager desktop to remind you that the application is still present in memory (see fig. A.2). Double-click the application icon to switch to that program. See *icon* and *Microsoft Windows*.

Application icons

Fig. A.2   *Application icons of several minimized applications.*

application program   See *application software*.

application program interface (API)   System software that provides a complete set of functions and resources on which programmers can draw to create user interface features, such as pull-down menus, command names, dialog boxes, keyboard commands, and windows. In network systems, an API establishes how programs use the various network features.

An application program interface benefits users by decreasing the time required to learn new programs, thereby encouraging users to use more programs.

application shortcut key   In Microsoft Windows 386 Enhanced mode, a shortcut key you assign to launch or bring an application to the foreground. You assign the keyboard shortcut, such as Alt+Ctrl+W for Word for Windows, using the Properties command on the File menu. Application shortcut keys are also available in applications such as DESQview, WordPerfect Office, and PC Tools Desktop to launch and switch between programs. See *386 Enhanced mode, Microsoft Windows,* and *shortcut key.*

application software   Programs that perform specific tasks, such as word processing or database management; unlike system software that maintains and organizes the computer system and utilities that help you maintain and organize the system. See *application, database management program, page layout program, spreadsheet program, system software, utility program,* and *word processing program.*

application window   In a graphical user interface, an application's main window, containing a title bar, the application's menu bar, and a work area. The work area can contain one or more document windows. See *document window* and *Microsoft Windows.*

A Programming Language   See *APL (A Programming Language).*

archie   In UNIX-based systems linked to the Internet, a program that lets the user search an index of files that can be downloaded from other servers using anonymous FTP. Archie now indexes approximately 2.1 million files on some 1,200 publicly accessible servers. See *anonymous FTP, file transfer protocol (FTP), Gopher, Internet,* and *UNIX.*

a

architecture   The physical structure or design of a computer and its components, from its internal operating structure and specific chips to the programs that make it run.

The term *architecture* is frequently used to describe the internal data-handling capacity of a computer. The 8-bit architecture of the Intel 8088 microprocessor, for example, is determined by the 8-bit data bus that transmits only one byte of data at a time. See *microprocessor.*

archival backup   A backup procedure in which a backup program backs up all files on the hard disk by copying them to floppy disks, tape, or some other backup medium. See *hard disk backup program* and *incremental backup.*

archive   A compressed file designed for space-efficient storage that contains one or more files.

Programs for compressing and decompressing IBM PC-compatible files are readily available as shareware. Look for the ARC program created by Systems Enhancement Associates and PKZIP by PKWare, Inc. The programs are available from many bulletin board systems (BBSs); look for files named ARC*x* or PKZ*x*, where the *x*'s represent the version number. The Macintosh file compression utility of choice is StuffIt, a shareware program created by Raymond Lau.

Almost all BBSs store files in archives to save hard drive space. You must use a file decompression program (PKUNZIP, for example) to extract archived files. See *file compression utility.*

archive attribute   In DOS, a hidden code, stored with a file's directory entry, that indicates whether the file has been changed since it was last copied using XCOPY or a backup utility.

DOS always sets the archive attribute to ON when you save a file. When you back up files using XCOPY or a backup utility, you can have the archive attribute turned off. If you later modify the file, DOS turns on the archive attribute when you save the file. The next time you back up files, you can tell the backup utility or XCOPY to back up only files that have changed, which is determined by checking the archive attribute.

TIP: *When the archive bit is off, you can't use XCOPY to copy a large directory of files to floppy disks without resetting the archive attribute. Use the ATTRIB command to turn the archive attribute back on.*

ARCnet   See *Attached Resource Computer Network (ARCnet).*

area graph   In presentation graphics, a line graph in which the area below the line is filled in to emphasize the change in volume from one time period to the next. The x-axis (categories axis) is the horizontal axis, and the y-axis (values axis) is the vertical axis.

When more than one data series are displayed, each series is shown in a distinctive cross-hatching pattern or shade of gray (as shown in fig. A.3). See *column graph, line graph, presentation graphics, x-axis,* and *y-axis.*

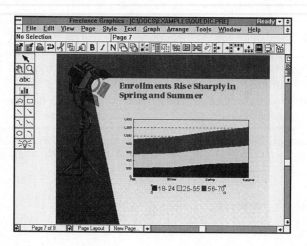

Fig. A.3   *An area graph.*

argument   Words, phrases, or numbers you enter on the same line as a command or a statement to expand or modify how that command or statement operates.

a

In the dBASE expression USE *customer*, USE is the command, and *customer* is the argument. In Lotus 1-2-3, the arguments of built-in functions are enclosed in parentheses, as in @SUM(B1..B3). See *argument separator* and *parameter*.

argument separator   In spreadsheet programs and programming languages, a comma or other punctuation mark that sets off one argument from another in a command or statement.

The argument separator is essential in commands that require more than one argument. Without the separator, the program can't tell one argument from another.

> **TIP:** *If you're having trouble getting a command or function to work, make sure that you know exactly how many arguments the command or function requires and that you've separated the arguments with the correct separator. Some programs don't allow spaces after the separator. If you're used to pressing the space bar after typing a comma, you may have to delete unnecessary spaces.*

arithmetic operator   A symbol that tells a program the arithmetic operation to perform, such as addition, subtraction, multiplication, and division.

In most computer programs, addition is represented by a plus sign (+), subtraction by a hyphen or minus sign (–), multiplication by an asterisk (*), division by a slash (/), and exponent by a caret (^). See *logical operator* and *relational operator*.

arithmetic-logic unit (ALU)   The portion of the central processing unit (CPU) that makes all the decisions for the microprocesser, based on the mathematical computations and logic functions it performs.

ARLL   See *Advanced Run-Length Limited (ARLL)*.

ARPAnet   A wide area network supported by the U.S. Defense Advanced Research Projects Agency (DARPA) and intended to support advanced scientific research.

Because it's a part of NSFNet, access to ARPAnet is restricted to a small group of advanced researchers. See *Internet*, *NSFNet*, and *wide area network*.

array   In programming, a fundamental data structure consisting of a single- or multidimensional table that the program treats as one data item. Any information in the array can be referenced by naming the array and the location of the item in the array.

arrow keys   See *cursor-movement keys*.

artificial intelligence (AI)   A computer science field that tries to improve computers by endowing them with some of the characteristics associated with human intelligence, such as the capability to understand natural language and to reason under conditions of uncertainty.

Ironically, the AI applications thought to be too difficult, such as playing world-class chess, have been easier than expected; and those thought to be easy, such as translating one human language to another, have been very difficult. For example, after spending large amounts of time and money, a U.S. Department of Defense computer system translated the Russian phrase "The spirit is willing but the flesh is weak" to "The vodka is excellent but the meat is rotten."

Douglas Lenat, an artificial intelligence researcher, points out that the computer can't work with a sentence, such as "Mr. Lincoln is in Washington, D.C.," without additional information, such as "When a person is in a city, his or her left foot is also in the city." If you've ever wondered whether you're smarter than a computer, this example should put all doubts to rest. See *expert system*.

artificial life   A scientific research area devoted to the creation and study of computer simulations of living organisms.

Computer viruses—those rogue, self-replicating programs released by pranksters and saboteurs—have forced a renewal of the debate on the definition of life. And UCLA researchers have created a computer "ant farm" with simulated "ants"—tiny programs that "live" or "die" based on their capability to survive, with the survivors passing on their characteristics to the next generation. Besides forcing us to re-examine our definition of life, artificial life research may create more effective technology. By applying the ant farm concept to real-life problems, we can program computer-generated solutions to compete for survival based on their capability to perform a desired task well.

ascender In typography, the portion of the lowercase letters *b*, *d*, *f*, *h*, *k*, *l*, and *t* that rises above the height of the letter *x*. The height of the ascender varies in different typefaces. See *descender*.

ascending order A sort in which items are arranged from smallest to largest (1, 2, 3) or from first to last (a, b, c). Ascending order is the default sort order for virtually all applications that perform sorting operations. See *descending sort*.

ASCII *as-kee* Acronym for American Standard Code for Information Interchange, a standard computer character set consisting of 96 upper- and lowercase letters, plus 32 non-printing control characters, each of which is numbered, to achieve uniformity among different computer devices.

Devised in 1968, the ASCII character set includes the English-language text characters, but not the accented letters and graphics characters required for many foreign languages and technical applications. Therefore, most modern computers use an extended ASCII character set containing the needed characters. See *extended character set*.

ASCII art Low-brow art in a high-tech medium, using only the ASCII character set (see fig. A.4). Smileys—sideways faces, such as a :-) happy face and :-(frowning face—provide emotional and social context for electronic mail messages, and provide yet another genre for ASCII art. See *smiley*.

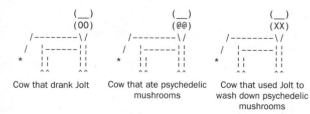

```
            ( __ )                      ( __ )                      ( __ )
           ( OO )                      ( @@ )                      ( XX )
       /--------\ /                /--------\ /                /--------\ /
      /   |------| |              /   |------| |              /   |------| |
    *     | |    | |            *     | |    | |            *     | |    | |
          ^ ^    ^ ^                  ^ ^    ^ ^                  ^ ^    ^ ^
   Cow that drank Jolt      Cow that ate psychedelic    Cow that used Jolt to
                                   mushrooms            wash down psychedelic
                                                             mushrooms
```

Fig. A.4 *Examples of ASCII art.*

ASCII character set   A character set consisting only of the characters included in the original 128-character ASCII standard. See *extended character set.*

ASCII file   A file that contains only characters drawn from the ASCII character set. No special formatting (such as boldface or underlining) is in an ASCII file. See *binary file.*

ASCII sort order   A sort order determined by the sequence used to number the standard ASCII character set. Words or lines that begin with spaces or punctuation come first, followed by those beginning with numbers. Next sorted are words or lines that begin with uppercase letters, followed by those beginning with lowercase letters.

> **❗ CAUTION:** *Programs that sort data in ASCII sort order may violate publication guidelines; all capitalized words, for instance, come before words beginning with lowercase letters. Also, an ASCII sort doesn't alphabetize foreign language characters properly. See* dictionary sort.

aspect ratio   In computer graphics, the ratio of the width of an image to its height. When changing the size of a graphic, maintaining the width-to-height ratio is important to avoid distortions.

assembler   A program that transforms an assembly language program into machine language so that the computer can execute the program. See *assembly language, compiler,* and *machine language.*

assembly language   A low-level programming language in which each program statement corresponds to an instruction that the processing unit can carry out.

Assembly languages are procedural languages. They tell the computer what to do in precise detail, requiring as many as two dozen lines of code to add two numbers. Assembly language programs are difficult and tedious to write, and the final result isn't transferred easily from one type of computer to another. The programs are designed for the specific capabilities and instruction sets of a given processing unit.

In its favor, assembly language code is compact, operates quickly, and, when assembled, is more efficient than a compiled program written in a high-level language. Some programs, such as operating systems, must run at the maximum speed possible and, therefore, are written in assembly language. Assembly language programs also consume less memory than compiled programs written in a high-level language. See *BASIC, C, compiler, high-level programming language, machine language, Pascal,* and *procedural language.*

assign   To give a value to a named variable.

assignment statement   In computer programming, a program statement that places a value into a variable. In BASIC, for example, the statement LET A=10 places the value 10 into the variable A. See *BASIC.*

associate   In Microsoft Windows, to create a link between data files and a specific application program using a file extension (such as .DOC). When you open an associated file, the application that created it is launched and the file retrieved into an open window. When you install a Windows application, the installation utility tells Windows which extension—such as .DOC or .WB1— the program uses.

You can tell whether a file is associated with an application by looking at the file name in the File Manager. Associated files are shown with a document icon—a page with lines on it. If an application's files aren't automatically associated, you can use the Associate command from the File Manager's File menu to create an association.

associated document   A file linked at the system level with the application that created it. You can start an application by choosing one of its associated documents.

MS-DOS doesn't support document associations; you can't start Lotus 1-2-3, for example, by choosing the document FALLQTR.WK1. In Microsoft Windows, Windows applications automatically establish associations with their documents, but you must manually associate non-Windows applications and documents using the Associate command on the File menu in File Manager.

In the Macintosh Finder and MultiFinder, all documents are associated with the applications that created them. The association is controlled by the creator type code, a four-letter code that identifies the application used to create the file. See *creator type*, *Finder*, *Microsoft Windows*, and *MultiFinder*.

TIP: *If you're using an application that doesn't automatically assign extensions—WordPerfect 5.1 for DOS, for example— you can start saving that application's files using an extension you make up. If you save all your WordPerfect files with an extension such as WP, you can use the Associate command to tell Windows to associate all WP files with WordPerfect.*

asterisk   In DOS, the wild-card symbol (*) that stands for one or more characters; unlike the question mark (?) wild card, which stands for only one character. An asterisk is also the arithmetic symbol for multiplication. See *arithmetic operator* and *question mark*.

Asymetrix ToolBook   A program development environment and hypertext authoring tool for Microsoft Windows that lets non-programmers develop Windows applications quickly. Asymetrix Corporation publishes the program, which resembles the HyperCard application in the Macintosh environment. See *HyperCard*, *hypertext*, and *Microsoft Windows*.

asynchronous communication   A method of data communication in which the transmission of bits of data isn't synchronized by a clock signal, but is accomplished by sending the bits one after another, with a start bit and a stop bit to mark the beginning and end, respectively, of each data unit. Because this results in lower communication speeds, telephone lines can be used for asynchronous communication. See *baud rate, bus, modem, synchronous communication,* and *Universal Asynchronous Receiver/ Transmitter (UART).*

asynchronous digital subscriber loop (ADSL)   A transmission method that can deliver through existing telephone lines a single compressed, high-quality video signal at a rate of 1.5M per second in addition to an ordinary telephone conversation.

ADSL-1, the lowest-bandwidth ADSL standard, can provide a VCR-quality video signal and telephone service to 75 percent of American and 80 percent of Canadian homes without replacing existing telephone wiring. ADSL may provide the key to a National Information Infrastructure (NII), in which high-bandwidth intercommunity services connect to low-bandwidth copper wiring for service delivery to the home. See *National Information Infrastructure (NII).*

AT bus   The 16-bit expansion bus used in the IBM Personal Computer AT, as distinguished from the 8-bit bus of the original IBM Personal Computer and the 32-bit bus of computers using the Intel 80386 and 80486 microprocessors. Most 80386 and 80486 machines contain AT-compatible expansion slots for backwards compatibility. See *expansion bus, Intel 80386DX, Intel 80386SX, Intel 80486DX, Intel 80486SX, local bus,* and *Micro Channel Bus.*

TIP: *For the fastest video updating with Microsoft Windows, select a computer that offers a local bus video system, in which the video circuitry is directly connected to the microprocessor's high-speed internal circuits.*

AT command set   A standard for software control of modems developed by Hayes Microcomputer Products and initially offered in the company's Smartmodems. The AT command set, so named because AT (short for ATtention) begins many of the commands, is widely emulated by so-called "Hayes-compatible" modems and has become the standard for personal computer modems.

AT keyboard   An 84-key keyboard introduced with the IBM Personal Computer AT (Advanced Technology) in response to complaints about the original IBM Personal Computer keyboard, which used a keyboard layout different from that of office type-writers. The AT keyboard is considered a minimal standard today; most IBM and IBM-compatible computers come equipped with an enhanced 101-key layout. See *keyboard layout*.

Attached Resource Computer Network (ARCnet)   A popular local area network originally developed by Datapoint Corporation for IBM-compatible computers, now available from several vendors. ARCnet interface cards are inexpensive and easily installed. ARCnet networks use a star topology, a token-passing protocol, and coaxial or twisted-pair cable. The network can trans-mit data at speeds of 2.5M per second. See *coaxial cable, local area network (LAN), network interface card, network protocol, network topology,* and *twisted-pair cable*.

attenuation   *ah-`ten-yew-ay-shun*   In local area networks, the loss of signal strength when the system's cables exceed the maxi-mum range stated in the network's specifications. Attenuation prevents successful data communications. You can use a device called a *repeater* to extend a network's cable. See *local area network (LAN)* and *repeater*.

attribute   In many word processing and graphics programs, a character emphasis, such as boldface and italic, and other charac-teristics, such as typeface and type size. In WordPerfect, for ex-ample, attributes include appearance (boldface, underline, double underline, italic, outline, shadow, small caps, strikeout, and redline) and size.

a

In MS-DOS and Microsoft Windows, information about a file that indicates whether the file is a read-only file, a hidden file, or a system file. See *archive attribute* and *file attribute*.

audit trail   In an accounting program, any program feature that automatically keeps a record of transactions so that you can backtrack to find the origin of specific figures that appear on reports.

authoring language   A computer-assisted instruction (CAI) application that provides tools for creating instructional or presentation software. A popular authoring language for Macintosh computers is HyperCard, provided free with every Macintosh computer. Using HyperCard, educators can develop instructional programs quickly and easily.

AutoCAD   A computer-aided design (CAD) program developed by AutoDesk and widely used for professional CAD applications. See *computer-aided design (CAD)*.

auto-dial/auto-answer modem   A modem that can generate tones to dial the receiving computer and can answer a ringing telephone to establish a connection when a call is received. See *modem*.

AUTOEXEC.BAT   In DOS, a batch file that DOS executes when you start or restart the system.

AUTOEXEC.BAT isn't mandatory, but when you're running a computer to which you've attached several devices and several major software applications, the file is essential for efficient operation. AUTOEXEC.BAT files commonly include PATH statements that tell DOS where to find application programs and the commands to install a mouse or operate your printer. All this information must be provided at the start of every operating session; AUTOEXEC.BAT does the task for you. See *batch file*, *CONFIG.SYS*, and *path*.

Although you may need to add commands to AUTOEXEC.BAT yourself, most programs come with an installation program that adds any needed commands, even creating the file, if necessary. Because these changes can be difficult to reconstruct, be careful to leave AUTOEXEC.BAT undisturbed and to keep a copy of the file in a safe place. Should you accidentally erase the file, you can copy it into the root directory of your hard drive.

automatic backup   An application program feature that saves a document automatically at a period the user specifies, such as every 5 or 10 minutes. After a power outage or system crash, you can retrieve the last automatic backup file when you restart the application. This feature can help you avoid catastrophic work losses.

CAUTION: *The automatic backup feature isn't a substitute for regularly saving your work.*

automatic font downloading   The transfer of down-loadable fonts from the hard disk to the printer by a utility program as the fonts are needed to complete a printing job. See *downloading utility* and *printer font.*

automatic hyphenation   See *hyphenation.*

automatic mode switching   The automatic detection and adjustment of a display adapter's internal circuitry to the video output of a program on an IBM PC-compatible computer. Most Video Graphics Array (VGA) adapters, for example, switch to adjust to CGA, MDA, EGA, or VGA output from applications.

automatic recalculation   In a spreadsheet, a mode in which cell values are recalculated every time any cell changes in the worksheet. Automatic recalculation can be switched to manual calculation while you're entering data into a large spreadsheet if recalculation slows data entry unacceptably. See *background recalculation* and *manual recalculation.*

automation   The replacement of human skill by automatic machine operations.

Word processing software is an excellent example of the potential of automation. These programs automate tasks as simple as centering text and as complex as sorting a mailing list into ZIP-code order.

Using automation technology, a small firm can compete more effectively. Equipped with a desktop computer and a variety of application programs, virtually anyone can carry out a sophisticated financial analysis, create a presentation-quality business chart, or publish an attractive newsletter or brochure.

autorepeat key   A key that repeatedly enters a character as long as you hold down that key.

autosave   See *timed backup.*

autostart routine   A set of instructions contained in read-only memory (ROM) that tells the computer how to proceed when you switch on the power. See *basic input/output system (BIOS)* and *Power-On Self-Test (POST).*

autotrace   In a graphics program, such as Adobe Illustrator, a command that transforms an imported bit-mapped image into its object-oriented counterpart. Object-oriented graphics print at the printer's maximum resolution (up to 300 dots per inch for laser printers). Using the autotrace tool, you can transform low-resolution graphics into art that prints at a higher resolution. See *bit-mapped graphic, object-oriented graphic,* and *paint program.*

A/UX   Apple Computer's version of the UNIX operating system. To use A/UX, you need a Macintosh with a Motorola 68020 or 68030 microprocessor and 4M of random-access memory (RAM). See *UNIX.*

AUX   In DOS, an abbreviation for *auxiliary port,* the communications (COM) port DOS uses by default—usually COM1.

auxiliary battery   In a notebook computer, a small, built-in battery that can power the computer for a few minutes while you insert a freshly charged battery pack. See *battery pack* and *notebook computer*.

auxiliary storage   See *secondary storage*.

axis   See *x-axis*, *y-axis*, and *z-axis*.

back end   The portion of a program that accomplishes the processing tasks that the program is designed to perform. In a local area network, the back-end application may be stored on the file server; front-end programs handle the user interface on each workstation. See *client/server architecture* and *front end*.

background   In computers that can do more than one task at a time, the environment in which tasks (such as printing a document or downloading a file) are carried out while the user works with an application in the foreground.

In a computer system that lacks multitasking capabilities, background tasks are carried out during brief pauses in the execution of the system's primary (foreground) tasks. Many word processing programs use this technique to provide background printing. See *multitasking*.

background communication   Data communication, such as downloading a file from a bulletin board, that takes place in the background while the user concentrates on another application in the foreground. See *multitasking*.

background noise   The random or extraneous signals that infiltrate a communications channel, unlike the signals that convey information. Background noise can be slight, causing only symbols to appear occasionally on-screen instead of the text messages you expect, or can be severe enough to end your connection. Any data you try to send or receive under these conditions is likely to contain errors.

background pagination   See *pagination*.

background printing   The printing of a document in the background while a program is active in the foreground. Background printing is particularly useful if you frequently print long documents or use a slow printer. With background printing, you can continue to work while the document prints.

Background printing is automatic in programs such as
WordPerfect, and is a menu option in others, such as Lotus 1-2-3
Release 3 and Microsoft Word for DOS. Otherwise, consider
commercially available print spooling programs or connect your
computer and the printer with a hardware device called a print
buffer. See *multitasking*, *print queue*, and *print spooler*.

background recalculation   In spreadsheet programs, such
as Lotus 1-2-3 Release 3.4, an option that causes the program to
perform recalculations in the background while you continue to
enter data into the spreadsheet.

background tasks   In a multitasking operating system, the
operations occurring in the background (such as printing, sorting
a large file, or searching a database on a bulletin board) while you
work in another program in the foreground.

backlit display   A liquid crystal display (LCD) commonly
used in notebook and laptop computers. The back of the screen
is illuminated to improve the screen's legibility, but at the cost of
decreased battery endurance. See *liquid crystal display (LCD)*.

backplane   A motherboard in a personal computer.

Originally, the term described early bus-oriented designs where
all the expansion was located on a single circuit board at the rear
of the computer case. More recent designs place the motherboard
on the bottom of the case with the expansion slots on the back of
the motherboard, but the term *backplane* is still used by some,
especially if the microprocessor plugs into the motherboard rather
than resides on it. See *motherboard*.

backspace   A key used to delete the character to the left of the
cursor's position, or the act of moving one space to the left by
using the cursor-movement keys.

backup   A copy of installed application software or of data files
you've created. Also, the act of copying files to another disk.

b

> ➤ **TIP:** *Make a copy of all software installation disks whenever you buy new software. Use the copies to install the program and keep the originals in a safe off-site location.*

Hard disks do fail, and when they do you may lose some or all of your programs and documents. Regular backup procedures are required for successful use of a hard disk system. See *archival backup*, *backup procedure*, *full backup*, and *incremental backup*.

backup procedure   A regular maintenance procedure that copies all new or altered files to a backup storage medium, such as floppy disks or a tape drive.

Whether you use your computer for home or business purposes, you should back up your hard disk on a regular basis—at least weekly. If you don't, you expose yourself to the possibility of professional embarrassment, lost customers and profits, and lost time while you re-create the documents. See backup utility.

backup utility   A utility program designed specifically to back up program and data files from a hard disk to a backup medium such as floppy disks or a tape drive.

Backup utility programs include commands to schedule regular backups, to back up only selected directories or files, and to restore all or only a few files from a backup set. An excellent backup utility that you can run in Windows or from a DOS prompt is MSBackup, included with MS-DOS 6.0 and 6.2. The MS-DOS User's Guide explains several backup strategies and provides instructions for using the program. You may prefer to buy another backup utility, such as Norton Utilities, FastBack Plus, or Central Point Backup.

Because backup utilities use a file format that can result in a file being split between two disks, use a backup utility to copy a file that's larger than the largest capacity floppy disk your computer can use.

Rather than use floppy disks for making backups, consider buying a quarter-inch cartridge tape drive. Tape drives with a 250M capacity are now available for $200 or less. Not only will you avoid swapping disks in and out, you can use the scheduler program that's included with most backup utilities to schedule automatic, background backup operations. See *archival backup, backup, backup procedure, incremental backup, quarter-inch cartridge (QIC),* and *save.*

backward chaining   In an expert system, a commonly used method of drawing inferences from IF/THEN rules. A backward chaining system starts with a question such as "How much is this property worth?" and searches through the system's rules to determine which ones allow the system to solve the problem and what additional data you must provide.

Expert systems simulate the expertise of a professional in fields such as medical diagnosis, property assessment, identification of an unknown substance's toxicity, and acceptability of life insurance applications. These programs engage the user, who isn't an expert in these fields, in a dialog.

In a forward chaining system, you begin by supplying all the data. Because backward chaining systems ask you only for the information required, it's easier for people who aren't computer experts to use the software. See *expert system, forward chaining,* and *knowledge base.*

backward compatible   Compatible with earlier versions of a program or earlier models of a computer. Windows 3.1, for example, is backward compatible with applications designed to run on Windows 3.0, but won't run on IBM PCs and PC compatibles equipped with the Intel 8088 microprocessor, even though millions of these machines exist.

backward search   In a database, spreadsheet, or document, a search that begins at the cursor's location and proceeds backward toward the beginning of a database or document (rather than the default forward search).

bad break   An improperly hyphenated line break. See *hyphenation.*

b

A
B
C

bad page break   In a document or spreadsheet, a page break inserted by the program that divides text at an inappropriate location. Headings can be left dangling at the bottom of pages (widows); tables of text can be split; and a single line of text (orphans) can be left at the top of a page. A common flaw in documents produced on computers, bad page breaks can be caught by a final, careful review of the document using the program's print preview command. See *block protection, orphan, soft page break,* and *widow.*

bad sector   An area of a floppy or hard disk that won't reliably record data. Almost all hard disks have some bad sectors as a result of manufacturing defects. The operating system locks these sectors out of reading and writing operations so you can use the disk as though the bad sectors didn't exist.

Bad sectors on floppy disks can present serious problems. If a bad sector appears after you use the disk, you can almost be certain that the data on that sector has been lost. You may be able to salvage the data using utility programs such as Norton Utilities or PC Tools. See *bad track table.*

bad track table   A list attached to or packaged with a hard disk. The bad track table lists the bad sectors or the defective areas of the disk. Almost every hard disk comes off the assembly line with some defects. During the low-level format, these defective areas of the disk are locked out so that system software can't access them. See *low-level format.*

ball bat   In UNIX, a common slang term for an exclamation point (!). Also called a *bang character.*

band   In a database management program's report function, an area set aside for a certain type of information, such as a header area or data from fields. See *database management program* and *report.*

bandwidth   A measurement, expressed in cycles per second (hertz) or bits per second (bps), of the amount of information that can flow through a channel. The higher the frequency, the higher the bandwidth.

bang character   See *ball bat*.

bank switching   A way of expanding memory beyond an operating system's or microprocessor's address limitations by switching rapidly between two banks of memory.

A 64K bank of memory between 640K and 1M is set aside. When more memory is needed, the bank, or *page*, is switched with a 64K page of free memory. This is repeated with additional 64K pages of memory. When the computer requires data or program instructions not now in memory, expanded memory software finds the bank containing the data and switches it with the current bank of memory. Although effective, bank switching results in memory access times that are slower than true, extended memory.
See *expanded memory (EMS)*.

bar code   A printed pattern of wide and narrow vertical bars used to represent numerical codes in machine-readable form.

Bar codes conforming to the Universal Product Code (UPS) are printed on most products sold in supermarkets. When an optical scanner reads the bar code at the checkout counter, the point-of-sale computer matches the product number with its database of price lists and rings up the correct amount.

Using U.S. Postal Service-approved bar codes, the ZIP code of the addressee can be encoded as a POSTNET bar code, which is then printed just above or below the mailing address. Commonly found on preprinted return-addressed envelopes, the latest versions of word processing programs such as WordPerfect and Word for Windows include an option to print the POSTNET bar code on envelopes. See *bar code reader*.

bar code reader   An input device equipped with a stylus that scans bar codes; the device then converts the bar code into a number on-screen. See *bar code*.

bar graph   In presentation graphics, a graph with horizontal bars commonly used to show the values of unrelated items (see fig. B.1). The x-axis (categories axis) is the vertical axis, and the y-axis (values axis) is the horizontal axis.

b

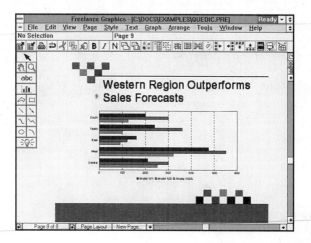

Fig. B.1 *A bar graph.*

A similar graph that uses vertical bars is called a column graph.
In practice, however, both are called bar graphs. For a professional
presentation, use a bar graph (horizontal) to focus on a value (such
as the dollar value or number of bushels of rice, wheat, and millet
harvested in several regions or countries). Use a column graph to
focus on change (bushels of wheat, rice, and millet harvested in
1980, 1985, 1990, and projected for 1995, for example). See
column graph, line graph, paired bar graph, x-axis, and *y-axis.*

baseband   In local area networks, a communications method
in which the information-bearing signal is placed directly on the
cable in digital form without modulation.

Computer signals can be conveyed over cables in two ways:
by analog signals or by digital signals. An analog communication
network is called a *broadband network.*

Digital communication networks are called *baseband networks.*
Since the signals from a computer are digital, the amount of circuitry required for a baseband network to convey the signal to and
from the computer is considerably less. Also, because many baseband networks can use twisted-pair (ordinary telephone) cables,
they're cheaper to install than broadband networks that require
coaxial cable. However, a baseband system is limited in its

geographic extent and provides only one channel of communication at a time. Most personal computer local area networks are baseband networks. See *broadband*.

base font The font that's used in a document. Changes such as italics or bold and larger or smaller sizes are variations of the base font. You can change to a different typeface at any point in the document, but if you change the base font while working in a document, the font change is applied for the entire document. In most word processors, you can choose a default base font for all documents or for just the document you're now editing.

base memory See *conventional memory*.

base-level synthesizer In multimedia, the minimum capabilities of a music synthesizer required by Microsoft Windows 3.1 and its Multimedia Personal Computer (MPC) specifications. A base-level synthesizer must be capable of playing at least six simultaneous notes on three melodic instruments, and three simultaneous notes on three percussion instruments. See *extended-level synthesizer*, *Multimedia Personal Computer (MPC)* and *Musical Instrument Digital Interface (MIDI)*.

baseline In typography, the lowest point that characters reach (excluding descenders). For example, the baseline of a line of text is the bottom of letters such as *a* and *x*, excluding the lowest points of *p* and *q*. See *descender*.

BASIC An easy-to-use (but widely criticized) high-level programming language available on personal computers. Developed in 1964, BASIC (Beginner's All-Purpose Symbolic Instruction Code) is a procedural language that tells the computer what to do step by step.

BASIC programs run in an interactive environment, complete with a text editor, debugger, and an interpreter that translates and executes the BASIC source code line by line. Because you develop a program interactively, trying alternatives and testing program integrity each step of the way, the process of program construction

b

is highly conducive to learning. Recently created compilers transform BASIC code into stand-alone executable programs.

BASIC may be easy to learn, but the programs execute slowly, making the language a poor choice for professional applications. Newer versions have appeared, such as Microsoft's QuickBASIC and Borland's TurboBASIC, that include modern control structures, named subroutines, and a compiler. Some commercially viable software (and many shareware programs) are written in a compiled BASIC, although C is far more popular for professional program development.

New programming techniques are giving BASIC a new lease on life. For example, Microsoft's Visual BASIC, designed for Windows programming, uses the Windows graphical interface and event-oriented programming to create an impressive-looking application. See *C, compiler, control structure, debugger, interpreter, Pascal, procedural language, QuickBASIC, spaghetti code,* and *structured programming.*

BASICA   An interpreter for the Microsoft BASIC programming language. BASICA is supplied on the MS-DOS disk provided with IBM personal computers. See *GW-BASIC.*

basic input/output system (BIOS)   *by-ose*   A set of programs encoded in read-only memory (ROM) on IBM PC-compatible computers. These programs handle startup operations (the POST) and the low-level control for hardware such as disk drives, the keyboard, and monitor.

The BIOS programs of IBM personal computers are copyrighted, so manufacturers of IBM PC-compatible computers must create a BIOS that emulates the IBM BIOS or buy an emulation from companies such as Phoenix Technologies and American Megatrends, Inc. Some system components have a separate BIOS. The BIOS on a hard drive controller, for example, stores a table of tracks and sectors on the drive. See *Power-On Self Test (POST).*

batch file   A file containing a series of DOS commands executed one after the other, as though you had typed them. The mandatory .BAT file extension causes COMMAND.COM to process the file one line at a time. Batch files are useful when you need to type the same series of DOS commands repeatedly. Almost all hard disk users have an AUTOEXEC.BAT file, a batch file that DOS loads at the start of every operating session.

The following example shows how a simple batch file can help you back up your precious data files to floppy disks using the XCOPY command. Add the /M parameter to copy only changed files and to mark each file when it's copied, /S to copy the contents of any subdirectories, and /V to verify that each copy matches the original file. Name the file BACKUPS.BAT and run it daily or weekly.

```
ECHO OFF
ECHO Insert a blank disk in drive A: Press Enter when ready.
PAUSE
MKDIR A:\wp
MKDIR A:\123
XCOPY C:\WP60\WPDOCS A:\WP /S/M/V
XCOPY C:\123R24\FILES A:\123 /S/M/V
```

If you get a Disk full message, insert a blank disk and run BACKUPS.BAT again. Continue until all files have been copied. See *AUTOEXEC.BAT*.

batch processing   A mode of computer operation in which program instructions are executed one after the other without user intervention.

Batch processing efficiently uses computer resources but isn't convenient—especially if you discover a programming or data input error while the computer is spewing out reams of useless printout. In interactive processing, you see the results of your commands on-screen so that you can correct errors and make necessary adjustments before completing the operation. Reserve batch processing for well-tested routines such as system backups. See *interactive processing* and *multiuser system*.

battery pack   A rechargeable battery that supplies power to the computer, usually a laptop or notebook, when external (main) power isn't available. Most battery packs use nickel-cadmium (NiCad) batteries, which have two significant drawbacks: they're prone to becoming incapable of accepting a full charge, and

b

cadmium is an extremely toxic substance. Increasing in use are nickel metal hydride (NiMH) battery packs, which provide increased capacity without either drawback. See *auxiliary battery* and *notebook computer*.

> **TIP:** *NiCad batteries are prone to "remember" the last, lowest charge level and progressively fail to accept a full charge. To prevent this phenomenon, known as* memory effect, *every 5-6 times you run the computer on battery power, fully discharge the battery and then completely recharge it.*

baud *bawd* A variation or change in a signal in a communications channel. See *baud rate* and *bits per second (bps)*.

baud rate The maximum number of changes that can occur per second in the electrical state of a communications circuit.

Under RS-232C communications protocols, 300 baud is likely to equal 300 bits per second (bps), but at higher baud rates, the number of bits per second transmitted is usually twice the baud rate because two bits of data can be sent with each change. Therefore, the transfer rate of modems, for example, is usually stated in bps. See *asynchronous communication, bits per second (bps), modem, serial port, serial printer*, and *telecommunications*.

bay See *drive bay*.

BBS See *bulletin board system (BBS)*.

BCD See *binary coded decimal (BCD)*.

bed In multimedia, the instrumental music that provides the enveloping background for a presentation.

Bell 103A In the United States, a modulation protocol for computer modems governing sending and receiving data at a speed of 300 bits per second. See *CCITT protocol, modem*, and *modulation protocol*.

Bell 212A   In the United States, a modulation protocol for computer modems governing sending and receiving data at a speed of 1200 bits per second. See *CCITT protocol, modem,* and *modulation protocol.*

bells and whistles   An application program's or computer system's advanced features. Many people say that bells and whistles, such as mail-merging capabilities in a word processing program, aren't desirable for novices, and they recommend programs that lack such features. This notion not only requires that you buy additional software as your skills improve, it actually discourages learning by eliminating the opportunity to explore more complex features. If advanced features don't clutter the user interface, you should buy full-featured software you can grow into. A feature that seems hopelessly advanced right now may turn out to be vital. See *mail merge.*

benchmark   A standard measurement used to test the performance of different brands of equipment.

benchmark program   A utility program used to measure a computer's processing speed so that its performance can be compared to that of other computers running the same program.

A variety of standard benchmark tests are available. You should look for results of tests that are applicable to the way you work. Tests such as Dhrystone and Whetstone, for example, test the CPU thoroughly but don't test the performance of system components such as disk drives and internal communications. The speed of components and application programs also affect performance. Look for benchmark tests such as Khornerstone and SPECmark, or try using those included with Norton Utilities and PC Tools. See *cache memory, central processing unit (CPU), throughput,* and *utility program.*

Berkeley UNIX   A version of the UNIX operating system, developed by the University of California at Berkeley, that takes full advantage of the virtual memory capabilities of Digital Equipment Corporation (DEC) minicomputers.

b

The Berkeley version of UNIX, often called BSD (Berkeley System Distribution) UNIX, has been relegated to a subsidiary role by AT&T's promotion of its own UNIX System 5. BSD UNIX, however, is still preferred in technical, academic, and educational environments, in which the system's features meet special needs. See *UNIX*.

Bernoulli box   An innovative removable mass storage device developed by Iomega Corporation for IBM PC-compatible and Macintosh computers. The Bernoulli box is named for the Swiss scientist who discovered the principle of aerodynamic lift.

Bernoulli boxes have removable cartridges containing flexible disks that can hold up to 44M of programs and data. Unlike floppy disk drives, however, these disks spin at high speeds; the latest Bernoulli boxes are capable of up to 22-millisecond access times.

The flexible disk is resistant to head crashes; you can drop a Bernoulli cartridge to the floor without damaging the disk or data. Bernoulli cartridges are removable and relatively inexpensive, making them an excellent choice for a virtually unlimited mass storage system. See *hard disk* and *secondary storage*.

beta site   The company, university department, or individual authorized to beta test software. When developing a program or a version of an existing program, a company chooses out-of-house beta sites where the program is subjected to demanding, heavy-duty usage. This process reveals the program's remaining bugs and shortcomings.

beta software   In computer software testing, a preliminary version of a program that's widely distributed before commercial release to users who test the program by operating it under realistic conditions. See *alpha test*, *beta site*, and *beta test*.

beta test   The second stage in the testing of computer software, before commercial release. Beta tests usually are conducted outside the company that manufactures the software. See *alpha test*.

Bézier curve *beh-zee-ay* A mathematically generated line that can display non-uniform curves. Bézier curves are named after the French mathematician Pierre Bézier, who first described them. In a Bézier curve, the location of two midpoints—called *control handles*—is used to describe the overall shape of an irregular curve. In computer graphics applications, by dragging the control handles (shown as small boxes on-screen), you manipulate the complexity and shape of the curve.

bibliographic retrieval service An on-line information service that specializes in maintaining huge computerized indexes to scholarly, scientific, medical, and technical literature.

The two leading information firms are BRS Information Technologies (Latham, N.Y.) and DIALOG Information Services (Menlo Park, Calif.). Serving mainly corporate and institutional customers, these companies' fees average more than $1 per minute. Copies of articles and documents are available, but the price is steep. Personal computer users can access, at substantially lower rates, special menu-driven night and weekend versions of these services, BRS/After Dark and Knowledge Index. Try the University of Maryland Info Database for information without charge. See *on-line information service*.

> **TIP:** *Before signing on, find out whether your local library makes databases available on CD-ROM disks. If so, you can search these databases for free. Because no clock is ticking away, you can make full use of the interactive searching potential of this information.*

Big Blue Slang for International Business Machines (IBM) Corporation, which uses blue as its corporate color.

binary coded decimal (BCD) A method of coding long decimal numbers so that they can be processed with precision in a computer, which uses a fixed number of places, such as 8 or 16, to code numerical values.

Most personal computers process data in 8-bit chunks called *bytes*, but that size causes problems for number crunching.

When working with binary numbers, the biggest number that can be represented with 8 bits is 256. Some programs get around this limitation by using BCD notation, a way of coding decimal numbers in binary form without really translating them into binary. To code the number 260, BCD fits the codes for 2, 6, and 0 into three adjacent bytes. Larger numbers are no problem; the number of bytes set aside in memory to store the number is simply increased. See *precision*.

binary file   A file containing data or program instructions in a computer-readable format. Using the DOS TYPE command or a word processing program, you can't display the actual contents of a binary file.

> **TIP:** *Don't panic if you open a strangely named file and see an appalling collection of happy faces, spades, clubs, and other odd symbols: chances are that you've opened a binary file accidentally. Just close the file and try again.*

binary numbers   A number system with a base (or radix) of 2, unlike the number systems most of us use, which have bases of 10 (decimal numbers), 12 (measurement in feet and inches), and 60 (time).

Binary numbers are preferred for computers for precision and economy. Building an electronic circuit that can detect the difference between two states (high current and low current, or 0 and 1) is easy and inexpensive; building a circuit that detects the difference among 10 states (0 through 9) is much more difficult and expensive. See *bit*.

binary search   A search algorithm that avoids a slow search through hundreds or thousands of records by starting in the middle of a sorted database and determining whether the desired record is above or below the midpoint. Having reduced the number of records to be searched by 50 percent, the search proceeds to the middle of the remaining records, and so on, until the desired record is found. See *algorithm*.

binary transfer   A file transfer protocol that allows you to transfer binary (compiled) files to a remote computer using terminal software.

binding offset   A measured amount to shift text away from the edge of the page at the time of printing to leave room for binding the document. Binding offset is used only for documents printed or reproduced on both sides of the page (duplex printing); the text is shifted to the left on *verso* (left, even-numbered) pages and to the right on *recto* (right, odd-numbered) pages. Synonymous with *gutter*.

If you're planning to bind a document printed or reproduced on only one side of the page, just increase the left margin to make room for the binding.

BIOS   See *basic input/output system (BIOS)*.

bit   The basic unit of information in a binary numbering system (*bi*nary digi*t*).

The electronic circuitry in computers detects the difference between two states (high current and low current) and represent these states as one of the two numbers in a binary system: 1 or 0. These basic high/low, either/or, yes/no units of information are called *bits*. Because building a reliable circuit that tells the difference between a 1 and a 0 is easy and inexpensive, computers are accurate in their internal processing capabilities, typically making fewer than one internal error in every 100 billion processing operations. See *byte*.

bit map   The representation of a video image stored in a computer's memory as a set of bits. Each *pic*ture *ele*ment (pixel), corresponding to a tiny dot on-screen, is controlled by an on or off code stored as a bit (1 for on or 0 for off) for black-and-white displays. Color and shades of gray require more information. The bit map is a grid of rows and columns of the 1's and 0's that the computer translates into pixels to display on-screen. See *bit, bit-mapped graphic, block graphics, graphics accelerator board*, and *pixel*.

b

bit-mapped font   A screen or printer font in which each character is composed of a pattern of dots. To display or print bit-mapped fonts, the computer or printer must keep a full representation of each character in memory.

When referring to bit-mapped fonts, the term *font* should be taken literally as a complete set of characters of a given typeface, weight, posture, and size. If you want to use Palatino (Roman) 12 and Palatino Italic 14, for example, you must load two complete sets of characters into memory. You can't scale bit-mapped fonts up or down without introducing grotesque staircase distortions, called *aliasing* (see fig. B.2).

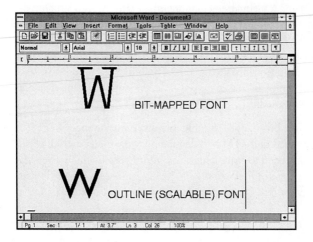

Fig. B.2   *Aliasing visible in the diagonal lines of a bit-mapped font compared with an outline font.*

A separate file of characters for each font size and type you use requires a large amount of disk space, and each file uses a large amount of printer memory. Outline fonts (also called *scalable fonts*) are constructed from mathematical formulas and can be scaled up or down without distortion. See *aliasing, outline font, printer font,* and *screen font.*

bit-mapped graphic   A graphic image formed by a pattern of pixels (screen dots) and limited in resolution to the maximum screen resolution of the device being used. Bit-mapped graphics are produced by paint programs such as MacPaint, SuperPaint, GEM Paint, PC Paintbrush, and some scanners.

Considered inferior to object-oriented graphics for most applications, bit-mapped graphics may have rough edges caused by the square shape of pixels. The irregular patterns are visible when the image includes diagonal lines (refer to fig. B.2) and curves. These graphics usually print at the resolution of the video display now in use, even if the printer is capable of a higher resolution, although programs such as Windows Paintbrush include an option to print using the printer resolution.

Resizing a bit-mapped graphic image without introducing distortions is almost impossible. Scaling up the graphic produces a chunky effect because the lines thicken proportionately; scaling down causes the bits to run together, resulting in an inky effect. Unlike object-oriented graphics (in which each object, such as a line, can be edited or moved independently), bit-mapped graphic images are difficult to edit or modify.

Finally, bit-mapped graphics are notorious memory hogs. You may need up to 1M of video memory to store a map of all the tiny dots needed to form a high-resolution graphic image. See *aliasing, Encapsulated PostScript (EPS) file, object-oriented graphic, paint program, pixel, resolution,* and *scanner.*

BITNET   A wide area network that links more than 1,000 colleges and universities in the United States, Canada, and Europe.

BITNET (Because It's Time Network) was developed by EDUCOM, a non-profit educational consortium, for scholarly communication. Services provided include electronic mail and file transfer. BITNET is used heavily by geographically separated scholars who are working jointly in a narrowly defined research area. See *Internet.*

bits per second (bps)   In asynchronous communications, a measurement of data transmission speed. In personal computing, bps rates frequently are used to measure the performance of modems and other serial communications devices, such as serial ports. The bps rates are enumerated incrementally: 110 bps, 150 bps,

300 bps, 600 bps, 1200 bps, 2400 bps, 4800 bps, 9600 bps, 19200 bps, 38400 bps, 57600 bps, and 115200 bps. See *asynchronous communication, baud rate,* and *modem.*

BIX   A complete on-line computer service owned by the parent company of Delphi but operated as an independent entity. BIX offers e-mail; more than 200 conferences, including conferences for more than 90 hardware manufacturers and software publishers; real-time conferencing; software downloads; and direct access to the WIX (Windows Information Exchange) on-line service, which features a number of Windows-related conferences.

BIX also offers Internet access and includes for Internet access a Windows front end called InterNav. You can access the Internet without InterNav and actually use more services than are available on the InterNav interface, although InterNav will be upgraded soon to extend its features.

black letter   In typography, a family of typefaces derived from German handwriting of the medieval era. Black letter typefaces often are called *Fraktur* (after the Latin word *fractus,* meaning *broken*) because the medieval scribes who created this design lifted their pens from the line to form the next character—fracturing the continuous flow of handwriting.

blank cell   In a spreadsheet program, a cell that contains no values, labels, or formatting different from the worksheet's global formats.

bleed   In desktop publishing, a photograph, text box, or other page-design element that extends to the edge of the page, such as the thumb tab index at the edge of this page. This usually isn't possible if you're printing with a laser printer, which can't print in a 1/4-inch strip around the page's perimeter.

blessed folder   The Macintosh folder containing a System file and a Finder file.

The blessed folder is like a DOS directory named in the PATH command because the System Folder is the only folder the System consults when it can't find a file. Macintosh users, therefore, are obliged to place all the configuration files required by their application programs in this folder, which can quickly grow so large that keeping track of its contents is difficult. See *System* and *System Folder*.

> **TIP:** *Moving the System and Finder files into another folder is called blessing a folder. The procedure of changing the blessed folder can be automated using a free utility called the Folder Blesser, available in the Macintosh Systems forum (GO MACSYS) on CompuServe.*

block   A unit of information that's processed or transferred. The unit may vary in size.

In communications, a unit of information passed from one computer to another is a block. If, for example, you use XMODEM, a communications protocol for transferring files, 128 bytes is considered a block. Under DOS, a block transferred to or from a disk drive is 512 bytes.

In word processing, a unit of text that you mark so that you can use a block operation to move, copy, or otherwise affect that text. See *block operation*.

block definition   See *selection*.

block graphics   On IBM PC-compatible computers, graphics formed on-screen by graphics characters in the extended character set.

The graphics characters in the IBM extended character set are suitable for creating and shading rectangles but not for fine detail. Because the block graphics characters are handled the same way as ordinary characters, the computer can display block graphics considerably faster than bit-mapped graphics. See *bit-mapped graphic* and *graphics character*.

block move   A fundamental editing technique in word processing in which a marked block of text is cut from one location and inserted in another. Synonymous with *cut and paste*.

b

A
B
C

block operation   The act of transferring a block of information from one area to another. In word processing, an editing or formatting operation—such as copying, deleting, moving, or underlining—performed on a marked block of text. See *block move*.

block protection   In word processing and page layout programs, a command that prevents the insertion of a soft page break in a specific block of text. See *bad page break* and *soft page break*.

blurb   In desktop publishing, a brief explanatory subheading that's set below or next to a headline.

.BMP   In Microsoft Windows, an extension indicating that the file contains a Windows-compatible bit-mapped graphic.

board   See *adapter* and *circuit board*.

body type   The font (usually 8- to 12-point) used to set paragraphs of text, distinguished from the font used to set headings, captions, and other typographical elements.

Serif typefaces, such as Century, Garamond, and Times Roman, are preferred over sans serif typefaces for body type because they're more legible. See *display type*, *sans serif*, and *serif*.

boilerplate   A block of text used over and over in letters, memos, or reports.

TIP: *Use boilerplates to achieve big gains in your writing productivity. If your job involves answering routine inquiry letters, develop boilerplate responses to questions on such matters as warranty, sales terms, and the like, and attach these passages to glossaries—named storage areas for boilerplate text and other frequently used items—or save the text in a file. Then you can write a letter just by inserting two or three glossaries or files, and then adding a few personalized touches. See* glossary.

boldface   A character emphasis visibly darker and heavier in weight than normal type. Each entry word in this dictionary is in boldface type. See *emphasis* and *weight*.

bomb   See *crash*.

book weight   A typeface that's darker and heavier than most typefaces, but not so dark and heavy as bold. Book weight fonts are used to set lengthy sections of text so that they're easy to read and produce a pleasing gray tone on the page. See *font* and *weight*.

Boolean operator   `boo-lee-en*   See *logical operator*.

boot   To initiate an automatic routine that clears the memory, loads the operating system, and prepares the computer for use. The term *boot* is derived from the saying "pull yourself up by the bootstraps." Personal computers must do just that because random-access memory (RAM) doesn't retain program instructions when the power is shut off.

Included in the computer's read-only memory (ROM) BIOS are startup and hardware testing programs that execute when the power is switched on (a cold boot). Unlike RAM, ROM circuits retain data and program instructions without requiring power.

After a system crash or lockup occurs, you usually must reboot the computer. First try performing a warm boot using the Reset button or by pressing Ctrl+Alt+Del to restart the system without the stress on electronic components caused by switching the power off and on again. See *cold boot, Power-On Self-Test (POST),* and *warm boot*.

boot sector   The first track on an IBM PC-compatible disk (track 0). After you turn on the power, the bootup software in ROM tells the computer to read the first block of data on this track and load whatever program is found there. If a system disk is read, the program in the boot record directs the computer to the root directory to load MS-DOS. See *boot*.

b

bowl   In typography, the curved strokes that enclose or partially enclose a blank space, called the *counter*, that's part of a letter, such as the blank space in the letter *a* or *c*.

bps   See *bits per second (bps)*.

branch   In DOS, one or more subdirectories located within a directory. In Microsoft Windows File Manager and other graphical file manager utilities, directory branches can be displayed or hidden, depending on your needs (see fig. B.3).

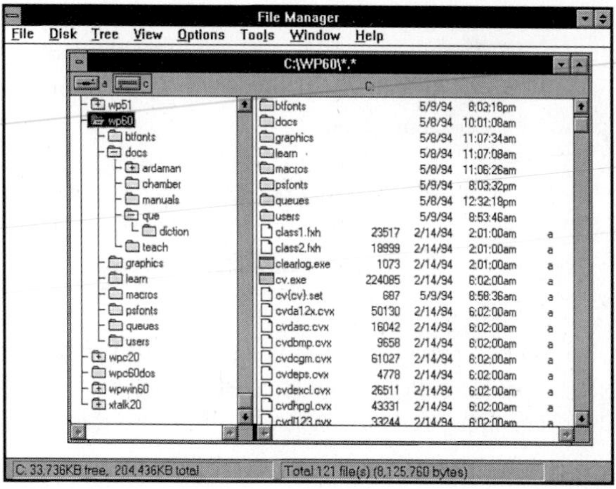

Fig. B.3   *A directory tree with a branch in Microsoft Windows.*

branch control structure   In computer programming, a control structure that tells a program to branch to a set of instructions only if a specified condition is met. If a program detects that a vital data file has been irretrievably corrupted, for example, the program branches to display a message that says something like `The file you want to open is corrupted`. Synonymous with *selection*. See *control structure* and *IF/THEN/ELSE*.

break   A user-initiated signal that interrupts processing or receiving data. See *Control+Break*.

break-out box   A testing device inserted into a communications cable or between a serial port and a serial cable that allows each signal to be tested separately.

breakpoint   A location in a program where it pauses to let the user decide what to do next.

➡ **TIP:** *If you're writing a complex macro, include several breakpoints so that you can check the progress and decide whether to continue.*

bridge   In local area networks, a device that allows two networks (even ones dissimilar in topology, wiring, or communications protocols) to exchange data.

broadband   In local area networks, an analog communications method characterized by high bandwidth. The signal usually is split, or *multiplexed*, to provide multiple communications channels.

Because a computer's signals are digital signals, they must be transformed by a process called *modulation* before they can be conveyed over an analog-signal network. A modem performs this task.

A broadband system uses analog transmissions. Because the microcomputer is a digital device, a device similar to a modem is required at either end of the transmission cable to convert the signal from digital to analog and back again.

Broadband communications can extend over great distances and operate at extremely high speeds. A broadband network can, like a cable TV network, convey two or more communication channels at a time (the channels are separated by frequency). Therefore, a broadband network can handle voice and data communications. See *analog, analog transmission, bandwidth, baseband, digital,* and *local area network (LAN).*

b

broadcast message   In a computer network, a message to all system users that appears when you log on to the system. For example, broadcast messages are used to inform users when the system will be shut down for maintenance.

brownout   A period of low-voltage electrical power caused by unusually heavy demand. Brownouts can cause computers to operate erratically or to crash, either of which can result in loss of data. If brownouts frequently cause your computer to crash, you may need to buy an uninterruptible power supply to work with your machine. See *uninterruptible power supply (UPS)*.

browse   To use a dialog or list box to look for a document or directory (see fig. B.4). In a database management program, to use a dialog or list box to look for a data record.

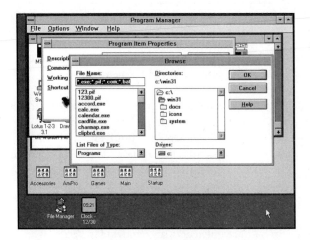

Fig. B.4 *A Microsoft Windows Browse dialog box.*

TIP: *When you use the Browse dialog box, restrict the display of files by choosing an appropriate option in the List Files of Type list box.*

Browse mode   In a database management program, a mode in which data records are displayed in columns for quick, on-screen review (see fig. B.5). Synonymous with *list view* or *table view* in some programs. See *edit mode.*

```
Records   Organize   Fields   Go To   Exit
FIRST_NAME    LAST_NAME    AREA_CODE  PHONE_NO  MALE  BIRTH_DATE  ANNUAL_PAY
James C       Smith        206        123-4567  T     07/04/60        34500.00
Albert K.     Zeller       212        457-9801  T     09/28/59        27900.00
Doris A.      Gregory      503        284-0567  F     07/04/62        16900.00
Harry M.      Nelson       315        576-8235  T     02/15/58        29000.00
Tina B.       Baker        415        787-3154  F     10/12/56        25900.00
Kirk D.       Chapman      618        625-7045  T     00/04/61        19750.00
Mary W.       Thompson     213        432-6783  F     06/18/55        24500.00
Charles M.    Duff         206        456-9873  T     07/22/64        13500.00
Winston E.    Lee          503        365-0512  T     05/14/39        34900.00
Thomas T.     Hanson       206        573-5005  T     12/24/45        28950.00




Browse   C:\data\dbdata\EMPLOYEE   Rec 1/10          File            NumCaps
```

Fig. B.5   *Records displayed in Browse mode.*

brush style   In typography, a typeface design that simulates script drawn with a brush or broad-pointed pen.

brute force   In computer programming, a technique for solving a difficult problem by repeating a simple procedure many times. Computer spell-checkers use a brute-force technique. They don't really "check spelling"; they merely compare all the words in your document to a built-in dictionary of correctly spelled words.

BSD UNIX   See *Berkeley UNIX.*

BTW   In on-line conferences, an acronym for *By The Way.*

buffer   A unit of memory given the task of holding information temporarily, especially while waiting for slower components to catch up.

b

A
B
C

→ **TIP:** *A major advantage exists using Microsoft Windows in 386 Enhanced mode. When you print a file, the print instructions are delivered directly to Print Manager so you can regain control of your applications. Windows then prints in the background, doling out information to the printer at the requisite, glacial pace.*

bug   A programming error that causes a program or a computer system to perform erratically, produce incorrect results, or crash. The term *bug* was coined when a real insect was discovered to have fouled up one of the circuits of the first electronic digital computer, the ENIAC.

Bugs can have serious consequences. Five days before the first manned moon attempt, a bug was discovered in NASA's program that performed trajectory calculations based on the assumption that the moon's gravity was repulsive! See *glitch*.

built-in font   A printer font encoded permanently in the printer's read-only memory (ROM). All laser printers offer at least one built-in typeface, also called a *resident font.* You should consider buying a printer with several typefaces, including a Roman-style serif font such as Times Roman or Dutch, and a clean sans serif font such as Helvetica or Swiss.

Because the terms *font* and *typeface* are often used interchangeably, it's important that you find out exactly which is included in the printer you're interested in buying. Check the printer's literature for a list of the built-in fonts and whether they're scalable. See *cartridge font, downloadable font, font, scalable font,* and *screen font.*

built-in function   In a spreadsheet program, a ready-to-use formula that performs mathematical, statistical, trigonometric, financial, and other calculations.

A built-in function begins with a special symbol (usually @ or =), followed by a keyword, such as AVG or SUM, that describes the formula's purpose. Most built-in functions require one or more arguments enclosed in parentheses and separated by commas. In Lotus 1-2-3, for example, the @ROUND function requires you to provide the number to be rounded (or a cell reference) and the number of decimal places to round the number. The function to round the value in cell C5 to two decimal places is @ROUND(C5,2). Synonymous with *@function*. See *argument*, *argument separator*, *function*, and *keyword*.

built-in pointing device   In notebook computers, a trackball or movable peg that's built into the computer's case in a fixed position. See *clip-on pointing device*, *freestanding pointing device*, *mouse*, *snap-on pointing device*, and *trackball*.

CAUTION: *Before buying a notebook computer that has a built-in pointing device, try it out to make sure that you're happy with the trackball's position and performance.*

bulk storage   Magnetic media that can store data. Synonymous with *mass storage*. See *secondary storage*.

bullet   Originally, a hollow (○) or solid circle (•) about the height of a lowercase letter, used to set off items in a list. Today, squares, triangles, pointing fingers, and a variety of other graphics characters are used as bullets.

Often combined with an indent, bullets are used when listing items whose content is roughly equal in emphasis or significance. When listing items that vary in significance or are arranged chronologically, using numbers is more effective. See *hanging indent* and *indentation*.

bulleted list chart   In presentation graphics, a text chart that lists a series of ideas or items of equal weight (see fig. B.6). See *presentation graphics*.

b

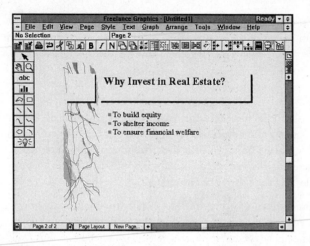

Fig. B.6 *A bulleted list chart.*

bulletin board system (BBS)   A telecommunications utility, usually set up by a personal computer hobbyist for the enjoyment of other hobbyists.

Bulletin boards can be great fun. Late at night, you can dial a BBS, leave messages, upload and download public domain software and shareware, and play Space Invaders. However, a little caution is necessary since the advent of computer viruses. When you log on to a BBS for the first time, look for information about automated virus protection used by the BBS. Nowadays, most BBSs scan all uploaded files before writing the file to the host computer's hard drive. If you find no virus checking on a certain BBS, don't use it as a source to download files. Since you can find all the popular software on almost every BBS, look elsewhere for a software source. See *chat forum, communications program, cybersex, dirty, Fidonet, telecommunications,* and *virus.*

bulletproof   Capable of resisting external interference and recovering from situations that would crash other programs. See *fault tolerance.*

bundled software Software included with a computer sys-tem as part of the system's total price. Also, several programs that are packaged and sold together, now frequently called *software suites.*

burn-in Operating a newly assembled computer system to screen for failures. Semiconductor components such as memory chips and microprocessors tend to fail either in the first few hours of operation or late in their lives. Responsible computer retailers, therefore, run systems continuously for 24 to 48 hours before releasing the systems to customers.

Sometimes used—incorrectly—to refer to permanently burning, or etching, the screen phosphors of a computer monitor when the same image is constantly on-screen. This phenomenon is really called *ghosting.* See *ghost* and *screen saver.*

bus An internal electrical pathway along which signals are sent from one part of the computer to another. Personal computers have a processor bus design with three pathways:

- The data bus sends data back and forth between the memory and the microprocessor.

- The address bus identifies which memory location will come into play.

- The control bus carries the control unit's signals.

An extension of the data bus, called the *expansion bus,* connects the computer's expansion slots to the processor. The data, address and expansion buses are wired in parallel rows so that all the bits being sent can travel simultaneously, like cars side by side on a 16- or 32-lane freeway.

Three bus architectures are commonly found in today's IBM PC and PC-compatible marketplace:

b

- *Industry Standard Architecture (ISA) bus.* Synonymous with AT bus, this is the 16-bit bus initially developed for IBM's AT (Advanced Technology) computers. The bus includes 8-bit expansion slots for compatibility with earlier adapters, and 16-bit slots for AT-compatible adapters.

- *Micro Channel Architecture (MCA) bus.* A proprietary, 32-bit bus used in high-end IBM PS/2 computers.

- *Enhanced Industry Standard Architecture (EISA) bus.* A 32-bit bus that, unlike the MCA bus, is backward compatible with ISA adapters.

The 32-bit bus width is only part of the equation. Although the pathways in the processor bus operate at the speed of your microprocessor, the expansion bus operates at much slower speeds— EISA at 8.33 MHz and MCA at 10 MHz. Local bus, a high-speed data path that directly links the computer's processing unit to several expansion slots, was developed to speed video display in graphics-intense programs such as Microsoft Windows. See *address bus, data bus, expansion bus*, and *local bus*.

> **TIP:** *Confused about which bus to choose when you're buying a new PC? If you're running Microsoft Windows, choose a system with local bus video. Such systems offer significantly faster screen updating with graphics-intensive Windows applications.*

bus mouse   A mouse connected to the computer by a dedicated mouse adapter inserted into an available expansion slot. See *serial mouse*.

bus network   In local area networks, a decentralized network topology used by AppleTalk and EtherNet, for example, in which a single connecting line, the *bus*, is shared by a number of nodes, including workstations, shared peripherals, and file servers (see fig. B.7).

In a bus network, a workstation sends every message to all other workstations. Each node in the network has a unique address, and its reception circuitry monitors the bus for messages being sent to the node, ignoring all other messages.

Fig. B.7 *An illustration of a bus network.*

> **TIP:** *Bus networks have a significant advantage over competing network designs (star networks and ring networks); the failure of a single node doesn't disrupt the rest of the network. Extending a bus network also is a simple matter; just lengthen the bus and add nodes, up to the system's maximum (about 1,000 feet without a repeater). See* node *and* repeater.

button   In graphical user interfaces, a dialog box option used to execute a command, choose an option, or open another dialog box. See *Cancel button, default button, OK button, pushbutton,* and *radio button.*

button bar   See *icon bar* and *toolbar.*

byline   In desktop publishing, the author's name (often including organizational affiliation and address) positioned directly after the article's title.

byte   *bite*   Eight contiguous bits, the fundamental data unit of personal computers. Storing the equivalent of one character, the byte is also the basic unit of measurement for computer storage. Because computer architecture is based (for the most part) on binary numbers, bytes are counted in powers of two.

b

The terms *kilo* (in kilobyte) and *mega* (in megabyte) are used to count bytes but are misleading: they derive from decimal (base 10) numbers. A kilobyte actually is 1,024 bytes, and a megabyte is 1,048,576 bytes. Many computer scientists criticize these terms, but the terms give those who think in decimal numbers a nice handle on the measurement of memory. See *bit* and *kilobyte (K)*.

C A high-level programming language widely used for professional programming. Developed by Dennis Ritchie of Bell Laboratories in 1972, C is preferred by most major professional software companies. A general-purpose procedural language, C combines the virtues of high-level programming languages with the efficiency of an assembly language.

Because the programmer can embed instructions that directly reach the bit-by-bit representation of data inside the processing unit, compiled C programs run significantly faster than programs written in other high-level programming languages. C programs are highly portable, being easily and quickly rewritten to run on a new computer as long as the target environment has a C compiler.

AT&T's Bell Laboratories was prohibited from copyrighting C or UNIX because of the antitrust regulations in effect before the breakup of the Bell system. Therefore, C compilers and UNIX are in the public domain and have been adopted by virtually all colleges and universities, resulting in a steady stream of computer science graduates well versed in the C language and the UNIX operating system. That, and the language's portability, are the important factors in its widespread adoption by professional programmers who hope to find the widest possible market for their products. See *algorithm, assembly language, control structure, high-level programming language, portable computer, procedural language, syntax,* and *UNIX.*

C++ A high-level programming language developed by Bjarne Stroustrup at AT&T's Bell Laboratories. Combining all the advantages of the C language with those of object-oriented programming, C++ has been adopted as the standard house programming language by several major software vendors, such as Apple Computer. See *C* and *object-oriented programming language.*

C: In personal computers, the default letter assigned to the first hard drive.

cache *cash* A storage area that keeps frequently accessed data or program instructions readily available so that you don't have to retrieve them repeatedly.

Caches improve performance by storing data or instructions in faster sections of memory and by using efficient design to increase the likelihood that the data needed next is in the cache. See *cache memory*, *hardware cache*, and *internal cache*.

cache controller A chip, such as the Intel 82385, that manages the retrieval, storage, and delivery of data to and from memory or the hard disk.

A cache controller performs a number of complex tasks. When data or instructions are requested by the central processing unit (CPU), the cache controller intercepts the request and handles the delivery from RAM. The cache controller then determines where in the cache to store a copy of the just-delivered data, when to fetch data or code from adjacent addresses in RAM in case it's needed next, where in the cache to store this new data, and which data to discard if the cache is full. The cache controller also keeps an up-to-date table of the addresses of everything it's holding. Despite the magnitude of these duties and the small amount of memory actually used (32K to 256K), a well-designed cache controller must predict and have stored in the cache what the CPU needs next with an accuracy greater than 95 percent. See *cache memory*, *Intel 82385/82485*, and *set-associative*.

cache memory A special section of fast memory chips set aside to store the information most frequently accessed from RAM. Synonymous with *external cache*.

Cache memory is a small section, usually 32K to 512K, of ultra-fast static random-access memory (SRAM) chips with its own bus to the central processing unit (CPU), used to store data and code requested by the CPU. When the CPU requests this data again, it's delivered at the speed of the microprocessor. Because the cache communicates directly with the CPU, the bus can be wider to improve memory performance further. Cache memory is distinguished from a software cache, an area of ordinary RAM set aside to store information frequently accessed from disk drives. See *software cache*, *static random-access memory (SRAM)*, and *wait state*.

CAD   See *computer-aided design (CAD)*.

CADD   See *computer-aided design and drafting (CADD)*.

CAI   See *computer-assisted instruction (CAI)*.

calculated field   In a database management program, a field that contains the results of calculations performed on other fields. Current balance and total score are examples of calculated fields. Synonymous with *derived field*. See *data field*.

call   In programming, a statement that transfers program execution to a subroutine or procedure. When the subroutine or procedure is complete, program execution returns to the command following the call statement.

callout   In desktop publishing, items of text that name parts of an illustration, usually with a line or arrow pointing to the part of the illustration the text describes.

camera-ready copy   A finished, printed manuscript or illustration ready to be photographed by a printing company for reproduction.

Cancel button   An option in a graphical user interface dialog box that you use to cancel a command and return to the active document. Equivalent to pressing Esc.

canonical form   In mathematics and computer programming, an expression that conforms to established principles learned only through practice, apprenticeship, and interaction with experts. It's possible to write a programming expression that's entirely correct but not in canonical form, thus preventing social acceptance in learned mathematical and computer science societies. Most people, however, are concerned with getting the right answer.

cap height   In a typeface, the height of capital letters, measured in points, from the baseline. See *baseline*.

 # A B C

Caps Lock key   A toggle key that locks the keyboard so that you can enter uppercase letters without pressing the Shift key. When you're in uppercase mode, most keyboards have a light that illuminates; many programs also display a message, such as CAPS LOCK or CAPS. The Caps Lock key has no effect on the number and punctuation keys.

caption   In desktop publishing, a descriptive phrase that identifies a figure, such as a photograph, illustration, or graph.

capture   To copy all or part of an image on-screen and convert it to a graphics file format to insert in a document or save on a disk.

In NetWare network software, a command used to create a connection between the LPT1 port of a workstation and the network printer. If you have a local printer attached to LPT1, you can redirect LPT2 to the network printer.

card   An electronic circuit board designed to fit into a slot of a computer's expansion bus. Synonymous with *adapter*. See *expansion bus*.

caret   A symbol (^) commonly found over the 6 key on computer keyboards. In spreadsheet programs, the caret is the symbol for exponent, or "to the power of." Caret also can be used to stand for the Ctrl key in computer documentation, as in "Press ^C."

carpal tunnel syndrome   See *repetitive strain injury (RSI)*.

carriage return   A signal that tells the printer to move to the left margin. Some printers also perform a line feed when executing a carriage return; such distinctions are handled by software printer drivers. See *Enter/Return* and *line feed*.

carrier sense multiple access with collision detection (CSMA/CD)   In local area networks, a widely used method for controlling a computer's access to the communication channel. With CSMA/CD, each component of the network (called a *node*) has an equal right to access the communication channel. If two computers try to access the network at the same time, the network uses a random number to decide which computer gets to use the network.

This channel access method works well with relatively small- to medium-sized networks (two or three dozen nodes) and is used by the two most popular network architectures: EtherNet and AppleTalk. When you have many workstations and network traffic volume is high, many data collisions occur, overloading and even locking up the system. Large networks, therefore, use alternative channel access methods, such as polling and token passing. See *AppleTalk, EtherNet, local area network (LAN), node, polling,* and *token passing.*

Cartesian coordinate system   *car-`tee-zhen*   A method, created by 17th century French mathematician René Descartes, of locating a point in a two-dimensional space by defining a vertical axis and a horizontal axis. A mouse uses the Cartesian coordinate system to locate the pointer on-screen. In some graphics applications, you can display the coordinates so that the pointer can be located precisely. See *digitizing tablet* and *mouse.*

cartridge   A removable module containing data storage media such as magnetic tape or disks. In computer printers, a removable module that expands the printer's memory or contains fonts in addition to the fonts resident in the printer.

cartridge font   A printer font supplied in the form of a read-only memory (ROM) cartridge that plugs into a receptacle on Hewlett-Packard LaserJet printers and clones.

Unlike downloadable fonts, a cartridge font is immediately available to the printer and doesn't consume space in the printer's RAM, which can be used up quickly when printing documents loaded with graphics. The popular cartridges contain multiple fonts, often more than 100. Most laser printers now use built-in fonts or software-generated fonts. See *font* and *typeface.*

cascading menus   A menu system where selecting a command on a pull-down menu causes another menu to appear, or *cascade,* next to the selected command. The presence of a cascading menu is usually indicated by a triangle at the right edge of the menu. Synonymous with *submenus*.

cascading windows In a user interface, two or more windows displayed so they overlap. This mode is convenient because you still can see the title bar and an edge of all the other windows you've opened (see fig. C.1). See *overlaid windows* and *tiled windows*.

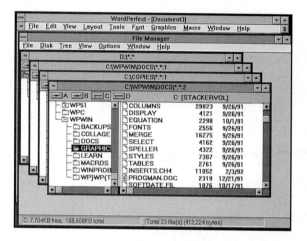

Fig. C.1 *Cascading windows in Microsoft Windows.*

case-sensitive Distinguishing the difference between upper- and lowercase letters. DOS isn't case-sensitive; you can type DOS commands in upper- or lowercase letters.

case-sensitive search A search in which a program tries to match the exact pattern of upper- and lowercase letters. A case-sensitive search for *Porter*, for example, matches *Porter* but not *PORTER*, *porter*, or *pOrter*.

cast-based animation In multimedia, an animation method in which each object in a production is treated as an individual graphic image (a *cast member*). You can manipulate each cast member individually by means of a script. See *script*.

catalog   In database management, a list of related database files you've grouped together so that you can easily distinguish them from others.

All relational database management programs can work with more than one file at a time. Frequently, the results of relational operations (such as a join) produce a new file. Also, you create several indexes and other files that support the application. A catalog helps you track all these related files in a unit. See *join* and *relational database management system (RDBMS)*.

cathode ray tube (CRT)   In a computer monitor, a vacuum tube that uses an electron gun (cathode) to emit a beam of electrons that illuminates phosphors on-screen as the beam sweeps across the screen repeatedly. The computer monitor is often called a CRT. The same technology is used in television. See *monitor, phosphor*, and *refresh*.

CAV   See *constant angular velocity (CAV)*.

CBT   See *computer-based training (CBT)*.

CCITT   See *Comité Consultatif International Téléphonique et Télégraphique (CCITT)*.

CCITT protocol   A number of standards for the transmission of data using a computer modem, serial port, or a network. The following protocols are in the V series:

Protocol	Description
CCITT V.21	Defines a standard for sending data at speeds of 300 bits per second. Used infrequently within the United States, where the Bell 103A standard is more common.
CCITT V.22	A standard for sending data at speeds of 1,200 bits per second. This standard is used infrequently within the United States, where the Bell 212A standard is more common.

Protocol	Description
CCITT V.22bis	Governs sending and receiving data at a speed of 2,400 bits per second. (*Bis* means again, or repeat. V.22bis repeats the 1,200 standard for 2,400 bits.)
CCITT V.32	A standard for sending data at speeds of 4,800 or 9,600 bits per second. High-speed modems using this standard are now available for less than $150.
CCITT V.32bis	A standard for sending data at speeds of 14,400 bits per second. A modem that conforms to this standard is downwardly compatible with V.32 modems, meaning that it can slow down to 9,600 bps to accommodate a slower modem on the other end of the line.
CCITT V.42	An error-checking standard that filters out line noise and eliminates errors that can occur when sending or receiving data. For error checking to function, both the sending and receiving modems must have error-checking capabilities conforming to the same error-checking protocol.
CCITT V.42bis	A standard for speeding transmissions by compressing data on the sending end and decompressing the data on the receiving end. If the data isn't already compressed, gains in effective transmission speeds of up to 400 percent can be realized.

CCITT V.21, V.22, and V.22bis are modulation protocols; V.32 and V.32bis are high-speed modulation protocols; V.42 is a standard error-checking protocol; and V.42bis is a data-compression protocol. Other CCITT protocols exist, including standards for serial transmission and arranging data in packets. See *Bell 103A, Bell 212A, data-compression protocol, error-correcting protocol, modem, modulation protocol,* and *packet.*

CD   See *compact disk (CD).*

CDEV   See *control panel device (CDEV).*

CD-I   See *Compact Disk-Interactive (CD-I)*.

CD-ROM   *cee-dee-rom*   Acronym for *compact disc-read only memory*, a read-only optical storage technology that uses compact disks.

CD-ROMs can store up to 650M of data, all of which can be made available interactively on the computer's display. New compression techniques let you pack up to 250,000 text pages on one CD-ROM disk.

CD-ROM was originally used for encyclopedias, dictionaries, and software libraries. Current uses include programs with large graphics and sound files, such as multimedia, games, font and clip-art libraries for desktop publishers, and for distribution of program software. Installing program software from CD-ROM avoids the lengthy process of swapping 10 to 20 disks.

Like all electronic devices, CD-ROM drives and disks are getting cheaper, making them an excellent choice if you're expanding a home computer system. The cost of a CD-ROM drive and a high-quality CD-based encyclopedia, for example, is considerably less than a traditional, print-based encyclopedia. If you're buying a CD-ROM drive for a Windows-compatible system, make sure that you look for a drive that conforms to the Multimedia Personal Computer (MPC) standard. See *compact disk (CD)*, *Multimedia Personal Computer (MPC)*, and *optical disk*.

CD-ROM disk drive   A read-only disk drive designed to read the data encoded on compact disks and to transfer this data to a computer.

Although audio compact disk players sell for as little as $99, CD-ROM drives cost two to four times that much. A CD-ROM disk drive, however, contains circuitry optimized to locate data at high speeds; audio CD players need to locate only the beginning of audio tracks, which they play sequentially. As the number of these drives increases, the price of CD-ROM drives will drop to more reasonable levels.

CD-ROM drives retrieve data much more slowly than computer disk drives. If you don't like waiting for the screen to update, spend more money to get one of the faster CD-ROM drives. An access time of 200 ms (milliseconds) to 250 ms is considered fast for currently available drives and is well worth the additional cost. Avoid drives with 800 ms access times. If you're buying your drive for a Windows-compatible MPC system, make sure that the CD-ROM drive can play CDs that store up to 600M of data, transfer data at rates of at least 150 kilobits per second, and access data in at least 400 ms. Also, make sure that the drive has headphone jacks, external speaker jacks, and a volume control. See *access time*, *compact disk (CD)*, and *millisecond (ms)*.

CD-ROM eXtended Architecture (CD-ROM XA)   A compact disk data storage standard jointly developed by Philips, Sony, and Microsoft for the storage of audio and visual data on compact disks so that you can simultaneously access the audio and visual portions.

CD-ROM XA   See *CD-ROM eXtended Architecture*.

cell   In a spreadsheet, a rectangle formed by the intersection of a row and column in which you enter information in the form of text (a label) or numbers (a value). See *constant*, *formula*, and *label*.

cell address   In a spreadsheet, a letter and number combination that identifies a cell's location on the worksheet by column and row (A3, B9, C2, and so on). If you refer to a cell in a formula, the cell address is called the *cell reference*. See *cell reference* and *formula*.

cell animation   An animation technique in which a background painting is held in place while a series of transparent sheets of celluloid containing objects are placed over the background painting, producing the illusion of movement.

Cell animation is much easier than drawing a new background for every frame in the animation sequence. A Macintosh animation program that uses a computerized version of cell animation is Macromedia Director.

cell definition   The actual contents of a cell in a spreadsheet, as displayed on the entry line. If you place a formula in a cell, the program displays the result of the calculation rather than the formula itself. See *cell protection, entry line, formula*, and *value*.

cell format   In a spreadsheet, the way the program displays the contents of cells. Label formats include aligning the text on the left, right, or center. Numeric formats include currency, percent, including commas, setting a number of decimal places, and date and time display. You can change the font and font size, and make values and labels bold and italicized. See *character-based program, current cell, global format, graphics spreadsheet, label, label alignment, numeric format, range format*, and *value*.

cell pointer   In DOS spreadsheet programs, the rectangular highlight that indicates the current cell. When you enter data in the spreadsheet, it's recorded in the current cell. See *cursor*.

cell protection   In a spreadsheet program, a format applied to a cell, a range of cells, or an entire file that prevents you from altering the contents of protected cells.

TIP: *With most spreadsheet applications, you can use a two-step process to create a worksheet in which the cell pointer can move only to cells where you want values entered. After you enter column and row labels and titles, unprotect the cells that will contain values (protected is the default format). Second, protect the rest of the worksheet, including those cells containing labels. The worksheet can then be saved to use as a data-entry form.*

cell reference   In a spreadsheet formula, the address of the cell that contains a value needed to solve the formula. Using cell references is the key to the power and usefulness of a spreadsheet program. You use cell references rather than values to write a formula, such as **+B1+B2**, where B1 and B2 are *cell addresses*. When used in a formula, they tell the program to go to the named cell (such as B1) and use the value in that cell to perform the calculation. If changing the values in the spreadsheet is necessary, you need to change only the value in the referenced cell.

A cell reference can refer to a cell containing a formula, which may contain its own cell references to other cells, which can themselves contain formulas, and so on. A change made to any constant in such a worksheet affects intermediate values and, ultimately, the bottom line. See *cell address, constant, formula, recalculation method, value,* and *what-if analysis.*

central mass storage   See *file server.*

central processing unit (CPU)   The computer's internal storage, processing, and control circuitry, including the arithmetic-logic unit (ALU), the control unit, and memory in the form of ROM and RAM. The ALU and control unit are wholly contained on a chip called the microprocessor chip; the memory is elsewhere on the motherboard or a card on the expansion bus. See *adapter, arithmetic-logic unit (ALU), control unit, expansion bus, microprocessor, motherboard,* and *primary storage.*

Centronics interface   The parallel printing port of IBM PC-compatible computers, named after the company (Centronics) that designed a predecessor to this interface standard. See *parallel port.*

CGA   See *Color Graphics Adapter (CGA).*

CGM   See *Computer Graphics Metafile (CGM).*

chain printing   The printing of separate files as a unit by placing commands at the end of the first file to direct the program to continue printing the second file, and so on. Full-featured word processing programs such as Microsoft Word allow chained printing with continuous pagination and, in some cases, the generation of a complete table of contents and index for the linked files. See *master document.*

chamfer   In desktop publishing and presentation graphics, a beveled edge between two intersecting lines.

channel access In local area networks, the method used to gain access to the data communication channel that links the computers. Three common methods are contention, polling, and token ring. See *contention, local area network (LAN), polling,* and *token-ring network.*

character Any letter, number, punctuation mark, or symbol that you can produce on-screen by pressing a key on the keyboard. A character uses one byte of memory. See *byte.*

character-based program A program that relies on the ASCII and extended ASCII character set that includes block graphics to create its screens and display the text you enter. Figure C.2 shows Lotus 1-2-3, a character-based DOS program, running with Norton Desktop for Windows, a graphics-based program. See *Microsoft Windows* and *windowing environment.*

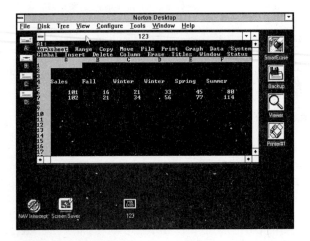

Fig. C.2 *A character-based program (1-2-3) and a graphics-based program (Norton Desktop).*

character graphics See *block graphics.*

character-mapped display A method of displaying characters in which a special section of memory is set aside to represent the display; programs generate a display by inserting characters into the memory-based representation of the screen. Therefore, the whole screen—not just one line—remains active, and the user or the program can modify characters anywhere on-screen. See *teletype (TTY) display*.

character mode   In IBM and IBM-compatible computers, a display mode in which the computer displays only those characters contained in its built-in character set. Synonymous with *text mode*. See *character set*, *character view*, and *graphics mode*.

> **TIP:** *If you're using an older DOS machine, you probably will get the best performance from programs that allow you to choose between character mode and graphics mode (such as Microsoft Word). Switch to graphics mode only when you need to preview formatting or graphics before printing.*

character set   The fixed set of keyboard codes that a particular computer system uses. See *ASCII*, *code page*, and *extended character set*.

characters per inch (cpi)   The number of characters that fit in an inch of type of a given font. Standard sizes drawn from typewriting are pica (10 cpi) and elite (12 cpi).

characters per second (cps)   A measurement of the speed of a communications or printer device.

character string   Any series of characters (including spaces) that a program treats as a group. In programming and database management, you distinguish character strings from reserved words (command names) by enclosing strings in quotation marks; as a result, the characters in the string give no instructions to the computer. In a database management query language, for example, the expression FIND "Wyoming" causes the computer to search for the first record that exactly matches the character string *Wyoming*. Synonymous with *string*.

character view   In some DOS applications, a mode in which the program switches the display adapter circuitry to character mode; also called *draft mode* by some programs. In character mode, the computer can display only those characters contained in the computer's built-in character set. See *character mode* and *graphics view*.

> **TIP:** *On all but the fastest machines, character view is noticeably faster than graphics view. Unless you need to see graphics and fonts on-screen, work in character view and switch to graphics view before printing.*

chat forum   In a computer bulletin board system (BBS), a special forum or conference that allows two or more callers, online at the same time, to engage in conversation with each other by taking turns typing questions and answers.

Bulletin boards usually feature conferences for specific software, such as WordPerfect or Gaming, and chat lines can be used by two afficiandos swapping information and hints. Other BBSs, such as SeniorNet, a San Francisco-based board designed to serve senior citizens' needs, includes a number of computer conference groups and chat lines where users can gather via computer. See *cybersex*.

check box   In a graphical user interface dialog box, a square box that you choose to toggle an option on or off. When the option is turned on, an x appears in the check box. A check box can appear alone or with other check boxes in a list of items. Unlike radio buttons, you can choose more than one check box. See *dialog box, graphical user interface (GUI)*, and *radio button*.

checksum   An acronym for SUMmation CHECK. In data communications, an error-checking technique in which the number of bits in a unit of data is summed and transmitted along with the data. The receiving computer then checks the sum. If the sum differs, an error probably occurred in transmission. A commonly used personal computer communications protocol called XMODEM uses the checksum technique.

In virus scanning software, such as Central Point Anti-Virus, checksums are calculated for every file in a directory and the results saved in a file stored in the directory. When the program is scanning, it compares the checksum information stored in the directory with the current checksum for each scanned file. A difference in the sum may indicate that the file has been infected by a virus that doesn't leave a recognized signature. See *XMODEM*.

checkwriting program   An accounting program designed to help individuals and small-business owners keep track of checking accounts, credit card accounts, tax records, and budgets using a blank check as its basic data entry form.

Chiclet keyboard   A keyboard, frequently found on calculators, that uses small rectangular keys the size of Chiclet chewing gum. Chiclet keys are difficult to use because the keys are too small and offer little tactile feedback. A Chiclet keyboard was featured on one of IBM's most notorious marketing failures, the PCjr home computer.

chip   A miniaturized electronic circuit mass-produced on a tiny chip or wafer of silicon.

The electronic age began in earnest with the 1947 invention of the transistor, a switching and amplifying device that replaced huge, power-hungry, and unreliable vacuum tubes. As important as the transistor was, it didn't solve the bigger problem: the necessity of wiring all those components together. Various automated procedures were devised, but some of the wiring and soldering had to be done by hand, making complex electronic devices very expensive.

In the late 1950s, Jack Kilby (an engineer at Texas Instruments) and Robert Noyce (an engineer at Fairchild Semiconductor) discovered that they could create an integrated circuit, a chip made out of semiconducting materials that could duplicate the function of several transistors and other electronic components. The first integrated circuits contained only a few components, but the same manufacturing techniques now can generate 16 million components on a chip so small that you can place it on the tip of your finger.

Of even greater economic and social significance than the chip's miniaturization is the fact that it can be mass-produced, and at very low prices. Today's Intel Pentium microprocessor, for example, sells for $1,000, but is the electronic equivalent of a mainframe computer priced at several million dollars just 20 years ago. The achievement of chip-manufacturing technology has spread the use of computer technology throughout society. See *integrated circuit* and *microprocessor*.

choose   In a program that uses menus and dialog boxes, the process of picking an option that begins an action.

Highlighting or selecting an option is often different from choosing it. In many programs, you can highlight an option without choosing it. To choose a highlighted option, press Enter. In Microsoft Windows and many DOS applications, to choose using the keyboard, move the selector or highlight to the item and then press Enter; or press the Alt key plus the underlined letter in the item name. To choose with the mouse, click buttons and menu commands; double-click icons and file names to execute commands or launch applications. See *highlighting* and *select*.

> **TIP:** *If you use a mouse, look for ways you can save time by double-clicking an option. In many applications, double-clicking an option highlights and chooses it in one quick action. To double-click, press the mouse button twice in rapid succession.*

Chooser   A Macintosh desktop accessory (DA) supplied by Apple Computer with the Mac's operating system—the System. The Chooser governs the selection of printer drivers, the programs that control communication with the printer. The Chooser displays the icons of the printer drivers now installed in the System Folder.

A major contrast between DOS applications and the Macintosh operating system is that the Macintosh provides printer drivers that work with any Mac application. Following the Mac's lead, Microsoft Windows provides printer drivers for all programs designed to take advantage of its graphical user interface.

When using network devices or communicating on an AppleTalk

network, you also use the Chooser to set up these network connections. See *character-based program, Microsoft Windows, printer driver, System,* and *System Folder.*

chord   In desktop publishing and presentation graphics, a straight line that connects the end points of an arc.

chrominance   In multimedia, the portion of a composite video signal that contains color information.

circuit board   A flat plastic board on which electrically conductive circuits are laminated. Synonymous with *printed circuit board.* See *adapter, card,* and *motherboard.*

circular reference   In a spreadsheet, an error condition caused by two or more formulas that reference each other. A circular reference occurs, for example, when the formula +B5 is placed in cell A1, and the formula +A1 is placed in cell B5; or when a formula totalling the values in the cells D1 through D4 is placed in D5, and the formula mistakenly refers to cells D1 through D5.

Circular references don't always result in errors. They can be used deliberately, for example, to create an iterative function in a worksheet: each recalculation increases the values of the two formulas. Circular references, however, frequently arise from unintentional typing errors and usually produce erroneous results. If you see an error message informing you that a circular reference exists in your worksheet, eliminate any unwanted circular references before placing confidence in the spreadsheet's accuracy. Spreadsheet programs usually have a command that displays a screen which includes a list of the cells containing circular references.

CISC   *sisk*   See *complex instruction set computer (CISC).*

Class A certification   A Federal Communications Commission (FCC) certification that a given make and model of computer meets the FCC's Class A limits for radio frequency emissions, which are designed for commercial and industrial environments.

Class B certification   A Federal Communications Commission (FCC) certification that a given make and model of computer meets the FCC's Class B limits for radio frequency emissions, which are designed for homes and home offices. Class B standards are tougher than Class A and are designed to protect radio and television reception in residential neighborhoods from excessive radio frequency interference (RFI) generated by computer usage. Class B computers also are shielded more efficiently from external interference.

Computers used at home are more likely to be surrounded by radio and television equipment. If you plan to use your computer at home, avoid computers that have only Class A certification (that is, they failed Class B).

clear   To remove data from a document. In the Windows and Macintosh environments, the Clear command (Edit menu) completely wipes out the selection, as opposed to Cut, which removes the selection to the Clipboard (from which you can retrieve the selection, if you later discover that you deleted it by mistake). Synonymous with *delete*.

> **TIP:** *Most applications can recover a cleared deletion if you choose Undo immediately after performing the clear. In Lotus 1-2-3, press Alt+F4 to Undo; in other programs, Undo is usually on the Edit menu. Don't move the pointer, choose another command, or type any other text before choosing Undo, or the deletion may be lost irretrievably.*

click   To press and quickly release a mouse button. You frequently see this term in instructions such as "Click the Bold check box in the Fonts dialog box." For users of IBM-compatible PCs, this instruction means, "Move the mouse pointer so that its tip touches the Bold check box and then click the left mouse button." (The right mouse button is often clicked on part of the screen, such as a scroll bar or selected text, to display context-sensitive menus.)

With some applications, you also can double-click to perform various functions. In dialog boxes, double-clicking an option is the same as choosing the option and clicking the OK button. In documents, double-clicking highlights an entire word. Double-clicking a program icon launches the application.

Most applications also support Shift+clicking, which extends a selection, such as a block of text or several files. With the selection on-screen, click the beginning of the selection, hold down the Shift key, and then click the end of the selection. See *double-click* and *Shift+click*.

client   In a network, a workstation with processing capabilities, such as a personal computer, that can request information or applications from the network server. In object linking and embedding, an application that includes data in another application, called the server application. See *client application, client/server network, file server, local area network (LAN), object linking and embedding (OLE)*, and *server application.*

client application   In object linking and embedding (OLE), an application in which you can create a linked object or embed an object. See *object linking and embedding (OLE)* and *server application.*

client-based application   In a network, an application that resides on a workstation and isn't available for use by others on the network. File server crashes don't affect client-based applications. Also, individual packages of software must be installed on workstations if network licenses haven't been bought. See *client/server network, file server, local area network (LAN)*, and *server-based application.*

client/server architecture   A design model for applications running on a network, in which the bulk of the back-end processing, such as performing a physical search of a database, takes place on a server. The front-end processing, which involves communicating with the user, is handled by smaller programs distributed to the client workstations. See *local area network (LAN)* and *wide area network (WAN).*

client/server network   A method of allocating resources in a network so that computing power is distributed among the computers in the network, but some shared resources are centralized in a file server. See *file server* and *peer-to-peer network*.

clip art   A collection of graphic images, stored on disk and available for use in a page layout or presentation graphics program. The term *clip art* is derived from a graphics design tradition in which packages of printed clip art are sold and actually clipped out by layout artists to enhance newsletters, brochures, and presentation graphics. Most page layout or presentation graphics programs can read graphics file formats used by clip art collections now available on disk (see fig. C.3).

Fig. C.3   *Print preview of a document using clip art.*

Clipboard   In a windowing environment such as Microsoft Windows or the Macintosh Finder, a temporary storage area in memory where material cut or copied from a document is stored until you paste the material elsewhere (see fig. C.4).

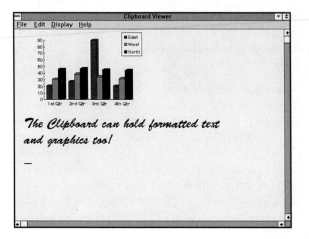

Fig. C.4   *The Clipboard window in Microsoft Windows.*

clip-on pointing device   A trackball mouse that clips on the side of the computer. See *built-in pointing device, freestanding pointing device, mouse, snap-on pointing device,* and *trackball.*

Clipper   A compiler developed by Nantucket Systems, Inc., for the dBASE software command language. Many application developers consider Clipper superior to the compiler offered by dBASE's publisher. See *compiler.*

clock   An electronic circuit that generates evenly spaced pulses at speeds of millions of cycles per second. The pulses are used to synchronize the flow of information through the computer's internal communication channels. Some computers also contain a circuit that tracks hours, minutes, and seconds. See *clock/calendar board* and *clock speed.*

clock/calendar board   A card that includes a battery-powered clock for tracking the system time and date and is used in computers that lack such facilities on their motherboards. See *adapter* and *motherboard.*

clock speed   The speed of the internal clock of a microprocessor that sets the pace—measured in megahertz (MHz)—at which operations proceed within the computer's internal processing circuitry.

Each successive model of microprocessor has produced a faster clock speed, from the original Intel 8088 operating at a speed of 4.77 MHz to the 80486- and Pentium-based systems running at speeds up to 100 MHz to the DEC Alpha family with processors now "trudging" along at 333 MHz. Higher clock speeds bring noticeable gains in CPU-intensive tasks, such as recalculating a spreadsheet, but isn't the only feature that determines performance. Disk-intensive operations can slow performance dramatically if the disk drives are sluggish.

Microprocessor design and caches can dramatically affect clock speed. A Pentium-based PC running at 66 MHz (with two caches and two pipelines) is twice as fast as a 486DX2 running at the same speed. When comparing clock speeds, compare only computers that use the same microprocessor.

Some computers come with two or more clock speeds you select using the keyboard or a button located on the computer's front panel. These computers offer this feature to accommodate certain older programs that can't run at faster clock speeds. Most Windows applications are designed to run at the fastest speed that your system can run.

If you plan to run Windows applications, you need an 80386-based system that runs at a minimum of 16 MHz with zero wait states. Experienced Windows users prefer 80486 systems that run at 33 MHz or more. See *Intel 80386DX, Intel 80386SX, Intel 80486DX, Intel 80486SX,* and *wait state.*

clone   A functional copy of a hardware device, such as a personal computer that successfully runs the software and uses all the peripherals intended for an IBM Personal Computer; or a functional copy of a program, such as a spreadsheet program that reads Lotus 1-2-3 files and can recognize most or all the commands and add-ins. See *IBM PC-compatible computer.*

close   In a program that can display more than one document window, to exit a file and remove the window from the display.

CAUTION: *In many applications, you must save your work before you close a window. If you haven't saved your work, the program probably displays an alert box warning you to save. To abandon your work, confirm that you don't want to save the document. See* document window.

close box   In a graphical interface, a box at the left end of the title bar of a window, which may include a pull-down menu, that is used to close the window. A close box available in all Macintosh windows is used only to close the window. Similar boxes in Windows applications are called control menu boxes. See *control menu.*

closed bus system   A computer design in which the computer's internal data bus doesn't contain receptacles and isn't easily upgraded by users. See *open bus system.*

cluster   On a floppy or hard disk, the basic unit of data storage. A cluster includes two or more sectors.

When DOS stores a file on disk, DOS writes the file into dozens or even hundreds of contiguous clusters. If enough contiguous clusters aren't available, DOS locates the next empty cluster and writes more of the file to the disk, continuing this process until the entire file is saved. The file allocation table (FAT) tracks how files are distributed among the clusters on a disk. See *contiguous, file allocation table (FAT), file fragmentation,* and *sector.*

CLV   See *constant linear velocity (CLV).*

CMOS   See *Complementary Metal-Oxide Semiconductor (CMOS).*

coaxial cable   In local area networks, a high-bandwidth connecting cable in which an insulated wire runs through the middle of the cable. Surrounding the insulated wire is a second wire made of solid or mesh metal.

Coaxial cable is much more expensive than twisted-pair cable (ordinary telephone wire) but can carry more data. Coaxial cables are required for high-bandwidth broadband systems and for fast baseband systems such as EtherNet. See *bandwidth, broadband, local area network (LAN),* and *twisted-pair cable.*

COBOL   A high-level programming language specially designed for business applications.

Short for COmmon Business Oriented Language, COBOL is a compiled language that originated in a 1959 committee representing business, government, defense, and academic organizations. Released in 1964, the language was the first to introduce the data record as a principal data structure. Because COBOL is designed to store, retrieve, and process corporate accounting information and to automate such functions as inventory control, billing, and payroll, the language quickly became the language of choice in businesses. COBOL is the most widely used programming language in corporate mainframe environments.

COBOL programs are verbose but easy to read because most commands resemble English; however, readability can be easily lost through the use of spaghetti code and poor internal documentation.

Versions of COBOL are available for personal computers, but business applications for personal computers are more frequently created and maintained in C or Xbase. See *high-level programming language, remark,* and *spaghetti code.*

code   To express a problem-solving algorithm in a programming language. See *algorithm.*

code page   In DOS, a table of 256 codes for an IBM PC-compatible computer's character set. The two kinds of code pages are classed as follows:

- *Hardware code page.* The character set built into the computer's ROM.

- *Prepared code page.* A disk-based character set you can use to override the hardware code page.

A B C

Prepared code pages contain character sets in which characters 0
through 127 are those available in the ASCII character set, and
128 through 255 are appropriate for the specific foreign language.
MS-DOS 6.2 includes code pages for 26 languages. To override
the hardware code page, use the CHANGE CODE PAGE
(CHCP) command. Your printer and keyboard also can be configured to use a specific foreign language code page. See *character set*.

codes See *hidden codes*.

code snippet One or more lines of programming code embedded in a user-defined menu option or button. The code
defines what the button or option does.

cold boot Starting a computer by turning on the system's
power switch. See *boot* and *warm boot*.

cold link A method of copying information from one document (the source document) to another (the target document) so
that a link is created. To update the link, choose a command that
opens the source document, reads the information, and recopies
the information if it has changed. See *dynamic data exchange
(DDE)*, *hot link*, *Inter-Application Communication (IAC)*, and
System 7.

collapse When creating an outline or viewing a disk directory
tree (such as in Microsoft Windows' File Manager), the process of
hiding all the outline levels or subdirectories below the selected
outline heading or directory.

> **TIP:** *In the Microsoft Windows File Manager, you can double-
> click the directory icon to collapse a directory quickly.*

collate See *sort*.

collating sequence See *sort order*.

collision   In local area networks, a garbled transmission that results when two or more workstations transmit to the same network cable at exactly the same time. See *local area network (LAN)*.

color   In typography, the quality of the printed portion of the page, which should be perceived by the eye as an even shade of gray. Defects such as rivers, bad word breaks, poor character spacing, or uneven line spacing disrupt this even appearance.

To maintain good color, use consistent word spacing, avoid widows and orphans, use kerning as necessary (especially for display type), and avoid hyphen ladders. See *hyphen ladder, kerning, orphan, river,* and *widow*.

Color Graphics Adapter (CGA)   A bit-mapped graphics display adapter for IBM PC-compatible computers. This adapter displays four colors simultaneously with a resolution of 200 pixels horizontally and 320 lines vertically, or displays one color with a resolution of 640 pixels horizontally and 200 lines vertically.

Color graphics adapters can drive composite color monitors and RGB monitors, but screen resolution is lower than that of EGA and VGA adapters. See *bit-mapped graphic, composite color monitor, Enhanced Graphics Adapter (EGA), RGB monitor,* and *Video Graphics Array (VGA)*.

color monitor   A computer display device that can display an image in multiple colors, unlike a monochrome monitor that displays one color on a black or white background.

color scheme   A named collection of screen colors you can select from a menu to change a program's on-screen appearance.

In Microsoft Windows, you can choose Colors from the Control Panel to display the Color dialog box, where you can choose from a variety of preset color schemes (see fig. C.5). If Microsoft's color schemes don't suit you, you can paint each element of the screen to your liking.

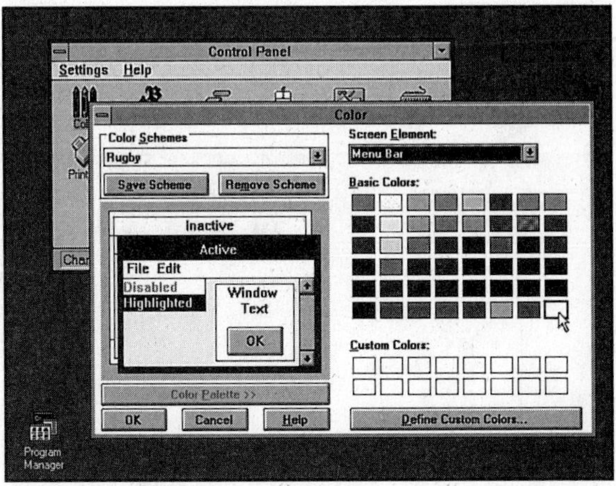

Fig. C.5 *The Color dialog box.*

color separation   The separation of a multicolor graphic into
several layers of color, with each layer corresponding to one of the
colors that'll be printed when a professional printer reproduces the
graphic. See *Pantone Matching System (PMS)*.

column   In character-based video displays, a vertical one-
character-wide line down the screen. In a spreadsheet, a vertical
block of cells usually identified by a unique alphabetical letter.
In a database management program, the terms *column* and *field* are
sometimes used synonymously.

column graph   In presentation and analytical graphics, a
graph with vertical columns. Column graphs are commonly used
to show the values of items as they vary at precise intervals over a
period of time (see fig. C.6). The x-axis (categories axis) is the
horizontal axis, and the y-axis (values axis) is the vertical axis. Such
graphs are often called bar graphs, but technically speaking, bar
graphs have horizontal bars.

Column graphs, which suggest that the information was obtained
at intervals, differ from line graphs, which suggest a continuous
change over time. Column graphs are more honest than line

graphs in some cases, because a line graph suggests that you're making data observations all along instead of once a month or once every two weeks.

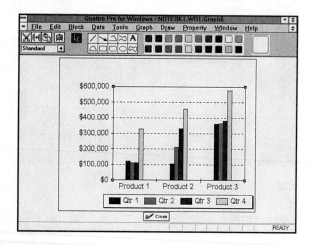

Fig. C.6 *A column graph with clustered columns.*

When you display more than one data series, clustering the columns (as in fig. C.6) or overlapping them (see fig. C.7) is helpful. With caution, you also can create a three-dimensional effect to differentiate the columns, if it really helps clarify the data (see fig. C.8). See *bar graph, histogram, line graph, stacked column graph, x-axis,* and *y-axis.*

column indicator   In word processing programs, such as Microsoft Word, a message in the status bar that shows the current number of horizontal spaces, or columns, the cursor has moved across the screen.

column text chart   In presentation graphics, a chart showing related items as side-by-side columns of text (see fig. C.9).

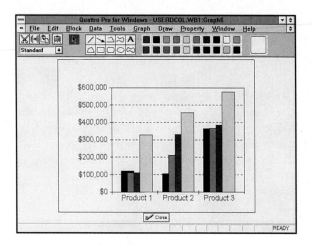

Fig. C.7 *Overlapped columns.*

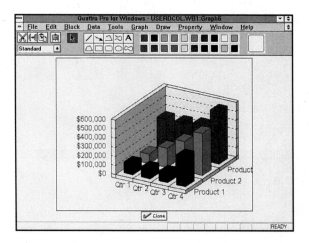

Fig. C.8 *A three-dimensional column graph.*

column-wise recalculation In spreadsheet programs, a recalculation order that calculates all the values in column A before moving to column B, and so on.

CAUTION: *If your spreadsheet program doesn't offer natural recalculation, use column-wise recalculation for worksheets in which columns are summed and the totals are forwarded. Row-wise recalculation may produce erroneous results. See* natural recalculation, optimal recalculation, *and* row-wise recalculation.

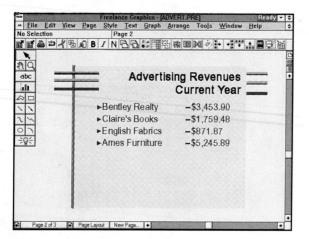

Fig. C.9 *A column text chart.*

COM In DOS, a device name that refers to the serial communications ports available in your computer. Your computer can have up to four COM ports, designated by DOS as COM1, COM2, COM3, and COM4.

When used as a file name extension, .COM indicates an executable program file limited to 64K. To run a .COM file, type the file name and press Enter.

combinatorial explosion   A barrier to the solution of a problem that occurs when the possibilities that must be computed are too numerous.

Combinatorial explosions vex the designers of chess software, which must frequently compute and analyze tens of thousands of alternative moves in a turn. Because people rely on as-yet poorly understood intuitive processes to narrow down the range of possibilities to a manageable number, the best chess champions can still beat the best chess programs. See *artifical intelligence*.

Comité Consultatif International Téléphonique et Télégraphique (CCITT)   An international organization that sets standards for analog and digital communications involving modems, computer networks, digital signal transmission, and fax machines. In the United States, early modem communications standards were proprietary standards, such as the use of the Bell 103A standard for 300 baud telecommunications. Increasingly, U.S. firms are switching to CCITT standards. Commonly used, for example, is the V.22bis standard, which governs modem telecommunications at 2400 baud, and the CCITT Group 3 standards for fax machines. See *CCITT protocol*.

comma-delimited file   A data file, usually in ASCII file format, in which a user or program separates the data items by commas to facilitate the transfer of data to another program. See *ASCII*, *file format*, and *tab-delimited file*.

command   A user-initiated signal given to a computer program that initiates, terminates, or otherwise controls the execution of a specific operation. In command-driven programs, you type the command statement and its associated syntax and press Enter. In a menu-driven program, you choose a command from an on-screen menu. See *command-driven program*, *graphical user interface (GUI)*, and *menu-driven program*.

command button   In graphical user interfaces such as Microsoft Windows or the Macintosh Finder, a button in a dialog box that initiates an action such as carrying out a command with the options chosen, cancelling a command, or displaying another dialog box. You can quickly choose the default button just by pressing Return (for Macintoshes) or Enter (for Windows systems). See *pushbutton.*

COMMAND.COM   In DOS, a file that contains the command processor. This file must be present on the startup disk for DOS to run. See *command processor.*

CAUTION: *The COMMAND.COM file is one of three files that must be available to launch DOS. The other two files are hidden and therefore not as vulnerable to being erased by accident. COMMAND.COM is usually located in the root directory of your hard drive and can be easily deleted. Consult your DOS manual for instructions for formatting a floppy as a system disk (make two) and keep it handy in case you see* Missing Command Interpreter *when you boot your system. Place the system disk in the A drive and reboot.*

command-driven program   A system, utility, or application program that requires you to type command statements, with the correct syntax and nomenclature, to use the program's features. See *command, graphical user interface (GUI),* and *menu-driven program.*

Command key   On Macintosh keyboards, a key marked with ⌘ that's frequently used in combination with alphabetical keys to provide keyboard shortcuts for menu options. Apple standardized these shortcuts so that all Macintosh applications support them.

command language   See *software command language.*

command-line operating system   A command-driven operating system, such as MS-DOS, that requires you to type commands using the keyboard. See *graphical user interface (GUI).*

command processor   The part of an operating system that accepts input from the user and displays prompts and messages, such as confirmation and error messages. Also referred to as the *command interpreter*. See *COMMAND.COM* and *command-line operating system*.

comment   See *remark*.

comment out   In computer programming, to place a symbol (such as a semicolon) or a command at the beginning of a line that marks the line as documentation. The compiler ignores any lines preceded with this symbol.

Common User Access (CUA) Interface   In Microsoft Windows applications, a standard set of basic menu items, the arrangement of items on the menus, and basic keystrokes. These include Alt+F4 to close an application, Ctrl+F6 to switch to another window, and the location of File, Window, and Help on the menu bar. See *application program interface (API)*.

communications parameters   In telecommunications and serial printing, the settings (parameters) that customize serial communications for the hardware you're contacting. See *baud rate*, *communications protocol*, *full duplex*, *half duplex*, *parameter*, *parity bit*, and *stop bit*.

communications program   An application program that turns your computer into a terminal for transmitting data to and receiving data from distant computers through the telephone system.

A good communications program includes a command language you can use to automate cumbersome log-on procedures, several file-transfer protocols (such as XMODEM and Kermit), terminal emulation of several popular mainframe terminals (such as the DEC VT100), on-screen timing so that you can keep track of time charges, and a phone book for storing and retrieving telephone numbers. Many excellent communications programs available are shareware, such as PC-Talk and QMODEM for IBM PC-compatible computers. See *terminal* and *terminal emulation*.

communications protocol   The standards that govern the transfer of information among computers on a network or using telecommunications. The computers involved in the communication must have the same settings and follow the same standards to avoid errors.

When you use a modem to access a bulletin board or information service, such as CompuServe, choose the communications protocol established by the host computer system, including baud rate, data bits, duplex, parity, and stop bits. The baud rate must be that of the modem with the lower rate. Most communications services use eight data bits and one stop bit; full duplex also is common. Review any documentation you have for an on-line service to find out which settings to use.

You may have to specify an additional parameter called *handshaking*. This parameter establishes the way one computer tells the other device when to wait. Almost all computers and many peripheral devices use XON/XOFF handshaking, the default for most communications programs. If you're having trouble establishing communication with an on-line service, press Enter twice and try these settings:

Parity: No
> Data bits: 8
> Stop bits: 1
> Duplex: Full

If you can't see what you're typing, switch to half duplex. If the preceding settings don't work, hang up and dial again with these settings:

Parity: Even
> Data bits: 7
> Stop bits: 1
> Duplex: Full or half

If you're using half duplex and see any typed text echoed, such as HHEELLLLOO, switch to full duplex.

 See *asynchronous communication, baud rate, communications parameters, communications program, file transfer protocol (FTP), handshaking, mode, modem, parity bit, protocol, stop bit,* and *terminal emulation.*

communications settings See *communications parameters* and *communications protocol*.

comp In desktop publishing, a complete mock-up of a page layout design, showing what the final printed page will look like.

compact disk (CD) A plastic disk, 4.75 inches in diameter, that uses optical storage techniques to store up to 72 minutes of music or 650M of digitally encoded computer data.

In an optical storage medium, digital data is stored as microscopic pits and smooth areas with different reflective properties. A precisely controlled beam of laser light shines on the disk so that the reflections can be detected and translated into digital data.

CDs originally provided read-only data storage. The computer can read information from the disk, but you can't change this information or write new information to the disk. Therefore, this storage medium accurately is termed CD-ROM (read-only memory). Erasable optical disk drives are now available and are expected to have a major impact on secondary storage techniques in the next decade. See *CD-ROM disk drive*, *erasable optical disk drive*, *optical disk*, and *secondary storage*.

Compact Disk-Interactive (CD-I) A compact-disk standard designed for interactive viewing of audiovisual compact disks using a television set and a CD-I player. Designed for education, training, and entertainment, CD-I has been slow to find a market.

company network A wide area network, such as DEC ENET (the internal engineering network of Digital Equipment Corporation), that often has automatic gateways to cooperative networks such as ARPAnet or BITNET for functions such as electronic mail and file transfer.

comparison operator See *relational operator*.

compatibility   The capability of a device, program, or adapter to function with or substitute for a given make and model of computer, device, or program. Also, the capability of one computer to run the software written to run on another computer.

To be truly compatible, a program or device should operate on a given system without changes; all features should operate as intended and run, without changes, all the software the other computer can run. See *clone*.

 TIP: *In IBM PC-compatible computing, a frequently used index of 100% IBM compatibility is a computer's capability to run Microsoft Flight Simulator.*

compiler   A program that reads the statements written in a human-readable programming language, such as Pascal or Modula-2, and translates the statements into a machine-readable executable program. Compiled programs run significantly faster than interpreted ones because the program interacts directly with the microprocessor and doesn't need to share memory space with the interpreter. See *interpreter* and *machine language*.

Complementary Metal-Oxide Semiconductor (CMOS)   An energy-saving chip made to duplicate the functions of other chips, such as memory chips or microprocessors. CMOS chips are used in battery-powered portable computers and in other applications where reduced electrical consumption is desired.

CMOS also refers to a special CMOS chip that operates the real-time clock included on a motherboard and stores the basic system configuration, including the floppy and hard drive types, amount of installed memory, and wait state settings. These settings are retained while the computer is off with only a nominal battery support. See *chip*.

complex instruction set computer (CISC)   *sisk*   A central processing unit (CPU) that can recognize as many as 100 or more instructions, enough to carry out most computations directly.

Most microprocessors are CISC chips. The use of RISC technology, however, is becoming increasingly common in professional workstations and is expected to migrate to personal computers in the mid 1990s. See *central processing unit (CPU)* and *reduced instruction set computer (RISC)*.

compose sequence   A series of keystrokes that lets you enter a character not found on the computer's keyboard. In Lotus 1-2-3, for example, you can enter é by pressing Alt+F1 and then typing **233**.

composite   See *comp*.

composite color monitor   A monitor that accepts a standard video signal that mixes red, green, and blue signals to produce the color image. Display quality is inferior to that of RGB monitors. See *composite video* and *RGB monitor*.

composite video   A method for broadcasting video signals in which the red, green, and blue components, as well as horizontal and vertical synchronization signals, are mixed together.

Composite video, regulated by the U.S. National Television Standards Committee (NTSC), is used for television. Some computers have composite video outputs that use a standard RCA phono plug and cable such as on the backplane of a hi-fi or stereo system. See *composite color monitor* and *RGB monitor*.

compound device   In multimedia, a device (such as a MIDI sequencer) that reproduces sound or other output that you record in a specific media file, such as a MIDI file. See *Musical Instrument Digital Interface (MIDI)*.

compound document   In object linking and embedding (OLE), a single file created by two or more applications. When you use OLE to embed a Microsoft Excel chart into a Microsoft Word document, for example, the resulting file contains the Word text as well as the Excel object. The object contains all the information Excel needs to open the chart for editing. This information results in file sizes considerably larger than normal. See *object linking and embedding (OLE)*.

compressed file   A file converted by a file compression utility to a special format that minimizes the disk storage space required. See *file compression utility*.

CompuServe   The largest and most successful personal computer on-line information service. A for-profit version of a bulletin board system (BBS) coupled with the resources of an on-line information service, CompuServe offers file downloading, electronic mail, current news, up-to-the-minute stock quotes, an on-line encyclopedia, and conferences on a wide variety of topics. The outmoded and challenging character-based user interface, however, has encouraged the creation of front-end programs such as CompuServe Navigator and TAPCIS, either of which you should consider using. See *America Online, bulletin board system (BBS), GEnie, on-line information service,* and *Prodigy.*

compusex   See *cybersex.*

computation   The successful execution of an algorithm, which can be a textual search or sort, as well as a calculation. See *algorithm.*

computer   A machine that can follow instructions to alter data in a desirable way and to perform at least some of these operations without human intervention. Computers represent and manipulate text, graphics, symbols, and music, as well as numbers. See *analog computer* and *digital computer.*

computer addiction   See *computer dependency.*

computer-aided design (CAD)   The use of the computer and a CAD program to design a wide range of industrial products, ranging from machine parts to modern homes. CAD has become a mainstay in a variety of design-related fields, such as architecture, civil engineering, electrical engineering, mechanical engineering, and interior design. CAD applications are graphics- and calculation-intensive, requiring fast processors and high-resolution video displays. CAD programs often include sophisticated statistical analysis routines that help designers optimize their applications, as well as their extensive symbol libraries. All these features require huge amounts of processing power—a requirement that kept CAD off early personal computers.

Like many other professional computer applications based on expensive mainframe or minicomputer systems, however, CAD is migrating to powerful personal computers, such as those based on the Intel 80486 and Motorola 68040 microprocessors. CAD software for personal computers blends the object-oriented graphics found in draw programs with precision scaling in two and three dimensions, to produce drawings with an intricate level of detail. See *draw program* and *object-oriented graphic*.

computer-aided design and drafting (CADD)　The use of a computer system for industrial design and technical drawing. CADD software closely resembles computer-aided design (CAD) software, but has additional features that allow the artist to produce drawings conforming to engineering conventions.

computer-assisted instruction (CAI)　The use of programs to perform instructional tasks, such as drill and practice, tutorials, and tests.

Unlike human teachers, a CAI program works patiently with bright and slow students alike. Ideally, CAI can use sound, graphics, and on-screen rewards to engage a student in learning with huge payoffs. In practice, however, a great deal of CAI software is badly designed: the software is stilted, boring, and emphasizes drill and practice, often in a way that suggests remedial instruction.

With the advent of multimedia, however, CAI may be entering a new era. Multimedia machines equipped with compact disks, video, and sound may function to open new worlds to students by placing immense reservoirs of knowledge and experience in every classroom. Authoring languages, such as HyperTalk, make developing high-quality instructional software much easier. See *authoring language*, *HyperTalk*, and *multimedia*.

computer-based training (CBT)　The use of computer-aided instruction (CAI) techniques to train for specific skills, such as operating a numerically controlled lathe.

computer dependency   A psychological disorder characterized by compulsive and prolonged computer usage. For example,
medical authorities in Denmark have reported the case of an
18-year-old who spent up to 16 hours a day with his computer.
Doctors found that he was talking to himself in a computer programming language.

Computer Graphics Metafile (CGM)   An international
graphics file format that stores object-oriented graphics in device-
independent form so you can exchange CGM files among users of
different systems (and different programs). A CGM file contains
the graphic image as well as the instructions required for another
program to create the file.

Personal computer programs that can read and write to CGM file
formats include Harvard Graphics and Ventura Publisher. It's the
standard format used by Lotus 1-2-3. See *object-oriented graphic*
and *Windows Metafile Format (WMF)*.

computer system   A complete computer installation—
including peripherals, such as disk drives, monitor, mouse, operating system software, and printer—in which all the components are
designed to work with each other.

CON   In DOS, the device name for console, which refers to
the keyboard and monitor. The command COPY CON
C:AUTOEXEC.BAT, for example, creates a file called
AUTOEXEC.BAT and stores in this file all the characters you
type after giving the command. To finish copying text from the
keyboard, press Ctrl+Z and then press Enter. See *console*.

concatenation   To link together two or more units of
information, such as text or files, so that they form one unit. In
spreadsheet programs, concatenation is used to combine text in a
formula by placing an ampersand between the formula and text.

In DOS, you easily can combine two or more files by using a
straightforward variation of the COPY command. To combine

C

files, you list all the source files, using plus signs to separate them. The following command combines all the DOC files into one backup file named REPORT.BAK:

```
COPY REPORT1.DOC+REPORT2.DOC REPORT.BAK
```

concordance file   A file containing the words you want a word processing program to include in the index the program constructs.

To index a document, you have only one choice with most programs: you must mark each occurrence of each word throughout the manuscript. The best word processing programs, such as WordPerfect, use a concordance file to simplify the manual part of indexing. The concordance file contains one sample of each word you want indexed. When you give the command that starts the indexing operation, the program uses the concordance file as a guide and performs the marking operation.

concurrency control   In a local area network (LAN) version of an application program, the features built into the program that govern what happens when two or more people try to access the same program feature or data file.

Many programs not designed for networks can run on a network and allow more than one person to access a document, but it may result in one person accidentally destroying another person's work. Concurrency control addresses this problem by enabling multiple access where such access can occur without losing data and by restricting multiple access where access could result in destroyed work. See *file locking, LAN-aware program,* and *LAN-ignorant program.*

concurrency management   The capability of an application written for use on a local area network (LAN) to ensure that data files aren't corrupted by simultaneous modification or multiple input.

concurrent processing   See *multitasking.*

condensed type   Type narrowed in width so that more characters can fit into an inch of type. In dot-matrix printers, condensed type usually is set to print 17 cpi. See *characters per inch (cpi)*.

CONFIG.SYS   In DOS, an ASCII text file in the root directory that contains configuration commands. DOS consults this file at system startup.

If no CONFIG.SYS file is on the startup disk, DOS uses default configuration values. Many programs work well with the default configuration settings, but newer versions of popular programs usually require more files and buffers than the default values. Further, to set up and configure high memory and extended memory, you must include in a CONFIG.SYS file commands to install the HIMEM.SYS and EMM386.EXE device drivers. Nonstandard peripherals and some application programs also may require the inclusion of device drivers or other commands in a CONFIG.SYS file in the root directory so that these configurations are modified. See *American National Standards Institute (ANSI), ANSI.SYS, ASCII, buffer, driver, mouse, peripheral*, and *root directory*.

> **CAUTION:** *If an application program you're using has written a CONFIG.SYS file to your startup disk, don't erase the file. Make a backup copy CONFIG.SYS so that if it's accidentally erased, you can restore it on the hard drive.*

configuration   The choices made in setting up a computer system or an application program so that it meets the user's needs.

Properly configuring your system or program is one of the more onerous tasks of personal computing and, unfortunately, hasn't been eliminated by the arrival of windowing environments. In Microsoft Windows, for example, you must perform some manual configuration to obtain maximum performance from Windows and to take full advantage of the memory available on your system. Along the way, you may be obliged to distinguish among upper memory, high memory, extended memory, and expanded memory, in addition to the usual kinds of memory.

When established, the configuration is saved to a configuration file, where it's vulnerable to accidental erasure. Windows, for example, stores the user's configuration choices in a file called WIN.INI, which you should be very careful not to erase. Besides creating configuration files, programs also frequently perform surreptitious changes to AUTOEXEC.BAT and CONFIG.SYS, the two files DOS consults when you start your system. If you delete these files, your system may not perform as you expect, and applications—if they run at all—may revert to their preconfigured states or prevent you from choosing certain commands.

configuration file   A file created by an application program that stores the choices you make when you install the program so that they're available the next time you start the program. In Microsoft Word, for example, the file MW.INI stores the choices you make from the Options menu.

> **TIP:** *More than a few users have accidentally erased configuration files when trying to free up disk space. Make copies of files with extensions such as .CFG, .INI, or .SET. To avoid re-creating erased configuration files, you can use the copy of the configuration file.*
>
> *To avoid disturbing configuration and other vital program files, don't store your documents in your application's directory. If you store them elsewhere, you're less likely to erase vital application files when you're deleting unwanted documents.*

confirmation message   An on-screen message asking you to confirm a potentially destructive action, such as closing a window without saving your work. See *alert box.*

connectivity   The extent to which a given computer or program can function in a network setting.

connectivity platform   A program or utility designed to enhance another program's capability to exchange data with other programs through a local area network. Oracle for the Macintosh, for example, provides HyperCard with the connectivity required to search for and retrieve information from large corporate databases. See *HyperCard* and *local area network (LAN)*.

console   A display terminal, consisting of a monitor and keyboard. In multiuser systems, *console* is synonymous with *terminal*, but console also is used in personal computer operating systems to refer to the keyboard and display. See *CON*.

constant   In a spreadsheet program, a number you type directly into a cell or place in a formula. See *cell definition* and *key variable*.

constant angular velocity (CAV)   In data storage media such as disk drives, a playback technique in which the disk rotates at a constant speed. This technique results in faster data retrieval times as the read/write head nears the spindle; retrieval times slow as the read/write head moves toward the perimeter of the disk. See *constant linear velocity (CLV)*.

constant linear velocity (CLV)   In compact disk players, a playback technique that speeds or slows the rotation of the disk to ensure that the velocity of the disk is always constant at the point where the disk is being read. To achieve constant linear velocity, the disk must spin more slowly when reading or writing closer to the spindle. In contrast to CLV devices, constant angular velocity (CAV) devices such as hard disks access data at differing rates, depending on the distance of the read/write head from the drive spindle. See *constant angular velocity (CAV)*.

contention   In local area networks, a channel access method in which access to the communication channel is based on a first-come, first-served policy. See *carrier sense multiple access with collision detection (CSMA/CD)*.

context-sensitive help   In an application package, a user-assistance mode that displays documentation relevant to the command, mode, or action you now are performing. Context-sensitive help reduces the time and keystrokes needed to get on-screen help. After pressing Format (Shift+F8) in WordPerfect 6 for DOS, for example, rather than search for the desired information manually from an index or menu, press Help (F1) to see a help screen explaining the options available on the Format menu.

context switching   Changing from one program to another without exiting either program, when the programs are loaded in a multiple-loading program.

Unlike the true multitasking possible with Microsoft Windows and DESQview, a multiple-loading program doesn't allow background programs to continue executing, but does allow you to switch rapidly from one program to another. When combined with a graphical user interface and cut-and-paste facilities provided by a clipboard, context switching lets you move data rapidly and easily from one application to another. See *multiple program loading* and *multitasking*.

contiguous   Adjacent; placed one next to or after the other. In Microsoft Windows, for instance, the permanent swap file must occupy contiguous sectors on the disk. The file's maximum size—and, consequently, Windows' capability to create virtual memory for your system—is limited by the number of contiguous sectors available. See *permanent swap file*, *sector*, *swap file*, and *virtual memory*.

> **TIP:** *Before creating a permanent swap file for Microsoft Windows, run a disk optimizing utility to free up the maximum number of contiguous free sectors.*

continuous paper   Paper manufactured in one long strip, with perforations separating the pages, so you can feed the paper into a printer with a tractor-feed mechanism. Synonymous with *continuous-feed paper*.

continuous tone   An illustration, whether black-and-white or color, in which tones change smoothly from the darkest to the lightest, without noticeable gradations.

control   In a Windows program, a dialog box feature (such as a check box, radio button, or list box) that allows the user to choose options.

Control+Break   In DOS, a keyboard command that cancels the execution of a program or command at the next available break point.

control code   In the American Standard Code for Information Interchange (ASCII), a code reserved for hardware-control purposes, such as advancing a page on the printer. ASCII has 32 control codes. See *ASCII*.

Control (Ctrl) key   In IBM PC-compatible computing, a key frequently pressed in combination with other keys to issue program commands. In WordStar, for example, pressing Ctrl+Y deletes a line.

controller   See *disk drive controller*.

controller card   An adapter that connects disk drives to the computer. Most personal computer controller cards contain circuitry to connect one or more floppy disks and a hard disk. See *adapter*.

control menu   In Microsoft Windows, a pull-down menu, found in all windows and dialog boxes, that contains options for managing the active window (see fig. C.10). The control menu icon, a button containing a bar shaped like a hyphen, is on the left end of the title bar. The contents of the menu vary, but the menu usually includes commands to move, size, maximize, and minimize windows, as well as to close the current window or switch to another application window or the next document window.

TIP: *To display the control menu of an application window or a dialog box quickly, press Alt+space bar. To open a document window's control menu, press Alt+hyphen. You can use the keyboard to select commands on the control menu.*

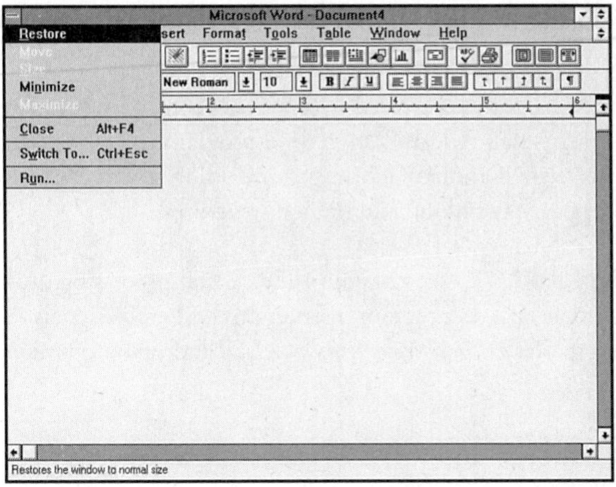

Fig. C.10 *The control menu.*

control panel   In Lotus 1-2-3, the top three lines of the screen. The top line contains the current cell indicator and the mode indicator. The second is the entry line and the third line is blank. When you press the slash key to use menu mode, the second and third lines contain menus and prompts.

In the Macintosh and Windows systems, the control panel is a utility window that lists options for hardware devices, such as the mouse, monitor, and keyboard.

control panel device (CDEV)   *see-dev*   Any Macintosh utility program placed in the System Folder that appears as an option in the Control Panel.

control structure   A logical organization for an algorithm that governs the sequence in which program statements are executed.

Control statements govern the flow of control in a program by specifying the sequence in which the program's steps are carried out. Control structures include branch structures that cause a special set of instructions to be executed if a specified situation is encountered; loop structures that execute over and over until a condition is fulfilled; and procedure/function structures that set aside distinct program functions or procedures into separate modules, which are invoked from the main program.

In personal computing, you likely will use control structures even if you don't plan to learn a high-level programming language since most software command languages, including macro commands, include a variety of loop and branch structures.

control unit   A component of the central processing unit (CPU) that obtains program instructions and emits signals to carry them out. See *arithmetic-logic unit (ALU)* and *central processing unit (CPU)*.

conventional memory   In any IBM PC-compatible computer, the first 640K of the computer's random-access memory (RAM).

The Intel 8086 and 8088 microprocessors, which were available when the IBM Personal Computer (PC) was designed, can directly use 1M of RAM. The PC's designers decided to make 640K of RAM accessible to programs, reserving the rest of the 1M memory space for internal system functions.

640K has since proven to be insufficient, however, because of programs that demand more memory and users who want to run more than one program at a time. For this reason, many users equip their systems with extended or expanded memory and the memory management programs required to access this memory. See *expanded memory (EMS)*, *expanded memory manager (EMM)*, *extended memory*, *extended memory manager*, *Microsoft Windows*, *protected mode*, *real mode*, and *upper memory area*.

conventional programming   The use of a procedural programming language, such as BASIC, FORTRAN, or assembly language, to code an algorithm in machine-readable form. In conventional programming, the programmer must be concerned with the sequence in which events occur within the computer. Non-procedural programming languages let the programmer focus on the problem without worrying about the precise procedure the computer must follow to solve the problem. See *declarative language* and *procedural language*.

convergence   The alignment of the red, blue, and green electron guns in a monitor to create colors on-screen. If they aren't perfectly aligned, poor convergence results, causing a decrease in image sharpness and resolution. White area also tends to show colors around the edges.

cooperative network   A wide-area computer network, such as BITNET or UUCP, in which the costs of participating are borne by the linked organizations. See *BITNET*, *company network*, *research network*, and *UUCP*.

coprocessor   A microprocessor support chip that takes over a specific processing operation, such as handling mathematical computations or displaying images on the video display. See *microprocessor* and *numeric coprocessor*.

copy   The material—including text, graphic images, pictures, and artwork—to be assembled for printing. Also, to reproduce part of a document at another location in the document or in another document.

copy fitting   In desktop publishing, a method used to determine the amount of copy (text), in a specified font, that can fit into a given area on a page or in a publication.

copy protection   Hidden instructions included in a program intended to prevent you from making unauthorized copies of software. Because most copy-protection schemes impose penalties on legitimate owners of programs, such as forcing them to insert a specially encoded "key disk" before using a program, most business software publishers have given up using these schemes. Copy protection is still common, however, in recreational and educational software.

core dump   In mainframe computing, a debugging technique that involves printing out the entire contents of the computer's core, or memory. In contemporary slang, the term refers to a person who, when asked a simple question, recites everything he or she remembers about a subject. See *dump*.

corrupted file   A file that contains scrambled and unrecoverable data. Files can become corrupted due to bad sectors (surface flaws on the disk), disk drive controller failures, or software errors.

cost-benefit analysis   A projection of the costs and benefits of installing a computer system. The analysis compares the costs of operating an enterprise with and without the computer system and calculates the return (if any) on the original investment.

CAUTION: *Cost-benefit analyses often involve overly optimistic assumptions about the tangible cost savings of installing a computer system. With a word processing program, for example, you can revise a document faster, but you may keep working to achieve perfection, spending more time than you originally would have.*

Computerization also may prove more costly than standard methods if the enterprise must carry out its business in an inefficient or unprofitable way. More than a few businesses buy the wrong program or find that expensive software proves to be inflexible as business needs change. See re-engineering.

counter   In typography, the space fully or partially enclosed by the strokes that form a letter, such as the blank space inside the letter a or o. See *bowl.*

Courier   A monospace typeface, commonly included as a built-in font in laser printers, that simulates the output of office typewriters. For example: `This is Courier type.`

courseware   Software developed for computer-assisted instruction (CAI) or computer-based training (CBT) applications. See *computer-assisted instruction (CAI)* and *computer-based training (CBT).*

cpi   See *characters per inch (cpi).*

C

CP/M (Control Program for Microprocessors) An operating system for personal computers that uses the 8-bit Intel 8080 and Zilog Z-80 microprocessors.

CP/M was created in the late 1970s as floppy disk drives became available for early personal computers. Designed for computers with as little as 16K of random-access memory (RAM), CP/M is a command-line operating system still widely used on the more than 4 million 8-bit computers (such as Morrow, Kaypro, and Osborne) still in existence.

MS-DOS, a clone of CP/M, was designed to facilitate the translation of 8-bit CP/M business software for the new 16-bit IBM Personal Computer environment. IBM originally approached CP/M's publisher, Digital Research, to write the operating system for its new computer, but Microsoft Corporation got the job instead.

CPM See *critical path method (CPM)*.

cps See *characters per second (cps)*.

CPU See *central processing unit (CPU)*.

cracker A computer hobbyist who, for kicks, tries to thwart computer security systems by gaining access to the systems. Many in the computer hobbyist community believe this activity beneficially exposes flaws and loopholes in computer system security that can be exploited by criminals; however, many states have laws that say that accessing without permission a computer that isn't your own is a serious crime. This is true even if the cracker does no damage to the data found in the computer. See *hacker* and *hacker ethic*.

crash An abnormal termination of program execution, usually (but not always) resulting in a frozen keyboard or an unstable state. In most cases, you must cold boot the computer to recover from a crash. See *cold boot*.

CRC   See *cyclic redundancy check (CRC)*.

creator type   In the Macintosh, a four-letter code that identifies the program used to create a document. The code associates the document with the application so that you can start the application by opening the document. See *associated document*.

creeping featurism   An unfortunate tendency in computer programming where software developers add more and more features in an attempt to keep up with the competition. The result is a program that's hopelessly complex, sluggish, and hogs disk space. See *feature*.

crippled version   A freely distributed version of a program that lacks one or more crucial features that have been deliberately disabled in an attempt to introduce the user to the program in the hope that the user will buy the full version. Synonymous with *working model*. See *demo*.

criteria range   In a spreadsheet program that includes database functions, the range of cells that contains the conditions, or *criteria*, you specify to govern how a search is conducted or an aggregate function is calculated.

critical path method (CPM)   In project management, a technique for planning and timing the execution of tasks where you identify a critical path—a series of tasks that must be completed in a timely fashion if the entire project is to be completed on time. The software helps the project manager identify the critical path.

cropping   A graphics editing operation in which you trim the edges from a graphic to make it fit into a given space or to remove unnecessary parts of the image.

cross-hatching   A pattern of parallel and crossed lines added to areas solid in a graph to distinguish one data range from another.

A B C

CAUTION: *In graphs, the overuse of cross-hatching may create moiré vibrations, which result from visual interference between cross-hatching patterns. If your graph seems to flicker, reduce the cross-hatching. See* moiré effect.

cross-linked files   In DOS, a file-storage error that occurs when the file allocation table indicates that two files claim the same disk cluster. Like lost clusters, cross-linked files occur when the computer is interrupted (by a system crash or a power outage) while it's writing a file.

To repair cross-linked files, run CHKDSK frequently with the /f switch. Repairing files quickly can minimize the extent of data loss. See *file allocation table (FAT)* and *lost cluster.*

cross-platform computing   The use of virtually identical user interfaces for programs running on a variety of different (and often incompatible) computer architectures. The Windows and Macintosh versions of Microsoft Word, for example, resemble each other closely enough that Microsoft publishes the same manual for both versions of the program.

cross-post   In a computer newsgroup such as EchoMail (Fidonet) or USENET (Internet), to mail a contribution to two or more discussion groups simultaneously. Cross-posting is rarely warranted and is often taken as a netiquette violation by someone who doesn't care to get involved in the give-and-take of discussion within a specific group. See *netiquette.*

cross-reference   In word processing programs, a code name used to refer to material discussed elsewhere in a document.

Cross-references, such as "See the discussion of burnishing methods on page 19," are helpful to the reader, but they can become a nightmare if you add or delete text. The best word processing programs (such as WordPerfect and Microsoft Word) contain cross-reference features, enabling you to mark the original text and assign a code name to the marked text, such as BURNISH.

Then you type the code name (not the page number) when you want to cross-reference the original text. When you print your document, the program substitutes the correct page number for the code name. If you add or delete text later and print again, the cross-references are updated to reflect the new page numbers.

crosstalk   The interference generated by cables too close to one another. You sometimes hear crosstalk on the telephone. When speaking long-distance, hearing other voices or entire conversations in the background of your conversation isn't uncommon. Crosstalk often prevents error-free transmission of data.

CRT   See *cathode ray tube (CRT)*.

CSMA/CD   See *carrier sense multiple access with collision detection (CSMA/CD)*.

Ctrl   See *Control (Ctrl) key*.

Ctrl+Break   See *Control+Break*.

CUA   See *Common User Access (CUA) Interface*.

cumulative trauma disorder   See *repetitive strain injury (RSI)*.

current cell   In a spreadsheet program such as Lotus 1-2-3, the cell in which the pointer is positioned. Synonymous with *active cell*.

current cell indicator   In Lotus 1-2-3, a message in the upper-left corner that displays the address of the cell in which the pointer is positioned.

current directory   The directory that DOS or an application uses by default to store and retrieve files. Synonymous with *default directory*.

Within an application, the current directory is usually determined by the application program defaults and is often the directory in which the program's files are saved. Some applications, however, let you specify another directory where you want to save data files, which then becomes the current directory.

current drive   The drive the operating system uses for an operation unless you specify otherwise. Synonymous with *default drive*.

current graph   In Lotus 1-2-3, the graph that the program creates when you open the Graph menu and choose View, and that's retained in memory until you save the graph or quit the worksheet.

cursor   An on-screen blinking character that shows where the next character will appear. See *pointer*.

cursor-movement keys   The keys that move the cursor on-screen. Synonymous with *arrow keys*.

The arrow keys move the cursor in the direction indicated by the arrow on each key—one character left or right or one line up or down. Like the keys in the typing area, these keys are autorepeat keys. If you hold down the key, the cursor keeps moving in the direction indicated.

The enhanced keyboard includes separate cursor keys that perform the same function as the arrow keys on the numeric keypad. Some programs configure additional keys so that they move the cursor. These keys include Home, End, Tab, Page Up, and Page Down, and are often combined with other keys, such as Shift+Tab. See *keyboard* and *scroll*.

cut and paste   See *block move*.

cut-sheet feeder   A paper-feed mechanism that feeds separate sheets of paper into the printer, where a friction-feed mechanism draws the paper through the printer.

You can buy cut-sheet feeding mechanisms as optional accessories for dot-matrix and letter-quality printers, but they're standard equipment with laser printers and high-quality inkjet printers. See *friction feed* and *tractor feed.*

cyberphobia   An exaggerated and irrational fear of computers. Noted by the psychotherapist Craig Brod and others, cyberphobia stems from the stress individuals encounter as they try to cope with an increasingly computer-driven society.

An unhappy postal inspector fires five bullets at the terminal. An employee, fearing that computers would eliminate her job, vomits all over the keyboard when forced to sit at her new computer. As personal computing technology spreads throughout society, cyberphobic acts increasingly find their way into crime and news reports. Alert employers that offer training to employees new to the world of computers can help ease employee transition to a computerized work environment.

cyberpunk   A genre of science fiction that depicts a dystopian future dominated by worldwide computer networks, battling artificial intelligences, monopoly capitalism, and a world culture as ethnically eclectic as it is politically apathetic and alienated. On this stage are chronicled the exploits of hackers who use hallucinogenic drugs, cyborg implants, and trance states to carry out criminal and heroic missions within the networks' fabulous realms of virtual reality.

The originator of the genre is William Gibson in his 1982 book *Neuromancer,* which coined the term *cyberspace.* Curiously, Gibson knew little about computing when he wrote the book—on a typewriter. See *cyberspace.*

cybersex   A form of long-distance eroticism made possible by a real-time computer chat forum; synonymous with *compusex.* To stimulate your virtual partner, you relay a favorite sexual fantasy or describe in vivid terms what you would be doing if the person were actually present.

Cybersex occurs in "chat" lines on adult bulletin boards, in which you exchange messages with another person who is also connected to the same system. These chat lines offer explicit sex—one of the reasons people call them. See *bulletin board system (BBS)*, *chat forum*, and *teledildonics*.

cyberspace   The virtual space created by computer systems.

One definition of space is "a boundless three-dimensional extent in which objects and events occur and have relative position and direction." In the 20th century, computer systems are creating a new kind of space that fits this definition: cyberspace. (The term *cyber* refers to computers.)

In virtual reality, cyberspace can be directly experienced by donning a headset that displays a world that doesn't really exist. Walking through this world, you can "pick up" objects, navigate through "rooms," and perform other actions that seem quite real to the person wearing the headset.

Cyberspace can be created by computer systems less sophisticated than the ones that power virtual reality experiments. Electronic mail advocates will readily testify that the ability to communicate with other users, located all over the world, breaks down social and spatial boundaries in an exhilarating way. See *cyberpunk*, *hacker ethic*, and *virtual reality*.

cyclic redundancy check (CRC)   An automatic error-checking method used by DOS when writing data to the disk. When DOS later reads data from the disk, the same error-check is conducted, and the results of the two checks are compared to make sure that the data hasn't changed. If you see an error message such as CRC ERROR READING DRIVE C, it signals serious problems with the disk. A similar CRC checking procedure also is commonly used by file compression utilities (such as PKZIP) and when transferring files using data communications.

TIP: *If DOS can't read a file due to a CRC error, don't give up hope. A disaster recovery program such as Diskfix (included with PC Tools) or PKZIPFIX may be able to recover the file.*

cylinder   In disk drives, a unit of storage consisting of the set of tracks that occupy the same position. On a double-sided disk, a cylinder includes track 1 of the top and the bottom sides. On hard disks in which several disks are stacked on top of one another, a cylinder consists of track 1 on both sides of all the disks.

Cyrix   A manufacturer of computer chips. See *Cx486DRX²* and *Cx486SRX²*.

Cx486DRX²   A clock-doubling 486 microprocessor originally released by Cyrix in October 1992 as the Cx486DRu². The chip is available in three speed-doubling configurations: 20/40, 25/50, and 33/66. The chip is used to replace a 386 chip in an existing system.

Cx486SRX²   A clock-doubling 486 microprocessor originally released by Cyrix in October 1992 as the Cx486DRu². The chip is available in four speed-doubling configurations: 16/32, 20/40, 25/50, and 33/66. The chip is used to replace a 386 chip in an existing system.

data is the plural of the Latin word *datum*, data is commonly used to represent both singular and plural.

database   A collection of related information about a subject organized in a useful manner that provides a base or foundation for procedures such as retrieving information, drawing conclusions, and making decisions. Any collection of information that serves these purposes qualifies as a database, even if the information isn't stored on a computer. In fact, important predecessors of today's sophisticated business database systems were files kept on index cards and stored in file cabinets.

Information usually is divided into distinct data records, each with one or more data fields. For example, a video store's record of a children's film may include the following information:

TITLE	The Blue Fountain
CATEGORY	Children
RATING	G
RETAIL PRICE	$24.95
RENTED TO	325-1234
DUE DATE	12/31/92

See *data field* and *data record.*

database design   The choice and arrangement of data fields in a database so that fundamental errors (such as data redundancy and repeating fields) are avoided or minimized. See *data redundancy* and *repeating field.*

database driver   In Lotus 1-2-3 Release 3.0, a program that lets 1-2-3 exchange data with database programs such as dBASE.

database management   Tasks related to creating, maintaining, organizing, and retrieving information from a database. See *data manipulation.*

d

DA   See *desk accessory (DA)*.

daemon   *dee-mon*   In UNIX systems, a utility program that works unobtrusively in the background, performing tasks such as receiving incoming electronic mail. The user isn't aware of the daemon's presence.

daisy chain   A method of connecting together several devices along a bus and managing the signals for each device. Devices that use a SCSI interface, such as a CD-ROM, hard disk, and scanner, can be daisy-chained to one SCSI port. See *Small Computer System Interface (SCSI)*.

daisywheel printer   An impact printer that simulates the typescript produced by an office typewriter. The term *daisywheel* refers to the metal or plastic disk consisting of characters mounted on spokes connected to a hub, resembling a daisy. To produce a character, the printer spins the wheel until that character is in front of a hammer that strikes the character against an inked ribbon, transferring the image to paper.

Because you can remove and replace daisywheels, these printers can print multiple typefaces. However, changing fonts within a document is tedious, because you must change the daisywheel manually.

Once the ultimate in printing technology, daisywheel printers have all but disappeared from the market because of their slow speed and the development of inexpensive laser printers that can change fonts and typefaces within a document. See *impact printer*.

DASD   See *Direct Access Storage Device (DASD)*.

data   Factual information such as text, numbers, sounds, and images, in a form that can be processed by a computer. Although

database management program   An application program that provides the tools for data retrieval, modification, deletion, and insertion. Such programs also can create a database and produce meaningful output on the printer or on-screen. In personal computing, three kinds of database management programs exist: flat-file, relational, and text-oriented. See *band, flat-file database management program, relational database management,* and *table-oriented database management program.*

D E F

database management system (DBMS)   In personal computing, a program that organizes data in a database, providing information storage, organization, and retrieval capacities, sometimes including simultaneous access to multiple databases through a shared field (relational database management). See *flat-file database management program.*

database structure   In database management, a definition of the data records in which information is stored, including the number of data fields; a set of field definitions that specify the type, length, and other characteristics of the data that can be entered in each field; and a list of field names. See *data type.*

CAUTION: *Rare is the database structure that doesn't require changes after you start entering data. Many database management programs, however, either don't let you redefine the database structure, or require a cumbersome procedure that may corrupt the data. If you're using such a program, perform exhaustive tests on sample data before typing hundreds of data records.*

data bus   An internal electronic pathway that allows the microprocessor to exchange data with random-access memory (RAM). The width of the data bus, usually 16 or 32 bits, determines how much data can be sent at one time. See *bus, microprocessor,* and *random-access memory (RAM).*

data communication   The transfer of information from one computer to another. The transfer can occur via direct cable connections, as in local area networks, or over telephone lines using modems. See *local area network (LAN)* and *telecommunications.*

data-compression protocol   In computer modems, a standard for automatically compressing data when it's sent and decompressing data when it's received. With data compression, you can realize gains of up to 400 percent in effective transmission speed. The two most common data compression protocols are V.42bis and MNP-5. See *CCITT protocol* and *MNP-5.*

> **TIP:** *If you use your modem frequently to exchange lengthy files with others, consider a modem that offers automatic data compression, which is much more convenient than manually compressing files using programs such as PKZIP.*

data deletion   In a database management program, an operation that deletes records according to specified criteria.

Many database programs don't actually delete the records in such operations; they merely mark the records so that they aren't included in data retrieval operations. Therefore, you usually can restore the deleted records if you make a mistake. Check your program manual.

data dictionary   In a database management program, a list of all the database files, indexes, views, and other files relevant to a database application. A data dictionary also can include data structures and any information pertinent to the maintenance of a database.

data-encoding scheme   The technique a disk drive controller uses to record bits of data on the magnetic surface of a floppy disk or hard disk. Disk drives are categorized by the data-encoding scheme the drive uses. See *Advanced Run-Length Limited (ARLL),* *disk drive controller, Modified Frequency Modulation (MFM),* and *Run-Length Limited (RLL).*

data-entry form   In a database management program, an on-screen form that makes entering and editing data easier by displaying only one data record at a time. The data fields are listed vertically, as in figure D.1. You also can create a custom data-entry form (see fig. D.2).

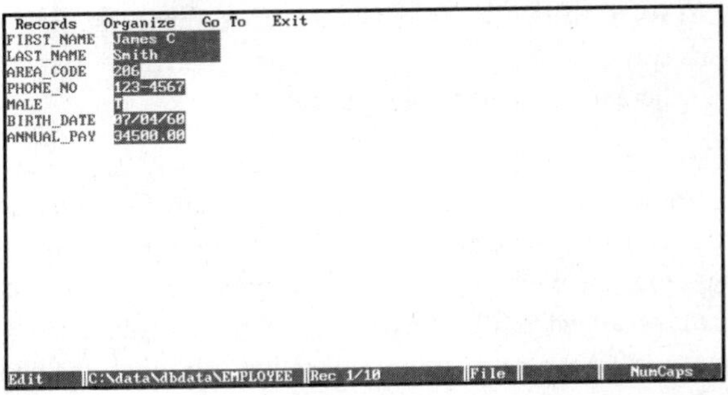

Fig. D.1 *A standard data-entry form in dBASE.*

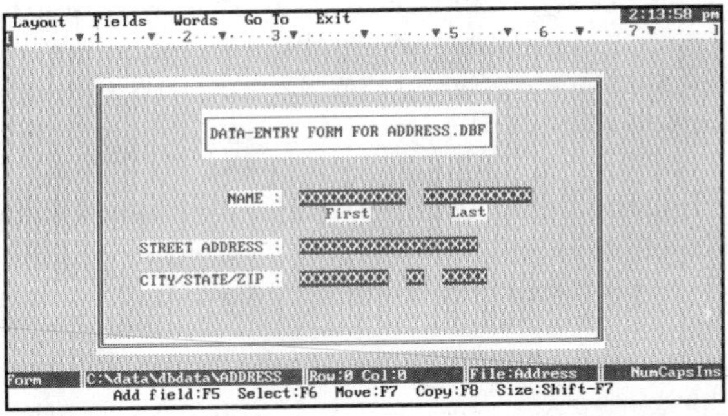

Fig. D.2 *A custom data-entry form in dBASE.*

data field In a database management program, a space reserved for a specified piece of information in a data record. In a table-oriented database management program, in which all retrieval operations produce a table with rows and columns, data fields are displayed as vertical columns.

Data fields in a simple mail list database might be FIRSTNAME, LASTNAME, COMPANY, ADDRESS, CITY, ST, and ZIP. See *database, field definition,* and *table-oriented database management program.*

data file   A disk file containing the work you create with a program; unlike a program file which contains instructions for the computer.

data independence   In database management, the storage of data in a way that allows you to access that data without knowing exactly where it's located or how it's stored.

Ideally, you should be able to say to the computer, "Give me information on Acme International" rather than "Go to record #1142 and match the text string Acme International." The newer database management programs include command languages, called *query languages*, that let you phrase questions based on content rather than the data's physical location. Although the best query languages require you to know some procedures, such as which database to search, databases are evolving toward complete data independence. In the future, anyone using a corporate computer should be able to send out a query on a network, searching the company's shared databases and the small, personal ones on some of the computers connected to the network. See *query language* and *Structured Query Language (SQL)*.

data insertion   In a database management program, an operation that adds new records to the database. Unlike appending records, however, insertion lets you add records anywhere in the database. See *append*.

data integrity   The accuracy, completeness, and internal consistency of the information stored in a database. A good database management program ensures data integrity by making it difficult (or impossible) to accidentally erase or alter data. Relational database management programs help to ensure data integrity by eliminating data redundancy. See *data redundancy*.

data interchange format (DIF) file   In spreadsheet programs and some database programs, a standard file format that simplifies importing and exporting data between different spreadsheet programs. Originally developed by Software Arts—the creators of VisiCalc—DIF is supported by Lotus 1-2-3, Quattro Pro, and most other spreadsheet programs.

d

data manipulation   In database management, the use of the basic database manipulation operations—data deletion, data insertion, data modification, and data retrieval—to make changes to data records.

data mask   See *field template*.

data modification   In database management, an operation that updates one or more records according to specified criteria. You use a query language to specify the criteria for the update. For example, the following statement, written in a simplified form of Structured Query Language (SQL), tells the program to find records in which the supplier field contains *CC*, and then increase the value in the price data field by 15 percent:

```
UPDATE inventory
SET price = price * 1.15
WHERE supplier = "CC"
```

See *query language* and *Structured Query Language (SQL)*.

data privacy   In local area networks, limiting access to a file so that other users in the network can't display the contents of that file. See *encryption*, *field privilege*, *file privilege*, and *password protection*.

data processing   Preparing, storing, or manipulating information with a computer. See *word processing program*.

data record   In a database management program, a complete unit of related data items stored in named data fields. In a database, *data record* is synonymous with *row*.

A data record contains all the information related to the item the database is tracking. In a video store's database, for example, the data record lists the information for each tape the store stocks. Most programs display data records in two ways: as data-entry forms and as data tables. In a table-oriented relational database management system, the data records are displayed as horizontal rows and each data field is a column. See *relational database management system (RDBMS)*.

data redundancy   In database management, the repetition of the same data in two or more data records.

Generally, you shouldn't enter the same data in two different places within a database—someone may mistype just one character, destroying accurate retrieval. To the computer, *Acme* isn't *Acmee*. The program fails to retrieve both data records if you search for all the records with Acme in the COMPANY field. Integrity is a serious issue for any database management system.

Relational database management programs can reduce the data redundancy problem. Suppose that you're running a retail operation, and you create a simple inventory database to help you track items in stock. In the SUPPLIER field, you enter abbreviations such as USPSI instead of Ultra-Sophisticated Products Suppliers Intl. In a second database, you create records for all your suppliers, including a SUPPLIER field where the abbreviation for the company name is entered (USPSI in this example) and other fields for the address information.

Because you type the full name and address of the company just once, in the second database the address can't be typed two different ways. Of course, you still can mistype the code USPSI; however, a short code is easier to type, and errors are easier to catch.

data retrieval   In database management programs, an operation that retrieves information from the database according to the criteria specified in a query.

A database management program is most useful when you want to access only a few records: all the customers in Florida or those who haven't been contacted in the last 90 days. By using queries, you can tell the program to sort the data, perhaps by customer last name, or to select only certain records, such as customers in Atlanta. In some programs, the query can specify which fields to display after the matching records are selected.

A program that displays data tables as the result of retrieval operations is a table-oriented database management program. Record-oriented database management programs are less useful because they display all the information on all the data records retrieved.

d

data series   In business and presentation graphics, a collection of values that all pertain to a single subject, such as the third-quarter sales of three products.

In spreadsheet programs, a column, row, or block of values that increases or decreases a fixed amount. When creating a data series, you indicate a beginning value, the amount to increase or decrease the value, and an ending value.

data table   In a database management program, an on-screen view of information in a columnar (two-dimensional) format, with the field names at the top. Most database management programs display data tables as the result of sorting or querying operations (see fig. D.3). See *data-entry form*.

Records	Organize	Fields	Go To	Exit				
LAST_NAME	FIRST_NAME	ADDRESS		CITY	STATE	ZIP	MALE	BIR
Harvey	Jane W.	9709 Broadway		Vancouver	WA	98665	F	08/
Bush	Alfred G.	13456 N. 95th St		Seattle	WA	98105	T	08/
Johnson	Robert J.	3245 Oak Street		Portland	OR	97203	T	06/
Morgan	Albert C.	1354 S. 78th Ave		Portland	OR	97202	T	05/
Watson	James L.	3091 S.W. Powell		Portland	OR	97201	T	09/
Ball	Thomas	9440 Rockcreek R		Beaverton	OR	97201	T	12/
Morrow	Peter T.	2046 Skyline Dri		Fremont	CA	94538	T	04/
Peters	Cathy K.	3467 First Avenu		Los Angele	CA	94321	F	03/
Swanson	Linda K.	1345 Bayview R		San Mateo	CA	94105	F	10/
Peterson	Janet	3090 Oceanview R		San Diego	CA	92121	F	11/
King	Steven W.	2771 Plaza Drive		Pittsburgh	PA	15230	T	01/
Taylor	George F.	123 Main Street		New York	NY	10021	T	05/
Browse	C:\data\dbdata\BYZIP		Rec 1/12		File			NumCaps

Fig. D.3   *A data table in dBASE.*

In spreadsheet programs, a form of what-if analysis where a formula is calculated many times using different values for one or two of the arguments in the formula. The results are displayed in a table.

data type   In a database management program, a classification you give to a data field that governs the kind of data you can enter. In dBASE, for example, you can choose among the following data types:

- *Character field (or text field).* Stores any character you can type at the keyboard, including numbers. The program can't, however, perform computations on character fields. A character field can contain approximately one line of text.

- *Memo field.* Stores any type of text; useful for entering notes about the information contained in a record. A memo field can contain more text than a character field.

- *Numeric field.* Stores numbers in such a way that the program can perform calculations on them.

- *Logical field.* Stores information in a true/false, yes/no format.

- *Date field.* Stores dates so that the program can recognize and compare them.

See *field template.*

DBMS   See *database management system (DBMS).*

DDE   See *dynamic data exchange (DDE).*

debugger   A utility, often included in program compilers or interpreters, that helps programmers find and fix syntax errors and other errors in the source code. See *compiler, interpreter, source code,* and *syntax error.*

debugging   The process of locating and correcting errors in a program.

decimal tab   In a word processing or page layout program, a tab stop configured so that values align at the decimal point.

declarative language   A programming language that frees the programmer from specifying the exact procedure the computer needs to follow to accomplish a task. Programmers use the language to describe a set of facts and relationships so that the user may then query the system to get a specific result.

d

For example, Structured Query Language (SQL) allows you to perform a search by asking to see a list of records showing specific information instead of by telling the computer to search all records for those with the appropriate entries in specified fields. See *data independence, expert system,* and *procedural language.*

decrement   To decrease a value. See *increment.*

decryption   The process of deciphering data from an encrypted form so you can read the data. See *encryption.*

dedicated file server   In a local area network, a computer dedicated exclusively to providing services to the users of the network and running the network operating system.

Some file servers can be used for other purposes. In peer-to-peer networks, for example, all the networked computers are potential file servers, although they're being used for stand-alone applications. See *file server.*

default button   In graphical user interfaces such as Microsoft Windows, the highlighted button automatically selected as your most likely choice in a dialog box. You can press Enter to choose this button quickly. See *pushbutton.*

default directory   See *current directory.*

default extension   The three-letter extension an application program uses to save and retrieve files unless you override the default by specifying another extension.

Using the default extension makes retrieving files easier. Many programs, such as Lotus 1-2-3 and Microsoft Word, assign extensions if you don't provide one. During retrieval operations, such programs display a list of only the files that use the default extension, making retrieving a file easier. If you give the file a different extension, the file doesn't appear on the list. You still can retrieve the file, but you must remember the file's name or change the File Name entry to *.* so that all files are listed. See *extension* and *file name.*

default font   The font that the printer uses unless you tell it otherwise. Synonymous with *initial base font.*

default numeric format   In a spreadsheet program, the numeric format that the program uses for all cells unless you choose a different one. See *numeric format.*

default printer   The printer a program automatically uses when you choose Print. If you change printers for a single print job, some programs return to the printer designated as the default when the document is closed. Others treat the currently selected printer as the default printer until you select another printer.

default setting   The setup a program uses unless you specify another setting. In Lotus 1-2-3, for example, the default column width is nine characters.

An important step toward the mastery of an application program is learning the program defaults and how to change these settings so the program works the way you want. Most programs save the changes you make so they're the default settings thereafter, but some options can't be saved under any circumstances. Microsoft Word, for example, saves the printer driver you select, but it doesn't save settings such as the number of copies you want to print (the default is always 1); WordPerfect lets you change the default number of copies if you routinely make more copies.

default value   A value a program uses when you don't specify one.

defragmentation   A procedure in which all the files on a hard disk are rewritten on disk so that all parts of each file are written to contiguous sectors. The result is an improvement of up to 75 percent in the disk's speed during retrieval operations. During normal operations, the files on a hard disk eventually become fragmented so that parts of a file are written all over the disk, slowing down retrieval operations.

d

> **TIP:** *MS-DOS 6 includes DEFRAG, a defragmentation utility. Run DEFRAG no more than once a month to obtain maximum system performance without undue wear on your hard disk.*

Delete (Del) key   A key that erases the character at the cursor.

Use the Backspace and Delete keys to correct mistakes as you type. If you discover that you've made a typing error, press Backspace to erase to the left and then retype. Use the Delete key to erase a character at the cursor.

delimiter   A code, such as a space, tab, or comma, that marks the end of one section of a command and the beginning of another section. Delimiters also are used to separate data into fields and records when you want to export or import data using a database format. For example, using delimiters makes it easy to export a merge file created using a word processing program or to import data into a spreadsheet program and have lines of data divided logically into columns.

Delphi   A full-service on-line computer network, established in 1982 as an on-line encyclopedia.

Today, DELPHI has grown to offer a variety of business and financial services; news and analysis; special interest group forums for every major category of computer; a range of real-time conferences; entertainment in the form of games, Hollywood gossip, and movie reviews; trivia tournaments; and astrological predictions. There are also forums on many topics of interest; news, weather, and sports information; a gateway to the DIALOG Information Service and Grolier's Academic American Encyclopedia; shopping; travel support services; and special regional gateways to major cities (note that DELPHI/Miami and DELPHI/Argentina are Spanish-language versions of DELPHI).

delurk   In a computer newsgroup, to post a message or a follow-up reply that identifies the contributor and declares his or her affiliation with the newsgroup's values; typically, this is done after a long period in which the person has been a *lurker*, logging on only to read the postings without contributing. See *lurk* and *virtual community*.

demo   An animated presentation or a preview version of a computer program distributed without charge in an attempt to acquaint potential customers with a program's features.

demodulation   In telecommunications, the process of receiving and transforming an analog signal into its digital equivalent so that a computer can use the information. See *modulation* and *telecommunications*.

demount   To remove a disk from a disk drive. See *mount*.

density   A measurement of the amount of information (in bits) that can be packed reliably into a square inch of a magnetic secondary storage device, such as a floppy disk. See *double density*, *high density*, and *single density*.

dependent worksheet   In Microsoft Excel, a worksheet that contains a link, or reference formula, to data in another Excel worksheet, called the *source worksheet*, on which it depends for the data. More than one worksheet can depend on a single source worksheet. In other spreadsheet programs, such as Lotus 1-2-3 and Quattro Pro, a worksheet containing a link is called a *target worksheet*. See *external reference formula* and *source worksheet*.

> **TIP:** *If you include links in worksheets, group the dependent worksheet and the source worksheet as a workgroup or workspace to ensure that the changes you make in the source worksheet are always reflected in the dependent worksheet.*

derived field   See *calculated field*.

descender   The portion of a lowercase letter that hangs below the baseline. Five letters of the alphabet have descenders: g, j, p, q, and y. See *ascender*.

descending sort   A sort that reverses the normal ascending sort order. Rather than sort A, B, C, D and 1, 2, 3, 4, for example, a descending sort lists D, C, B, A and 4, 3, 2, 1.

descriptor   In database management, a word used to classify a data record so that all records containing the word can be retrieved as a group. In a video store's database, for example, the descriptors Adventure, Comedy, Crime, Horror, Mystery, or Science Fiction can be entered in a field called CATEGORY to indicate where the film is shelved in the store. See *identifier* and *keyword*.

desk accessory (DA)   In a graphical user interface, a set of utility programs that assists with day-to-day tasks such as jotting down notes, performing calculations on an on-screen calculator, maintaining a list of names and phone numbers, and displaying an on-screen calendar (see fig. D.4). See *Font/DA Mover*, *graphical user interface (GUI)*, and *utility program*.

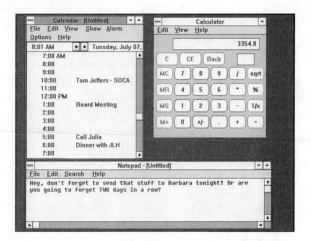

Fig. D.4   *Desk accessories in Microsoft Windows.*

desktop   In a graphical user interface, a representation of your day-to-day work, as though you were looking at an actual desk with folders full of work to do. In Microsoft Windows, this term refers specifically to the background of the screen, on which windows, icons, and dialog boxes appear (see fig. D.5). You can

change the desktop color and pattern by choosing Colors in the
Control Panel. See *graphical user interface (GUI)*.

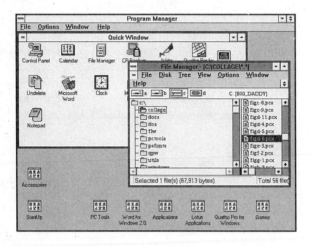

Fig. D.5 *A Microsoft Windows desktop.*

desktop computer A personal computer or professional
workstation designed to fit on a standard-sized office desk that's
equipped with sufficient memory and disk storage to perform
business computing tasks. See *laptop computer*.

desktop pattern In Microsoft Windows, a graphical
pattern—called *wallpaper*—displayed on the desktop (the background "beneath" windows, icons, and dialog boxes). To change
the desktop pattern, choose Desktop from the Control Panel.

desktop presentation The use of a slide show feature available in a presentation graphics program (and some spreadsheet
programs) to create a display of charts or other illustrations that
can be run on a desktop computer. You can tell the program to
run the presentation automatically or to give you a menu of options. See *presentation graphics program* and *slide show*.

desktop publishing (DTP) The use of a personal computer
as an inexpensive production system for creating typeset-quality
text and graphics.

d

Desktop publishers often merge text and graphics on the same page and print pages on a high-resolution laser printer or typesetting machine (see fig. D.6). Desktop publishing software lets one person produce typeset-quality text and graphics with a personal computer, enabling an organization to reduce publication costs by as much as 75 percent.

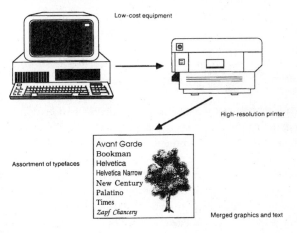

Fig. D.6 *The elements of desktop publishing.*

One drawback is that desktop publishing has one foot in technology and the other foot in the world of art. Using a page layout program doesn't guarantee that a document meets professional design standards. By observing a few rules, however, virtually anyone can produce a price list, brochure, or report that doesn't embarrass an organization.

desktop video A multimedia application in which a personal computer, coupled with a videocassette recorder or laser disk player, is used to control the display of still or motion images.

destination The record, file, document, or disk to which information is copied or moved, as opposed to the source. See *source.*

destination document In object linking and embedding (OLE), the document in which you insert or embed an object.

When you embed a Microsoft Excel object (such as a chart) into a Word for Windows file, for example, the Word document is the destination document. See *object linking and embedding (OLE)* and *source document.*

destination file   In many DOS commands, the file into which data or program instructions are copied. See *source file.*

device   Any hardware component or peripheral, such as a printer, modem, monitor, or mouse, that can receive and/or send data. Some devices require special software, called *device drivers.* See *device driver.*

device contention   The technique that Microsoft Windows uses to handle simultaneous requests from multitasked programs to access devices. Device contention is used in Windows' 386 Enhanced mode in which two or more programs can run simultaneously. If two programs try to access the same device at the same time, Windows gives one of the programs preference. You can modify how Windows gives preference using the 386 Enhanced option from the Control Panel group. See *device.*

device driver   A program that provides the operating system with the information needed for it to work with a specific device, such as a printer.

DOS doesn't need DEVICE commands to work with most keyboards, monitors, and printers. To use other devices, the driver must be loaded using a DEVICE or DEVICEHIGH command in the CONFIG.SYS file. The following command, for example, tells DOS to use a mouse driver:

```
DEVICE = MOUSE.SYS
```

CAUTION: *After you install a mouse on your system, beware of accidentally erasing the CONFIG.SYS file. If you do, the mouse won't work.*

d

device independence   The capability of a computer program, operating system, or programming language to work on a variety of computers or computer peripherals, despite their electronic variation. Examples of device independence include UNIX and PostScript. UNIX, an operating system for multiuser computer systems, is designed to run on a wide variety of computers, from PCs to mainframes. PostScript, a page description language for high-quality printing, is used by many printer manufacturers. See *PostScript* and *UNIX*.

D E F

device name   In DOS, a three-letter abbreviation that refers to a peripheral device. See *AUX, CON,* and *LPT*.

diagnostic program   A utility program that tests computer hardware and software to determine whether they're operating properly.

TIP: *Most computers initiate a diagnostic check at the start of every operating session. A particular focus of attention is the memory. If any errors are found, you see an error message, and the computer doesn't proceed. If you run into this problem, start the computer again. If you see the error message again, you may have to replace a memory chip. Because the error message specifies the location of the faulty chip, make sure that you write down the number you see in the message.*

dialog box   In a graphical user interface, an on-screen message box that conveys or requests information from the user (see fig. D.7). See *graphical user interface (GUI)*.

dictionary sort   A sort order that ignores the case of characters as data is rearranged. See *sort* and *sort order*.

DIF   See *data interchange format (DIF) file*.

digital   A form of representation in which distinct objects, or digits, are used to stand for something in the real world—

temperature or time—so that counting and other operations can be performed precisely. Information represented digitally can be manipulated to produce a calculation, a sort, or some other computation. In an abacus, for example, quantities are represented by positioning beads on a wire. A trained abacus operator can perform calculations by manipulating beads at high rates of speed by following an algorithm—a recipe for solving the problem. In digital electronic computers, two electrical states correspond to the 1s and 0s of binary numbers, and the algorithm is embodied in a computer program. See *algorithm, analog, binary numbers, computation*, and *program*.

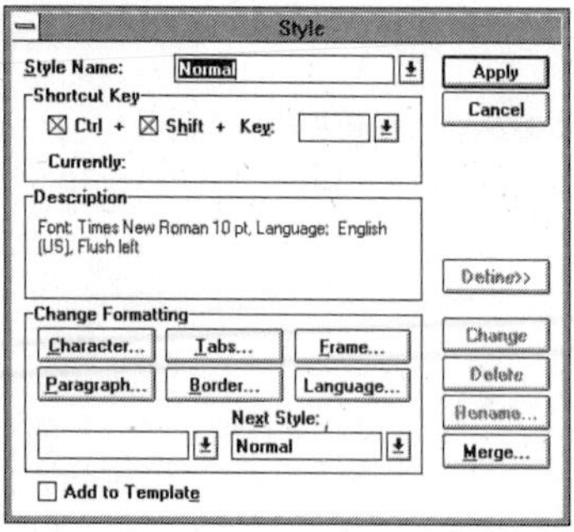

Fig. D.7 *A typical dialog box (Style) in Microsoft Windows.*

digital computer   A computer that uses the digits 0 and 1 to represent information, and then uses at least partly automatic procedures to perform computations on this information. See *analog computer* and *computer*.

Digital Darkroom   An image-enhancement program developed by Silicon Beach Software for Macintosh computers. The program uses computer processing techniques to edit and enhance scanned black-and-white photographic images.

digital monitor   A cathode-ray-tube (CRT) display that accepts digital output from the display adapter and converts the digital signal to an analog signal. Digital monitors can't accept input unless the input conforms to a prearranged standard, such as the IBM Monochrome Display Adapter (MDA), Color Graphics Adapter (CGA), or Enhanced Graphics Adapter (EGA). All these adapters produce digital output.

Digital monitors are fast and produce sharp, clear images. However, they have a major disadvantage: they display only a limited number of color values instead of continuously variable colors. For the Video Graphics Array (VGA) standard, IBM chose to use analog monitors so you can display continuously variable images. See *analog monitor, Color Graphics Adapter (CGA), digital, Enhanced Graphics Adapter (EGA), monochrome display adapter (MDA),* and *Video Graphics Array (VGA).*

digital transmission   A data communications technique that passes information encoded as discrete, on-off pulses. Digital transmission doesn't require digital-to-analog converters at each end of the transmission; however, analog transmission is faster and can carry more than one channel at a time. See *analog transmission.*

digitize   The process of transforming analog data into digital form. A scanner converts a continuous-tone image into bit-mapped graphics. CD-ROMs contain many digital (separate and discrete) measurements of the pitch and volume of sound. See *CD-ROM, digitizing tablet,* and *scanner.*

digitizing tablet   In computer-aided design, a peripheral device, usually measuring 12×12 or 12×18 inches and 1/2 inch thick, that is used with a pointing device called a cursor to convert graphics, such as pictures and drawings, into digital data that a computer can process. The location of the cursor on the tablet is sensed magnetically in relation to a wire grid embedded within the tablet, and the position is tracked on-screen. Synonymous with *graphics tablet.* See *Cartesian coordinate system.*

dimmed   The display of a menu command, icon, or dialog box option in a different color or shade of gray to indicate that the selection isn't available now.

dingbats   Ornamental characters—such as bullets, stars, pointing hands, scissors, and flowers—used to illustrate text. Dingbats originally were used between columns or, more commonly, between paragraphs, to provide separation. See *Zapf Dingbats*.

DIP   See *dual in-line package (DIP)* and *document image processing (DIP)*.

DIP switch   One or more toggle switches enclosed in a small plastic housing, called a dual in-line package (DIP). This housing is designed with downward-facing pins so it can be inserted into a socket on a circuit board or soldered directly to the circuit board. DIP switches are frequently used to provide user-accessible configuration settings for computers, printers, and other electronic devices.

CAUTION: *If you must remove the computer or printer case to change DIP switch settings, ALWAYS unplug the computer or printer first. Although your computer's electronic circuits use low-voltage DC, the power supply uses high voltages and may contain a capacitor that stores extremely high voltages for system start-up purposes. DON'T TOUCH THE POWER SUPPLY, even when the system is unplugged! To change a DIP switch, use a toothpick or another small pointed device. Don't use a pencil; lead shavings can damage the internal workings of a DIP switch. See dual in-line package (DIP).*

Direct Access Storage Device (DASD)   *daze-dee* Any storage device, such as a hard disk, that offers random or direct access to the stored data; in contrast to a sequential device (such as a tape unit). See *random access* and *sequential access*.

direct-connect modem   A modem equipped with a jack like the standard jack found in a telephone wall outlet, both of which accept an RJ-11 plug. The modem can be connected directly to the telephone line using ordinary telephone wire, unlike an acoustic coupler modem designed to cradle a telephone headset. See *acoustic coupler*.

direct memory access (DMA) channels   In a computer, a channel that's used to transfer data from memory to peripheral devices, such as hard disk controllers, network adapters, and tape backup equipment. Requests for data are handled by a special chip called a *DMA controller*, which operates at one-half the microprocessor speed.

The AT bus design includes two DMA controller chips: the first providing four 8-bit wide DMA channels, and the second providing four 16-bit wide channels. One channel is reserved to cascade the four channels on the other chip, leaving seven channels. When data is transferred using DMA channels, the CPU is bypassed completely, leaving it free to process other requests.

directory   An index you can display of the files stored on a disk or on a portion of a disk. The contents of a disk aren't obvious to the eye. The operating system keeps an up-to-date record of the files stored on a disk, with ample information about the file's content, time of creation, and size.

In DOS, the DIR command displays a disk directory. A typical DOS directory display is as follows:

```
Volume in drive C has no label
Volume Serial Number is 1B87-9988
Directory of C:\DOS

    .              <DIR>            04-20-93   11:02a
    ..             <DIR>            04-20-93   11:02a
EMM386    EXE     120,926 09-30-93    6:20a
COMMAND   COM      54,619 09-30-93    6:20a
HIMEM     SYS      29,136 09-30-93    6:20a
CHKDSK    EXE      12,241 09-30-93    6:20a
SETVER    EXE      12,015 12-07-93    7:12p
ANSI      SYS       9,065 09-30-93    6:20a
HELP      HLP     296,844 09-30-93    6:20a
UNDEL     EXE     194,375 01-28-93    1:00a
QBASIC    EXE     194,309 03-10-93    6:00a
DBLSPACE  EXE     177,034 09-30-93    6:20a
MSD       EXE     158,470 03-10-93    6:00a
      127 file(s)      4,284,480 bytes
                      27,369,472 bytes free
```

This disk directory contains the following information:

- *Volume label.* You can name a disk when it's formatted; the name is called a volume label. You also can name the disk later using the VOL command. If you give the disk a volume label, you see the name at the top of the directory.

- *Volume serial number.* Each disk is assigned a unique serial number when it's formatted using the DOS FORMAT command. The serial number is used to determine whether you've changed floppy disks in drives that don't have change line support.

- *Current directory.* The full name of the directory being displayed.

- *Directory entries.* Both the current and parent directories are listed using their directory markers. Any subdirectories are listed by directory name. Directory entries are indicated by displaying <DIR> in the third column of the directory table.

- *File name.* DOS file names have two parts: file name and extension. The first two columns of the directory table show the file name and the extension of each file on the disk.

- *File size.* The fourth column shows the size of each file (in bytes).

- *Date last modified.* The fifth column shows the date on which you last modified the file or created the directory.

- *Time last modified.* The sixth column shows the time when you last modified the file or created the directory.

- *Number of files.* The total number of files listed in the directory table.

- *Total bytes.* The total bytes in the fourth column.

- *Space remaining.* The number of bytes of available storage space on the disk is shown at the bottom of the directory. This information is important because you can't write a file to a disk with insufficient room.

d

> **TIP:** *If your computer isn't equipped with a clock/calendar board, be sure to set the system time and system date manually when you start the computer. DOS uses this information to create the date and time listings in disk directories. If the date and time aren't set, the dates listed for files are incorrect.*

D E F

See *clock/calendar board, current directory, directory markers, parent directory* and *subdirectory.*

directory markers   In DOS, symbols displayed in a directory table that represent the current directory (.) and the parent directory (..). See *current directory, directory, parent directory,* and *subdirectory.*

directory sorting   The organized display of the files in a disk directory, sorted by name, extension, or date and time of creation. DOS 5.0 added parameters to the DIR command enabling directory sorting, which was previously possible only by combining the DIR command with the DOS SORT command or with add-on utility programs.

directory tree   A graphical representation of a disk's contents that shows the branching structure of directories and subdirectories. The Microsoft Windows File Manager, for example, displays a directory tree (see fig. D.8).

dirty   Full of extraneous signals or noise. A dirty telephone line causes problems when you try to log on with a modem to a distant computer system or BBS. You'll know if the line's dirty: you'll see many extraneous characters on-screen. Log off, hang up, and dial again. See *bulletin board system (BBS)* and *modem.*

Also, a file that has been changed but hasn't yet been saved.

disable   To temporarily disconnect a hardware device or program feature; to make it unavailable for use.

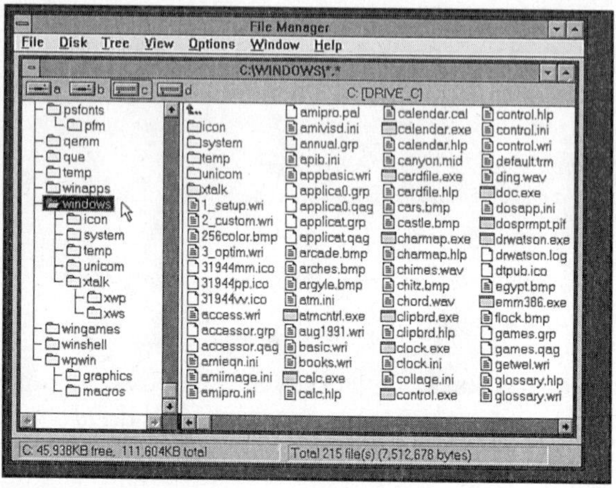

Fig. D.8 *A directory tree.*

disk See *floppy disk* and *hard disk*.

disk buffer See *cache controller*.

disk capacity The storage capacity of a floppy disk or hard disk, measured in kilobytes (K) or megabytes (M). The capacity of a floppy disk depends on the size of the disk and the density of the magnetic particles on its surface. The two most popular disk sizes are 5 1/4 inch and 3 1/2 inch. Single-sided disks were once common but are all but obsolete now; double-sided disks are the norm. Also standard today are the double-density and high-density disks. Extra-high density disks are available, but aren't common.

The remaining variables are the operating system you use to format the disk and the capabilities of the disk drive you're using. The following table shows the relationship of the variables and the resulting capacity:

Size	Density	System	Drive	Capacity
3 1/2"	DD	MS-DOS	Standard	720K

Size	Density	System	Drive	Capacity
3 1/2"	DD	Mac	Standard	800K
3 1/2"	HD	Mac	Superdrive	1.4M
3 1/2"	HD	MS-DOS	High density	1.44M
3 1/2"	HD	MS-DOS	Extra-high density	2.88M
5 1/4"	DD	MS-DOS	Standard	360K
5 1/4"	HD	MS-DOS	High density	1.2M

TIP: *If you're shopping for an IBM PC-compatible computer, bear in mind that higher capacity drives aren't much more expensive ($10 to $30) than their lower capacity counterparts.*

disk drive   A secondary storage device such as a floppy disk drive or a hard disk. This term usually refers to floppy disk drives.

A floppy disk drive is an economical secondary storage medium that uses a removable magnetic disk that can be recorded, erased, and reused over and over. The recording and erasing operations are performed by the read/write head that moves over the surface of the disk, giving the drive its random-access capabilities.

Floppy disk drives are too slow to serve as the main data storage for today's personal computers, but are needed to copy software and disk-based data onto the system and for backup operations. For business applications, a minimum configuration is one hard disk and one floppy disk drive. See *floppy disk, random access, read/ write head,* and *secondary storage.*

disk drive controller   The circuitry that controls the physical operations of the floppy disks and/or hard disks connected to the computer. Until recently, most disk drive controllers were plug-in controller cards with cabling for the floppy disks and a hard disk. A clear trend toward including this circuitry on the computer's motherboard now exists. With the advent of the Intelligent Drive

Electronics (IDE) standard, which transfers much of the controller circuitry to the drive itself, the inclusion of the remaining circuitry on the motherboard has become much more simple.

Wherever it's positioned, the disk drive controller circuitry performs two functions: it uses an interface standard (such as ST-506/ST-412, ESDI, or SCSI) to establish communication with the drive's electronics, as well as a data encoding scheme (such as MFM, RLL, or ARLL) to encode information on the magnetic surface of the disk. See *Advanced Run-Length Limited (ARLL), Enhanced System Device Interface (ESDI), Modified Frequency Modulation (MFM), Run-Length Limited (RLL), Small Computer System Interface (SCSI)*, and *ST-506/ST-412.*

diskless workstation   In a local area network (LAN), a workstation that has a CPU and RAM but lacks its own disk drives. Diskless workstations abandon all benefits of personal computing except the software. In large organizations, data processing managers have believed that it's far better to let professionals choose the software, so everyone produces and uses compatible data. Also, personal computers raise serious security issues for organizations. Anyone can come into your office and, if you aren't around and haven't secured your system, copy a disk containing valuable information.

The diskless workstation returns the personal computer's control to the hands of system administrators and resolves security issues, but with serious loss of speed, flexibility, and originality and with greater vulnerability to the effects of a disk or system crash and access by hackers. See *distributed processing system* and *personal computer.*

disk operating system   See *operating system.*

disk optimizer   See *defragmentation.*

display   See *monitor.*

d

display adapter   See *video adapter*.

display type   A typeface, usually 14 points or larger and differing in style from the body type, used for headings and subheadings. See *body type*.

D E F

> **TIP:** *Use a sans serif typeface such as Avant Garde or Helvetica for display type. For body type, use serif fonts such as Times Roman or New Century Schoolbook, because serif fonts are more readable than sans serif fonts. See* sans serif *and* serif.

distributed bulletin board   A collection of computer conferences, called *newsgroups,* automatically distributed throughout a wide area network so that individual postings are available to every user. The conferences are organized by topic, embracing such areas as ecology, politics, current events, music, specific computers and computer programs, and human sexuality. See *follow-on post, Internet, moderated newsgroup, post, thread, unmoderated newsgroup,* and *USENET.*

distributed processing system   A computer system designed for multiple users that provides each user with a fully functional computer. In personal computing, distributed processing takes the form of local area networks, in which the personal computers of a department or organization are linked by high-speed cable connections.

Distributed processing offers some advantages over multiuser systems. If the network fails, you can still work. You also can select software tailored to your needs. You can start a distributed processing system with a modest initial investment; you need only two or three workstations and, if desired, a central file server. You add more workstation nodes as needed.

A multiuser system, however, requires a major initial investment in the central computer, which must be powerful enough to handle system demands as the system grows. Multiuser systems

have legitimate applications—for example, in point-of-sale terminals, in which you gain by making sure that all information is
posted to a central database. See *file server, local area network
(LAN),* and *multiuser system.*

dithering   In color or grayscale printing and displays, the min-
gling of dots of several colors to produce what appears to be a new
color. With dithering, you can combine 256 colors to produce
what appears to be a continuously variable color palette, but at the
cost of sacrificing resolution; the several colors of dots tend to be
mingled in patterns rather than blended well.

docking station   A cabinet containing disk drives, video
circuits, and specially designed receptacles that's designed to house
a notebook computer. When the notebook is inserted into the
docking station, devices attached to the docking station can be
used by the notebook computer.

> **TIP:** *If you have a high-speed notebook or laptop with a large
> hard drive and at least 4M of RAM, a docking station may be
> a less expensive alternative to purchasing a desktop computer.*

document   A file containing work you've created, such as a
business report, a memo, or a worksheet. The term strongly con-
notes the authority of an original—that is, fixed text—with a
clearly named author. The meaning of the term *document* has
shifted in two ways, thanks to the computer.

First, computers make document revision easy. Second, develop-
ments in groupware and hypertext make group authoring easy.
Both points were first noted, with alarm, by newspaper reporters,
who found that, after electronic editing systems were installed,
editors would simply make changes to their stories without asking
their permission. With today's network technology, a document
can become text in flux, constantly accessed and modified by
many people—and, with dynamic data exchange (DDE), even by

d

the computer itself, as it detects changes in supporting documents and updates dynamic links automatically. See *dynamic data exchange (DDE)*, *groupware*, and *word processing*.

documentation   The instructions, tutorials, and reference information that provide you with the information you need to use a computer program or computer system effectively. Documentation can appear in printed form or in on-line help systems.

document base font   The base font you've told a word processing program to use for only one document. You can choose Times Roman as the initial base font for all documents, for example, but for a letter you're now writing, override that choice by choosing Helvetica as the document base font. You can choose other fonts within this letter, but the program uses Helvetica unless you give an explicit command to the contrary. See *base font* and *initial base font*.

document comparison utility   A utility program or word processing command that compares two documents created with a word processing program. If the two documents aren't identical, the program displays the differences between them, line by line.

Document comparison utilities are useful in collaborative writing. Suppose that you create a document and send a copy to the person working with you on the project, who makes changes and returns an altered version to you. By using a document comparison utility, you can see the differences between the two documents on-screen. In figure D.9, for example, altered or added passages are shown as highlighted text, and the original version is shown in strikethrough text. See *redlining*.

document file icon   In Microsoft Windows, the icon of a document associated with an application. You can open the document and launch the application simultaneously just by double-clicking a document file icon. See *associate* and *associated document*.

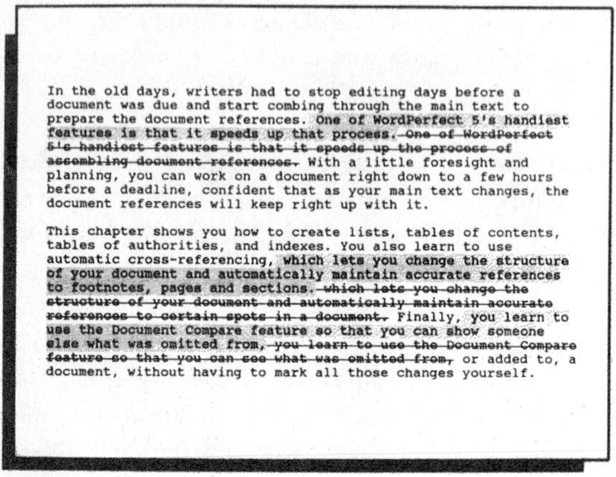

In the old days, writers had to stop editing days before a document was due and start combing through the main text to prepare the document references. ~~One of WordPerfect 5's handiest features is that it speeds up that process.~~ ~~One of WordPerfect 5's handiest features is that it speeds up the process of assembling document references.~~ With a little foresight and planning, you can work on a document right down to a few hours before a deadline, confident that as your main text changes, the document references will keep right up with it.

This chapter shows you how to create lists, tables of contents, tables of authorities, and indexes. You also learn to use automatic cross-referencing, which lets you change the structure of your document and automatically maintain accurate references to footnotes, pages and sections. ~~which lets you change the structure of your document and automatically maintain accurate references to certain spots in a document.~~ Finally, you learn to use the Document Compare feature so that you can show someone else what was omitted from, ~~you learn to use the Document Compare feature so that you can see what was omitted from,~~ or added to, a document, without having to mark all those changes yourself.

Fig. D.9 *Two versions of a document compared by a document comparison utility.*

document format   In a word processing program, a set of formatting choices that control the page layout of the entire document. Examples of document formats include margins, headers, footers, page numbers, and columns.

document image processing (DIP)   A system for the imaging, storage, and retrieval of text-based documents that includes scanning documents, storing the files on optical or magnetic media, and viewing when needed using a monitor, printer, or fax.

The goal of a document image processing system is a "paperless office." According to one recent estimate, a four-drawer file cabinet costs about $25,000 to fill, and another $2,160 per year to maintain. Moreover, 1 out of every 33 documents is lost (usually by incorrect filing), at a cost of more than $100 per lost document trying to recover the missing information. For that much money, you can buy a pretty nifty document image processing system, scan the documents into a document database, and stick the originals into storage boxes in sequential order.

d

The DIP solution has its shortcomings, though. Today's optical character recognition (OCR) technology, while vastly improved, is still slow, prone to error, and performs poorly when text size is smaller than 9 points, although you can pass the scanned documents through a spelling checker to shorten proofreading time. Moreover, retrieving documents using keywords has many known shortcomings. See *optical character recognition (OCR)* and *paperless office*.

D
E
F

document processing   The use of computer technology during every stage of the in-house production of documents, such as instruction manuals, handbooks, reports, and proposals. A complete document processing system includes all the software and hardware needed to create, organize, edit, and print such documents, including generating indexes and tables of contents. See *desktop publishing (DTP)* and *word processing program*.

document window   In multidocument programs as diverse as Word for Windows and WordPerfect 6.0 for DOS, a window within an application program that displays the document you're creating or altering. You can open more than one document window within an application window. See *Microsoft Windows*.

domain   An area of interest.

On the Internet, the highest subdivision, usually a country. However, in the United States, the subdivision is by type of organization, such as commercial, educational, and government.

DOS   See *MS-DOS* and *operating system*.

Doskey   A utility provided with MS-DOS (5.0 and later) that allows you to type more than one DOS command on a line, store and retrieve previously used DOS commands, create stored macros, and customize all DOS commands.

DOS prompt   In MS-DOS, a letter representing the current disk drive followed by the greater-than symbol (>), which together inform you that the operating system is ready to receive a command. See *prompt*.

→ **TIP:** *You can change the default DOS prompt. To insert a colon after the drive letter and show the current directory, add this line to your AUTOEXEC.BAT file:*

```
PROMPT=$P$G
```

dot file   In UNIX, a file that has a name preceded by a dot. Such a file normally isn't displayed by UNIX file-listing utilities. Dot files are frequently used for user configuration files, such as a file that lists the newsgroups the user regularly consults.

dot-matrix printer   An impact printer that forms text and graphic images by hammering the ends of pins against a ribbon in a pattern (a matrix) of dots.

Dot-matrix printers are relatively fast, but their output is generally poor quality because the character isn't well formed. Some dot-matrix printers use 24 pins instead of 9, to improve print quality. Also, many of today's dot-matrix printers offer a near-letter-quality (NLQ) mode that produces substantially better results by passing over a line several times, offsetting the dots to form a solid character. Dot-matrix printers usually can produce printout in more than one font. These printers also can be extremely noisy. See *font, impact printer, near-letter quality (NLQ),* and *non-impact printer.*

! **CAUTION:** *In IBM PC-compatible computing, no widely accepted standard exists for printer control commands. De facto standards have been established by Epson and IBM. Many dot-matrix printers recognize the Epson or IBM commands, but others don't. If you plan to buy a dot-matrix printer, make sure that your software includes a printer driver for the model.*

dot pitch   The size of the smallest dot that a monitor can display. Dot pitch determines a monitor's maximum resolution. High-resolution monitors use dot pitches of approximately 0.31 mm or less; the best monitors use dot pitches of 0.28 mm or less.

d

To keep the electron beam from activating the wrong part of the screen, color monitors use a *shadow mask*—a metal sheet with fine perforations. These perforations are arranged so that the beam strikes one hole at a time, corresponding to one dot on-screen. The smaller the hole in the shadow mask, the higher the resolution.

High-resolution monitors use dot pitches of approximately 0.31 mm or less; the best monitors use dot pitches of 0.28 mm or less.

D
E
F

dot prompt   In dBASE, the prompt, a lone period on an otherwise empty screen, for the command-driven interface of the program.

dots per inch (dpi)   A measure of printer resolution that counts the dots that the device can produce per linear inch.

In describing screen resolutions, the practice is to state the resolution in horizontal pixels (picture elements) by vertical lines, rather than state a dpi figure. The resolution of a Super VGA monitor, for example, is 800 horizontal pixels by 600 vertical lines.

double-click   To click a mouse button twice in rapid succession. In many programs, double-clicking extends the action that results from single-clicking; double-clicking anywhere in a word, for example, selects the whole word rather than just one character. Double-clicking is also used to initiate an action. In a file list, for example, double-clicking a file name selects and opens the file.

double density   A widely used recording technique that packs twice as much data on a floppy or hard disk as the earlier, single-density standard. See *high density, Modified Frequency Modulation (MFM), Run-Length Limited (RLL),* and *single density.*

DO/WHILE loop   In programming, a loop control structure that continues to carry out its function until a condition is satisfied. A DO/WHILE control structure establishes a test that, if true, causes the program to execute the next instructions until an ENDDO is reached. The program now loops back to the DO/WHILE and repeats the process again. When the test finally proves false, the sequential control structure takes over again, and the program moves on to the next statement. See *loop*, *sequence control structure*, *software command language*, and *syntax*.

Dow Jones News/Retrieval Service   An on-line information service from Dow Jones, the publishers of the Wall Street Journal and Barron's, that offers a computer-searchable index to financial and business publications and to up-to-date financial information, such as stock quotes. See *on-line information service*.

downloadable font   A printer font that's transferred from the hard disk to the printer's memory at the time of printing. Often called *soft fonts*, downloadable fonts are the least convenient of the three types of printer fonts you can use. Downloading can consume from 5 to 10 minutes at the start of every operating session. See *bit-mapped font*, *built-in font*, *cartridge font*, *downloading utility*, *font*, *font family*, *outline font*, *page description language (PDL)*, and *PostScript*.

> **TIP:** *After you print a document that requires several downloadable fonts that you no longer need, switch your printer off and on before proceeding, especially if the next document contains graphics. The power interruption clears the printer's memory and makes room for the computations needed to generate the graphic image.*

downloading   Transferring a copy of a file from a distant computer to a disk in your computer using data communication links. See *file transfer protocol (FTP)* and *modem*.

downloading utility   A utility program that transfers downloadable fonts from your computer or printer hard disk to the printer's random-access memory (RAM). Downloading utilities usually are included with the downloadable fonts you buy. You may not need the utility if the word processing or page layout program you're using has downloading capabilities built in, as do Word-Perfect, Microsoft Word, Ventura Publisher, and PageMaker.

downward compatibility Hardware or software that runs without modification when using earlier computer components or files created with earlier software versions. VGA monitors, for example, are downwardly compatible with the original IBM PC if you use an 8-bit VGA adapter that fits in the PC's 8-bit expansion bus.

dpi See *dots per inch (dpi)*.

drag To move the mouse pointer while holding down a mouse button.

drag and drop In Microsoft Windows 3.1 and Macintosh programs running under System 7, a technique that allows you to perform operations on objects by dragging the object with the mouse to an application icon. You can open a document by dragging it to an application, or install icons in other group windows by dragging the icon to the desired window. Drag a selection of files and drop them on the A drive face in the File Manager to copy the files to a floppy disk.

> **TIP:** *Windows 3.1 implements drag-and-drop in the File Manager, so you can copy and move files quickly and easily. To copy a file from one drive to another, click the file and drag the pointer to the file's destination (see fig. D.10).*

drag-and-drop editing An editing feature that allows you to perform a block move or copy by highlighting the block and then using the mouse to drag a special pointer to the text's new location. When you release the mouse button, the text appears in the new location. Some DOS programs, such as WordPerfect 6.0, implement drag-and-drop editing. See *block move*.

DRAM See *dynamic random-access memory (DRAM)*.

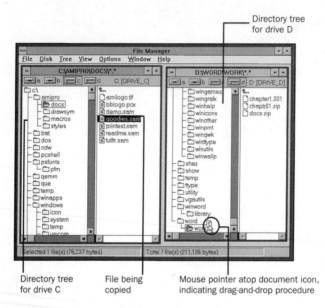

Directory tree
for drive D

Directory tree   File being   Mouse pointer atop document icon,
for drive C   copied   indicating drag-and-drop procedure

Fig. D.10 *Using drag-and-drop to copy a file from drive C to drive D.*

draw program A computer graphics program that uses object-oriented graphics to produce line art. A draw program stores the components of a drawing, such as lines, circles, and curves, as mathematical formulas rather than as a configuration of bits on-screen, as paint programs do. Unlike images created with paint programs, line art created with a draw program can be sized and scaled without introducing distortions. Draw programs produce output that prints at a printer's maximum resolution. See *object-oriented graphic* and *paint program.*

draw tool In any program that includes graphics capabilities, a command that transforms the cursor into a "pen" for creating object-oriented (vector) graphics. Draw tools typically include options for creating lines, circles, ovals, polylines, rectangles, and Bézier curves. See *object-oriented graphic.*

drive See *disk drive.*

d

drive bay   A receptacle or opening into which you can install a hard or floppy disk drive. Common in today's IBM and IBM-compatible personal computers are half-height bays. See *half-height drive*.

drive designator   In DOS, an argument that specifies the drive to be affected by the command. The command FORMAT B:, for example, tells DOS to format the disk in drive B. *B:* is the drive designator.

driver   A disk file that contains information needed by a program to operate a peripheral such as a monitor or printer. See *device driver*.

drop cap   An initial letter of a chapter or paragraph, enlarged and positioned so that the top of the character is even with the top of the first line, and the rest of the character descends into the second and subsequent lines (see fig. D.11). See *initial* and *stickup initial*.

> This is a 24 point
> Helvetica Big First
> Char. with Space For
> Big First: Normal.
> Ventura automatically
> aligns the top of the
> character with the top of
> the first line of text and
> calculates the number
> of lines to indent.

Fig. D.11   *A drop cap created with Ventura Publisher.*

drop-down list box   In industry-standard and graphical user interfaces, a list of command options that displays as a single-item text box until you select the command, which causes a list of options to drop down (or pop up). After you "drop down" the list, you can choose one of its options. The drop-down list box lets a programmer provide many options without taking up much space on-screen. See *graphical user interface (GUI)* and *industry-standard user interface*.

dropouts   Characters lost in data transmission for some reason. On slower systems, for example, a fast typist may find that some typed characters don't make it into a word processing program's file; this is caused by an interruption of user input when the program must access the disk for some reason. The computer's type-ahead buffer, which is supposed to handle this situation, can accommodate only a dozen or so characters. The user soon learns to pause when the disk drive's activity light comes on.

dropout type   White characters printed on a black background.

drop shadow   A shadow placed behind an image, slightly offset horizontally and vertically, creating the illusion that the topmost image has been lifted off the surface of the page.

drunk mouse   A mouse whose pointer seems to jump wildly and irritatingly just as you're about to select something. Many users suspect that this malady is caused by a computer virus, but it's attributable to something far more mundane: plain old dirt.

About once every two weeks, pop the ball out of your mouse and take a look inside. On Microsoft mice, you'll see two metal bars that are supposed to spin as the mouse ball moves. If you're experiencing the drunk mouse syndrome, chances are good that one or both of these bars is coated with finger grease. To remove it, dip a cotton swab in copious amounts of isopropyl alcohol and rub the dirt until it's completely gone. Then wipe grease off the ball using a soft cloth dampened with isopropyl alcohol.

DTP   See *desktop publishing (DTP)*.

dual in-line package (DIP)   A standard packaging and mounting device for integrated circuits. DIP is the favored packaging for DRAM chips, for example. The package, made of hard plastic material, encloses the circuit; the circuit's leads are connected to downward-pointing pins that stick in two parallel rows. The pins are designed to fit securely into a socket; you also can solder them directly to a circuit board. See *single in-line package (SIP)*.

d

CAUTION: *Don't try to install or remove DIP circuits unless you know what you're doing. You can easily bend or break the pins.*

dual y-axis graph   In presentation and analytical graphics, a line or column graph that uses two y-axes (values axes) when comparing two sets of data measured differently. In figure D.12, for example, sales (of battery-operated hand warmers, perhaps?) are measured in dollars, and temperatures are measured in degrees. See *paired bar graph*.

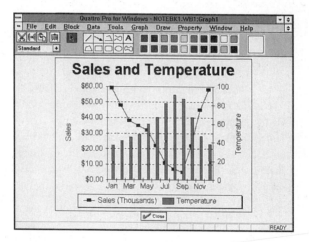

Fig. D.12   *A dual y-axis graph.*

dumb terminal   See *terminal*.

dump   To transfer the contents of memory to a printer or disk storage. Programmers use memory dumps while debugging programs to see exactly what the computer is doing when the dump occurs. See *Print Screen (PrtSc)*.

duplex   See *full duplex* and *half duplex*.

duplex printing   Printing or reproducing a document on both sides of the page so that the verso (left) and recto (right) pages face each other after the document is bound. (A document always begins on an odd-numbered recto page; verso pages have even numbers.) See *binding offset*.

Dvorak keyboard   An alternative keyboard layout in which 70 percent of the keystrokes take place on the home row (compared to 32 percent with the standard QWERTY layout). A Dvorak keyboard is easier to learn and faster to use. However, every time you return to a QWERTY keyboard, you must go back to the hunt-and-peck method. See *QWERTY*.

dynamic data exchange (DDE)   In Microsoft Windows and Macintosh System 7, an interprocess communication channel (IPC) through which programs can actively exchange data and control other applications. To be capable of DDE, the programs must conform to Microsoft Corporation's specifications.

DDE allows simultaneously running programs to exchange data, even as the information changes. With a telecommunications link to a stock-reporting service such as Dow-Jones News/Retrieval Service, for example, a DDE-capable spreadsheet program (such as Microsoft Excel) can receive real-time data from the on-line service, record changes in the price of key stocks, and recalculate the entire worksheet as the change occurs.

Underlying DDE is a client/server model. The application that supplies information is called the *server application*, whereas the application that receives information is called the *client application*. Most DDE-capable applications can function as both client and server for DDE purposes and can even provide data to more than one client.

Microsoft's object-linking and embedding (OLE) standards have helped to simplify the user's task in setting up dynamic links in Windows and Macintosh systems. In OLE terms, you just paste data from one application to another using the Paste Link or Paste Special command (Edit menu). Thereafter, DDE updates the destination document if the source document changes. If the client application isn't running when you update the source document, you see an alert box when you open the destination document, informing you that the source data has changed and asking you

d

whether you want to update it. See *client application, dynamic link, interprocess communication (IPC), object linking and embedding (OLE), server application,* and *System 7.*

dynamic link   A method of linking data so that it's shared by two programs. When data is changed in one program, the data is likewise changed in the other when you use an update command. See *hot link.*

dynamic object   A document or portion of a document pasted or inserted into a destination document using object linking and embedding (OLE) techniques. A linked object is automatically updated if you make changes to the source document. An embedded object includes information to allow you to open the application used to create the object and edit the object. See *object linking and embedding (OLE).*

dynamic random-access memory (DRAM)   A random-access memory (RAM) chip that represents memory states by using capacitors that store electrical charges. Because the capacitors eventually lose their charges, DRAM chips must refresh continually (hence *dynamic*).

Dynamic RAM chips vary in their access times—the speeds with which the central processing unit (CPU) can obtain information encoded within them. These access times are rated in nanoseconds (billionths of a second); a chip marked 12, for example, has an access time of 120 ns. Such access times may seem remarkably fast, but a poky (relatively speaking, of course) 25 MHz 386 completes a processor cycle every 80 ns. To make matters worse, dynamic RAM chips must precharge between each access, so the cycle time for these 120 ns chips is doubled. See *central processing unit (CPU), nanosecond (ns), static random-access memory (SRAM),* and *wait state.*

TIP: *Faster chips rated at 60-80 ns are common, though they won't keep up with 486 66 MHz processors. Fortunately, efficient memory design and a cache of faster SRAM chips, standard on most computers sold today, will see that data is delivered almost as fast as the processor needs it. All you need to add is a software cache.*

Easter egg   A message or screen that's buried within a computer program and accessible only through an undocumented procedure.

The TECO operating system featured a famous Easter egg. Many file-creation commands began with MAKE—and sooner or later, the designers knew that someone would type **MAKE LOVE**. The response?

    NOT WAR?

Logically, if you type **MAKE WAR**, TECO responds,

    NOT LOVE?

Buried within the data fork of the Macintosh System File is the message Help! Help! We're being held prisoner in a system software factory! Reportedly, at least 12 Easter eggs are buried in Macintosh system software.

An Easter egg was hidden in each pane in the Windows logo in Word for Windows. A notorious Word for Windows Easter egg depicts WordPerfect as a green monster that's vanquished by a tiny hero, who squashes the competing program with a Word icon, as other tiny figures cheer and celebrate.

EBCDIC   See *Extended Binary Coded Decimal Interchange Code (EBCDIC)*.

echoplex   A communications standard for computers in which the receiving station acknowledges and confirms the reception of a message by echoing the message back to the transmitting station. See *full duplex* and *half duplex*.

edge connector   The part of an expansion board that plugs into an expansion slot. See *adapter* and *expansion slot*.

EDI   See *Electronic Data Interchange (EDI)*.

edit mode   A program mode that makes correcting text and data easier (see fig. E.1). In Lotus 1-2-3, for example, press F2 (Edit) to display the contents of a cell in the second line of the control panel, where you can use editing keys to correct errors or add characters.

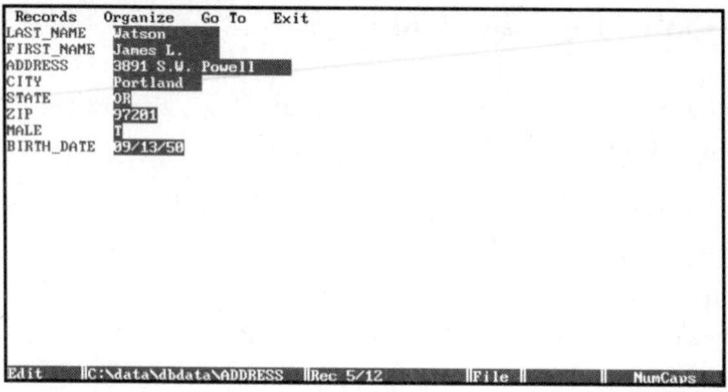

```
 Records    Organize   Go To   Exit
LAST_NAME    Watson
FIRST_NAME   James L.
ADDRESS      3091 S.W. Powell
CITY         Portland
STATE        OR
ZIP          97281
MALE         T
BIRTH_DATE   09/13/50
```
```
 Edit     IIC:\data\dbdata\ADDRESS   IIRec 5/12      IIFile II          NumCaps
```

Fig. E.1 *A dBASE data record displayed in edit mode.*

editor   See *text editor.*

edutainment   Computer application programs designed to tell the user about a subject but presented in the form of a game that is sufficiently entertaining or challenging to hold the interest of the user.

A long-time best seller is the Microsoft Flight Simulator, bought by most users as a game but actually used as a prelude to professional flight instruction in many flight schools. Almost as well known is the Carmen Sandiego series of games, such as Where In the World is Carmen Sandiego? and Where in Europe is Carmen Sandiego? More recently, Sierra On-Line has released a Sierra Discovery Series that covers several topics, such as Ecoquest, The Search for Cetus, which teaches ecology, marine biology, environmental ethics, and logic. Each game is a problem-solving adventure rated for specific age groups but entirely satisfying for adult game players as well.

EEMS   See *Enhanced Expanded Memory Specification (EEMS).*

EGA   See *Enhanced Graphics Adapter (EGA).*

EISA   See *Extended Industry Standard Architecture (EISA).*

electrocutaneous feedback   A primitive method of providing tactile feedback in virtual reality systems by administering a low-voltage shock to the user's skin. The user feels a mild buzz. Varying the voltage and frequency of the current produces variations in the buzz that the user can learn to discriminate. See *virtual reality.*

Electronic Data Interchange (EDI)   A standard for the electronic exchange of business documents, such as invoices and purchase orders, that was developed by the Data Interchange Standards Association (DISA).

Using field codes, such as BT for Bill To or ST for Ship To, EDI specifies the format in which data is transmitted electronically. By ensuring that all EDI-based communications have the same data in the same place, this protocol allows companies to exchange purchase orders and other documents electronically.

Electronic Frontier Foundation   A non-profit organization based in Washington, D.C., dedicated to encouraging and ensuring that everyone has access to the newly emerging communications technologies. As part of this effort, EFF sponsored the writing (by Adam Gaffen) of *The Big Dummy's Guide to the Internet*, almost 300 pages of Internet information for people with little or no experience with network communications. The guide is available for downloading from several networks. See *Internet*.

electronic mail   The use of a network to send and receive messages. Also called *e-mail*.

Linked by high-speed data connections that cross national boundaries, electronic mail lets you compose messages and transmit them in seconds to one or more recipients in your office, to headquarters in another state, or to an international location. It isn't necessary for a recipient to be present when the message is received; a message such as You have mail waiting is displayed the next time the recipient logs on to the system.

The Internet, an extensive system of computer linkages, is providing the solution to e-mail incompatibility. Electronic mail vendors such as MCI Mail and CompuServe now offer links to the Internet, extending the Internet's reach. The result is an explosion of electronic mail. See *freenet, Internet,* and *netiquette*.

elite   A typeface that prints 12 characters per inch. See *pitch*.

e-mail   See *electronic mail.*

embedded chart   In Microsoft Excel, a chart created within a worksheet rather than as a separate chart document.

embedded formatting command   A text formatting command placed directly in the text to be formatted. In some programs, the command doesn't affect the appearance of the text on-screen, which can make the program more difficult to use. In other programs, such as WordPerfect, only a few embedded commands—full justification or a font change—don't change the screen display. Windows applications and recent releases of the most popular DOS word processing programs include a graphical display where formatting is displayed immediately. Synonymous with *off-screen formatting.* See *hidden codes, on-screen formatting,* and *what-you-see-is-what-you-get (WYSIWYG).*

embedded object   In object linking and embedding (OLE), an object created with one application that has been wholly inserted, or embedded, into a destination document created by another application. The object can be text, a chart, graphic, or sound. See *linked object* and *object linking and embedding (OLE).*

em dash   A continuous dash equal in width to one em, the width of the capital letter *M* in a given typeface, often used to introduce parenthetical remarks. The following sentence contains em dashes:

> The butler—or someone who knows what the butler knows—must have done it.

See *en.*

em fraction   A single-character fraction that occupies one em of space and uses a diagonal stroke ($^1/_4$) rather than a piece fraction made from three or more characters (1/4). See *en fraction.*

EMM   See *expanded memory manager (EMM).*

D E F

EMM386.EXE   In MS-DOS running on an 80386 or higher computer equipped with extended memory, an expanded memory emulator that allows DOS applications to use the extended memory as though it were expanded memory. EMM386.EXE also allows the user to load device drivers and programs into the upper memory area. See *device driver, expanded memory (EMS), expanded memory emulator, extended memory,* and *upper memory area.*

emoticon   See *smiley.*

emphasis   The use of a non-Roman type style—such as under-lining, italic or bold typefaces, and small caps—to highlight a word or phrase. See *type style.*

EMS   See *Lotus-Intel-Microsoft Expanded Memory Specification (LIM EMS).*

emulation   The duplication of the functional capability of one device in another device, or a device designed to work exactly like another. In telecommunications, for example, a personal computer emulates a dumb terminal for on-line communication with a distant computer. See *terminal.*

en   A unit of measurement in typesetting that equals half the width of an em space, the width of the capital letter *M* in the current typeface. En dashes are used in place of the English words *to* or *through,* as in January 9–14 or pp. 63–68. See *em dash.*

en fraction   A single-character fraction that occupies one en of space and uses a horizontal stroke. See *em fraction* and *en.*

Encapsulated PostScript (EPS) file   A high-resolution graphic image stored in PostScript page description language. The EPS standard allows the transfer of high-resolution graphic images between applications. EPS images can be sized without sacrificing image quality (see fig. E.2).

A major drawback of EPS graphics is that a PostScript-compatible laser printer is required to print them. The resolution when printed is determined by the printer; 300 or 600 dpi with laser printers, but up to 2,540 dpi possible on Linotronic. A second drawback is that with most application programs, the image isn't visible on-screen unless a PICT- or TIFF-format screen image has been attached to the EPS file.

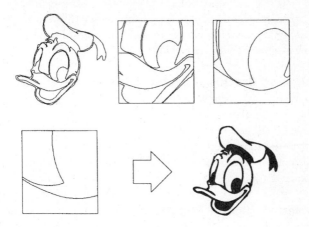

Fig. E.2 *An EPS graphic image scaled to various sizes without distortion.*

As an alternative to expensive PostScript printers, developers have created programs that interpret and print EPS files on standard dot-matrix printers or non-PostScript laser printers. One such program is GoScript (LaserGo, Inc.). See *PostScript*.

encryption The process of enciphering, or encoding, data so that users who don't possess the necessary password can't read the data. See *decryption*.

End key A key on IBM PC-compatible keyboards with functions that vary from program to program. Frequently, the End key is used to move the cursor to the end of the line or the bottom of the screen, but the assignment of this key is up to the programmer.

endnote A footnote positioned at the end of the document or section rather than the bottom of the page. Many word processing programs let the user choose between footnotes and endnotes.

end user The person who uses a computer and its application programs at home or at work to perform tasks and produce results.

Enhanced Expanded Memory Specification (EEMS)
An enhanced version of the original Lotus-Intel-Microsoft Expanded Memory Specification (LIM EMS) that allows DOS applications to use more than 640K of memory. Version 4.0 of EMS supports the original version of EMS and the enhanced version (EEMS). See *bank switching, expanded memory (EMS)*, and *Lotus-Intel-Microsoft Expanded Memory Specification (LIM EMS)*.

Enhanced Graphics Adapter (EGA)   A color, bit-mapped, graphics display adapter for IBM PC-compatible computers. The EGA adapter displays up to 16 colors simultaneously with a resolution of 640 pixels horizontally by 350 lines vertically. The 16 colors are selected from the EGA color palette that contains 64 colors, if you count black and shades of gray. See *Color Graphics Adapter (CGA)*, *Super VGA*, and *Video Graphics Array (VGA)*.

Enhanced Graphics Display   A color digital monitor designed to work only with the IBM Enhanced Graphics Adapter (EGA).

Enhanced System Device Interface (ESDI)   An interface standard for hard disk drives. Drives using the ESDI standard transfer at 10 to 15 megabits of data per second, 2 to 3 times as fast as the earlier ST-506/ST-412 interface standard.

ESDI drives have virtually disappeared from the market. IDE drives with access speeds of 12 milliseconds (ms) or faster, up to 1,750M capacity, are very inexpensive and don't require any additional circuitry. See *IDE drive, interface standard*, and *ST-506/ST-412*.

Enter/Return   A key that confirms a command, sending the command to the central processing unit (CPU); synonymous with *carriage return*. In word processing, the Enter/Return key starts a new paragraph. On early IBM PC keyboards, this key is labeled with a hooked left arrow. On more recent AT and enhanced keyboards, *Enter* is printed on the key. (*Return* appears on Macintosh keyboards.)

Most IBM PC-compatible keyboards have an Enter key located to the right of the typing area, and a second one in the lower right corner of the numeric keypad. These two keys have identical functions in most but not all programs.

entry-level system   A computer system considered to be the minimal system for undertaking serious applications with the computer, such as using electronic spreadsheets or word processing software.

The definition of *entry-level system* changes rapidly. Ten years ago, an entry-level system—incapable of running the latest versions of today's most popular software—had at least one 360K floppy disk drive, a monochrome text monitor, and 256K of RAM.

Contributing to the steady increase in "minimum" system requirements are two trends. First, computers get cheaper even as they become more powerful. Second, programmers keep creating bigger and more complex programs to run on these more powerful computers. Yesterday's 80286 is still a useful machine—as long as you run yesterday's software.

entry line   In a spreadsheet program, the second line of the control panel, on which the characters you type appear. The program doesn't insert the characters into the current cell until you press Enter. If the cell has contents, cell contents are displayed in the upper left corner of the control panel.

envelope printer   A printer designed specifically to print names, addresses, and U.S. Postal Service POSTNET bar codes on business envelopes. Most envelope printers can print POSTNET bar codes. Businesses that use the bar codes receive an attractive discount on postal rates and receive faster and more accurate delivery of their business correspondence.

If you have a laser printer, you may not need an envelope printer because laser printers can print POSTNET codes. Envelope printers, however, do a better job of handling high-volume printing jobs. See *bar code*.

environment   The hardware and/or operating system for application programs, such as the Macintosh environment. In DOS, the environment also is a space in memory reserved for storing variables that can be used by applications running on your system. See *environment variable*.

environment variable   An instruction stored in the DOS environment that controls, for example, how to display the DOS prompt, where to store any temporary files, and the path of directories DOS searches to find commands. The PATH, COMSPEC, PROMPT, and SET commands in the AUTOEXEC.BAT file all define environment variables.

TIP: *After you install Microsoft Windows, make a copy of the AUTOEXEC.BAT file that Windows created or modified during installation. This file contains a SET command that tells Windows where to store the many temporary files it creates. If you erase this file, you can use the copy to restore it to the root directory.*

EOF   Abbreviation for *end of file*.

EOL   Abbreviation for *end of line*.

EPROM   See *erasable programmable read-only memory (EPROM)*.

EPS   See *Encapsulated PostScript (EPS) file*.

equation typesetting   Embedded codes within a word processing document that cause the program to print multiline equations, including mathematical symbols such as integrals and summation signs. The best word processing programs, such as WordPerfect and Microsoft Word, now offer WYSIWYG ("what-you-see-is-what-you-get") on-screen equation editors, which let you see the equation as you build it. See *what-you-see-is-what-you-get (WYSIWYG)*.

erasable optical disk drive   A read/write data storage medium that uses a laser and reflected light to store and retrieve data on an optical disk.

Unlike CD-ROM and write-once, read-many (WORM) drives, erasable optical disk drives can be used like hard disks: You can write and erase data repeatedly. Storage capacities are sizable; current drives store up to 650M of information. They're expensive and much slower than hard disks, however, making them attractive primarily to organizations that need access to huge amounts of supplementary information, such as engineering drawings or technical documentation. See *CD-ROM disk drive, optical disk, secondary storage,* and *write-once, read-many (WORM).*

erasable programmable read-only memory (EPROM)

A read-only memory (ROM) chip that can be programmed and reprogrammed.

The erasability of EPROM chips matters to computer manufacturers, who often find that they need to reprogram ROM chips containing bugs. PROM chips, which can't be reprogrammed, must be discarded when a programming error is discovered.

EPROM chips are packaged in a clear plastic case so that the contents can be erased using ultraviolet light. To reprogram the EPROM chip, a PROM programmer is necessary. See *programmable read-only memory (PROM)* and *read-only memory (ROM).*

TIP: *Because of the slight possibility that EPROM chips may be damaged by ultraviolet light, avoid exposing your computer's innards to bright sunlight.*

ergonomics
The science of designing machines, tools, computers, and the physical work area so that people find them easy and healthful to use.

error-correcting protocol
In computer modems, a method for filtering out line noise and repeating transmissions automatically if an error occurs. Error correction requires the use of sending and receiving modems that conform to the same error correction protocols. When error correction is in use, a reliable link is established. Two widely used error-correcting protocols are MNP-4 and V.42. See *CCITT protocol, MNP-4,* and *reliable link.*

error handling
The way a program copes with errors, such as the failure to access data on a disk or a user's failure to press the appropriate key. A poorly written program may fail to handle errors at all, leading to a system lockup. The best programmers anticipate possible errors and provide information that helps the user solve the problem. See *error trapping.*

error message In application programs, an on-screen message informing you that the program can't carry out a requested operation. Early computing systems assumed users to be technically sophisticated, and frequently presented cryptic error messages. Applications for general use should display more helpful error messages that include suggestions about how to solve the problem, such as

```
You are about to lose work you have not saved.
Choose OK if you want to abandon this work.
Choose Cancel to return to your document.
```

error trapping An application's capability to recognize an error and perform a predetermined action in response to that error.

Esc A key that can be implemented differently by application programs. Esc usually is used to cancel a command or an operation.

escape code A combination of Esc (ASCII value 27) and one or more ASCII characters that can be used to change screen colors, control the cursor, create special prompts, reassign keys on the keyboard, and change the settings of your printer (to compressed type or bold, for example). Synonymous with *escape sequence*.

ESDI See *Enhanced System Device Interface (ESDI)*.

EtherNet A local area network hardware, protocol, and cabling standard, originally developed by Xerox Corporation, that can link up to 1,024 nodes in a bus network.

A high-speed standard using a baseband (single-channel) communication technique, EtherNet provides for a raw data transfer rate of 10 megabits per second, with actual throughputs in the range of 2 to 3 megabits per second. EtherNet uses carrier sense multiple access with collision detection (CSMA/CD) techniques to prevent network failures when two devices try to access the network at the same time. See *AppleTalk, bus network, carrier sense multiple access with collision detection (CSMA/CD)*, and *local area network (LAN)*.

D E F

> **CAUTION:** *Several firms, such as 3Com and Novell, manu-*
> *facture local area network hardware that uses EtherNet proto-*
> *cols, but the products of one firm often are incompatible with*
> *the products of another.*

EtherTalk   An implementation of EtherNet local area network
hardware, jointly developed by Apple and 3Com, designed to work
with the AppleShare network operating system. EtherTalk transmits
data via coaxial cables at the EtherNet rate of 10 megabits per second,
in contrast to AppleTalk's 230 kilobits per second rate.

ETX/ACK handshaking   See *handshaking.*

even parity   In asynchronous communications, an error-
checking technique that sets an extra bit (called a *parity bit*) to
1 if the number of 1 bits in a 1-byte data item adds up to an even
number. The parity bit is set to 0 if the number of 1 bits adds up
to an odd number. See *asynchronous communication, odd parity,*
and *parity checking.*

event   In an event-driven environment, an action—such as
moving or clicking the mouse—that generates a message. See *event*
handler and *event-driven program.*

event handler   In an event-driven environment, a block of
program code designed to handle the messages generated when a
specific kind of event occurs, such as a mouse click.

event-driven environment   A program or operating system
that normally functions in an idle loop, waiting for events to occur, such as a mouse click, keyboard input, or messages from
devices. When an event occurs, the program exits the idle loop
and executes the program code designed to handle the specific
event. This code is called an *event handler.* After the event is
handled, the program returns to the idle loop. Microsoft Windows
and Macintosh system software are event-driven environments.
See *event-driven program.*

event-driven language   A programming language that creates programs that respond to events such as input, incoming data,
or signals received from other applications. Such programs keep
the computer in an idle loop until an event occurs, at which time
they execute code that's relevant to the event. HyperTalk, the
language included with the HyperCard application packaged with
every Macintosh, is an event-driven language. See *object-oriented
programming language*.

event-driven program   A program designed to react to user-
initiated events, such as clicking a mouse, rather than force the user to
go through a series of prompts and menus in a predetermined way.

Macintosh application programs are event-driven. Unlike conventional programs that have an algorithm for solving a problem, the
central feature of a Mac program is the main event loop that forces
the program to run in circles while waiting for the user to do
something, such as click the mouse.

eWorld   An on-line computer service introduced June 20, 1994,
designed specifically for the Macintosh by Apple Corporation.
eWorld offers stock quotes, e-mail, conferences, news, sports,
weather, and Apple/Macintosh information such as names of dealers.
AppleLink, the Apple on-line business service, has been merged with
eWorld. eWorld also provides a variety of conferences, files, and
other information for the Macintosh.

.EXE   In DOS, an extension that indicates a file is an executable
program. To run the program with DOS, simply type the file
name (but not the extension) and press Enter.

executable file   See *executable program*.

executable program   A computer program that's ready to
run on a given computer. To be executable, the program must
have been translated, usually by a compiler, into the machine
language appropriate for the computer.

→ **TIP:** *In DOS, you can tell whether a file is an executable pro-gram by looking at the extension: .EXE and .COM files are executable programs.*

D
E
F

execute To carry out the instructions in an algorithm or program.

expand In an outlining utility or a graphical disk directory (such as the Microsoft Windows File Manager), to reveal all the subordinate entries below the selected outline heading or direc-tory. In File Manager, for example, you can expand a directory quickly by double-clicking the directory icon.

expandability The capability of a computer system to accom-modate more memory, additional disk drives, or adapters.

Computers vary in their expandability. When shopping for a com-puter, consider only systems configured the way you want but with space for growth. Look for one or two empty drive bays, three to five empty expansion slots, and make sure that it's upgradable to the maximum amount of RAM the microprocessor can address.

expanded memory (EMS) In IBM PC-compatible computers, a method of getting beyond the 640K DOS memory barrier by swapping programs and data in and out of the main memory at high speeds.

When the IBM Personal Computer was designed, the first IBM PCs were available with as little as 16K of RAM. The IBM PC architecture and DOS, the PC's operating system, were designed to use a maximum of 640K of RAM. It quickly became obvious that programs such as spreadsheets would benefit from greater amounts of memory.

Expanded memory originally used hardware (an expanded memory board) and a programming trick to get beyond the 640K

RAM barrier. A 64K area called a *page frame* is reserved in the area between 640K and 1,024K so that program instructions and data can be switched in and out in pages, or *banks*, of 64K. When the computer requires a 64K page not currently paged in, expanded memory software finds the page and switches it into the page frame. Such swapping (*bank switching*) occurs so quickly that the computer seems to have more than 640K of RAM.

Expanded memory is still used by many DOS applications. Fortunately, the DOS expanded memory emulator, EMM386.EXE, can automatically configure RAM above 1M as expanded memory without additional hardware. Also, the Windows memory management scheme uses extended memory (XMS) to make extended or expanded memory available as demanded by the programs you're running.

If you're using an older program or a game that requires expanded memory, use MS-DOS 6.2's MEMMAKER or PC-DOS 6.1's RAMBoost utility to set aside some of your system's extended memory (XMS) so that it appears to these programs to be expanded memory (EMS). MEMMAKER automatically configures EMM386.EXE. See *bank switching, expanded memory emulator, extended memory,* and *Lotus-Intel-Microsoft Expanded Memory Specification (LIM EMS)*.

expanded memory board   An adapter that adds expanded memory to an IBM-compatible computer. See *expanded memory*.

expanded memory emulator   A utility program for 80386 and 80486 IBM-compatible computers that uses extended memory to simulate expanded memory to accommodate older programs and the many games that require it. See *EMM386.EXE, expanded memory,* and *extended memory*.

expanded memory manager (EMM)   A utility program that manages expanded memory in an IBM-compatible computer equipped with an expanded memory board. See *EMM386.EXE, expanded memory,* and *expanded memory board*.

expanded type   A typeface that places characters farther apart or makes the characters wider so that there are fewer characters per inch.

expansion board   See *adapter*.

expansion bus   An extension of the computer's data bus and address bus that includes a number of receptacles (slots) for adapter boards.

Because each generation of microprocessors has a wider data bus, the expansion bus of IBM PC-compatible computers has changed. The original IBM Personal Computer and XT, based on the 8/16-bit 8088 chip, used an expansion bus with 62-pin expansion slots; the IBM Personal Computer AT, based on the 16-bit 80286, uses the same 62-pin expansion slot plus a supplemental 36-pin expansion slot.

IBM PC-compatibles based on the 32-bit Intel 80386 microprocessor require a 32-bit data bus structure to connect with memory. Because even these computers use 16-bit peripherals such as disk drives and video displays, however, some of them set aside adequate room for memory expansion on the motherboard and use the standard AT-style expansion bus for peripherals. 386DX and 486-based machines have several expansion slots for full 32-bit adapters in addition to 16-bit expansion slots.

Several competing bus architectures are available now, but all are eclipsed in performance by local bus designs, which can directly connect up to three high-speed devices to the microprocessor using the same data path width. See *address bus, bus, Extended Industry Standard Architecture (EISA), local bus, Micro Channel Bus, microprocessor,* and *motherboard*.

expansion card   See *adapter*.

expansion slot   A receptacle connected to the computer's expansion bus, designed to accept adapters. See *adapter*.

expert system   A computer program that contains much of the knowledge used by an expert in a specific field and that assists non-experts as they try to solve problems.

Expert systems contain a base of knowledge expressed in a series of IF/THEN rules and an engine capable of drawing inferences from this knowledge base. The system prompts you to supply information needed to assess the situation and come to a conclusion. Most expert systems express conclusions with a confidence factor, ranging from speculation to educated guess to firm conclusion.

Creating an expert system is more difficult than it appears. A surprisingly high proportion of expertise is based on experientially learned rules of thumb, such as cleaning the video board contacts with an ink eraser if the computer doesn't start. Some rules are little more than hunches or guesses. See *artificial intelligence (AI)* and *PROLOG*.

exploded pie graph   A pie chart in which one or more of the slices has been offset slightly from the others to emphasize the data represented by the exploded slice (see fig. E.3). See *pie graph*.

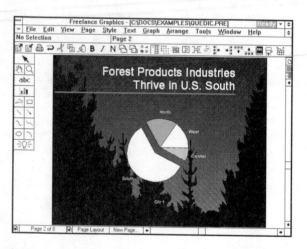

Fig. E.3   *An exploded pie graph.*

export   To save data in a format that another program can read. Most programs can export a document in ASCII format, which almost any program can read and use. When saving a document using one of the recent versions of word processing programs, you can choose the format from a list of dozens of other programs. See *import*.

Extended Binary Coded Decimal Interchange Code (EBCDIC)   A standard computer character set coding scheme used to represent 256 standard characters. IBM mainframes use EBCDIC coding, and personal computers use ASCII coding. Communications networks that link personal computers to IBM mainframes must include a translating device to mediate between the two systems.

extended character set   In IBM PC-compatible computing, a 256-character set stored in the computer's read-only memory (ROM) that includes, in addition to the 128 ASCII character codes, a collection of foreign language, technical, and block graphics characters. The characters with numbers above ASCII code 128 sometimes are referred to as *higher-order characters.*

Extended Graphics Array (XGA)   An IBM video display standard intended to replace its older, 8514/A standard and to bring 1,024 by 768 resolution to IBM and IBM-compatible video displays. An XGA board equipped with sufficient memory (1M) can display 65,536 colors at its low-resolution mode (640 by 480) and 256 colors at its high-resolution mode (1,024 by 768). For downward compatibility with software that supports earlier standards, XGA boards also support the VGA standard. The XGA standard faces stiff competition from makers of extended VGA (high-resolution Super VGA) video adapters. See *Super VGA, video adapter, Video Graphics Array (VGA),* and *video standard.*

Extended Industry Standard Architecture (EISA)   A 32-bit expansion bus design introduced by a consortium of IBM PC-compatible computer makers to counter IBM's proprietary Micro Channel Bus. Unlike the Micro Channel Bus, the EISA bus is downwardly compatible with existing 16-bit peripherals such as disk drives and display adapters.

EISA machines, once the state-of-the-art in personal computing, have been eclipsed by models that offer local buses, in which video circuits, disk drives, and other devices are directly connected to the processor. See *expansion bus, local bus,* and *Micro Channel Bus.*

extended-level synthesizer . In the Microsoft Windows Multimedia Personal Computer (MPC) specification, a synthesizer that can play a minimum of 16 simultaneous notes on nine melodic instruments, and 16 simultaneous notes on eight percussive instruments. See *base-level synthesizer* and *Multimedia Personal Computer (MPC)*.

extended memory In 80286 or later IBM-compatible computers, the random-access memory (RAM), if any, above 1M (megabyte) that usually is installed directly on the motherboard of 80286 and later computers and is directly accessible to the microprocessor.

An 80286-based computer can address up to 16M of main memory directly, whereas an 80386-based computer can address 4 gigabytes. That's the good news. The bad news is that initially only a few MS-DOS applications, such as Lotus 1-2-3, were written to use this memory. Microsoft Windows, coupled with the eXtended Memory Specification (XMS), provided a set of standards and an operating environment that allowed all programs to access extended memory.

Sometimes you see *extended memory* defined as "the memory above 640K." Computers sold with 1M of RAM, for example, are said to contain 640K of conventional memory and 384K of extended memory. (Microsoft Windows documentation defines extended memory this way.) Technically, this definition is incorrect; extended memory begins at 1,024K (1M). However, many extended memory managers can configure the upper memory area, the memory between 640K and 1M, as though it were extended memory and allow programs to access part of this memory. See *conventional memory, expanded memory (EMS), extended memory manager, eXtended Memory Specification (XMS), Microsoft Windows,* and *upper memory area.*

TIP: *2M of extended memory is required to operate Microsoft Windows, although 4M is the minimum if you want acceptable performance, and 8M for good performance.*

extended memory manager A utility program that lets certain DOS programs access extended memory. The programs must be written to conform to the XMS memory standard. See *conventional memory, extended memory, eXtended Memory Specification (XMS)*, and *HIMEM.SYS*.

eXtended Memory Specification (XMS) A set of standards and an operating environment that allows all programs to access extended memory.

Developed jointly by AST Research, Intel Corporation, Lotus Development, and Microsoft Corporation, XMS requires a utility program known as an *extended memory manager*, such as HIMEM.SYS (which is provided with DOS 5.0 and later and with Microsoft Windows). In Standard and 386 Enhanced modes, Windows lets MS-DOS applications use all the extended memory available, provided that these applications conform to the XMS guidelines, which most popular applications now do. In fact, many MS-DOS applications now make use of extended memory without help from Windows. See *extended memory* and *HIMEM.SYS*.

extended VGA See *Super VGA*.

extensible Capable of accepting new, user-defined commands.

extension A three-letter suffix added to a DOS file name that describes the file's contents. The extension is optional. It must be preceded by a period. See *file name*.

external command A DOS command that executes a program file. The program file must be present in the current drive, directory, or path. FORMAT and DISKCOPY are examples of external commands. See *internal command*.

external command (XCMD) In HyperTalk programming, a user-defined command (written in a language such as Pascal or C) that uses built-in Macintosh routines to perform tasks not normally available within HyperCard.

A popular XCMD is ResCopy, which is widely available in public domain or shareware stack-writing utilities. ResCopy allows a HyperTalk programmer to copy external commands and external resources from one program or stack to another. See *external function (XCFN)* and *ResEdit*.

external function (XCFN)   In HyperTalk programming, a program function (written in a language such as Pascal or C) that's external to HyperTalk but returns values to the program that can be used within the HyperTalk program. For example, Resources, an XCFN widely available in public domain or shareware stack-writing utilities, returns a list of all named resources in a file of a specified type. See *external command (XCMD)*.

external hard disk   A hard disk equipped with its own case, cables, and power supply. External hard disks generally cost more than internal hard disks of comparable speed and capacity.

external modem   A modem with its own case, cables, and power supply, designed to plug into the serial port of a computer. See *internal modem*.

external reference formula   In Microsoft Excel and other DDE-capable spreadsheet programs, the name of a formula placed in a cell that creates a link to another spreadsheet. See *dynamic data exchange (DDE)*.

external table   In Lotus 1-2-3 Release 3, a database created with a database management program (such as dBASE VI) that 1-2-3 can access directly with the /Data External command.

extremely low-frequency (ELF) emission   A magnetic field generated by commonly used electrical appliances such as computer display monitors, electric blankets, hair dryers, and food mixers, and extending one to two meters from the source.

ELF fields are known to cause tissue changes and fetal abnormalities in laboratory test animals and may be related to reproductive anomalies and cancers among frequent users of computer displays. Despite repeated assurances that computer displays are safe, evidence continued to accumulate of reproductive disorders among pregnant computer users.

Scientific researchers worldwide are beginning to document serious tissue changes and abnormalities in laboratory animals after exposure to ELF fields. Studies in the late 1980s suggested that using computer monitors in excess of 20 hours per week brought about a significant increase in the rate of human miscarriage. Government regulators and industry spokesmen claimed that these studies had serious methodological flaws or failed to provide a theoretical explanation that could draw a link between ELF and living cell abnormalities.

A study conducted by the U.S. Environmental Protection Agency concluded that the evidence suggested "modestly elevated" risks of cancer (especially leukemia, lymphoma, and cancer of the nervous system) after prolonged exposure to ELF fields. At the same time, a study by Columbia University and Hunter College demonstrated a link between ELF fields and a dramatically increased rate of DNA transcription in living cells.

CAUTION: *Emissions are strongest at the back and sides of the monitor. Avoid sitting behind a monitor and reduce exposure further by remaining an arm's length away from the screen. Better still, you may be able to replace your current display with a low-emissions model that meets the Swedish standards. See MPR II.*

facing pages The two pages of a bound document that face each other when the document is open. See *recto* and *verso*.

facsimile machine See *fax machine*.

FAQ *fak* Acronym for *Frequently Asked Questions*, a file that's regularly posted to a computer newsgroup containing answers to questions that new users frequently ask. A FAQ represents the accumulated wisdom of long-time users of the newsgroup and makes for excellent, informative reading. See *Fidonet*, *Internet*, and *newsgroup*.

> **TIP:** *If a FAQ doesn't appear on the list of postings, you can post a message asking someone to send you a copy.*

FAT See *file allocation table (FAT)*.

fatal error A processing error from which the program can't recover. Exiting the program without having to restart the computer may be possible, but you'll probably lose any unsaved data.

fault tolerance The capability of a computer system to cope with internal hardware problems without interrupting the system's performance, often by using backup systems automatically brought on-line when a failure is detected. The need for fault tolerance is indispensable whenever computers are assigned critical functions, such as guiding an aircraft to a safe landing or ensuring a steady flow of medicines to a patient. Fault tolerance also is beneficial for non-critical, everyday applications. See *bulletproof* and *Microsoft Windows NT*.

fax Sending and receiving printed pages between two locations using a telephone line. *Fax* is a shortened term for *facsimile*.

Fax machines let you send anything printed or written on paper—scribbles, newspaper clippings, photographs—which is then printed by the receiving fax machine, thus providing a paper copy to keep, or perhaps sign and fax back to the sender.

Faxing became universally popular after a European standards organization (CCITT) established specifications for the transmission of fax information at a rate of 9600 baud. See *Comité Consultatif International Téléphonique et Télégraphique (CCITT)* and *fax machine*.

fax board A circuit board that fits into an expansion slot in a computer, providing many of the features of a fax machine at a lower cost, as well as crisper output and convenience. If you are traveling, or in a remote location, you can use a laptop with a fax board to fax materials to and from any place with a phone.

Fax boards send a coded image of a computer-generated document and receive that image in the form of a file that can then be printed, if desired, using the DOS PRINT command. You must scan or record printed or handwritten material by using special video equipment before sending the material using a fax board. Some fax boards are send-only; others can receive and send faxes. See *modem*.

> **TIP:** *Don't settle for a send-only fax board that supports 4800 bps transmission speeds; 9600 bps send-receive boards aren't much more expensive and provide twice the transmission speed.*

fax machine A device that can send and receive images of pages via a phone line. A fax machine scans a sheet of paper and creates an image in a coded form that's then transmitted. A fax machine on the other end receives and translates the code, and then prints a replica of the original page.

fax modem   See *fax board*.

fax program   An application program that allows you to use a computer fax board. Generally, fax programs allow you to compose and send faxes, complete one of a variety of fax cover pages included with the program, as well as receive and print them. When you receive documents that include text, the newest fax programs use optical character recognition to convert the faxed image back into text so the document can be edited using any of the popular word processing programs. See *optical character recognition (OCR)* and *fax board*.

fax server   A personal computer or a self-contained unit that provides fax capabilities to all the workstations in a local area network. See *fax board* and *local area network (LAN)*.

FCC certification   An attestation, formerly made by the U.S. Federal Communications Commission, that a given brand and model of a computer meets the FCC's limits for radio frequency emissions. There are two certification levels: Class A, for computers to be used in industrial and commercial locations (specifically, mainframes and minicomputers), and Class B, for computers to be used in home locations, including home offices. All personal computers are explicitly defined as Class B equipment. See *Class A certification*, *Class B certification*, and *radio frequency interference (RFI)*.

FDHD   Acronym for *floppy drive high density*. See *SuperDrive*.

feathering   Adding an equal amount of space between each line on a page or column to force vertical justification. See *vertical justification*.

feature   A capability of a program. Occasionally, programs contain undocumented features. Of recent concern is creeping featurism where, in an attempt to remain competitive, manufacturers load programs with extra features that slow a program's operation and clutter the interface. See *creeping featurism*.

female connector   A computer cable terminator and connection device with receptacles designed to accept the pins of a male connector. See *male connector*.

femto- *fem-toe* Prefix indicating one quadrillionth, or a millionth of a billionth (10^{-15}).

TIP: *For the truly curious,* atto- *indicates a billionth of a billionth (10^{-18}) and* zepto- *indicates one quadrillionth of a billionth (10^{-21}).*

D E F

fiber optics A data transmission medium, consisting of glass fibers, that carries light instead of electrical signals. A detector at the receiving end converts the light back into electrical signals. Fiber optics, now used for transmission over long distances, offers immense bandwidth and protection from electromagnetic interference, radioactivity, and eavesdropping.

Fidonet A set of data exchange standards and procedures that permit privately operated computer bulletin board systems (BBS) to exchange data, files, and electronic mail internationally, using the world telephone system.

At an agreed-on time when telephone rates are low, subscribing BBSs send e-mail messages and files to a regional host, which in turn distributes them to other bulletin boards. Responses, called *echoes*, eventually find their way back to the host bulletin board. A popular Fidonet feature is EchoMail, a set of moderated conferences based on a variety of popular subjects, such as *Star Trek*, model aircraft, and political issues. See *bulletin board system (BBS)*, *FAQ, Internet, moderated newsgroup, unmoderated newsgroup*, and *wide area network*.

field See *data field*.

field definition In a database management program, a list of the attributes that define the type of information you can enter into a data field. The field definition also determines how the field's contents appear on-screen.

In dBASE, for example, the field definition includes the field name, the type and maximum length of data that can be entered, number of decimal places if the field is numeric, and the index attribute, if any. See *data type* and *field template*.

field name   In a database management program, a unique name given to a data field that helps you identify the field's contents.

In dBASE, field names are limited to 10 continuous characters without spaces. Some programs don't impose such stringent limitations. Even so, keep field names short. That way, when you display data in a columnar format, you'll be able to see more columns of data on-screen.

TIP: *Exercise care when naming fields to be sure the name describes the data contained in each data field, such as CITY. You see the field names on data-entry forms and data tables. Try creating two- or three-word field names using underscore characters, such as LAST_NAME or P_O_BOX. If you name a field MX388SMRPS, nobody else will know what the name means.*

field privilege   In a database management program, a database definition that establishes what you can do with the contents of a data field in a protected database. See *data field*.

field template   In database management programs, a field definition that specifies which kind of data you can type in the data field. If you try to type data into a field that doesn't match the field template, the program displays an error message. Synonymous with *data mask*.

In dBASE, for example, field templates for character fields can restrict data to Y (for Yes) or N (for No), T (for True) or F (for False), or only numbers or only letters. Field templates available for numeric fields include displaying commas in numbers larger than 999 and accepting spaces and + or – signs.

Use field templates as often as possible. They help prevent users from adding inappropriate information to the database. See *data type*.

file   A document or other collection of information stored on a disk and identified as a unit by a unique name. When a file is saved, the data may be scattered among dozens or even hundreds of non-contiguous clusters on the disk. The file allocation table is an index of the order in which those clusters are linked to equal a file. To the user, however, files appear as units on disk directories and are retrieved and copied as units. See *file allocation table (FAT)* and *secondary storage*.

file allocation table (FAT)   A hidden table of every cluster on a floppy or hard disk. The FAT records how files are stored in distinct—and not necessarily contiguous—clusters.

A file allocation table uses a simple method, much like a scavenger hunt, to keep track of data. The address of the first cluster of the file is stored in the directory file. In the FAT entry for the first cluster is the address of the second cluster used to store the file. In the entry for the second cluster is the address of the third cluster, and so on until the last cluster entry, which contains an end-of-file code. Because this table is the only way to know how data can be found on a disk, DOS creates and maintains two copies of the FAT in case one is damaged. See *file fragmentation*.

file attribute   A hidden code stored with a file's directory that contains its read-only or archive status and whether it's a system, hidden, or directory file. See *archive attribute*, *hidden file*, *locked file*, and *read-only attribute*.

file compression utility   A utility program that compresses and decompresses infrequently used files so that they take up 40 to 90 percent less room on a hard disk. File compression utilities are commonly used to decompress files downloaded from a bulletin board system (BBS), to store files on floppy disks in a more compact form, and to make room on a hard disk by compressing older or infrequently used files. Another utility is used to decompress a file.

Specialty file compression utilities that compress only certain types of files, such as downloadable font files, are also available. These programs usually load a special driver that remains in memory to decompress and recompress the files as needed. See *archive*, *bulletin board system (BBS)*, and *compressed file*.

file conversion utility   A utility program that converts text or graphics files created with one program to the file format used by another program. The best application programs now include a conversion utility that can handle a dozen or more file formats.

file defragmentation   See *defragmentation*.

file deletion   The apparent removal of a file name from a directory using the DOS DEL or ERASE command, which changes the first letter of the file name so the name isn't displayed in a directory listing. The contents of the file aren't removed from the disk. With a Macintosh, drag the file to the Trash icon, open the Special menu, and then choose Empty Trash.

You can redisplay a file using an undelete program. Utilities are also available that look for data on a disk one cluster at a time. To prevent the recovery of sensitive data, use a delete utility from programs such as PC Tools or, for the Macintosh, a shareware program such as Complete Delete that erases the data from the disk. See *shareware*, *undelete utility*, and *utility program*.

CAUTION: *If you accidentally delete a file, stop working. Don't perform any additional operations that write information to the disk. Immediately use the UNDELETE command included with MS-DOS, beginning with version 5, to replace the first letter of the file name.*

file extension   See *extension*.

file format   The patterns and standards a program uses to store data on disk. Few programs store data in ASCII format. Most use a proprietary file format that other programs can't read, ensuring that customers continue to use the company's program and enabling programmers to include special features that standard formats may not allow. See *file conversion utility*, *native file format*, and *proprietary file format*.

f

> **TIP:** *If you can't convert a document to a format you can use, try a data conversion service. Look in the Yellow Pages or in the back advertising sections of popular personal computer magazines for these services.*

D
E
F

file fragmentation   The allocation of a file in non-contiguous sectors on a floppy or hard disk. Fragmentation occurs because of multiple file deletions and write operations.

After you create and erase many files on a disk, the remaining files aren't stored in contiguous clusters. When you later save a file or install a new program, DOS stores the data in the available clusters between the existing files. The disk drive's read/write head must travel longer distances to retrieve a file that's scattered all over the disk. *Defragmenting* can improve disk efficiency by as much as 50 percent by rewriting files so that they are placed in contiguous clusters. See *defragmentation*.

file locking   On a network, a method of concurrency control that ensures the integrity of data. File locking prevents more than one user from accessing and altering a file at the same time. See *concurrency control* and *local area network (LAN)*.

file management program   A program that lets you manage files, directories, and disks by displaying a disk's directory structure and listing existing files. Commands available on the program's menus are used to move and copy files, create directories, and perform other housekeeping tasks that help improve disk performance and protect your data. The Microsoft Windows File Manager and XTree Gold are popular file management programs.

file name   A name assigned to a file when the file is first written on a disk. Every file on a disk must have a unique name.

In DOS and early versions of OS/2, file names have two parts: the file name and the extension. These names must conform to the following rules.

- *Length.* You may use up to eight characters for the file name and up to three characters for the extension. The extension is optional.

- *Delimiter.* If you use the extension, you must separate the file name and extension with a period.

- *Legal characters.* You may use any letter or number on the keyboard for file names and extensions, but not spaces. You also may use the following punctuation symbols:

  ’ ~ ! @ # $ ^ & ( ) _ – { }

In the Macintosh environment, you can use up to 32 characters for file names, and file names can contain any character (including spaces), with the exception of the colon (:).

file privilege   In dBASE, an attribute that determines what you can do with a protected database on a network. The options are DELETE, EXTEND, READ, and UPDATE. See *field privilege*.

file recovery   Restoring an erased disk file. See *undelete utility*.

file server   In a local area network, a personal computer that stores on its hard disk the application programs and data files for all the workstations in the network.

In a peer-to-peer network, all workstations act as file servers, because each workstation can provide files to other workstations. In the more common client/server network architecture, a single, high-powered machine with a huge hard disk is set aside to function as the file server for all the workstations (clients) in the network. See *network operating system (NOS)*.

file transfer protocol (FTP)   In asynchronous communications, a standard that ensures the error-free transmission of program and data files via the telephone system. The FTP program is named for UNIX file transfer protocol (FTP) that governs the transmission of data. See *anonymous FTP*, *archie*, *asynchronous communication*, *Gopher*, *Internet*, *Kermit*, and *XMODEM*.

file transfer utility   A utility program that transfers files between different hardware platforms, such as the IBM Personal Computer and the Macintosh, or between a desktop and a laptop computer. Popular file transfer utilities include MacLink Plus, which links PCs and Macs via their serial ports, and Brooklyn Bridge, which links desktop IBM computers with IBM PC-compatible laptops.

filespec   In MS-DOS, a complete statement of a file's location, including a drive letter, path name, file name, and extension, such as C:\REPORTS\REPORT1.WK1. Synonymous with *path name*.

fill   In spreadsheet programs, an operation that enters the same text, value (numbers, dates, times, or formulas), or a sequence of values in a worksheet. In Lotus 1-2-3, for example, you use the /Data Fill command to fill a range with values, indicating the value in the first cell, the amount to increase or decrease each number placed in the range, and the number where Lotus should stop filling. Synonymous with *data series*.

filter   In DOS and UNIX, taking input from a device or file and sending it through a command that modifies the information before displaying the result. The DOS filters are MORE (scrolls long output screen by screen), FIND (searches for text), and SORT (sorts the display in order of ASCII characters).

filter command   In DOS, a command that takes input from a device or file, changes the input by passing it through a filter, then sends the result to the screen or printer. The DOS filters are MORE (scrolls long output screen by screen), FIND (searches for text), and SORT (sorts in order of ASCII characters).

To send a file through a filter, use the less-than symbol (<). For example, the following command sorts the lines in a file called LIST.TXT:

```
SORT < list.txt
```

To route another command's output through a filter, use a *pipe*
(¦). The following command, for example, sends the output of
the TREE command through the MORE filter:

```
TREE C:\ ¦ MORE
```

To redirect the output, use the greater-than symbol (>). To sort
the file LIST.TXT and save the sorted result as the file
ALPHA.TXT, for example, use:

```
TYPE LIST.TXT ¦ SORT > ALPHA.TXT
```

Finder   A file and memory management utility provided by
Apple for Macintosh computers. This utility allows you to run
one application at a time.

Often mistakenly referred to as the Macintosh's operating system, the
Finder is nothing more than a shell that can be replaced by other shell
programs such as XTreeMac. Although the Finder's icons and menus
have contributed to the Mac's success, the program's limitations
quickly become apparent on systems equipped with large hard disks.
An improved Finder that shipped with System 7 addresses many of
the program's shortcomings. See *MultiFinder*.

firmware   Broadly, the system software that's stored in a
computer's read-only memory (ROM) or elsewhere in the computer's circuitry, such as the BIOS chips in IBM PC-compatible
computers. You can't modify firmware.

fixed disk   See *hard disk*.

fixed length   In a database management program, a field whose
length is set and can't vary, as opposed to a variable-length field,
which can adjust to accommodate entries of different lengths.

fixed numeric format   In spreadsheet programs, a numeric
format in which values are rounded to the number of decimal
places you specify. Also, commas aren't used in numbers greater
than 999. See *numeric format*.

fixed-frequency monitor   An analog monitor designed to
receive input signals at only one frequency; in contrast, a multiscanning monitor automatically adjusts to match the incoming

signal. Most of the VGA monitors sold with inexpensive entry-level 80386SX systems are fixed-frequency monitors. See *analog monitor* and *multiscanning monitor*.

Fkey   A Macintosh utility program executed by pressing the Command (⌘) and Shift keys with a number key from 0 to 9—the keys that simulate the function keys on IBM PC keyboards. Four Fkey utilities are included with the Macintosh system software, and additional Fkey utilities (and software to manage them) are available through shareware and commercial sources.

flame   In electronic mail, a slang term meaning to lose one's self-control by writing a message that uses derogatory, obscene, or inappropriate language. See *flame bait*, *flame war*, *moderated newsgroup*, and *rave*.

flame bait   In an unmoderated computer newsgroup, a posting that contains opinions that prompt abusive remarks and personal attacks, and ultimately launch a flame war. Flame-bait topics include abortion, homosexuality, and the desirability of upgrading to Microsoft Windows. See *flame*, *flame war*, *moderated newsgroup*, and *unmoderated newsgroup*.

flame war   In an unmoderated computer newsgroup, an unproductive and long-running debate that's marked by high emotion and little information.

> **TIP:** *If a newsgroup you're following erupts in a flame war, learn how to create a kill file that contains a list of subjects that you want excluded automatically from the messages displayed on your screen. See* flame, flame bait, kill file, *and* unmoderated newsgroup.

flat   Lacking structure; stripped of structural information that would permit more efficient retrieval of information. A file system without subdirectories in which files can be grouped is said to be *flat*, as is a database management program that doesn't offer the capability to place data in a series of related tables. Flat information structures take up less memory and were common on early computers that had 64K of RAM or less.

flat-file database management program   A database management program that stores, organizes, and retrieves information from one file at a time. Such programs lack relational database management features. See *data integrity* and *relational database management.*

flat-panel display   A thin display screen used in notebook and laptop computers that uses one of several display technologies, such as electroluminescence, gas plasma displays, liquid crystal displays (LCD), or thin film transistors (TFT). A backlit display makes the display easier to read. See *laptop computer* and *notebook computer.*

flatbed scanner   A scanner with a flat scanning area large enough to accommodate a letter-sized page (8 1/2 by 11 inches) of material. A sheet feeder to automate scanning multiple-page documents is an available option. See *digitize* and *scanner.*

flicker   A visible distortion that occurs when you scroll the screen of a video monitor that uses a low refresh rate. Also, a visible distortion apparent in light areas on an interlaced monitor. See *interlacing* and *refresh.*

floating graphic   A graph or picture that hasn't been fixed in an absolute position on the page, so it moves up or down on the page as you delete or insert text above the graphic.

floating-point calculation   A method for storing and calculating numbers so that the location of the decimal isn't fixed but floating (the decimal moves around as needed so that significant digits are taken into account in the calculation). Floating-point calculation can be implemented in numeric coprocessors or in software, improving the accuracy of computer calculations.

floppy disk   A removable and widely used data storage medium that uses a magnetically coated flexible disk of Mylar enclosed in a plastic envelope or case (see fig. F.1).

Software publishers provide their applications on floppy disks. At one time, they also were the only medium for data storage for personal computers, but the availability of inexpensive hard disks has relegated floppy disks to the sidelines.

f

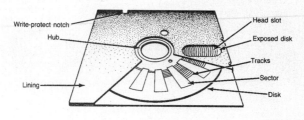

Fig. F.1 *A 5 1/4-inch floppy disk.*

Hard disks are preferred for many reasons: floppy disk drives are more than 10 times slower, the disks are damaged more easily, and they offer less storage. However, floppy disks are essential for getting programs and data into your computer and for backup purposes.

Most floppy disks used in personal computing come in two sizes: 5 1/4 and 3 1/2 inches. Floppy disks are available in single sided or double sided and standard double density or high density. Single-sided disks are rarely used these days, and high-density disks are becoming more popular than double-density disks.

The single-sided disks used in the original IBM Personal Computer held only 160K; the drives introduced soon after accommodated 320K on a double-sided disk. In 1983, PC DOS Version 2.0 increased the figure to 360K for double-sided disks. With the IBM Personal Computer AT came MS-DOS 3.0 and the capability of storing 1.2M on a high-density 5 1/4-inch disk. Later IBM PC-compatible computers came with 3 1/2-inch drives that could store 720K or 1.44M with high-density disks.

Macintoshes use 3 1/2-inch disks. The original Macintosh stored 400K on single-sided disks; this figure was doubled to 800K when double-sided disk drives were introduced. A floppy drive high density (FDHD) drive that could store 1.4M on high-density floppies was introduced in 1988; this technically sophisticated drive can read and write DOS disks, giving Mac users an easy way to exchange data with users of IBM PC-compatible computers. See *double density, hard disk, head slot, high density, read/write head, single-sided disk,* and *write-protect notch.*

CAUTION: *5 1/4-inch disks are more susceptible to damage than 3 1/2-inch disks, which are encased in rigid plastic and have a sliding door that covers the access hole (the drive opens the door after you insert the disk). Avoid pressing down hard with a ball-point pen as you label a 5 1/4-inch disk, and be careful not to get fingerprints on the actual surface of the disk, which is easy to touch through the open access hole. Always keep 5 1/4-inch disks in protective envelopes when you aren't using them, and don't leave the disk in the drive when the computer is turned off; the disk may accumulate dust.*

Although less susceptible than 5 1/4-inch disks, 3 1/2-inch disks can be damaged. Keep both types of disks away from moisture, heat, dust, and strong magnetic fields.

floptical disk   A removable optical disk the size of a 3 1/2-inch floppy disk but with a capacity of 20M to 25M. See *optical disk*.

floptical drive   A data storage device that uses laser technology to illuminate optical tracts on a floptical disk.

The reflected light is sensed by a photo detector, which generates a signal that allows more precise positioning of the read/write heads. The pattern of tracks, created when the disk is manufactured, is extremely compact, making it possible to create 3 1/2-inch floptical disks the same size as the familiar 3 1/2-inch floppy disks but capable of storing 21M of information. Floptical drives, manufactured by companies such as Iomega, can read and write on standard 3 1/2-inch floppy disks.

flow   A feature that allows text in a page layout to wrap around graphics and to move automatically from column to column (called *newspaper* or *snaking columns*). Page layout and better word processing programs can format text this way. See *newspaper columns* and *page layout program*.

flow chart   A chart that contains symbols referring to computer operations, describing how the program performs.

f

flush left In word processing, the alignment of text along the left margin, leaving a ragged right margin. See *justification*.

flush right In word processing, aligning text along the right margin, leaving a ragged left margin. Flush right alignment is seldom used except for decorative effects or cover pages. See *justification*.

folder In the Macintosh Finder, an on-screen representation of a file folder on the desktop and into which you can place files so that the display isn't overly cluttered with files.

follow-on post In an on-line newsgroup, a contribution that's posted in response to a previous posting. Unlike a reply, a follow-on post is public and will be seen by everyone who follows the newsgroup. See *distributed bulletin board*, *netiquette*, and *newsgroup*.

TIP: *Consider replying to a message instead of posting a follow-on message. In USENET, posting a message worldwide eventually costs hundreds of dollars, which have to be paid for by government and organizational subsidies. Post a follow-on message only if you truly believe your response is of sufficient value to all the members of the newsgroup.*

font One complete collection of letters, punctuation marks, numbers, and special characters with a consistent and identifiable typeface, weight (roman or bold), posture (upright or italic), and font size. Often used incorrectly in reference to a typeface or font family. Two kinds of fonts exist: bit-mapped fonts and outline fonts. Each comes in two versions: screen fonts and printer fonts. See *bit-mapped font*, *book weight*, *font family*, *outline font*, *posture*, *printer font*, *screen font*, *typeface*, *type size*, and *weight*.

font cartridge A plug-in ROM cartridge—designed to fit into a receptacle on a printer—that contains one or more fonts and expands the printer's font capabilities. See *cartridge font*.

Font/DA Mover   A utility program provided with Macintosh
system software that adds fonts and desk accessories to the System
Folder of the computer's startup disk. See *desk accessory (DA)* and
startup disk.

font downloader   See *downloading utility*.

font family   A set of fonts in several sizes and weights that
share the same typeface. The following list illustrates a font family
in the Helvetica typeface:

Helvetica Roman 10

Helvetica bold 10

Helvetica italic 10

Helvetica Roman 12

Helvetica bold 12

Helvetica italic 12

Helvetica bold italic 12

In Microsoft Windows, a font family includes several similar typefaces. Arial, Small Fonts, and MS Sans Serif are all considered part
of the Swiss font family, for example.

font ID conflict   In the Macintosh environment, a system
error caused by conflicts between the identification numbers
assigned to the screen fonts stored in the System Folder.

The Macintosh System and many Mac applications recognize and
retrieve fonts by the identification number, not by name. The original Mac operating system let you assign only 128 unique numbers,
so you inadvertently could assemble a repertoire of screen fonts with
conflicting numbers, causing printing errors. Beginning with System
6, a New Font Numbering Table (NFNT) scheme was introduced
that let you assign 16,000 unique numbers, reducing—but not ruling
out—the potential for font ID conflicts.

font metric   The width and height information for each character in a font. The font metric is stored in a width table.

font smoothing   In high-resolution laser printers, the reduction of aliasing and other distortions when text or graphics are printed. See *aliasing*.

font substitution   Substituting an outline font in place of a bit-mapped screen font for printing purposes. In the Macintosh environment, the Apple LaserWriter printer driver substitutes the outline fonts Helvetica, Times Roman, and Courier for the screen fonts Geneva, New York, and Monaco. Because spacing may be unsatisfactory, use screen fonts that are equivalent to the printer font.

footer   In a word processing or page layout program, repetitive material that's printed at the bottom of the pages of the document. See *header*.

footnote   In a word processing or page layout program, a reference or note positioned at the bottom of the page. Most word processing programs number footnotes automatically and renumber them if you insert or delete a note. The best programs can float lengthy footnotes to the next page so that no more than half the page is taken up by footnotes. See *endnote*.

TIP: *If you're creating documents that require excellent footnoting capabilities, make sure that you can format the footnotes properly. For example, many publishers require double-spacing of all text, even footnotes, but some word processors can't perform this task.*

footprint   The amount of space occupied by a computer case on a desk.

forced page break   A page break inserted by the user; the page always breaks at this location. Synonymous with *hard page break*.

forecasting   Using a spreadsheet program, a method of financial analysis that involves the projection of past trends into the future.

CAUTION: *Implementing a forecast with a spreadsheet program is easy, but remember that any model is only as good as the assumptions it's based on. Seasonal variables, a change in the prime rate, and other factors may be overlooked or unexpected.*

foreground task   In a computer capable of multitasking, the job being performed in the active window. In Microsoft Windows, the share of the processor's time devoted to foreground tasks depends on whether the task is a Windows or DOS application, and on the foreground and background settings established in the Scheduling section of the 386 Enhanced feature in the Windows Control Panel.

In other environments, such as networks and DOS, a foreground task is a job given priority status before background tasks are executed. Background printing or calculation, for example, takes place in brief pauses during the execution of the foreground task.

form feed   A command that forces the printer to eject the current page and start a new page.

format   The arrangement of information for storage, printing, or displaying.

The format of floppy disks and hard disks is the magnetic pattern laid down by the formatting utility. In a document, format includes margins, the font and alignment used for text, headers, footers, page numbering, and the way numbers are displayed. In a database management program, the format is the physical arrangement of field names and data fields in a data-entry form on-screen. When information is saved as a file, the format is a proprietary structure that may include printer control information or a specific method for storing graphic images.

formatting   An operation that establishes a pattern for the display, storage, or printing of data. In operating systems, an operation that prepares a floppy disk for use in a particular computer system by laying down a magnetic pattern. See *format, high-level format,* and *low-level format.*

formula   In a spreadsheet program, a cell definition that defines the relationship between two or more values. In a database management program, an expression that tells the program to perform calculations on numeric data contained in one or more data fields. See *calculated field, cell definition, precedence,* and *value.*

formula bar   In Microsoft Excel, the bar below the Toolbar where you enter or edit formulas and that displays the address of the current cell.

FOR/NEXT loop   A loop control structure that carries out a procedure a specified number of times. Suppose that you have a list of 10 items. A FOR/NEXT loop to change each item might read: "Set the count to 1. Select to the end of the line. Apply formatting. Move down one line. Then set the count to the previous count plus 1. Keep doing this until the count is equal to 10." See *loop, macro,* and *pseudocode.*

FORTH   A high-level programming language that offers direct control over hardware devices. Developed in 1970 by an astronomer named Charles Moore to help him control the equipment at the Kitt Peak National Radio Observatory, FORTH—short for FOuRTH-generation programming language—has been slow to gain acceptance as a general-purpose programming language. Because FORTH accepts user-defined commands, one FORTH programmer's code may be unintelligible to another programmer. FORTH sometimes is preferred for laboratory data acquisition, robotics, machine control, arcade games, automation, patient monitoring, and interfaces with musical devices. See *high-level programming language.*

FORTRAN   A high-level programming language well suited to scientific, mathematical, and engineering applications.

D
E
F

Developed by IBM in the mid 1950s and released in 1957, FOR-TRAN—short for FORmula TRANslator—was the first compiled high-level programming language. The nature of FORTRAN shows the predominance of scientific applications in the early history of computing; the language allows you to describe and solve mathematical calculations. Still highly suited to such applications, FORTRAN is widely used in scientific, academic, and technical settings.

For anyone familiar with BASIC, FORTRAN is immediately recognizable. Indeed, FORTRAN was BASIC's progenitor, and unfortunately shares its shortcomings. Like BASIC, recent versions of FORTRAN are more structured and have fewer limitations. See *BASIC, high-level programming language, modular programming, Pascal,* and *structured programming.*

forum   See *newsgroup.*

forward chaining   In expert systems, an inference technique that requires the user to state all the relevant data before processing begins. A forward chaining system starts with the data and works forward through its rules to determine whether additional data is required and how to draw the inference. See *backward chaining, expert system,* and *knowledge base.*

fragmentation   See *file fragmentation.*

frame   In desktop publishing and word processing, a rectangular area absolutely positioned on the page. The frame can contain text, graphics, or both.

In Lotus 1-2-3, the shaded border across the top of the spreadsheet containing the column letters and down the left of the spreadsheet containing the row numbers.

free system resources   In Microsoft Windows, the amount of space that's left in the special memory area (actually, the GDI and USER heaps) that Windows sets aside to store information about windows, subwindows, and objects created by Windows programs. See *heap.*

f

CAUTION: *With Windows 3.1, extravagant amounts of RAM (that is, more than 8M) won't allow you to run unlimited numbers of programs simultaneously. If the free system resources decrease to 10 to 15 percent, Windows won't let you open additional applications.*

D
E
F

To find out the percentage of system resources now available, switch to Program Manager, open the Help menu, and then choose About Program Manager. The About Program Manager dialog box displays the percentage of system resources that remains free.

To free up system resources, close applications and windows you aren't using. Applications such as Microsoft Word for Windows or Excel may consume as much as 10 to 15 percent of available system resources, and opening additional windows within these applications can consume as much as 2 percent each. See *heap, Microsoft Windows* and *system resources.*

free-form text chart   In presentation graphics, a text chart used to handle information difficult to express in lists, such as lengthy explanations, directions, invitations, and certificates (see fig. F.2).

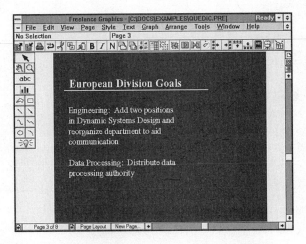

Fig. F.2   *A free-form text chart.*

freenet   A local or regional public-access computer network, accessible by modem, that provides a variety of computing resources as a community service. Generally provided by public library systems, freenets sometimes offer Internet access without charge. See *Internet*.

freestanding pointing device   A pointing device—such as a mouse or trackball—connected to the computer through the serial or mouse port that isn't otherwise attached to the computer. See *built-in pointing device, clip-on pointing device, mouse,* and *trackball.*

freeware   Copyrighted programs that have been made available without charge for public use. The programs may not be resold for profit. See *public domain software* and *shareware.*

freeze   To stop software development at a point where it's judged that the software is sufficiently stable for release.

frequency division multiplexing   In local area networks, a technique for transmitting two or more signals over one cable by assigning each to its own frequency. This technique is used in broadband (analog) networks. See *broadband, local area network (LAN),* and *multiplexing.*

frequency modulation (FM) recording   An early, low-density method of recording digital signals on computer media such as tape and disks. Synonymous with *single-density recording.* See *Modified Frequency Modulation (MFM)* and *single density.*

friction feed   A printer paper-feed mechanism that draws individual sheets of paper through the printer by using a platen to exert pressure on the paper. Friction-feed mechanisms usually require you to feed each sheet of paper by hand. For a document longer than a page or two, manual feeding can be tedious. See *cut-sheet feeder* and *tractor feed.*

fried   Burned out; short-circuited.

front end The portion of a program that interacts directly with the user. A front end can also be a separate program that acts as a user-friendly interface for a more difficult environment; for example, front-end interfaces for the Internet are being marketed.

In a local area network, this portion of the program may be distributed to each workstation so that the user can interact with the back-end application on the file server. See *back end* and *client/ server architecture*.

FTP See *file transfer protocol (FTP)*.

full backup A hard disk backup of every file on the entire hard disk. Synonymous with *global backup*. The procedure is extremely tedious if you're backing up to floppy disks, but it's necessary for secure computing. If it takes too long, consider adding a tape drive to your system. See *backup procedure* and *incremental backup*.

full duplex An asynchronous communications protocol in which the communications channel can send and receive signals at the same time. See *asynchronous communication, communications protocol, echoplex,* and *half duplex*.

full justification See *justification*.

full-motion video adapter A video adapter that can display moving video images—prerecorded or live—in a window that appears on the computer's screen. To display video images, the adapter is connected to a videocassette recorder, laser disk player, or a camcorder (for live images).

Most full-motion video adapters come with software that allows the development of a multimedia presentation, complete with wipes, washes, fades, animation, and sound. Full-motion video applications are expected to play a growing role in corporate and professional presentations and training applications.

full-page display   A computer monitor that can display a full page of text at a time, used most frequently with computer systems dedicated to desktop publishing. With a full-page display, you can view and edit an entire page of text, figures, or graphics at a time, giving a better grasp of the overall structure and organization of your document.

If you're thinking about equipping your DOS system with a full-page display, be aware that not all the programs you're using can take advantage of it. Check your programs' documentation. The Macintosh Finder and Windows 3.1, however, support a full-page display.

full-screen application   In Microsoft Windows, an application that takes up the entire screen after you launch it from Windows. Windows applications can be run in a window by clicking the maximize button at the right end of the title bar. DOS applications can be run in a window by pressing Alt+Enter.

> **TIP:** *When running DOS applications in a window, you can switch to other applications without halting the DOS application's execution. You can also use the Edit command on the control menu of a windowed DOS application to copy and move text between open applications using the Clipboard. See* control menu.

full-screen editor   A word processing utility, often included with application development systems, designed specifically for creating and editing computer programs. It therefore includes special features for indenting lines of program code, searching for non-standard characters, and interfacing with program interpreters or compilers. With MS-DOS Version 5.0, a good full-screen editor (MS-DOS Editor) has finally become part of that operating system's standard equipment. See *application development system, line editor,* and *programming environment.*

function   In programming languages and electronic spreadsheet programs, a named and stored procedure that returns a value. Typically, a spreadsheet program includes functions in categories such as finance, date and time, mathematics and trigonometry, statistics, lookup and reference, database manipulation, text processing, logical comparison, and engineering. In Microsoft Excel, for example, the NPV function returns the net present value of an investment, after you supply the data about periodic cash flow and the discount rate. Synonymous with *built-in function*.

function key   A programmable key—conventionally numbered F1, F2, and so on—that provides special functions, depending on the software you're using. See *Fkey*.

FYI   In on-line communications, an acronym for *For Your Information*. Also, an Internet document of answers to basic Internet questions. See *FAQ*.

G   Abbreviation for *gigabyte*.

gamut   In computer graphics, the range of colors that a color monitor can display.

gas plasma display   See *plasma display*.

gateway   In network computing, a device that connects two dissimilar local area networks or connects a local area network to a wide-area network, a minicomputer, or a mainframe. A gateway has its own processor and memory and may perform protocol conversion and bandwidth conversion.

Gateways typically are found in large organizations in which more than one local area network protocol is installed. A gateway called FastPath (by Kinetics), for example, provides a link between AppleTalk and EtherNet networks. See *bridge*, *Internet*, and *local area network (LAN)*.

general format   In most spreadsheet programs, the default numeric format in which all the numbers on either side of the decimal point (up to the furthest number that isn't a zero) are displayed, but without commas or currency signs. When a number is too large to display with the current column width, scientific notation is used.

General MIDI (GM)   In multimedia, a standard controlled by the MIDI Manufacturers' Association (MMA) that defines a set of 96 standard voices corresponding to traditional musical instruments, and an additional set of voices corresponding to non-melodic percussion instruments. When you use the standard code numbers from these sets to create a MIDI file, any GM-compatible synthesizer will reproduce the sounds in the file the way you intended them. See *Musical Instrument Digital Interface (MIDI)*.

general-purpose computer A computer that contains a sufficiently simple and general instruction set so that a wide variety of algorithms can be devised for the computer. Personal computers are general-purpose computers.

generate To produce something by setting in motion an automatic procedure. For example, after marking the entries and indicating the table, lists, and index locations, you can generate a table of contents, lists of figures, and an index in a word processing program when you choose the generate command. All the items are created automatically.

GEnie Developed by General Electric, an on-line information service that, like CompuServe, offers many of the attractions of a bulletin board system (BBS) and up-to-date stock quotes, conferences, Internet e-mail access, home shopping services, and news updates. See *on-line information service*.

ghost The effect of an image being displayed continuously on-screen. Such images "burn" into the screen phosphors, resulting in a ghost image. See *screen saver*.

GIF A bit-mapped color graphics file format for IBM-compatible computers. GIF, which originated on CompuServe, is commonly used to exchange graphics on bulletin board systems because it uses an efficient compression technique for high-resolution graphics, such as scanned pictures.

giga- A prefix indicating one billion (10^9).

gigabit `gig-uh-bit` A unit of measurement approximately equal to 1 billion bits (1,073,741,824). Usually used when indicating the amount of data that can be transferred or transmitted per second.

gigabyte `gig-uh-bite` A unit of measurement approximately equal to 1 billion bytes (1,073,741,824). Used when stating an amount of memory or disk capacity. One gigabyte equals 1,000M (megabytes).

GIGO   Acronym for "garbage in, garbage out," which is usually said in response to fouled-up output that's attributable to erroneous input (such as a mistyped command).

glitch   A momentary power interruption or some other inexplicable fluctuation in electronic circuits that causes computer systems to generate garbage output or, in the extreme, to crash. A glitch is a hardware problem; a software problem is called a *bug*. See *bug*.

global backup   See *full backup*.

global format   In a spreadsheet program, a numeric format or label alignment choice that applies to all cells in the worksheet. With most programs, you can override the global format by defining a format for certain cells.

> **TIP:** *If you're working on a financial spreadsheet, the values in your worksheet may require dollar signs and two decimal places. Choose currency as the global format when you begin the worksheet. See* label alignment, numeric format, *and* range format.

glossary   In a word processing program, a feature used to store frequently used phrases and boilerplate text for later insertion into documents when needed. See *boilerplate*.

GM   See *General MIDI (GM)*.

Gopher   In UNIX-based systems linked to the Internet, a menu-based program that helps you find files, programs, definitions, and other resources on topics you specify. Gopher was originally developed at the University of Minnesota and named after the school mascot.

Unlike FTP and archie, the Internet Gopher doesn't require you to know and use the details of host, directory, and file names. Instead, you browse through menus and press Enter when you find something interesting. You usually see another menu, with more options, until finally you select an option that displays

g

information. You can then read the information or save it to your disk storage area. See *anonymous FTP, archie, file transfer protocol (FTP), Internet,* and *World-Wide Web (WWW).*

grabber hand   In graphics programs and HyperCard, an on-screen image of a hand that you can position with the mouse to move selected units of text or graphics from place to place on-screen.

graphical user interface (GUI)   `goo-ee   A design for the part of a program that interacts with the user and uses icons to represent program features.

A GUI has its origins in ground-breaking research at Xerox Corporation's Palo Alto Research Center (PARC) in the early 1970s. Having found that people recognize graphic representations faster than they read words or phrases, the PARC team designed a user interface with graphic images called *icons.* An icon is a picture that closely resembles or reminds the viewer of the concept it represents. Examples of highly descriptive icons are a printer for print, scissors for cut, and the letters ABC with a check mark for spell check.

A GUI is usually associated with additional PARC innovations, such as the use of a mousable interface with pull-down menus, dialog boxes, check boxes, radio buttons, and the like. These features can be implemented quite easily on a character-based display, however, and many DOS programs that run PCs in character mode (as opposed to graphics mode) use these features.

Programs with a GUI require a computer with sufficient speed, power, and memory to display a high-resolution, bit-mapped display. See *check box, dialog box, drop-down list box, Microsoft Windows, mousable interface, pull-down menu, radio button,* and *scroll bar/scroll box.*

graphics   In personal computing, the creation, modification, and printing of computer-generated graphic images. The two basic types of computer-produced graphics are object-oriented graphics, also called *vector graphics,* and bit-mapped graphics, often called *raster graphics.*

Object-oriented graphics programs, usually called *draw programs,* store graphic images in the form of mathematical representations that can be sized and scaled without distortion. Object-oriented graphics programs are well suited for architecture, computer-aided design, interior design, and other applications in which precision and scaling capability are more important than artistic effects.

Bit-mapped graphics programs, often called *paint programs*, store graphic images in the form of patterns of screen pixels. Unlike draw programs, paint programs can create delicate patterns of shading that convey an artistic touch, but any attempt to resize or scale the graphic may result in unacceptable distortion. See *bit-mapped graphic*, *draw program*, *object-oriented graphic*, and *paint program*.

graphics accelerator board   An expansion board that includes a graphics coprocessor and all the other circuitry normally found on a video adapter. The graphics accelerator handles the graphics processing, freeing the central processing unit (CPU) for other important tasks and thereby dramatically improving your system's capability to run Windows and Windows applications. See *central processing unit (CPU)*, *graphics coprocessor*, *Microsoft Windows*, and *video adapter*.

graphics character   In a computer's built-in character set, a character composed of lines, shaded rectangles, or other shapes. You can combine graphics characters to form block graphics: simple images, illustrations, and borders. See *block graphics* and *character-based program*.

graphics coprocessor   A microprocessor specially designed to speed the processing and display of high-resolution video images. A graphics accelerator board that includes a graphics coprocessor can speed the display of programs, such as Windows, that use graphical user interfaces. Popular graphics coprocessors include the Weitek W5086 and W5186, as well as S3 Inc.'s 86C911. See *graphics accelerator board*.

graphics file format   In a graphics program, the way in which the information needed to display a graphic is arranged and stored on disk.

Little standardization exists for graphics file formats. Programs such as AutoCAD, GEM Draw, Lotus 1-2-3, Windows Paint, and PC

Paintbrush generate files in proprietary file formats that other programs can read only if specially equipped to do so, as many programs
are. WordPerfect 5.1, for example, can import any of these files, as
well as Encapulsated PostScript (EPS) and MacPaint, among the 14
formats it supports. WordPerfect 6 supports even more.

The Macintosh environment has a standard file format called *PICT*
that uses routines drawn from the Mac's QuickDraw toolbox. This
format, however, isn't satisfactory for many applications. Additional
formats include the MacPaint file format for 72-dpi bit-mapped
graphics, tagged image file format (TIFF) files for scanned images
stored at up to 300 dpi, and Encapsulated PostScript.

Microsoft Windows, unlike DOS, establishes graphics file format
conventions, and programs designed to run under Windows must
adhere to this format. See *Encapsulated PostScript (EPS) file*, *file
format*, *PICT*, *QuickDraw*, and *Tagged Image File Format (TIFF)*.

graphics mode   In video adapters, a display mode in which
everything on-screen—including text and graphics—is drawn
using *pixels*. Many adapters also offer a character mode, which
runs more quickly because it uses the computer's built-in, ready-
made characters rather than composes them individually. See
character mode and *graphics view*.

TIP: *Windows users who frequently run graphics-intensive
applications, such as desktop publishing programs, and find that
Windows runs sluggishly should consider adding a graphics accelerator board, which will result in impressive performance gains.*

graphics primitive   In an object-oriented (vector) graphics
program, the most basic unit of graphic expression, such as a line,
arc, circle, rectangle, or oval.

graphics scanner   A graphics input device that transforms a
picture into an image that can be displayed on-screen.

graphics spreadsheet   A spreadsheet program that displays
the worksheet by using bit-mapped graphics instead of relying on

the computer's built-in character set. Graphics spreadsheets such as Microsoft Excel and Lotus 1-2-3 for Windows include desktop publishing tools such as multiple typefaces, type sizes, rules, and screens (grayed areas). Also, printouts can combine spreadsheets and business graphs on one page.

graphics tablet An input device that lets you draw with an electronic pen on an electronically sensitive table. The pen's movements are relayed to the screen. See *pen computer.*

graphics view In some DOS applications, a mode in which the program switches the display circuitry to its graphics mode. In graphics mode, the computer can display bit-mapped graphics. On all except the fastest computers, graphics mode is significantly slower than character mode. See *character view.*

gray scale In computer graphics, a series of shades from white to black.

gray-scale monitor A monitor (and compatible display adapter) that can display a full range of shades from white to black.

TIP: *True gray-scale monitors are expensive and, in comparison to color monitors, offer few benefits to most users. They're essential, however, for a few applications, such as photographic image processing and retouching. A VGA monitor may suffice; it can display a minimum of 64 gray-scale levels.*

greeking Displaying a simulated version of a page on-screen, showing lines or bars instead of text so that the overall page layout design is apparent. Some word processing and page layout programs use a print preview feature that's similar to greeking.

Greek text A block of simulated text or lines used to represent the positioning and point size of text in a designer's composition of a page, used so that the aesthetics of the page design can be assessed.

green PC A computer system (not including printer) designed to operate in an energy-efficient manner.

g

Powerful green PCs—say, a 486DX2/66 with a 15-inch monitor
and 1M of video RAM—running at full power typically draw
from 90 to 130 watts, whereas standard systems draw 130 to 160
watts. A green PC also includes additional power modes, such as
turning of the hard disk drive and a power-saver mode. In power-
saver mode, entire systems draw between 28 and 36 watts, equal to
the power draw of a standard monitor. Green printers also are
appearing in the marketplace.

Translated into dollars, the power savings for the most efficient
system amounts to about $15 per year. Computers actually use
little power; in the office where PCs often stay on all day, the
annual electric bill per computer is about $30. However, when
you add up all the computers used by your state government offices, that's a lot of tax dollars.

group   In Microsoft Windows, a collection of program item icons
stored together in a single group window in Program Manager. Examples of groups include the Accessories, Main, and Games groups.

group icon   In Microsoft Windows, an icon that represents a
group window that's now minimized. When you open the group
icon, you see a group window, which contains the program item
icons (see fig. G.1).

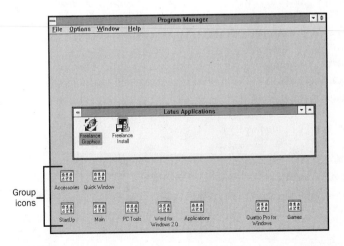

Fig. G.1   *Group icons in the Microsoft Windows Program Manager.*

groupware   Application programs that increase the coopera-
tion and joint productivity of small groups of co-workers. An
example of groupware is ForComment (by Broderbund Software),
designed to make collaborative writing easier. The program allows
each member of the group to insert comments and make changes
to the text, subject to the other members' approval.

Some industry observers thought that groupware was just a marketing gimmick after it was reported that Broderbund didn't use
ForComment for internal collaborative writing. The success of
Lotus Notes, a groupware program designed for minicomputer
and mainframe computer systems, may suggest otherwise. It's not
necessary to buy specialty software for this purpose, however.
Programs such as WordPerfect and Word for Windows include
features such as redline and strikethrough, user-selected text colors, and annotations with user initials that can be used to edit a
shared document on a network.

guest   In a local area network, an access privilege that allows
you to access another computer on the network without having to
provide a password. See *local area network (LAN)*.

GUI   See *graphical user interface (GUI)*.

guide   In a page layout program, a non-printing line that appears as a dotted line on-screen, showing the current location of
margins, gutters, and other page layout design elements.

guru   In computing, an expert who can talk about highly technical subjects in an intelligible way (a rare quality) and doesn't
mind doing so (even rarer).

gutter   See *binding offset*.

GW-BASIC   A version of the BASIC programming language
often licensed to PC-compatible computers. GW-BASIC is nearly
identical to the BASIC interpreter distributed with IBM PCs, but
each manufacturer is free to customize the language.

g

hack   An inordinately clever rearrangement of existing system resources that results, as if by magic, in a stunning improvement in system performance—or an equally stunning prank.

In the computer age, the term *hack* refers to a spectacular feat of programming prowess, in which a programmer finds a solution to a challenging problem by exploiting previously unknown system capabilities or combining known capabilities in a new and creative way. One of the most famous hardware hacks is Stephen Wozniak's design for the Apple II disk drive controller, which combined inexpensive, readily available chips in a way that greatly reduced the size and cost of the disk drive. But this sense of the term doesn't lose the connotation of "prank," for the best hacks work their magic in a way that seems fiendishly clever. See *hacker*, *hacker ethic*, and *phreaking*.

hacker   A computer enthusiast who enjoys learning everything about a computer system and, through clever programming, pushing the system to its highest possible level of performance.

During the 1980s, the press redefined the term to include hobbyists who break into secured computer systems. Sensationalist news accounts of the dangerous activities of "hackers" created a "hacker hysteria." In 1989, for example, the *New York Times* published an article headlined "Invasion of the Data Snatchers," culminating in a ridiculous series of Secret Service raids in which the computer systems of these "dangerous" individuals were confiscated.

Although some hackers are indeed *crackers* who enjoy the challenge of breaking into corporate and organizational computing systems, the media's redefinition of the term has cast a shadow over the activities of many of the most creative computer users. See *cracker*, *hack*, *hacker ethic*, and *phreaking*.

hacker ethic   A set of moral principles that were common to the first-generation hacker community (circa 1965-1982), described by Steven Levy in *Hackers* (1984). According to the hacker ethic, all technical information should, in principle, be freely available to all, so it's never unethical to gain entry to a system to explore and gain knowledge. However, it's always unethical to destroy, alter, or move data in such a way that could cause injury or expense to others. Unfortunately, in more and more states, this activity is against the law. See *cracker, cyberpunk, cyberspace, hack, hacker*, and *phreaking*.

half duplex   An asynchronous communications protocol in which the communications channel can handle only one signal at a time. The two stations alternate their transmissions. Synonymous with *local echo*. See *asynchronous communication, communications protocol, echoplex*, and *full duplex*.

half-height drive   A drive bay half the size of the 3-inch-high drive bays in the original IBM Personal Computer. Half-height drive bays and drives are standard in today's PCs.

TIP: *If you're shopping for a computer, make sure that it has plenty of drive bays. You may want to add an extra floppy disk drive or a second hard disk drive.*

halftone   A copy of a photograph prepared for printing by breaking down the continuous gradations of tones into a series of dots. Dark shades are produced by dense patterns of thick dots, and lighter shades are produced by less dense patterns of smaller dots.

A black-and-white photograph is a continuous-tone image of various shades of gray. Photographs don't photocopy well, since the fine gradations of gray tones are lost. Halftones of a photograph are created for printing; the photograph is copied using a halftone screen in front of the film. The screen breaks up the image into patterns of dots of varying size. However, high-end scanners are now producing excellent digitized photographs for magazines and newspapers. See *scanner* and *Tagged Image File Format (TIFF)*.

handle   In memory management, an access channel to a block of extended memory. When a program requests extended memory, HIMEM.SYS gives the program a handle to an extended memory block. The parameter /NUMHANDLES=*num* is used to inform HIMEM.SYS how many handles it'll have to manage. In Microsoft Windows, the global heap consists of all the tasks, called *objects*, that have been allocated memory; each object is assigned a handle.

In a graphical interface, handles are the small black squares around a selected object that are used to drag, size, or scale the object. See *draw program* and *object-oriented graphic*.

handler   A driver, utility program or subroutine that takes care of a task. The A20 handler, for example, is a routine that controls access to extended memory. If HIMEM.SYS can't gain control of the A20 address line, use the /MACHINE:*code* parameter to tell HIMEM.SYS what type of computer is being used, which usually solves the problem. Handlers can also be a set of programming instructions attached to a button. The instructions control what happens when the button is selected. Also, every type of interrupt is processed by a software handler. See *event-driven program* and *object-oriented programming language*.

G H I

handshaking   A method for controlling the flow of serial communication between two devices so that one device transmits only when the other device is ready. In hardware handshaking, a separate wire is used to send a signal when the receiving device is ready to receive; software handshaking uses special control characters.

Hardware handshaking is used for devices such as serial printers, because the device is nearby and a special cable can be used. Because the telephone system doesn't have an extra wire available, telephone connections used by modems require software handshaking. The two software handshaking techniques are ETX/ACK, which uses the ASCII character Ctrl+C to pause in data transmission, and XON/XOFF, which uses Ctrl+S to pause and Ctrl+Q to resume transmission.

hanging indent   A paragraph indentation in which the first line is flush with the left margin, but subsequent lines (called *turnover lines*) are indented.

hard   Permanent, physically defined, permanently wired, or fixed, as opposed to soft (changeable or subject to redefinition). The printed document is hard, because changing the printed document is difficult. A document still in the computer's memory is soft, because you can still make changes to it. See *hard copy*, *hard hyphen*, *hard return*, *hard space*, and *hard wired*.

hard card A hard disk and disk drive controller that are contained on a single plug-in adapter. You easily can add a hard disk to a system using a hard card: you just press the adapter into the expansion slot as you would any other adapter.

hard copy Printed output, distinguished from data stored on disk or in memory.

hard disk A secondary storage medium that uses several rigid disks coated with a magnetically sensitive material and housed, together with the recording heads, in a hermetically sealed mechanism. Typical storage capacities range from 60M to 500M, although 2 gigabyte hard disks are now available.

Developed by IBM in 1973, early hard disks were extremely expensive. With the increased success of the personal computer since the early 1980s, however, hard disks have been manufactured in huge quantities, and 150M and larger hard disks now are available for $1 or less per megabyte of storage capacity. Because hard drives are almost a necessity for personal computers today, they have become a standard element in computer systems.

A hard disk is a complex storage subsystem that includes two to five disks, the read/write head assembly, and the electronic interface that governs the connection between the drive and the computer (see fig. H.1).

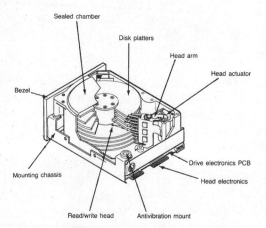

Fig. H.1 *The components of a hard disk drive.*

For years, all disks revolved at 3,600 rpm, with the read/write heads floating on a thin layer of air just above the magnetically encoded surface of the disk. The SCSI interface makes faster speeds possible; newer disks that revolve at speeds up to 5,400 rpm have improved disk access rates by as much as a third. Although 5 1/4-inch disks are common, the trend is toward 3 1/2-inch disks because the read/write heads reach the data more quickly. The technology used to position the read/write heads use voice coil motors. Older band-stepper technology is found only in XT and AT systems.

Hard drive interface standards include ST506, IDE, ESDI, and SCSI. You should develop a regular backup procedure. Hard disks occasionally fail, and they may take the data with them.

Some hard drives use removable cartridges, a significant advantage over normal hard drives. See *access time, backup, backup utility, Bernoulli box, Enhanced System Device Interface (ESDI), Integrated Drive Electronics (IDE), Run-Length Limited (RLL), secondary storage,* and *Small Computer System Interface (SCSI).*

hard disk backup program   A utility program that backs up hard disk data and programs onto floppy disks. See *backup utility* and *utility program.*

> **TIP:** *The best backup programs can perform incremental backups, in which the program backs up only those files that have changed since the last backup procedure.*

hard disk interface   An electronic standard for the connection of a hard disk to the computer. See *Enhanced System Device Interface (ESDI), hard disk, Integrated Drive Electronics (IDE),* and *Small Computer System Interface (SCSI).*

hard drive   See *hard disk.*

hard hyphen   In word processing programs, a special hyphen that acts as a regular character so that text can't word wrap at this hyphen. Synonymous with *non-breaking hyphen.* See *soft hyphen.*

→ **TIP:** *Use a hard hyphen for hyphenated names, even if the names aren't positioned near the end of a line. Remember, you may add or delete text in the paragraph later, and these changes are likely to push the name to the end of a line.*

hard page   A page break inserted by the user that remains in effect even after you later add or delete text above the break. In contrast, the soft return inserted by the program moves automatically as you add and delete text. Synonymous with *forced page break*.

hard space   In word processing programs, a space specially formatted as a regular character so that the text can't word wrap at the space's location. Hard spaces often are used to keep two-word proper nouns or month and date together, such as Key Biscayne, West Point, and January 25.

hard wired   A processing function built into the computer's electronic circuits rather than facilitated by program instructions. To improve computer performance, computer designers include circuits that perform specific functions, such as multiplication or division, at higher speeds. These functions are hard wired. The term *hard wired* also refers to the program instructions contained in the computer's read-only memory (ROM) or firmware. See *read-only memory (ROM)*.

hardware   The electronic components, boards, peripherals, and equipment that make up your computer system; distinguished from the programs (software) that tell these components what to do.

hardware cache   Cache memory on a hard disk controller or added directly to a disk drive. The cache memory stores frequently accessed program instructions and data, as well as additional tracks of data that may be needed next. When your computer requires data that's already in the hardware cache, it's accessed much faster than from the disk. The data is then delivered as fast as the expansion bus can carry it, which is not very fast unless you have the controller on a local bus. Both 32-bit and 16-bit cached disk controller cards are available. See *disk drive controller*.

h

hardware platform   A computer hardware standard, such as IBM PC-compatible or Macintosh. Devices or programs created for one platform won't run on others. See *device independence* and *platform independence*.

hardware reset   Restarting the system by pushing the computer's reset button. A hardware reset may be necessary after a system crash so severe that you can't use the keyboard restart command (in DOS, Ctrl+Alt+Del) to restart the computer. See *programmer's switch* and *warm boot*.

Hayes command set   A standardized set of instructions used to control modems. Common Hayes commands include the following:

AT	Attention (used to start all commands)
ATDT	Attention dial tone
ATDP	Attention dial pulse
+++	Enter command mode during communication session
ATH	Attention hang up

See *modem*.

Hayes-compatible modem   A modem that recognizes the Hayes command set. See *Hayes command set* and *modem*.

head   See *read/write head*.

head arm   In a disk drive, a rigid arm with a read/write head flexibly connected at one end and attached to a single moving assembly on the other end. Several head arms, one for each side of each platter in a hard disk, are attached to the same assembly so they can move as a unit. See *disk drive* and *read/write head*.

head actuator   `ak-chew-a-tor   In a disk drive, a mechanism that moves the assembly containing the read/write heads across the surface of the disk to the location where data is to be written or read. See *random access* and *sequential access*.

head crash   In a hard disk, the collision of a read/write head with the surface of the disk, resulting in damage to the disk surface and possibly to the head.

CAUTION: *Most disk drives can withstand some jostling, but you should avoid moving your computer or bumping its case while the drive is running.*

head seek time   See *access time*.

head slot   An opening in a floppy disk case. The access hole exposes a portion of the disk surface so that a read/write head can read information or write new information on the disk. See *floppy disk*.

head-mounted display (HMD)   A stereoscopic set of head-mounted goggles that produce a sensation of three-dimensional space. Head-mounted displays are an integral part of virtual reality systems, which allow users to feel as though they're exploring a real world that has actually been created within the computer system. See *stereoscopy* and *virtual reality*.

header   Repeated text, such as a page number and a short version of a document's title, that appears at the top of the pages in a document.

Some programs include odd headers and even headers, so you can define mirror-image headers for documents printed on both sides of the page. Use this feature to place the page number on the outside corner of facing pages. You can suppress the printing of a header on the first page of a document or a section of a document, and change headers within the document. Synonymous with *running head*. See *footer*.

heap   In Microsoft Windows, a special storage area in memory used for critical resources.

Several types of heaps are created during normal Windows operations, including a local heap, menu heap, and user heap, which are collectively called the *system resources*. These heaps are limited to a

64K size. When they're full, launching another application results in a Not enough memory message, even though plenty of memory may be available.

Windows also uses a global heap to store all the various types of objects now being used. Windows applications also use heaps.

Helvetica   A sans serif typeface frequently used for display type and occasionally for body type. One of the most widely used fonts in the world, Helvetica is included as a built-in font with many laser printers. The following example shows Helvetica type:

ABCDEFGHIJKLMNOPQRSTUVWXYZ

abcdefghijklmnopqrstuvwxyz 1234567890

G H I

Hercules Graphics Adapter   A monochrome display adapter for IBM PC-compatible computers. The Hercules Graphics Adapter displays text and graphics on a monochrome monitor with a resolution of 720 pixels horizontally and 320 lines vertically.

The Hercules (and Hercules-compatible) display adapter works only with graphics software that includes drivers for its non-IBM display format. Drivers for the Color Graphics Adapter (CGA), for example, don't work with Hercules cards. However, Hercules display adapters work with all programs that display monochrome text. See *monochrome display adapter (MDA)*.

hertz (Hz)   A unit of measurement of electrical vibrations; one Hz is equal to one cycle per second. See *megahertz (MHz)*.

heterogeneous network   A local area network that includes computers and devices from several manufacturers. Many firms create heterogeneous networks that successfully link Macintosh and Windows systems. See *local area network (LAN)*.

heuristic   A method of solving a problem by using rules of thumb acquired from experience. Heuristics rarely are stated formally in textbooks, but they're part of the knowledge that human experts use in problem solving. See *expert system* and *knowledge base*.

Hewlett-Packard Graphics Language   A page description language (PDL) and file format for graphics printing with the

HP LaserJet line of printers, HP plotters, and the high-end inkjet printers, now widely emulated by HP-compatible laser printers. See *Hewlett-Packard Printer Control Language (HPPCL)* and *page description language (PDL)*.

Hewlett-Packard Printer Control Language (HPPCL)

The proprietary printer control language introduced by Hewlett-Packard in 1984 with the company's first LaserJet printer. Like the Hayes command set in the modem world, HPPCL has become a standard. See *printer control language (PCL)*.

hexadecimal   A numbering system that uses a base (radix) of 16. Unlike decimal numbers (base 10), hexadecimal numbers include 16 digits: 0, 1, 2, 3, 4, 5, 6, 7, 8, 9, A, B, C, D, E, and F. Although binary numbers are ideally suited to the devices used in computers, they're inconvenient and hard to read. Binary numbers grow in length quickly; for example, 16 is 1111 in binary and 10 in hexadecimal format. Therefore, programmers use hexadecimal numbers as a convenient way of representing binary numbers.

hidden codes   The hidden text formatting codes embedded in a document by an on-screen formatting program.

Even a what-you-see-is-what-you-get (WYSIWYG) word processing program generates and embeds codes in your text as a result of formatting commands. The codes are necessary because the screen imaging technique may have no connection to the technique used to generate output to the printer. Most word processing programs hide these codes; in WordPerfect, however, you can view and edit the codes.

hidden file   A file with the hidden attribute set so that the file name isn't displayed when viewing a directory using the DIR command. You can't erase or copy hidden files.

Hierarchical File System (HFS)   A Macintosh disk storage system, designed for use with hard disks that's used to store files within folders so that only a short list of files appears in dialog boxes.

HFS is similar to the directory organization of DOS disks with one important exception—no path definition command exists,

h

except for checking the System Folder when an application searches for a file. See *path*.

> **TIP:** *Macintosh users should avoid the temptation of nesting too many levels of folders. Two or three nested levels reduces the amount of pointing or clicking when searching for a file; five or six increases the tedium. To automate the process, consider buying a file-location utility such as Findswell (Working Software) or Boomerang (ZetaSoft).*

high density   A floppy disk storage technique that uses extremely fine-grained magnetic particles. High-density disks are more expensive to manufacture than double-density disks, but can store 1M or more of information on one 5 1/4- or 3 1/2-inch disk. Synonymous with *quad density*.

high-density disk   See *floppy disk*.

high end   An expensive product at the top of a firm's offerings; includes features or capabilities likely to be needed only by the most discriminating users or professionals. See *low end*.

high-level format   A formatting operation that creates the boot record, file-allocation table, and root directory on a disk.

When you use the DOS FORMAT command to format a floppy disk, the computer performs a low-level format (creates tracks and sectors) in addition to the high-level format. When you use a hard disk, however, FORMAT performs just the high-level format.

IDE and SCSI drives are low-leveled at the factory, because they don't use the standard arrangement of tracks and sectors. For a hard disk that isn't low-level formatted, you have to run a program (usually provided on a floppy disk that comes with the hard disk) that performs the absolute format. See *boot sector*, *file allocation table (FAT)*, and *low-level format*.

high-level programming language   A programming language such as BASIC or Pascal that crudely resembles human language.

Each statement in a high-level language corresponds to several machine language instructions, so a programmer can write programs more quickly and concentrate on the problem that the program is designed to solve, instead of how the computer will carry out the program. However, programs written in a high-level language run slower. See *assembly language, low-level programming language,* and *machine language.*

higher-order characters   See *extended character set.*

highlight   A character, word, text block, or command displayed in reverse video, indicating the current location of the cursor. This term sometimes is used synonymously with *cursor.*

highlighting   The process of marking characters or command names in reverse video on-screen. Synonymous with *selecting.*

high/low/close/open graph   In presentation graphics, a line graph in which a stock's high value, low value, closing price, and average value are displayed (see fig. H.2). The x-axis (categories) is aligned horizontally, and the y-axis (values) is aligned vertically. Another application for a high/low/open/close graph is a record of daily minimum, maximum, and average temperatures. Synonymous with *HLCO chart.* See *column graph* and *line graph.*

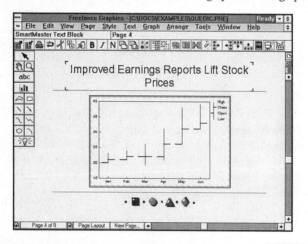

Fig. H.2   *A high/low/close/open graph.*

high memory   See *upper memory area.*

high memory area (HMA)   In a DOS computer, the first 64K of extended memory above 1M. Programs that conform to the eXtended Memory Specification (XMS) can use HMA as a direct extension of conventional memory. Beginning with MS-DOS 5.0, most of the portions of DOS that must be loaded into conventional memory can be loaded into the high memory area. See *conventional memory, extended memory,* and *eXtended Memory Specification (XMS).*

high resolution   In computer systems, using a sufficient number of pixels in display monitors or dots per inch when printing to produce well-defined text characters as well as smoothly defined curves in graphic images. A high-resolution video adapter and monitor can display 1,024 pixels horizontally by 768 lines vertically; a high-resolution printer can print at least 300 dots per inch (dpi). See *low resolution.*

HIMEM.SYS   A DOS device driver, supplied with Microsoft Windows and DOS, that configures extended memory and high memory so that programs conforming to the eXtended Memory Standard (XMS) can access it. See *CONFIG.SYS, device driver, eXtended Memory Specification (XMS), high memory area (HMA),* and *upper memory area.*

hinting   In digital typography, reducing the weight (thickness) of a typeface so that small-sized fonts print without blurring or losing detail on 300-dpi printers.

histogram   In a stacked column graph, placing the columns close together so that differences in the data items within each stack are emphasized (see fig. H.3).

By stacking data in a column, you emphasize the contribution each data item makes to the whole (as in a pie graph). By placing the columns next to each other, the eye is led to compare the relative proportions of one data item as the item varies from column to column.

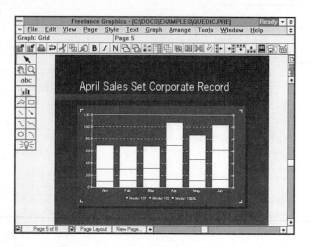

Fig. H.3 *A histogram.*

home computer   A personal computer specifically designed and marketed for home applications, such as educating children, playing games, balancing a checkbook, paying bills, and controlling lights or appliances.

Home key   A key on personal computer keyboards used frequently to move the cursor to the beginning of the line or the top of the screen, but the assignment of this key is up to the programmer.

homophone error   A type of spelling error that involves using an incorrect word that sounds the same as the correct word (*Two Bee Oar Knot Too Be*). The spell checking feature found in many application programs doesn't find homophone errors; grammar checking programs do find homophone errors.

hook   A software or hardware feature that's included so hobbyists and programmers can add custom features of their own design. For example, Microsoft Word for Windows is loaded with hooks that allow an expert to create custom dialog boxes, greatly extending the program's functionality for specific applications.

h

horizontal scroll bar See *scroll bar/scroll box.*

host In computer networks and telecommunications, the computer that performs centralized functions such as making program or data files available to other computers. See *Internet.*

hot key A keyboard shortcut that accesses a menu command.

> **TIP:** *In most programs, you can use keyboard shortcuts for many menu commands. If you see a bolded or an underlined character in a command or option name, you can access that command or option by holding down the Alt key and pressing that letter.*

G H I

hot link A method of copying information from one document (the source document) to another (the target document) so that the information is updated if you change the information in the source document.

In Microsoft Windows applications, you can create a hot link using the Paste/Link command. In Macintosh System 7, open the Edit menu and choose Publish in the source document, and then paste the link using Subscribe in the target document. See *dynamic data exchange (DDE), warm link,* and *object linking and embedding (OLE).*

HP-compatible printer A printer that responds to the Hewlett-Packard printer control language (PCL), which has become the standard for laser printing in the IBM and IBM-compatible computing world.

HPGL See *Hewlett-Packard Graphics Language.*

hung system A computer that has experienced a system failure and is no longer processing data, even though the cursor may still be blinking on-screen. The only option in most cases is to restart the system, which means losing any unsaved work.

> **TIP:** *If you're experiencing computer crashes frequently, try removing all the terminate-and-stay-resident (TSR) programs you're using. These programs, called INITs in the Mac world, can cause conflicts that produce hung systems. Add the programs again, one by one, testing between each addition, to determine whether one of them is causing the problem. Check the program documentation to see whether TSRs or INITs must be loaded in a specific order. Some operate in an unstable fashion unless they are the last program to be loaded at system startup. See* INIT *and* terminate-and-stay resident (TSR) program.

HyperCard   A software product, available with the Apple Macintosh computer, for developing information systems based on hypertext. See *HyperTalk* and *hypertext*.

hypermedia   A computer-assisted instructional application such as HyperCard that's used to add graphics, sound, video, and synthesized voice to the capabilities of a hypertext system. See *hypertext*.

HyperTalk   The scripting language provided with HyperCard, an accessory program shipped with every Macintosh. HyperTalk is an event-oriented language. To create a HyperTalk program, you begin by using HyperCard to create screen objects (cards with text fields, buttons, and other features), and then you write short, English-like programs, called *scripts*, that tell HyperCard what to do when one of these objects is manipulated. HyperTalk programming is fun and introduces a programming novice to the fundamental principles of object-oriented programming. The language is too slow, however, for professional program development, for which it was never intended. See *object-oriented programming language* and *SmallTalk*.

hypertext   The non-sequential retrieval of a document's text. The reader is free to pursue associative trails through the document by means of predefined or user-created links.

In a true hypertext application, you can highlight virtually any word in a document and immediately jump to other documents containing related text. Commands also are available that you use to create your own associative trails through the document. Hypertext applications are particularly useful for working with massive amounts of text, such as encyclopedias and multivolume case law reporters.

hyphenation   In word processing and page layout programs, an automatic operation that hyphenates words at the end of lines as needed. When used with caution and manual confirmation of each hyphen, a hyphenation utility can improve the appearance of a document, especially when using newspaper columns or large margins. See *hard hyphen, hyphen ladder,* and *soft hyphen.*

G
H
I

CAUTION: *Some programs break fundamental hyphenation rules, such as leaving only one or two characters on one side of the hyphen or hyphenating words on several consecutive lines. Another problem is homographs, two words spelled the same but with different meanings and pronunciations, for example:*

in-val-id *and* in-va-lid

min-ute *and* mi-nute

hyphen ladder   A formatting flaw caused by the repetition of hyphens at the end of two or more lines in a row. Synonymous with *hyphen stack.*

Hyphen ladders distract the eye and disrupt the text's readability. If you use automatic hyphenation, proofread the results carefully for hyphen ladders. Adjust word spacing and hyphenation manually, if necessary.

Hz   See *hertz (Hz).*

i486   See *Intel 80486 DX* and *Intel 80486SX*.

IAC   See *Inter-Application Communication (IAC)*.

I-beam pointer   In Macintosh and Windows applications, an I-shaped mouse pointer that appears when the pointer is moved over a screen area when you can edit text.

In Macintosh and Windows applications, the editing cursor appears as a thick, vertical bar *between* characters. The I-beam pointer is thin enough that you can position the pointer between characters with precision.

IBM 8514/A display adapter   A video adapter for IBM Personal System/2 computers that, with the on-board Video Graphics Array (VGA) circuitry, produces a resolution of 1,024 pixels horizontally and 768 lines vertically. The adapter also contains its own processing circuitry that reduces demand on the computer's central processing unit (CPU).

Introduced at the same time as the lower-resolution VGA and MCGA adapters, the 8514/A failed to attract much of a market because the 8514/A uses interlacing technology to achieve high resolution. The 8514/A and MCGA adapters have been discontinued. See *flicker, interlacing, non-interlaced monitor, Super VGA*, and *video adapter*.

IBM PC-compatible computer   A personal computer that runs all or almost all the software developed for the IBM Personal Computer, and accepts the IBM computer's cards, adapters, and peripheral devices. Synonymous with *clone*.

icon   In a graphical user interface, an on-screen symbol that represents a program, data file, or some other computer entity or function (see fig. I.1).

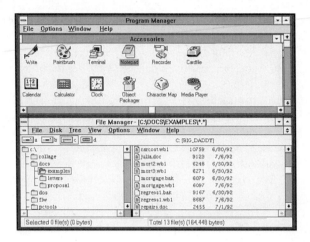

Fig. I.1   *On-screen icons representing Microsoft Windows Accessory programs.*

icon bar   An on-screen row of buttons, usually placed just above the document window, that allows the user to choose frequently accessed menu options without having to use the menus. On each button is a picture (icon) that shows the button's function. For example, the Print button displays a tiny picture of a printer.

IDE   See *Integrated Drive Electronics (IDE).*

IDE drive   On 80286 and more recent computers, a hard disk that contains most of the control circuitry within the drive itself. Designed to connect to computers containing an AT attachment on their motherboards, IDE drives combine the speed of ESDI drives with the integration of the SCSI hard drive interface. This performance is offered at a price lower than most ESDI and SCSI drives. See *Enhanced System Device Interface (ESDI), Integrated Drive Electronics (IDE),* and *Small Computer System Interface (SCSI).*

TIP: *If you're shopping for a computer and value is uppermost in your mind, look for a machine that includes an IDE interface and IDE drive. You need an ESDI or SCSI drive only if you run applications that demand the highest possible performance from your computer.*

identifier   In database management, a descriptor used to specify the uniqueness of the information contained in the data record. For example, the descriptor *Norway* appears in the data record of the only travel films that depict scenery from that country. See *descriptor*.

IEEE 802 standards   A series of telecommunications standards governing local area networks. Established by the Institute of Electrical and Electronic Engineers (IEEE), the standards include 10Base2 and 10Base-T cabling, network bridges, and the ring networks used by IBM's token-ring network. See *bridge, bus network, EtherNet, fiber optics, Institute of Electrical and Electronic Engineers (IEEE), star network,* and *token-ring network.*

IF/THEN/ELSE   A structure that conducts a test to see whether a condition is true. *If* the condition is true, *then* the program branches to option A, or *else* if the condition is false, the program branches to option B. IF/THEN/ELSE structures, with slight variations in the language, are used when writing macros, as merge codes, as functions in spreadsheet software, and as part of all high-level program languages.

The following example tests to see whether a file exists. If the file exists, the program tells the computer to open the file. If the file doesn't exist, the program tells the computer to create a file.

```
IF file_exists = true
    THEN open_file
    ELSE create_new_file
ENDIF
```

illegal character   A character that can't be used according to the syntax rules of command-driven programs and programming languages. Such characters usually are reserved for a specific program function. With DOS, for example, you can't assign a file name to a file if the name includes an asterisk (*). The asterisk is reserved for use as a wild-card symbol. Commas, spaces, slashes, and several other punctuation characters also are illegal characters for file names.

image compression   The use of a compression technique to reduce the size of graphics files, which usually consume inordinate amounts of disk space. A single 100K gray-scale TIFF file can be

reduced by as much as 96 percent to 4K or 5K for telecommunications or storage purposes. Some graphics programs compress
images automatically, but popular file compression programs such
as PKZIP (PKWARE, Inc.) also can do the job.

image processing   In computer graphics, the use of a computer to enhance, embellish, or refine a graphic image. Typical
processing operations include enhancing or reducing contrast,
altering colors so that the image is more easily analyzed, correcting
underexposure or overexposure, and outlining objects so that they
can be identified.

imagesetter   A professional typesetting machine that generates very high-resolution output on photographic paper or film.

Popular imagesetters include the Agfa Compugraphic, Linotronic,
and Varityper models that recognize PostScript commands. All are
capable of resolutions of 1,200 or more dots per inch (dpi), unlike
the 300-600 dpi resolution of laser printers. They also sell for
$30,000 and up, so if you have a PostScript-compatible word
processor or page layout program, take a disk to a service bureau
that owns one of these machines to obtain high-resolution output.
See *PostScript* and *service bureau*.

imaging model   The method of representing output on-
screen. In a graphical user interface, for example, the imaging
model is for the screen font to closely resemble the way the text is
printed. See *graphical user interface (GUI)* and *screen font*.

IMHO   In on-line conferences, acronym for *In My Humble
Opinion*.

impact printer   A printer that operates by pressing a physical
representation of a character against an inked ribbon, forming an
impression on the page. Impact printers are noisy, but they can
produce multiple copies of business forms using carbons. See *dot-
matrix printer*, *letter-quality printer*, and *non-impact printer*.

import   To load a file created by one program into a different
program. Harvard Graphics, for example, can import the PIC files
created by Lotus 1-2-3.

increment   To increase a value. See *decrement.*

incremental backup   A backup procedure in which a hard disk backup program backs up only the files changed since the last backup procedure. See *archival backup.*

incremental update   See *maintenance release.*

indentation   The alignment of a paragraph to the right or left of the document margins.

CAUTION: *Don't use the space bar or Tab key to indent text. If a printer uses proportional typefaces, the text won't align properly. This method also doesn't change the indentation of all the lines; you must change each line individually. Finally, if you edit the text, it won't automatically reformat correctly.*

Most word processing programs include commands that indent text from the left, right, or both margins (see fig. I.2). You also can create a hanging indent. See *hanging indent.*

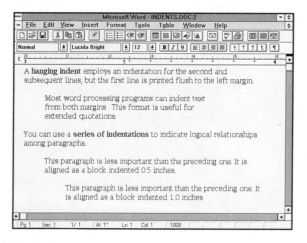

Fig. I.2   *Text indented from the left margin and from both margins.*

index   In database management programs, a compact file containing information (called *pointers*) about the physical location of records in a database file. When searching or sorting the database, the program uses the index rather than the full database. Such operations are faster than sorts or searches performed on the actual database.

In word processing programs, an index is an appendix that lists important words, names, and concepts in alphabetical order, and the page numbers where the terms appear. With most word processing programs, you must mark terms to be included in the index the program constructs. See *active index, concordance file, sort,* and *sort order.*

index hole   In a floppy disk, a hole that's electro-optically detected by the drive to locate the beginning of the first sector on the disk. See *floppy disk* and *sector.*

Industry Standard Architecture (ISA)   The bus design of IBM's AT (Advanced Technology) computer, which uses a 16-bit bus with several 8-bit slots for downward compatibility.

The AT bus added more than a simple doubling of the width of the data bus. The address bus was increased to 24 lines, enough to address 16M of memory. Downward compatibility was assured by adding a supplemental connector to the original 8-bit, 62-pin connector. Several new interrupt and DMA control lines were added. See *AT bus, bus, direct memory access (DMA) channels, Extended Industry Standard Architecture (EISA), local bus,* and *Micro Channel Architecture (MCA).*

industry standard user interface   An IBM standard for displaying programs on-screen; part of the company's Systems Application Architecture (SAA). The standard, called *Common User Access (CUA),* calls for many of the interface features found in graphical user interfaces: pull-down menus, dialog boxes with check boxes and option buttons, and highlighted accelerator keys for rapid keyboard selection of commands.

The CUA standard is now found in many character-based DOS applications. Strictly speaking, it isn't a graphical user interface (GUI) because it runs in character mode and doesn't represent computer resources as icons. But the CUA interface has just about every other GUI benefit, including a refreshing commonality of key assignments and procedures across applications: F1 brings up Help, F3 cancels or exits, F10 displays the menu, and so on. See *application program interface (API)*, *graphical user interface (GUI)*, *Microsoft Windows*, and *mousable interface*.

> **TIP:** *To avoid the big investment necessary to run Windows applications, you can set up a very nice, near-GUI system by choosing a library of CUA-compliant DOS applications and run a shell (such as the MS-DOS shell, WordPerfect Shell, or PC Tools Desktop). If you want to multitask, run them in DESQview.*

infection   The presence of a virus within a computer system or on a floppy disk. The infection may not be obvious to the user; many viruses, for example, remain in the background until a specific time and date, when they display prank messages or erase data. See *Trojan horse*, *virus*, and *worm*.

information service   See *bibliographic retrieval service*, *bulletin board system (BBS)*, and *on-line information service*.

information superhighway An international array of connections that's used to transmit data. The Internet, with its many world-wide connections, masses of data, millions of experienced users, and endless opportunities for the exchange of ideas and personal growth, is a main road system for the phenomenon now being called the *information superhighway*. The capability of fiber optic cable to transmit enormous quantities of data, and the growth of wireless data transmission and satellite-based systems promise to increase the power and extent of this highway. See *fiber optics* and *wireless wide area network*.

inheritance   In object-oriented programming, the passing of a message up through the levels of objects until an object is reached that traps the message.

In HyperTalk, for example, the lowest-level object is a button. If the user produces a message by clicking on the button, and the button contains no programming code (called a *handler*) that traps this message, the message is passed up to the next level of the hierarchy, the card; if the card has no handler, the message is passed to the stack; finally, if there's still no handler, the message goes to the highest level, HyperCard. See *object-oriented programming language*.

INIT   In the Macintosh environment, a utility program that executes during a system start or restart, such as SuperClock, which displays the current system date and time in the menu bar, and Adobe Type Manager, which uses outline-font technology to display Adobe screen fonts.

G
H
I

CAUTION: *Like terminate-and-stay resident (TSR) programs in the IBM environment, INITs can conflict with each other and cause system crashes. If your system is behaving erratically, try removing INITs one at a time from the System Folder and restarting your system; you may be able to determine whether an INIT is the culprit.*

initial   In typography, an enlarged letter at the beginning of a chapter or paragraph. Initials set down within the copy are *drop caps*, and initials raised above the top line of the text are *stickup caps* (see fig. I.3). See *drop cap*.

OREM IPSUM dolor sit amet, consectetuer adipiscing elit, sed diam nonummy nibh euismod tincidunt ut laoreet dolore magna aliquam erat volutpat. Ut wisi enim ad minim veniam, quis nostrud exerci tation ullamcorper suscipit lobortis nisl ut aliquip ex

a commodo consequat. Duis autem vel eum iriure dolor in hendrerit in vulputate velit esse molestie consequat, vel illum dolore eu feugiat nulla facilisis at vero eros et accumsan et iusto odio dignissim qui blandit praesent luptatum zzril delenit augue duis

ELUM COMMODO consequat. Duis autem vel eum iriure dolor in hendrerit in vulputate velit esse molestie consequat, vel illum dolore eu feugiat nulla facilisis

Lorem ipsum dolor sit amet, consectetuer adipiscing elit, sed diam nonummy nibh euismod tincidunt ut laoreet dolore magna aliquam erat volutpat. Ut wisi enim ad minim veniam,

Fig. I.3   *Examples of drop caps (S and Y) and stickup caps (T and L).*

! **CAUTION:** *You can create initials with many word processing and page layout programs, but to avoid a common formatting error, make sure that the letter aligns precisely at the base of a line of text.*

initial base font   The font used by word processing programs for all documents unless you instruct otherwise. The initial base font is part of the printer definition. Whenever you select a different printer, the initial base font may change.

You can override the initial base font for a particular document by choosing a document base font using the document menu or using the base font menu, and you can override this choice by formatting individual characters or blocks of characters within the document. See *document base font.*

initialization   In personal computing, the process of formatting a hard disk and floppy disks so that they are ready for use. See *format.*

initialize   To prepare hardware or software to perform a task. A serial port is initialized using the MODE command to set the baud, parity, data, and stop values, for example. In some programs, initializing can be setting a counter or variable to zero before running a procedure.

inkjet printer   A non-impact printer that forms an image by spraying ink from a matrix of tiny jets.

Inkjet printers are quiet and can produce excellent results. Hewlett-Packard's DeskJet and DeskWriter printers can produce text and graphics at resolutions of 300 dpi and better, rivaling the output of laser printers to the untrained eye. See *non-impact printer.*

i

CAUTION: *The ink used by most inkjet printers is water-soluble and smears easily.*

input   The information entered into the computer for processing purposes.

input device   Any peripheral that assists you in getting data into the computer: a keyboard, mouse, trackball, voice recognition system, graphics tablet, or modem.

input/output (I/O) redirection   In DOS and UNIX, the routing of a program's output to a file or device, or the routing of a program's input from a file rather than the keyboard.

Most DOS commands (such as DIR) send output to the screen, but you can easily redirect a command's output by using the greater-than sign (>). To redirect the output of DIR to the LPT1 (printer) port, for example, you type **DIR > lpt1** and press Enter. To redirect the command's output to a file, type **DIR > dir.txt** and press Enter. In DOS, input redirection is frequently used with filters. See *filter*, *MS-DOS*, and *UNIX*.

input/output (I/O) system   One of the chief components of a computer system's architecture, the link between the microprocessor and the remaining circuitry of the computer that passes program instructions and data to the central processing unit (CPU).

Insert (Ins) key   On IBM PC-compatible keyboards, a programmable key frequently (but not always) used to toggle between insert mode and overtype mode when entering text. See *insert mode* and *overtype mode*.

insert mode   In word processing programs, a program mode in which inserted text pushes existing text to the right and down. The Insert key is used to toggle between insert and overtype modes. See *overtype mode*.

insertion point   In Macintosh and Windows applications, the blinking vertical bar that shows the point at which text will appear when you start typing. The insertion point is similar to the cursor in DOS applications. See *cursor.*

installation program   A utility provided with an application program that helps you install the program on a hard disk and configure the program so that you can use it.

CAUTION: *In IBM PC-compatible computing, installation programs sometimes must change the CONFIG.SYS configuration file or the AUTOEXEC.BAT startup file on your hard disk. Some programs append instructions to the existing files, whereas others may actually delete files without asking you and write new ones in their place. If an old program stops working just after you install a program, the newly installed program may be the offender. Make a copy of both files before installing new programs in case the new program deletes the originals or modifies them so that they no longer work. See* CONFIG.SYS *and* AUTOEXEC.BAT.

Institute of Electrical and Electronic Engineers (IEEE)   *eye-trip-ul-ee*   A membership organization of engineers, scientists, and students. IEEE has also declared standards for computers and communications. Of particular interest is the IEEE 802 standard for local area networks, although the IEEE drew up a complete set of specifications for the AT bus, also called the *ISA bus.* See *AT bus, IEEE 802 standards,* and *Industry Standard Architecture (ISA).*

instruction   In computer programming, a program statement interpreted or compiled into machine language that the computer can understand and execute.

instruction cycle   The time it takes a central processing unit (CPU) to carry out one instruction and move on to the next.

instruction set   A list of keywords describing all the actions or operations that a central processing unit (CPU) can perform. See *complex instruction set computer (CISC)* and *reduced instruction set computer (RISC).*

integer   A whole number. If the number contains decimal places, the numbers to the left of the decimal point are the integer portion of the number.

integrated accounting package   An accounting program that includes all the major accounting functions: general ledger, accounts payable, accounts receivable, payroll, and inventory. Integrated programs update the general ledger every time an accounts payable or accounts receivable transaction occurs.

integrated circuit   A semiconductor circuit that contains more than one transistor and other electronic components. Synonymous with *chip*.

Integrated Drive Electronics (IDE)   A hard disk interface standard for 80286, 80386, 80486, and Pentium computers that offers high performance at low cost. The IDE standard transfers most of the controller electronics to the hard disk mechanism. For this reason, the IDE interface can be contained on the computer's motherboard; no controller card or expansion slot is necessary. See *controller card, hard disk interface,* and *IDE drive.*

integrated program   A program that combines two or more software functions, such as word processing and database management. Microsoft Works for DOS or Windows and ClarisWorks for Macintosh are examples of integrated programs.

Intel 8086   A microprocessor introduced in 1978 with a full 16-bit data bus structure (now obsolete).

The 8086 wasn't chosen for the first IBM Personal Computer, which used the slower 8088, because of the high cost of 16-bit peripherals and microprocessor support chips. By the time such peripherals became available at low prices, Intel had developed the Intel 80286 microprocessor.

Few personal computers, therefore, have used the 8086 chip. One exception is the use of the 8086 for the unsuccessful lower-end models of the PS/2 line, such as the Model 25. See *Intel 8088* and *Intel 80286.*

Intel 8088   A microprocessor introduced in 1978 with an 8-bit external data bus and an internal 16-bit data bus structure that operated at 4.77 MHz (now obsolete). The Intel 8088 could address up to 1M of random-access memory and was used in the original IBM Personal Computer.

This design compromise of the 8-bit external data bus and 16-bit internal data bus was deliberate. Intel designers wanted to introduce 16-bit microprocessor technology but take advantage of the inexpensive 8-bit peripherals (such as disk drives) and 8-bit microprocessor support chips.

Later versions of the chip have pushed its clock speed to approximately 10 MHz; such chips power computers known as Turbo XTs. See *Intel 8086.*

Intel 80286   A microprocessor introduced in 1984 with a 16-bit data bus structure and the capability to address up to 16M (megabytes) of random-access memory (RAM).

The Intel 80286 (now obsolete) powered the high-performance IBM Personal Computer AT. The 80286 offered increased clock speeds, eventually up to 20 MHz, but even the first 80286 AT achieved throughput about five times faster than an 8086.

Operating in real mode, the chip runs DOS programs in an 8086 emulation mode and can't use more than 1M of RAM (under DOS, the limit is 640K). The 80286 also runs in protected mode, where it can use up to 16M. However, DOS can't take advantage of this mode without the assistance of a memory-management program such as Microsoft Windows, which can run in Standard mode on an 80286. See *Standard mode* and *throughput.*

Intel 80287/Intel 80387/Intel 80487SX   Numeric coprocessors designed to work (respectively) with the 80286, 80386, and 80486. See *numeric coprocessor* and *Weitek coprocessors.*

Intel 80386DX   A microprocessor introduced in 1986 with a 32-bit data bus structure and capable of addressing up to 4 gigabytes of main memory directly.

The Intel 80386 represented a revolutionary advance over its predecessors. Not only did the chip introduce a full 32-bit data bus structure to IBM PC-compatible computing, the 80386 also brought
technical advances such as a much-improved memory architecture.

The 80386 includes a mode that allows the operating system to
divide memory into separate blocks of 640K so that DOS applications can run concurrently. You can, for example, run Lotus 1-2-3
and WordPerfect at the same time. To use this mode, however,
you need special software such as Quarterdeck Office Systems
DESQview or Microsoft Windows. See *Microsoft Windows.*

Intel 80386SL   A microprocessor based on the 80386DX chip
and designed with special power management circuitry, making it
ideal for low-power operation in portable computers such as laptops.

Intel 80386SX   A microprocessor introduced in 1988 with all
the electronic characteristics of the Intel 80386 32-bit microprocessor, except that it uses a 16-bit external data bus structure that allows
it to use the inexpensive peripherals developed for the Intel 80286.

Intel 80486DX   A microprocessor introduced in 1989 with a
full 32-bit data bus structure that can address 64 gigabytes of main
memory directly. The Intel 80486DX includes an 8K internal
cache to help avoid waiting for data to be delivered from memory.

Packing more than 1 million transistors into one tiny silicon chip,
the 80486 also incorporates the formerly separate numeric
coprocessor. A special hardware design, called a *pipeline,* allows the
80486 processor to execute an instruction in just one clock cycle,
or *tick*. For this reason, it's significantly faster than the 80386,
which requires two or more clock cycles to execute an instruction.
See *clock speed* and *Intel DX2 OverDrive.*

> **TIP:** *If you plan to use Microsoft Windows, choose a system
> based on the Intel 80486 microprocessor. Although Windows
> runs on an 80386, current versions of Windows applications
> are so demanding that they need 80486 speed to give you ad-
> equate performance.*

Intel 80486DX2   A microprocessor introduced early in 1992 that
runs instructions internally at twice the system speed. The 50 MHz
chip is a clock-doubled 25 MHz; the 66 MHz is a clock-doubled
33 MHz chip. The DX2 microprocessor is factory-installed. For
upgrading existing systems, the DX2 technology is available only
as the OverDrive chip.

Intel 80486DX4   An 80486DX microprocessor introduced
in 1993 with clock speeds of 75 MHz and 100 MHz, with an
85 MHz version expected to be released later in 1994. The design
uses clock-multiplying technology to allow the processor to run
three times faster than the system speed of a 25 MHz and 33 MHz
system. Also, the processor has a 16K internal cache to help speed
delivery of data from slower memory to this high-speed processor.

Intel 80486SL   A microprocessor based on the 80486DX chip
and designed with special power management circuitry, making it
ideal for low-power operation in portable computers such as laptops.

Intel 80486SX   A version of the 80486DX microprocessor,
introduced in 1990, with 300,000 fewer transistors and a disabled
numeric coprocessor. The 80486SX retains the full 32-bit data
bus structure of the 80486DX and therefore isn't comparable to
the 80386SX, which has a 16-bit external data bus structure—
a significant design compromise. You should choose the
80486DX, however, if your work commonly involves extensive
spreadsheet recalculations or statistical analysis.

> **TIP:** *An Intel 80486SX2 is also available. Similar to a DX2,
> the 486SX2/50 MHz is a clock-doubled 25 MHz chip.*

Intel 82385/82485   A cache controller chip that governs
external cache memory in personal computers using the Intel
80386 and 80486 microprocessors respectively. More recent versions of the 80486, including specifically the 80486DX2, use the
Intel 82495DX/82490DX chip. The Pentium uses the 82496/
82491 cache controller chip. See *cache controller* and *cache memory*.

Intel DX2 OverDrive   A user-installed processor upgrade designed to work with Intel 486 microprocessors. The OverDrive chip can be added to almost double the microprocessor's internal processing speed. The chip is available for 486SX/20, 25, and 33 systems, and 486DX/25 and 33 MHz systems. See *Intel 80486DX2, Intel 80486SX, Intel Pentium, microprocessor,* and *Zero Insertion Force (ZIF) socket.*

Intel P6   The "what's next?" in the ongoing development of ever-faster microprocessors, planned for release in 1995. (The Pentium was called P5 during its early development.) The P6 is expected to have 6+ million transistors and process at 250 MIPS (million instructions per second), executing more than two instructions per clock cycle. We'll see... See *Intel Pentium* and *million instructions per second (MIPS).*

Intel Pentium   The latest Intel microprocessor, the successor to the 80486. With more than 3 million transistors and two pipelines, the Pentium processes twice as many instructions as an 80486DX2 microprocessor. The design includes an 8K internal cache for data and another one for instructions, each using a more efficient write-back design. Improvements in the chip's mathematical processing circuitry offer performance gains of up to five times (compared to the fastest 486DX2 microprocessors) for math-intensive applications.

Intel Pentium OverDrive   A user-installed processor upgrade designed to work with Intel 80486SX and DX systems that have an OverDrive socket installed on the motherboard. A number of manufacturers are offering what they call Pentium OverDrive-upgradable 486 computers. The OverDrive chip doubles the processor's internal processing speed. OverDrive chips for Pentium systems are under development, and release is expected in the fall of 1994. See *Intel 80486DX2, Intel 80486SX, Intel Pentium, microprocessor,* and *Zero Insertion Force (ZIF) socket.*

interactive processing   A method of using the computer that displays the computer's operations on a monitor so that the user can catch and correct errors before the processing operation is completed.

Certain features of today's programs, however, recall the days when computer operations were performed in batches, invisible to the user. Word processing programs, for example, sometimes require you to embed formatting commands into the text without showing you their effects directly on-screen. See *batch processing*.

interactive videodisk   A computer-assisted instruction (CAI) technology that uses a computer to provide access to up to two hours of video information stored on a videodisk.

Like CD-ROM, videodisks are read-only optical storage media, but are designed for the storage and random-access retrieval of images, including stills and continuous video. You need a front-end program to access the videodisk information. With a videodisk of paintings in the National Gallery of Art, the user can demand, "Show me all the Renaissance paintings that depict flowers or gardens," and be led through a series of vivid instructional experiences while retaining complete control. See *computer-assisted instruction (CAI)*.

Inter-Application Communication (IAC)   In the Macintosh System 7, a specification for creating hot links and cold links between applications. See *cold link*, *hot link*, and *System 7*.

interface   The connection between two hardware devices, between two applications, or between a user and application programs that helps the reliable exchange of data.

interface standard   A set of specifications for the connection between the two hardware devices, such as the drive controller and the drive electronics in a hard disk. Common hard disk interface standards in personal computing include ST506, ESDI, and SCSI. Other standards exist for connections with serial and parallel ports, such as the Centronics interface. See *Centronics interface, Enhanced System Device Interface (ESDI), Small Computer System Interface (SCSI),* and *ST-506/ST-412*.

interlacing   A video monitor display technology that uses the monitor's electron gun to paint every other line of the screen with the first pass and the remaining lines on the second pass. When most of the screen display is a solid, light-color background, the eye perceives the alternating painted and fading lines as a slight flicker or shimmer. This technique provides higher resolution, but at the price of visual comfort.

TIP: *When you buy a monitor, make sure it's a non-interlaced monitor. See* non-interlaced monitor.

G
H
I

interleaved memory   A method of speeding the retrieval of data from dynamic random-access memory (DRAM) chips by dividing all the RAM into two or four large banks; sequential bits of data are stored in alternating banks. The microprocessor reads one bank while the other is being refreshed. Naturally, this memory arrangement doesn't improve speed when the CPU requests non-sequential bits of data. See *random-access memory (RAM)* and *dynamic random-access memory (DRAM)*.

interleave factor   The ratio of physical disk sectors on a hard disk that are skipped for every sector actually used for write operations.

With an interleave factor of 6:1, a disk writes to a sector, skips six sectors, writes to a sector, and so on. The computer figures out what it needs next and sends the request to the hard drive while the disk is skipping sectors. 80386SX and higher computers operate faster than hard disks, so a 1:1 interleave is standard today.

The interleave factor is set by the hard disk manufacturer but can be changed by software capable of performing a low-level format. Synonymous with *sector interleave*.

internal cache   *cash*   An 8K holding area for data included as part of the 80486 and Pentium microprocessor chip design. Synonymous with *primary cache*.

The cache included on the 486 chip uses a set-associative write-through design, while the two caches on the Pentium chip use a more efficient set-associative write-back scheme. Although small, these caches can achieve an excellent "hit" rate—that is, the number of times the data requested next is found in the cache.

To further improve performance, the cache feeds requested data directly to a pipeline designed to optimize delivery to the processing area. Part of the reason for the faster performance of the Pentium microprocessor is its use of two caches: one to handle data and the other for instructions. Each cache has its own direct pipeline. See *cache memory, Intel 80486DX, Intel Pentium, pipeline, set-associative, write-back*, and *write-through*.

internal command In DOS, a command such as DIR or COPY that's part of COMMAND.COM, and therefore is in memory and available whenever the DOS prompt is visible on-screen. See *external command*.

internal font See *printer font*.

internal hard disk A hard disk designed to fit within a computer's case and use the computer's power supply.

TIP: *Because internal hard disks don't require their own power supply, case, or cables, they generally cost less than external hard disks of comparable quality.*

internal modem A modem designed to fit into the expansion bus of a personal computer. See *expansion bus, external modem*, and *modem*.

Internet A system of linked computer networks, worldwide in scope, that facilitates data communication services such as remote login, file transfer, electronic mail, and newsgroups.

The Internet is a way of connecting existing computer networks that greatly extends the reach of each participating system. Its origins lie in a U.S. Department of Defense computer system called ARPAnet, an experimental network designed in 1969 to facilitate scientific collaboration in military research. ARPAnet featured a unique peer-to-peer communications philosophy where each computer in the system is fully capable of addressing any other computer.

Any computer network based on the ARPAnet design is best described as a collection of autonomous, local, and self-governing computing centers that are linked in a form of regulated anarchy. Motivating ARPAnet's design was a purely military need: The network had to be capable of withstanding an attack that could knock out huge chunks of it. The concept works well, as the United States and its allies learned in the Gulf War. Iraq's command and control network, modeled on ARPAnet technology, successfully resisted allied efforts to bring it down. That's why ARPAnet-derived technology is now on the export "No-No" list.

The Internet was originally designed to serve educational institutions, yet its technology allows virtually any system to link to it via an electronic gateway. In this way, thousands of corporate computer systems, as well as for-profit electronic mail systems such as MCI and CompuServe, have become part of the Internet. With more than 2 million host computers serving an estimated 20 million users, the Internet is exploding at the rate of a million new users each month.

TIP: *Almost anyone can gain access to the Internet. If you're a student or faculty member, ask your campus computing center how to access the Internet. Many large- and medium-sized corporations with electronic mail systems have Internet gateways. Increasingly, for-profit electronic mail services (such as CompuServe and MCI) offer Internet gateways, as do some local bulletin-board systems (BBSs). In some areas, free-nets provide Internet gateways at no charge.*

See *America Online, anonymous FTP, archie, ARPAnet, BITNET, BIX, Delphi, distributed bulletin board, electronic mail, FAQ, Fidonet, file transfer protocol (FTP), freenet, gateway, Gopher, host, MUD, net.god(dess), netiquette, NSFNet, packet-switching network, protocol, telnet, Transfer Control Protocol/Internet Protocol (TCP/IP), unmoderated newsgroup, USENET, Wide Area Information Server (WAIS), World-Wide Web (WWW),* and *wide area network.*

interpreter   A translator for a high-level programming language that translates and runs the program at the same time. Interpreters are excellent for learning how to program, because if an error occurs, the interpreter shows you the likely place (and sometimes even the cause) of the error. You can correct the problem immediately and execute the program again, learning interactively how to create a successful program. See *compiler*.

interprocess communication (IPC)   In a multitasking computing environment such as Microsoft Windows running in the 386 Enhanced mode, the communication of data or commands from one program to another while both are running, made possible by dynamic data exchange (DDE) specifications. In Microsoft Excel, for instance, you can write a DDE command that accesses changing data, such as stock prices, that's being received on-line in a communications program. See *dynamic data exchange (DDE)*.

interrupt   A signal to the microprocessor indicating that an event has occurred that requires the processor's attention. Processing is halted momentarily so that input/output or other operations can take place. When the operation is finished, processing resumes.

interrupt request (IRQ) lines   For IBM PC-compatible computers, the hardware lines over which peripherals (such as printers or modems) can get the attention of the microprocessor when the device is ready to send or receive data.

invisible file   See *hidden file*.

I/O   See *input/output (I/O) system*.

IPC   See *interprocess communication (IPC)*.

IRQ   See *interrupt request (IRQ) lines*.

italic   A typeface characteristic, commonly used for emphasis, in which the characters slant to the right. Two words in the following sentence are in italic. See *oblique* and *Roman*.

iteration   The repetition of a command or program statement. See *loop*.

jaggies See *aliasing*.

job A unit of work to be performed by the computer, especially one that doesn't require human intervention, such as a print job. This term originates from the world of mainframe data processing, in which an end user doesn't directly use the computer but submits a request that the data processing staff will carry out, much as one requests a print job from the printing department.

job control language (JCL) In mainframe computing, a programming language that allows programmers to specify batch processing instructions, which the computer then carries out. The abbreviation JCL refers to the job control language used in IBM mainframes. See *batch processing*.

job queue *cue* A series of tasks automatically executed, one after the other, by the computer.

In mainframe data processing during the 1950s and 1960s, the job queue was literally a queue, or waiting line. With interactive, multiuser computing and personal computing, you usually don't need to line up to get your work done (although jobs can still back up at a busy printer). The term is still used in WordPerfect, for example, where you can assign a job number to several files you want to print, and the program prints the files in the order you assign.

join In a relational database management program, a data retrieval operation in which a new data table is built from data in two or more existing data tables.

To understand how a join works and why join operations are desirable in database applications, suppose that for your video store you create a database table called RENTALS that lists the rented tapes with the phone number of the person renting the tape and the due date. You create another database table, called CUSTOMERS, in which you list the phone number, name, and credit card number of all your customers. To find out whether any customers are more than two weeks late returning a tape, you need to join information from the two databases. Suppose that you want to know the title and due date of the movie and the phone number and name of the customer. The following Structured Query Language (SQL) command retrieves the information:

```
SELECT TITLE, DUE_DATE, PHONE_NO, L_NAME, F_NAME
FROM RENTALS, CUSTOMERS
WHERE DUE_DATE=<05/07/92
```

This command tells the program to display the information contained in the data fields TITLE, DUE_DATE, PHONE_NO, L_NAME, and F_NAME, but only for those records in which the data field DUE_DATE contains a date equal to or earlier than May 7, 1992. The result is the following display:

TITLE	DUE_DATE	PHONE_NO	L_NAME	F_NAME
Alien Beings	05/07/92	499-1234	Jones	Terry
Almost Home	05/05/92	499-7890	Smith	Jake

See *join condition.*

join condition   In a relational database management program, a statement of how two databases are to be joined together to form a single table. The statement usually specifies a field common to both databases as the condition for joining records. See *join* and *relational database management.*

joystick   A control device widely used, as an alternative to the keyboard, for computer games and some professional applications, such as computer-aided design.

JPEG   Acronym for *Joint Photographic Experts Group,* but commonly used to refer to a lossy compression technique that can reduce the size of a graphics file by as much as 96 percent. The data compression technique results in the smoothing of the image and loss of detail, which can be apparent in some images. See *lossy compression.*

j

jumper   An electrical connector that allows the user to select a particular configuration on a circuit board. The jumper is a small rectangle of plastic with two or three receptacles. You install a jumper by pushing it down on two or more pins from a selection of many that are sticking up from the circuit board's surface. The placement of the jumper completes the electronic circuit for the configuration you want to use.

jump line   A message at the end of part of an article in a news-letter, magazine, or newspaper, indicating the page on which the article is continued. Page layout programs include features that make using jump lines for newsletters easier.

justification   The alignment of multiple lines of text along the left margin, the right margin, or both margins. The term *justification* often is used to refer to full justification, or the alignment of text along both margins. See *color*.

J
K
L

CAUTION: *When using a monospaced font, programs justify both margins by placing extra spaces between words, creating an uneven appearance. Proportional spaced fonts can have space added be-tween letters as well as words to create a more even appearance. Regardless, research has shown that text formatted with a ragged right margin is easier to read than fully justified text.*

K   Abbreviation for *kilobyte* (1,024 bytes).

KB   Alternative abbreviation for *kilobyte* (1,024 bytes).

Kermit   An asynchronous communications protocol that makes the error-free transmission of program files via the telephone system easier. Developed by Columbia University and placed in the public domain, Kermit is used by academic institutions because, unlike XMODEM, Kermit can be implemented on mainframe systems that transmit 7 bits per byte. See *asynchronous communication*, *communications protocol*, and *XMODEM*.

kernel   In an operating system, the core portions of the program that reside in memory and perform the most essential operating system tasks, such as handling disk input and output operations and managing the internal memory.

kerning   The adjustment of space between certain pairs of characters in display type, so that the characters print in an aesthetically pleasing manner.

Kerning is used for the body type in this book. The underlined pairs of characters in the next paragraph illustrate the use of kerning to decrease the space between the character pairs.

Some page layout programs include an automatic kerning feature, relying on a built-in database of letter pairs that require kerning (such as AV, VA, WA, YA, and so on). Manual kerning is possible with most page layout and some word processing programs (see fig. K.1).

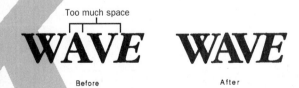

Fig. K.1   *Kerning with PageMaker.*

key assignments   The functions given to specific keys by
a computer program. Most of the keys on a personal computer
keyboard are fully programmable, meaning that a programmer can
use them in different ways. The best programs, however, stick to
standards in key assignments. See *industry standard user interface.*

keyboard   The most frequently used input device for all
computers. The keyboard provides a set of alphabetic, numeric,
punctuation, symbol, and control keys. When a character key is
pressed, a coded input signal is sent to the computer, which echoes
the signal by displaying a character on-screen. See *autorepeat key,
keyboard layout,* and *toggle key.*

keyboard buffer   A small area of primary storage set aside to
hold the codes of the last keystrokes you pressed on the keyboard
so that the computer can continue to accept your typing when the
computer is busy with other tasks.

keyboard layout   The arrangement of keys on the computer's
keyboard. A PC's keyboard layout uses the standard QWERTY
layout that typewriters have used for a century. However, three
different standards are used for arranging special computer keys
such as Control and Alt.

Early IBM Personal Computers used a standard 83-key layout that
attracted a good deal of criticism because of the placement of the
backslash key, the small Enter key, and the lack of lights for toggle
keys such as Scroll Lock, Num Lock, and Caps Lock (see fig. K.2).

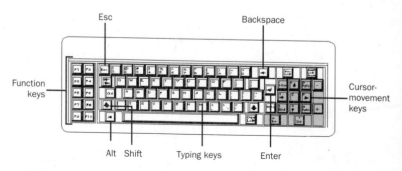

Fig. K.2   *The original PC keyboard.*

IBM introduced a new 84-key layout with the release of the IBM Personal Computer AT (see fig. K.3). The AT keyboard uses the standard Selectric typewriter key layout for the typing area, with indicator lights for Scroll Lock, Num Lock, and Caps Lock. The new 84th key, called Sys Rq, is used only when you're running an operating system other than MS-DOS.

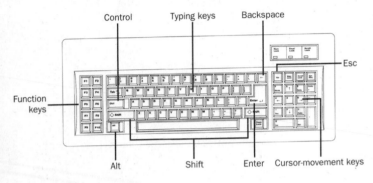

Fig. K.3 *The AT keyboard.*

The latest standard is an enhanced, 101-key layout (see fig. K.4). The 12 function keys (instead of 10) are lined up above the number keys, out of the reach of a normal hand position. The 101-key layout also has a separate cursor-control keypad.

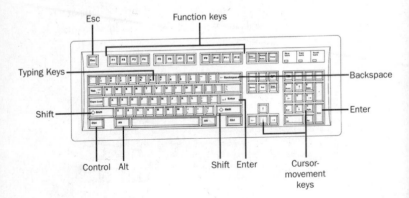

Fig. K.4 *The enhanced keyboard.*

The 101-key standard includes a relocated Control key at the lower left, requiring a contorted movement to reach it. Formerly, Control was situated left of the A key, within easy reach of your left pinkie. Many IBM PC-compatible computers use a corrected 101-key layout that places the Control key back beside the A key. See *Dvorak keyboard*.

TIP: *Fast typists should make sure that the keyboard has N-key rollover, enabling you to press an additional key even while the previous key is still engaged at the end of a stroke. To find out whether a keyboard has N-key rollover, hold down the A key and press S D F in rapid succession. You may see several a characters, but you also should see the s, d, and f.*

keyboard template   A plastic card or strip with an adhesive backing that you can press on the keyboard to explain the way a program configures the keyboard. Many applications provide keyboard templates, which are helpful when you're learning the program.

key disk   A computer software protection scheme that requires the user to insert a specially encoded floppy disk before the program will start. This is intended to prevent the recipients of illegal copies of the program from running the program on their machines.

Be wary of any program that uses a key disk copy-protection scheme. This method of preventing software penalizes legitimate users. If the disk becomes unusable for any reason (and floppy disks fail frequently), the owner of the program won't be able to use the program until a duplicate copy of the key disk is obtained from the software publisher—and that may take weeks.

key status indicator   An on-screen status message displayed by many application programs that informs you which, if any, toggle keys are active on the keyboard.

keystroke   The physical action of pressing down a key on the keyboard so that a character is entered or a command is initiated.

**J
K
L**

keystroke buffer A holding area in memory that's used to save your current keystrokes if you type something while the processor is busy with something else. If, for example, you begin typing while a file is being saved, the characters you type are placed in the keystroke buffer. When it's full (usually the buffer holds 20 characters), you'll hear a beep each time you press another key, indicating that your input isn't being accepted. When the processor completes its task, the characters in the buffer are sent to the screen.

key variable In a spreadsheet program, a constant placed in a cell and referenced throughout the spreadsheet using absolute cell references.

TIP: *The use of key variables is essential to good spreadsheet design. If you place a key variable, such as a tax or commission rate, in one cell and refer to the cell when its contents are needed in formulas, you need to make only one change if the rate changes. If you place the constant in all the formulas, you must change every formula to update your spreadsheet.*

keyword In programming languages (including software command languages), a word describing an action or operation that the computer can recognize and execute.

In a document summary, one or more words you can include to help you search for document summaries containing a specific word or phrase. Keywords can be used to indicate the subject of a document that doesn't contain the specific work within the document. An example might be a letter inquiring about green PCs and a keyword might be *environment*. See *green PC* and *query*.

kill file In a computer newsgroup, a file that contains a list of subjects or names that you don't want to appear on the list of messages available for you to read. If you no longer want to read messages from Edward P. Jerk, you can add this person's name to the kill file, and his contributions will be discarded automatically before they reach your screen.

k

Use kill files rather than post a complaint if you find certain topics that offend you. That way, you'll avoid being the recipient of vociferously worded replies that accuse you of ignorance, censorship, and worse, plus you won't see messages about this topic again. See *flame war*, *newsgroup*, and *USENET*.

kilo-   A prefix indicating one thousand (10^3).

kilobit   1,024 bits of information. See *kilobyte (K)*.

kilobyte (K)   The basic unit of measurement for computer memory and disk capacity, equal to 1,024 bytes. The prefix *kilo-* suggests 1,000, but the computer world contains twos, not tens: $2^{10} = 1,024$. Because one byte is the same as one character in personal computing, 1K of data can contain 1,024 characters (letters, numbers, or punctuation marks).

kludge   *klooj*   An improvised, technically inelegant solution to a problem, often a computer system assembled with poorly matched components.

knowbot   A program that searches through a network to locate specific information.

knowledge acquisition   In expert system programming, the process of acquiring and systematizing knowledge from experts. A major limitation of current expert system technology is that knowledge must be acquired by engineers and, in a slow and painstaking process, systematized so that the knowledge can be expressed in the form of computer-readable rules. See *expert system*, *knowledge engineer*, and *knowledge representation*.

knowledge base   In an expert system, the portion of the program that includes an expert's knowledge, often in IF/THEN rules (such as "If the tank pressure exceeds 600 pounds per square inch, then sound a warning").

J
K
L

knowledge domain   In artificial intelligence, an area of problem-solving expertise. Current artificial intelligence technology works well only in sharply limited knowledge domains, such as the configuration of one manufacturer's computer systems, the repair of a specific robotic system, or investment analysis for a limited range of securities. See *artificial intelligence (AI)*.

knowledge engineer   In expert system programming, a specialist who obtains the knowledge possessed by experts on a subject and expresses this knowledge in a form that an expert system can use. See *expert system* and *knowledge domain*.

knowledge representation   In expert system programming, the method used to encode and store the knowledge in a knowledge base.

Although several alternative knowledge representation schemes are used, most commercially available expert systems use the production system approach in which knowledge is represented in the form of production rules, which have the following form:

> UL>IF {condition} THEN {action}

A given rule may have multiple conditions as in the following example:

> IF {a person's intraocular pressure is raised}
> AND {the person has pain in the left quadratic region}
> THEN {immediate hospitalization is indicated}

label   In a spreadsheet program, text entered in a cell. In DOS batch files, a string of characters preceded by a colon that marks the destination of a GOTO command. See *value*.

label alignment   In a spreadsheet program, the way labels are aligned in a cell (flush left, centered, flush right, or repeating across the cell). Unless you specify otherwise, labels are aligned on the left of the cell. See *label* and *label prefix*.

label prefix   In most spreadsheet programs, a punctuation mark at the beginning of a cell entry that tells the program that the entry is a label and specifies how the program should align the label within the cell.

Programs that use prefixes enter the default label prefix—usually an apostrophe (')—when the cell entry begins with a letter. You can control the alignment of a label as you type it by beginning the label with one of these prefixes:

Label Prefix	Alignment
'	Flush left
^	Centered
"	Flush right
\	Repeating across the cell

J
K
L

➜ **TIP:** *If you begin a cell entry with a number, the program interprets the number as a value rather than a label; however, you can make a number into a label by starting the entry with a label prefix. In Lotus 1-2-3, for example, if you type '1991, the program interprets the entry as a label and formats the label flush left. See* label alignment.

label printer A printer designed specifically to print names and addresses on continuous labels.

LAN See *local area network (LAN)*.

LAN-aware program A version of an application program specifically modified so that the program can function in a network environment.

Network versions of transactional application programs—such as database management programs—create and maintain shared files. An invoice-processing program, for example, has access to a database of accounts receivable. The network versions of non-transactional programs—such as word processing programs—include file security features to prevent unauthorized users from gaining access to your documents. See *concurrency control, file locking, file server, LAN-ignorant program, local area network (LAN), non-transactional application,* and *transactional application.*

LAN backup program A program designed specifically to back up the programs and data stored on a local area network's file server. The best LAN backup programs automatically back up the file server at scheduled times, without user intervention.

landscape orientation The rotation of a page layout so that text and/or graphics are printed sideways on the paper. See *portrait orientation.*

LAN-ignorant program An application program designed for use only as a stand-alone program and that contains no provisions for use on a network (such as file locking and concurrency control). See *concurrency control.*

LAN memory management program A utility program designed specifically to free conventional memory so that you can run applications on a network workstation. Every workstation must run the network software, which can consume as much as 100K of conventional memory. As a result, workstations may not be capable of running certain memory-hungry applications. LAN memory managers move the network software—as well as device drivers, terminate-and-stay-resident (TSR) programs, and other utilities—into the upper memory area, extended memory, or expanded memory. A popular and well-rated LAN management program is NetRoom by Helix Software. See *conventional memory, device driver, expanded memory (EMS), extended memory, local area network (LAN), network operating system (NOS),* and *terminate-and-stay-resident (TSR) program.*

LAN server   See *file server* and *print server.*

laptop computer   A small, portable computer that's light and small enough to hold on your lap. The smallest laptop computers, which weigh less than 6 pounds and can fit in a briefcase, are called *notebook computers.*

A laptop can't be expanded or modified easily should your computing needs change. Also, the display is inferior to standard VGA displays, although color-active matrix displays compete well except for size. The limitations of laptop computers argue against buying one as a main system, especially when you consider that laptops are generally more expensive than desktop computers. However, many people have legitimate needs for a portable computer and find a 486 50 MHz laptop with 8M of RAM, a 200M hard drive, and a fax modem an excellent choice for their only computer. See *active matrix display, docking station,* and *notebook computer.*

large-scale integration (LSI)   In integrated circuit technology, placing up to 100,000 transistors on a single chip. See *very large scale integration (VLSI).*

laser font   See *outline font.*

laser printer   A high-resolution printer that uses a version of the electrostatic reproduction technology of copying machines to fuse text and graphic images to the page.

Although laser printers are complex machines, understanding how they work isn't difficult. The printer's controller circuitry receives the printing instructions from the computer and builds a bit map of every dot on a page (about 1M of memory is required to ensure adequate storage space for graphic images). The controller ensures that the print engine's laser transfers a precise replica of this bit map to a photostatically sensitive drum or belt. Switching on and off rapidly, the beam travels across the drum, and as the beam moves, the drum charges the areas exposed to the beam. The charged areas attract toner (electrically charged ink) as the drum rotates past the toner cartridge.

In a write-black engine, the beam charges the printed areas with a positive charge that attracts toner, resulting in better image detail. In a write-white engine, the beam charges the areas not printed, giving the areas a negative charge that repels toner, resulting in a denser image. An electrically charged wire pulls the toner from the drum onto the paper, and heat rollers fuse the toner to the paper. A second electrically charged wire neutralizes the drum's electrical charge. See *light-emitting diode (LED) printer*, *print engine*, and *resolution*.

latency   In disk drives, the delay while the disk rotates until the desired data is under the read/write head.

launch   To start a program.

layer   In some illustration and page-layout applications, an on-screen sheet on which you can place text or graphics so that they're independent of any text or graphics on other sheets. The layer can be opaque or transparent.

In SuperPaint, for example, you can create illustrations on two layers: a paint layer for bit-mapped graphics and a draw layer for object-oriented graphics. In FreeHand, you can draw or paint on up to 200 transparent layers. Commands typically named Bring to Front or Send to Back allow you to bring a background layer forward so that you can edit that layer.

layout   In desktop publishing and word processing, the process of arranging text and graphics on a page. In database management systems, the arrangement of report elements, such as headers and fields, on a printed page.

LCD   See *liquid crystal display (LCD)*.

LCD printer See *liquid crystal display (LCD) printer*.

leader In word processing, a row of dots or dashes that provides a path for the eye to follow across the page. Leaders often are used in tables of contents to lead the reader's eye from the entry to the page number. Most word processing programs let you define tab stops that insert leaders when you press the Tab key.

leading *leh-ding* The space between lines of type, measured from baseline to baseline. Synonymous with *line spacing*. The term originated from letterpress-printing technology, in which lead strips were inserted between lines of type to add spacing between lines.

leading zero The zeros added in front of numeric values so that a number fills up all required spaces in a data field. For example, three leading zeros are in the number 00098.54.

LED See *light-emitting diode (LED)*.

LED printer See *light-emitting diode (LED) printer*.

left justification Synonymous with *ragged-right alignment*. See *justification*.

legend In presentation graphics, an area of a chart or graph that explains what data is being represented by the colors or patterns used in the chart.

letter-quality printer An impact printer that offers the fully formed text characters produced by a high-quality office typewriter.

As with office typewriter technology, many letter-quality printers use daisywheels or similar printing mechanisms. A major drawback of these mechanisms is that they can't print graphics. This fact ensures a brisk market for dot-matrix printers that, despite their poorer quality for text output, can print charts and graphs. With the arrival of laser printers, the market for letter-quality printers has all but disappeared. See *impact printer*.

CAUTION: *If you plan to buy a letter-quality printer, make sure that your software includes a printer driver for the specific brand and model you're buying. Alternatively, check the printer manual to determine whether the printer can emulate a printer, usually a Diablo or Qume, that your software supports. Many letter-quality printers also recognize the Epson or IBM commands, but others don't.*

library   A collection of programs kept with a computer system and made available for processing purposes. The term often refers to a collection of library routines written in a given programming language such as C or Pascal. See *library routine.*

library routine   In programming, a well-tested subroutine, procedure, or function in a given programming language. The library routine handles tasks that all or most programs need, such as reading data from disks. The programmer can draw on this library to develop programs quickly.

ligature   In typography, two or more characters designed and cast as a distinct unit for aesthetic reasons, such as æ.

Five letter combinations beginning with f (fi, ff, fl, ffi, and ffl) and two diphthongs (æ and œ) commonly are printed as ligatures. Some outline fonts available for PostScript laser printers include ligatures for professional typesetting applications. See *outline font* and *PostScript laser printer.*

light-emitting diode (LED)   A small electronic device made from semiconductor materials. An LED emits light when current flows through it. LEDs are used for small indicator lights, but because they draw more power than liquid crystal displays (LCD), they rarely are used for computer displays.

light-emitting diode (LED) printer   A high-quality printer that closely resembles the laser printer in that it electrostatically fuses toner to paper; however, the light source is a matrix of light-emitting diodes. To create the image, the diodes flash on and off over the rotating print drum. See *laser printer* and *liquid crystal display (LCD) printer.*

light pen   An input device that uses a light-sensitive stylus so that you can draw on-screen, draw on a graphics tablet, or select items from menus.

LIM EMS   See *Lotus-Intel-Microsoft Expanded Memory Specification (LIM EMS)*.

line   In programming, one program statement. In data communications, a circuit that directly connects two or more electronic devices.

line adapter   In data communications, an electronic device that converts signals from one form to another so that you can transmit the signals. A modem is a line adapter that converts the computer's digital signals to analog equivalents so that they can be transmitted using standard telephone lines.

line art   In computer graphics, a drawing that doesn't contain halftones so that low- to medium-resolution printers can accurately reproduce the drawing. See *halftone*.

line chart   See *line graph*.

line editor   A primitive word processing utility that's often provided with an operating system as part of its programming environment. Unlike with a full-screen editor, you can write or edit only one line of program code at a time. See *full-screen editor* and *programming environment*.

> **TIP:** *Even if you're programming just for fun or for hobby purposes, obtain and use a full-screen editor.*

line feed   A signal that tells the printer when to start a new line. See *carriage return* and *Enter/Return*.

line graph   In presentation and analytical graphics, a graph that uses lines to show the variations of data over time or to show the relationship between two numeric variables (see fig. L.1). In general, the x-axis (categories) is aligned horizontally, and the y-axis (values) is aligned vertically. A line graph, however, may have two y-axes. See *bar graph*, *presentation graphics*, *x-axis*, and *y-axis*.

J
K
L

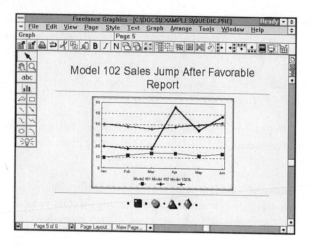

Fig. L.1 *A line graph.*

line spacing See *leading.*

link To establish a connection between two files or data items so that a change in one is reflected by a change in the second. A cold link requires user intervention and action, such as opening both files and using an updating command, to make sure that the change has occurred. A warm link occurs automatically. See *cold link* and *hot link.*

linked list See *list.*

linked object In object linking and embedding (OLE), a document or portion of a document (an object) created with one application that's inserted in a document created with another application.

Linking places a copy of the object, with hidden information about the source of the object, into the destination document. If you change the original document while the destination document is open, the object in the destination document is automatically updated. If the destination document isn't open, the object is updated the next time you open it. Object linking and embedding is possible only when you're using OLE-compatible applications on a Windows system, or on a Macintosh system running System 7. See *destination document, embedded object, object linking and embedding (OLE),* and *source document.*

> **TIP:** *To quickly edit a linked object, double-click the object. The computer automatically opens the application used to create the object. When you exit the source application, any changes you made appear in the object.*

linked pie/column chart See *linked pie/column graph.*

linked pie/column graph In presentation graphics, a pie graph paired with a column graph so that the column graph displays the internal distribution of data items in one slice of the pie (see fig. L.2).

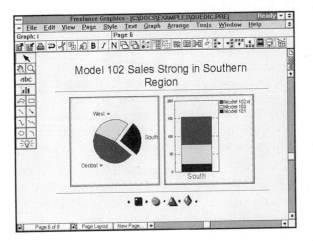

Fig. L.2 *A linked pie/column graph.*

For example, in an exploded pie graph emphasizing total sales for a region, the linked column graph could display a breakdown of the products sold in that region.

liquid crystal display (LCD) A low-power display technology used in laptop computers and small, battery-powered electronic devices such as meters, testing equipment, and digital watches. The display device uses rod-shaped crystal molecules that change their orientation when an electrical current flows through them.

LCD displays are flat and draw little power; therefore, they aren't bright enough for comfortable, sustained use. A compromise design uses a backlit screen that improves the LCD screen's readability and draws more power.

liquid crystal display (LCD) printer   A high-quality printer that closely resembles the laser printer in that it electro-statically fuses toner to paper; however, the light source is a matrix of liquid crystal shutters. The shutters open and close to create the pattern of light that falls on the print drum. See *laser printer* and *light-emitting diode (LED) printer*.

LISP   A high-level programming language, often used for artificial intelligence research, that makes no distinction between the program and the data. This language is considered ideal for manipulating text.

One of the oldest programming languages still in use, LISP (short for *list processing*) was developed by John McCarthy and his colleagues at the Massachusetts Institute of Technology in the early 1960s. LISP is a declarative language; the programmer composes lists that declare the relationships among symbolic values. Lists are the fundamental data structure of LISP, and the program performs computations on the symbolic values expressed in those lists.

In addition to its use in artificial intelligence research, LISP was used to write EMACS—a respected mainframe text editor that influenced the design and implementation of word processing packages such as WordPerfect and Sprint. Like other public do-main programming languages, however, a number of mutually unintelligible versions of LISP exist. A standardized, fully config-ured, and widely accepted version is Common LISP. See *declara-tive language* and *interpreter*.

list   In programming, a data structure that lists and links each data item with a pointer showing the item's physical location in a data-base. Using a list, a programmer can organize data in various ways without changing the physical location of the data. For example, the programmer can display a database so that it appears to be sorted in alphabetical order, even though the actual physical data records still are stored in the order in which they were entered.

live copy/paste   See *hot link*.

load   To transfer program instructions or data from a disk into the computer's random-access memory (RAM).

local area network (LAN)   Personal and other computers within a limited area that are linked by high-performance cables so that users can exchange information, share peripherals, and draw on programs and data stored in a dedicated computer called a *file server*.

Ranging tremendously in size and complexity, LANs may link only a few personal computers to an expensive, shared peripheral, such as a laser printer. More complex systems use central computers (file servers) and allow users to communicate with each other via electronic mail to share multiuser programs and to access shared databases. See *AppleTalk, baseband, broadband, bus network, EtherNet, file server, multiuser system, NetWare, network operating system (NOS), peer-to-peer network, ring network,* and *star network*.

local bus   A high-speed data path that directly links the computer's processing unit with one or more slots on the expansion bus. This direct link means the signals from an adapter (video or hard disk controller, for example) don't have to travel through the computer's expansion bus, which is significantly slower.

Expansion bus designs—such as the Industry Standard Architecture (ISA) bus, the Extended Industry Standard Architecture (EISA) bus, and IBM's proprietary Micro Channel Architecture (MCA) design)—all slow Windows down to an almost unacceptable level because redrawing the screen is held up while the video signals travel through the expansion bus. Although an Intel 80486 microprocessor can handle about 74M of data per second, the standard ISA expansion bus can move only 16M per second. A local bus design with circuits directly connected to the computer's processing unit can produce substantial performance gains. See *AT bus, Extended Industry Standard Architecture (EISA), Industry Standard Architecture (ISA), Micro Channel Architecture (MCA), Micro Channel Bus,* and *VL-Bus*.

J
K
L

➡ **TIP:** *If you're shopping for a system and planning to run Microsoft Windows, investigate systems that offer VESA-compatible local bus video cards. They outperform previous video adapters by a wide margin.*

local drive   In a local area network, a disk drive that's part of the workstation you are now using, as distinguished from a network drive (a drive made available to you through the network).

local echo   See *half duplex*.

local printer   In a local area network, a printer directly connected to the workstation you're using, as distinguished from a network printer (a printer made available to you through the network).

LocalTalk   The physical connectors and cables manufactured by Apple Computer for use in AppleTalk networks.

locked file   In a local area network, a file attribute that prevents applications or the user from updating or deleting the file.

logarithmic chart   See *logarithmic graph*.

logarithmic graph   In analytical and presentation graphics, a graph displayed with a y-axis (values) that increases exponentially in powers of 10.

On an ordinary y-axis, the 10 is followed by 20, 30, 40, and so on. On a logarithmic scale, however, 10 is followed by 100, 1,000, 10,000, and so on. This makes a logarithmic graph useful when great differences exist in the values of the data being graphed. In an ordinary graph, you can hardly see a data series or data item with small values (see fig. L.3); on a logarithmic chart, however, the small values show up much better (see fig. L.4). See *analytical graphics* and *presentation graphics*.

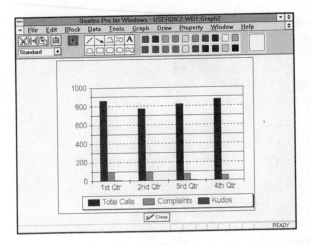

Fig. L.3 *A column graph with an ordinary y-axis.*

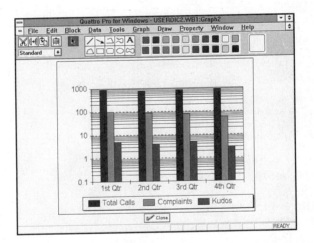

Fig. L.4 *A column graph with a logarithmic y-axis.*

logical Having the appearance of, and treated as, a real thing. The difference doesn't matter to the user. For example, a sheet of mailing labels is a page. Each label on the page is a logical page. See *logical drives* and *physical drive*.

logical drives   Sections of a hard drive that are formatted and assigned a drive letter, each of which is presented to the user as though it was a separate drive. Another way logical drives are created is by substituting a drive letter for a directory. Also, networks typically map directories to drive letters, resulting in logical drives. See *logical, partition,* and *physical drive.*

➜ **TIP:** *Partitioning a hard drive is no longer necessary. However, creating separate partitions allows you to install both DOS and OS/2 on your computer, each happily existing in its own partition.*

logical format   See *high-level format.*

logical operator   A symbol used to specify the logical relationship between two quantities or concepts. In query languages, the inclusive logical operator (OR) broadens the number of data records retrieved, and the exclusive logical operators (AND and NOT) restrict the number retrieved. Synonymous with *Boolean operator.*

Each of these queries illustrates the use of a logical operator and produces a different list of video tape titles:

```
The field RATING contains PG or PG-13.
The field CATEGORY contains Adventure and the field
RATING includes PG.
The field CATEGORY contains Adventure, but not the ones
in which the field RATING includes R.
```

logic board   See *motherboard.*

login name   In a computer network, a unique name assigned to you by the system administrator that's used as a means of initial identification. You must type this name, and also your password, to gain access to the system.

login security   In local area and mainframe networks, a validation process that requires you to type a password before gaining access to the system. See *local area network (LAN)* and *password protection.*

Logo   A high-level programming language well-suited to teaching fundamental programming concepts to children.

A special version of LISP, Logo was designed as an educational language to illustrate the concepts of recursion, extensibility, and other concepts of computing, without requiring math skills. The language also provides an environment in which children can develop their reasoning and problem-solving skills.

A key feature of Logo is *turtle graphics*, in which a graphic representation of a turtle creates images under program control. Program instructions tell the turtle to put down the pen and move forward, backward, left, or right. After the child succeeds in writing a program that defines a shape such as a rectangle, the program can be saved as a new command; this teaches the concept of extensibility. Through recursion, children can create and print geometric diagrams. See *LISP*.

log off   The process of terminating a connection with a computer system or peripheral device in an orderly way.

log on   The process of establishing a connection with, or gaining access to, a computer system or peripheral device.

In MS-DOS, *logging on* refers to the process of changing to another drive by typing the drive letter and a colon, and then pressing Enter. In computer networks, you may be required to type a security password to log on.

logon file   In a local area network, a batch file or configuration file that starts the network software and establishes the connection with the network when you turn on the workstation.

lookup function   A procedure in which the program consults stored data listed in a table or file.

lookup table   In a spreadsheet program, data entered in a range of cells and organized so that a lookup function can use the data—for example, to determine the correct tax rate based on annual income.

loop   In computer programming, a control structure in which a block of instructions repeats until a condition is fulfilled. See *control structure*, *DO/WHILE loop*, and *FOR/NEXT loop*.

J
K
L

lossless compression   A data compression technique that reduces the size of a file without sacrificing any original data; used by programs such as Stacker to compress all the program and document files on a hard disk. In lossless compression, the expanded or restored file is an exact replica of the original file before it was compressed. See *data-compression protocol* and *lossy compression*.

lossy compression   A data compression technique in which some data is deliberately discarded to achieve massive reductions in the size of the compressed file. Lossy compression techniques can reduce a file to 1/50 of its former size (or less), compared to the average of one-third achieved by lossless compression techniques. Lossy compression is used for graphics files in which the loss of data—such as information about some of the graphic's several million colors—isn't noticeable. An example is the JPEG compression technique. See *JPEG* and *lossless compression*.

lost chain   In MS-DOS, a group of clusters that are connected to each other in the file allocation table (FAT) but are no longer connected to a specific file.

lost cluster   A cluster that remains on the disk, even though the file allocation table (FAT) contains no record of its link to a file. Lost clusters can occur when the computer is turned off (or the power fails) or tries to perform other operations while a file is being written.

Lotus-Intel-Microsoft Expanded Memory Specification (LIM EMS)   An expanded memory standard that allows the programs that recognize the standard to work with more than 640K RAM under DOS. The LIM Version 4.0 standard, introduced in 1987, supports up to 32M of expanded memory and lets programs run in expanded memory.

CAUTION: *Software can't work with expanded memory unless specifically designed to do so. Applications such as WordPerfect, Lotus 1-2-3, and dBASE work with LIM 4.0 expanded memory, but less popular programs and shareware may not unless you use a windowing environment such as Quarterdeck's DESQview or Microsoft Windows. See* expanded memory (EMS) *and* extended memory.

low end   An inexpensive product at the bottom or near the bottom of a firm's offerings. Low-end products include only a few of the features available in more expensive products and may rely on obsolete or near-obsolete technology to keep costs down.

CAUTION: *You can still get IBM PC-compatible computers based on the Intel 8086, 8088, and 80286 microprocessors quite cheaply, but these computers can't take advantage of the 386 Enhanced mode of Microsoft Windows, in which Windows' technical advantages are fully available. See* 386 Enhanced mode *and* Microsoft Windows.

low-level format   Defining the physical location of magnetic tracks and sectors on a disk. This operation, sometimes called a *physical format*, is different from the high-level format that establishes the sections where DOS system files are stored and that records the free and in-use areas of the disk. See *high-level format*.

low-level programming language   In computer programming, a language, such as machine language or assembly language, that describes exactly the procedures to be carried out by the computer's central processing unit (CPU). See *assembly language*, *high-level programming language*, and *machine language*.

low resolution   In computer monitors and printers, a visual definition that results in characters and graphics with jagged edges. The IBM Color Graphics Adapter (CGA) and monitor, for example, can display 640 pixels horizontally, but only 200 lines vertically, resulting in poor visual definition. Higher resolutions produce well-defined characters or smoothly defined curves in graphic images. See *high resolution*.

LPT   In DOS, a device name that refers to a parallel port to which you can connect parallel printers.

LSI   See *large-scale integration (LSI)*.

lurk   To read a newsgroup without ever posting a message of your own. See *delurk*.

M   Abbreviation for *megabyte* (1,048,576 bytes).

MacBinary   A file transfer protocol for Macintosh computers that allows you to store Macintosh files on non-Macintosh computers without losing icons, graphics, and information about the file (such as the creation date). Most Macintosh communication programs send and receive files in MacBinary.

machine dependent   Capable of running on only a specific brand of hardware.

machine language   The native binary language recognized and executed by the computer's central processing unit (CPU). The language, symbolized by 0s and 1s, is extremely difficult to use and read. See *assembly language* and *high-level programming language.*

macro   A program consisting of keystrokes and an application's command language that, when run within the application, executes the keystrokes and commands to accomplish a task. Macros can automate tedious and often-repeated tasks (such as saving and backing up a file to a floppy) or create special menus to speed data entry.

Some programs provide a macro-recording mode in which the program records your keystrokes and then saves the recording as a macro. Others provide a built-in macro editor, where you type and edit macro commands directly. Such facilities often amount to a full-fledged software command language, including modern control structures such as DO/WHILE loops and IF/THEN/ELSE branches.

Full-featured application programs such as Microsoft Word, WordPerfect, and Lotus 1-2-3 include advanced macro capabilities. Commercially available macro programs such as SuperKey or AutoMac III provide macro capabilities for programs that lack them. See *DO/WHILE loop, IF/THEN/ELSE,* and *script.*

magnetic disk   In data storage, a random-access storage medium that's the most popular method for storing and retrieving computer programs and data files. In personal computing, common magnetic disks include 5 1/4-inch floppy disks, 3 1/2-inch floppy disks, and hard disks of various sizes.

The disk is coated with a magnetically sensitive material. Magnetic read/write heads move across the surface of the spinning disk under the disk drive's automatic control to the location of desired information. The information stored on a magnetic disk can be repeatedly erased and rewritten, like any other magnetic storage medium. See *3 1/2-inch disk, 5 1/4-inch disk, floppy disk, hard disk,* and *random access.*

magnetic media   In secondary storage, the use of magnetic techniques to store and retrieve data on disks or tapes coated with magnetically sensitive materials.

Like iron filings on a sheet of waxed paper, these materials are reoriented when a magnetic field passes over them. During write operations, the read/write head emits a magnetic field that reorients the magnetic materials on the disk or tape so that they're positively or negatively charged, corresponding to a bit of data. During read operations, the read/write head senses the magnetic polarities encoded on the tape.

magnetic tape   In secondary storage, a high-capacity mass storage and backup medium.

Although magnetic tape drives must use slow sequential access techniques, magnetic tape is inexpensive and offers a cost-effective way to store massive amounts of data; 250M tape cartridges are common. Magnetic tape drives are available for IBM Personal Computers and compatibles, and 250M tape drives are available for as little as $180. Most tape drives are used for hard disk backup purposes. See *sequential access.*

magneto-optical (MO) drive   A data storage device that uses laser technology to heat an extremely small spot on the magneto-optical (MO) disk so that the magnetic medium used in the MO disk becomes capable of having its magnetic orientation changed by the read/write head.

M N O

The write operation actually requires two passes to do the job. On the first pass, the target disk area is erased. On the second pass, the new data is written. The warmed spot cools quickly, at which point the magnetic medium becomes highly resistant to change—in fact, twice as resistant as a standard hard drive. The laser is then used, at a much lower intensity, to read the information on the disk.

The data on a magneto-optical drive is highly stable, unlike the floppy and hard disks, which tend to self-erase if the data isn't re-written regularly. Magneto-optical disks are removable cartridges, about the size of a 3 1/2-inch floppy disk but twice as thick. Unlike floppy disks, however, magneto-optical disks commonly have capacities of 128M or 230M.

On the negative size, the write time is slow because of the required two passes and because the read/write heads are more substantial than those found in hard drives, taking longer to speed up, slow down, and settle. The fast magneto-optical drives have an average seek time of 30 milliseconds (ms), compared to less than 15 ms for hard disk drives. The data transfer rate ranges from 1M per second for 128M disks to 2M per second for 230M disks. Although clearly slower than hard drives, magneto-optical drives are highly suitable for backup storage and for storing large programs or data that's accessed less often. The drives are expensive, with average prices of $750 for internal drives and $1,100 for external drives (four disks included) for good performers. Additional disks are about $40 for 128M of storage.

mailbox   In electronic mail, a storage location that holds messages addressed to an individual until he or she accesses the system. An on-screen message informs the user that mail is waiting.

mailing list   On the Internet or another network, a list of users who will receive copies of mail messages. Lists are usually divided by topic or work area. On the Internet, you can subscribe to mailing lists for topics that interest you.

mail merge   In word processing programs, a utility that draws information from a database—usually a mailing list—and incorporates it into a form document to create multiple copies of the document. Each copy of the document includes information from one record from the database.

The most common application of the mail merge utilities is to personalize form letters. You can create a letter containing text that's sent to all recipients, and then use mail merge to insert the correspondent's name, address, and (if desired) other personal information elsewhere in the letter. For example, "In all honesty, *Dr. Richards*, we have never received a complaint about this product before your letter of *October 3*."

Use the word processing program to create the database, called the *secondary file* or *data file*, and create a primary file (also called a *form document*) that contains the text you want to send. In place of the correspondent's name and address and any other information you want to insert from the data file, however, are codes that refer to fields in the name-and-address database. Finally, you give a command that prints one copy of the primary file for each record in the database.

TIP: *Most programs let you perform conditional merging that prints an optional passage of text if a database record meets a specified condition.*

M N O

mail package   A utility program that manages the sending and receiving of e-mail messages for a specific computer.

Some networks use a full-featured package such as WordPerfect Office that includes an e-mail program. More friendly or full-featured mail programs can also be bought separately. Microsoft Mail and cc:Mail are two popular mail programs.

mainframe   A multiuser computer designed to meet the computing needs of a large organization.

Originally, the term *mainframe* referred to the metal cabinet that housed the central processing unit (CPU) of early computers. The term came to be used generally to refer to the large central computers developed in the late 1950s and 1960s to meet the accounting and information-management needs of large organizations. The largest mainframes can handle thousands of dumb terminals and use gigabytes of secondary storage. See *minicomputer, personal computer,* and *workstation.*

main memory   See *random-access memory (RAM)*.

main program   In programming, the part of the program containing the master sequence of instructions, unlike the subroutines, procedures, and functions that the main program calls.

main storage   See *random-access memory (RAM)*.

maintenance release   A program revision that corrects a minor bug or makes a minor new feature available, such as a new printer driver. Maintenance releases are usually numbered in tenths (3.2) or hundredths (2.01), to distinguish them from major program revisions. Synonymous with *interim update*.

male connector   In computer cables, a cable terminator and connection device in which the pins protrude from the connector's surface. See *female connector*.

management information system (MIS)   A computer system, based on a mainframe, minicomputer, or PC network, designed to provide management personnel with up-to-date information on the organization's performance.

manual recalculation   In a spreadsheet program, a recalculation method that suspends the recalculation of values until you press a key that forces recalculation to take place.

Most spreadsheet programs recalculate all values within the spreadsheet after you change the contents of an individual cell. If you're using a slow computer and creating a large spreadsheet, you may want to choose the manual recalculation mode as you enter data. When you're finished, be sure to recalculate the spreadsheet and turn automatic recalculation on again. The word CALC or a similar indicator appears at the bottom of the spreadsheet to remind you to recalculate.

➔ **TIP:** *In the latest generation of spreadsheet software, such as Lotus 1-2-3 Release 3, recalculation occurs in the background. With these spreadsheet programs you don't need to use manual recalculation. See* automatic recalculation.

m

map   A representation of data stored in memory. See *bit map*.

MAPI   See *Messaging Application Program Interface (MAPI)*.

mapping   The process of converting data encoded in one format or device to another format or device. In database management, for example, the database index provides a way of mapping the actual records (which are stored on disk in a fixed order) to the display screen in useful ways.

In a local area network, mapping refers to assigning drive letters to specific volumes and directories.

marquee   In Microsoft Excel, a moving dotted line that surrounds a cell or a range of cells that you've cut or copied.

mask   A pattern of symbols or characters that, when imposed on a data field, limits the kinds of characters that you can type into the field. In a database management program, for example, the mask *Az* lets you type any alphabetical character, uppercase or lowercase, but not numbers or other symbols.

mass storage   See *secondary storage*.

master document   In word processing, a document that contains commands that tell the program to print additional documents at the commands' locations. The program prints all the documents as though they were one. See *chain printing*.

masthead   In desktop publishing, the section of a newsletter or magazine that gives the details of its staff, ownership, advertising, subscription prices, and so on.

math coprocessor   See *numeric coprocessor*.

maximize   To zoom or enlarge a window so that it fills the screen.

In Microsoft Windows, you maximize a window by clicking the maximize button (the right button in the upper right corner) or by choosing Maximize from the control menu. See *Microsoft Windows* and *minimize*.

M N O

MB   Alternative abbreviation for *megabyte* (1,048,576 bytes).

MCA   See *Micro Channel Architecture (MCA)*.

MCGA   See *MultiColor Graphics Array (MCGA)*.

MCI   See *Media Control Interface (MCI)*.

MDA   See *monochrome display adapter (MDA)*.

mean time between failures (MTBF)   The statistical average operating time between the start of a component's life and the time of its first electronic or mechanical failure.

TIP: *You shouldn't take MTBF figures too seriously when comparison shopping. The figures stem from laboratory tests performed under extreme conditions; the results are then statistically extrapolated to determine the MTBF. Little pressure exists for manufacturers to use an extrapolation procedure that revises the MTBF figure downward.*

mechanicals   In desktop publishing, the final pages or boards with pasted-up galleys of type and line art, sometimes with acetate or tissue overlays for color separations and notes, which you send to the offset printer. See *camera-ready copy* and *desktop publishing (DTP)*.

media   The plural of *medium*. See *secondary storage medium*.

Media Control Interface (MCI)   In Microsoft Windows, the multimedia extensions that greatly simplify the task of programming multimedia device functions such as Stop, Play, and Record. See *multimedia extensions*.

Media Player   An accessory provided with Microsoft Windows 3.1 that provides a control center for multimedia devices, such as CD-ROM drives. The buttons resemble the familiar controls of a tape player (see fig. M.1).

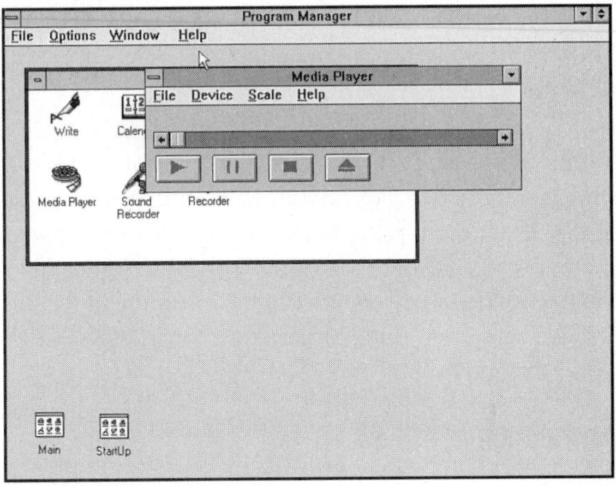

Fig. M.1 *Microsoft Windows Media Player.*

meg Common abbreviation for *megabyte.*

mega- Prefix indicating 1 million.

megabyte (M) A measurement of storage capacity equal to approximately 1 million bytes (1,048,576 bytes).

megaflop A benchmark used to rate professional workstations and scientific mainframe or minicomputers. A megaflop is equal to 1 million floating point operations per second.

megahertz (MHz) A unit of measurement equal to 1 million electrical vibrations or cycles per second; commonly used to compare the clock speeds of computers.

One million cycles per second sounds impressive, but by today's standards, the 4.77 MHz clock speed of the original IBM Personal Computer is considered intolerable. Clock speeds of 33 MHz, 50 MHz, and even 66 MHz are increasingly common in personal computing. See *clock speed* and *hertz (Hz).*

membrane keyboard A flat and inexpensive keyboard covered with a dust- and dirt-proof plastic sheet on which only the two-dimensional outline of computer keys appears. The user presses the plastic sheet and engages a switch hidden beneath.

M
N
O

Accurately typing on a membrane keyboard is more difficult, but such keyboards are needed in restaurants or other locations where users may not have clean hands.

memory   The computer's primary storage, such as random-access memory (RAM), as distinguished from its secondary storage, such as disk drives. See *primary storage* and *secondary storage*.

memory address   A code number that specifies a specific location in a computer's random-access memory. See *random-access memory (RAM)*.

memory cache   See *cache memory*.

memory controller gate array   Synonymous with *MultiColor Graphics Array (MCGA)*, a video display standard of the low-end models of IBM's Personal System/2 computers.

memory-management program   A utility program that increases the apparent size of random-access memory (RAM) by making expanded memory, extended memory, or virtual memory available for the execution of programs.

Memory-management programs include utilities provided with expanded memory boards, windowing environments such as Microsoft Windows, and virtual memory programs that set aside a portion of a hard disk and treat it as a RAM extension. See *EMM386.EXE, expanded memory (EMS), expanded memory emulator, extended memory*, and *HIMEM.SYS*.

memory map   An arbitrary allocation of portions of a computer's memory, defining which areas the computer can use for specific purposes.

Although the Intel 8088 microprocessor can use 1M of RAM, a portion of this potential memory space is reserved for functions such as the keyboard buffer and display adapters. This decision, although arbitrary, is irrevocable if MS-DOS is involved, because MS-DOS and its application programs can't operate unless the memory map remains exactly the way it was laid out when IBM designed the Personal Computer.

m

memory-resident program   See *terminate-and-stay-resident (TSR) program.*

memory word   See *word.*

menu   An on-screen display that lists available command choices. See *menu bar* and *pull-down menu.*

menu bar   In a user interface, a bar stretching across the top of the screen (or the top of a window) that contains the names of available pull-down menus. See *graphical user interface (GUI), industry standard user interface,* and *pull-down menu.*

menu-driven program   A program that provides you with menus for choosing program options so that you don't need to memorize commands. See *command-driven program.*

merge printing   See *mail merge.*

Messaging Application Program Interface (MAPI)   The Microsoft implementation of an application program interface that provides access to messaging services for developers. MAPI Version 3.2 provides resources to programmers for cross-platform messaging that's independent of operating system and underlying hardware, and to make applications mail-aware. MAPI can send messages to and from VIM programs. See *application program interface (API)* and *Vendor Independent Messaging (VIM).*

MFM   See *Modified Frequency Modulation (MFM).*

MHz   Abbreviation for *megahertz.*

micro-   Prefix for small. Also a prefix indicating one millionth, and an abbreviation (increasingly rare) for *microcomputer.*

Micro Channel Architecture (MCA)   The design specifications of IBM's proprietary Micro Channel Bus. An MCA-compatible peripheral is designed to plug directly into a Micro Channel Bus, but won't work with other bus architectures. See *local bus* and *Micro Channel Bus.*

M
N
O

Micro Channel Bus   A proprietary 32-bit expansion bus introduced by IBM for its high-end PS/2 computers.

Almost all non-IBM 80386 computers use a 32-bit bus structure for the microprocessor, but otherwise use the 16-bit AT expansion bus, for which a huge supply of cheap peripherals is available. In an attempt to define a 32-bit bus standard, IBM introduced Micro Channel Architecture (MCA) in 1987 and used the Micro Channel Bus on its high-end PS/2 models.

The MCA bus has many technical advantages, including the capability to use 32-bit peripherals, higher speed, greater reliability, and even the capability to use more than one central processing unit (CPU) in one computer. But the MCA standard isn't downwardly compatible with existing peripherals and adapters designed for the AT expansion bus; therefore, some industry analysts believe that MCA was designed primarily to recapture for IBM part of the lucrative market for peripherals and adapters.

IBM has offered the MCA technology to clone-makers under a licensing scheme, but few have taken up IBM on the offer. Instead, the major manufacturers of IBM compatibles have offered their own 32-bit bus design, called *Extended Industry Standard Architecture (EISA)*, followed by the local bus technology that connects video circuits and disk drives directly to the processor's internal data pathways. See *Extended Industry Standard Architecture (EISA)* and *local bus*.

microcomputer   Any computer with its arithmetic-logic unit (ALU) and control unit contained on one integrated circuit, called a *microprocessor*.

When personal computers—often referred to as microcomputers because their central processing units (CPUs) were microprocessors—first appeared in the mid to late 1970s, they were designed as single-user machines. Many computing professionals, however, at first didn't take microcomputers seriously. For them, the word *microcomputer* sounded like an amusing toy.

Since the mid 1980s, the distinction between minicomputers (as multiuser computers) and microcomputers (as single-user computers) has become blurry. Many microcomputers are substantially more powerful than the mainframes of just 10 years ago. You can transform some of today's more powerful microcomputers into minicomputers by equipping them with remote terminals. Also, many of today's minicomputers use microprocessors.

Differentiating among these machines by the function they're designed to perform makes the most sense:

- *Centralized computing systems.* Designed for use by several users simultaneously, most mainframe and minicomputer systems meet the needs of an organization or a department within an organization. The emphasis in such computer systems is on keeping programs, data, and processing capabilities under central control, so that end users gain access to these systems through remote terminals.

- *Stand-alone computers.* Designed for single-user applications, a stand-alone computer such as a personal computer designed for personal, home, or private use, that doesn't rely on external resources such as a central database or share computing resources with other people.

- *Distributed computing systems.* A network of personal computers designed to get computing power to the user without giving up the means to share external computing resources, such as access to a central database.

- *Professional workstation.* An advanced microcomputer that contains the display and processing circuitry needed by professionals such as engineers, financial planners, and architects.

Today's advanced personal computers are powerful enough to migrate around these categories with ease.

microprocessor   An integrated circuit that contains the arithmetic-logic unit (ALU) and control unit of a computer's central processing unit (CPU). See *Intel 8086, Intel 8088, Intel 80286, Intel 80386DX, Intel 80386SX, Intel 80486DX, Intel 80486SX, Motorola 68000, Motorola 68020*, and *Motorola 68030*.

Microsoft Mouse   A mouse and associated software for IBM and IBM-compatible personal computers, including IBM's PS/1 and PS/2 computers. Available in serial and bus versions, the Microsoft Mouse uses the optical-mechanical technology that most mouse users favor.

M N O

Microsoft Windows   A windowing environment and application user interface (API) that implements multitasking operations for DOS and brings to IBM-format computing some of the graphical user interface features of the Macintosh, such as pull-down menus, multiple typefaces, desk accessories, and the capability to move material from one program to another via the Clipboard. Because Windows provides all the functions needed to implement features such as menus, windows, and dialog boxes, all Windows applications have a consistent interface (see fig. M.2).

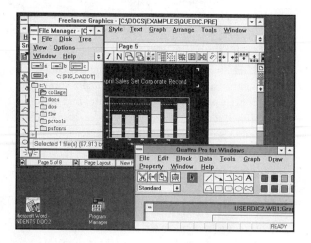

Fig. M.2   *The Microsoft Windows desktop with several open applications.*

Originally, Windows was to be little more than a preview of OS/2's Presentation Manager. Windows ran the few applications specifically developed for it in a graphical user interface environment and used expanded memory schemes such as the Lotus-Intel-Microsoft Specification 4.0. However, the new generation of IBM-format programs needed the protected mode of the Intel 80286 and 80386 microprocessors, with their 16M of undifferentiated memory space. Microsoft had taken the position that protected-mode programs must be developed for OS/2 and Presentation Manager.

Then DESQview (by Quarterdeck Systems) appeared with the capability to run MS-DOS programs in windows in protected mode, so Microsoft released Windows 3.0, which also runs

MS-DOS applications in protected mode. Version 3.0 was phenomenally successful, with Excel and Word for Windows gaining more users; other Windows users bought the program to simplify running more than one program at a time.

The 1992 release of Windows 3.1 consolidated Windows' popularity, offering major improvements in speed, Program Manager and File Manager, TrueType fonts, mouse control of MS-DOS applications, improved Help screens and multitasking, built-in screen savers, object linking and embedding (OLE) capability, and multimedia extensions. Although many MS-DOS users continue to prefer the greater speed and more direct user-control available in their favorite DOS applications, users with a more graphical bent agree that Microsoft Windows is a joy to use.

> **TIP:** *To run Windows, you need much more computing horsepower than you need to run comparable MS-DOS applications. A minimal Windows platform includes an 80386SX running at 16 MHz (but preferably 20 or 25 MHz), at least 4M of RAM, an 80M hard disk, a 16-bit VGA video adapter and VGA monitor, and an inkjet or laser printer. Better, get an 80486DX2 running at 66 MHz, 8M of RAM, a 200M hard disk, and a Super VGA adapter and monitor. See* free system resources *and* Microsoft Windows NT.

Microsoft Windows NT   A 32-bit version of Microsoft's popular graphical user interface that offers true multitasking for Intel-based personal computers and professional engineering workstations. This version of Windows dispenses with DOS and provides better access to system memory than Windows 3.1.

Windows NT runs exclusively in protected mode, allowing programmers to use up to 4 gigabytes of RAM without resorting to tricks. Also, Windows NT offers enhanced fault tolerance, file handling, network access, and security. On-screen, Windows NT looks just like the familiar Windows 3.1.

Freed from the restrictions of DOS, Windows NT addresses many of the shortcomings of Windows 3.1, making it attractive to multiuser computing systems that would otherwise use UNIX or OS/2. However, the gigantic memory requirements—70M of hard disk space and 16M of free RAM—rule out its use on all but the brawniest desktop systems. See *fault tolerance, Microsoft Windows, MS-DOS,* and *protected mode.*

micro-to-mainframe   The linkage of personal computers to mainframe or minicomputer networks.

MIDI   See *Musical Instrument Digital Interface (MIDI).*

MIDI cuing   In multimedia, a set of MIDI messages that determines the occurrence of events other than musical notes (such as recording, playing back, or turning on lighting devices). See *Musical Instrument Digital Interface (MIDI).*

MIDI file   A file containing musical data encoded according to MIDI specifications. In Microsoft Windows, MIDI files use the extension .MID. See *Musical Instrument Digital Interface (MIDI).*

MIDI port   A receptacle that allows you to connect a personal computer directly to a musical synthesizer. See *Musical Instrument Digital Interface (MIDI).*

migration   A change from an older computer hardware platform, operating system, or software version to a newer one. For example, industry observers expected corporations to *migrate* from MS-DOS to Microsoft Windows.

milli-   Prefix indicating one thousandth.

million instructions per second (MIPS)   A benchmark method for measuring the rate at which a computer executes microprocessor instructions. A computer capable of 0.5 MIPS, for example, can execute 500,000 instructions per second.

m

CAUTION: *MIPS ratings are associated with sophisticated mainframes and supercomputers; only with the 80486 and Pentium systems has the performance of personal computers improved to the point that their processing speed can be described in MIPS. However, MIPS measurements inadequately state a computer system's throughput—a performance measurement that takes into account the speed of internal data transfer to and from the memory and the speed of important peripherals such as disk drives. See* benchmark, Norton SI, super-computer, *and* throughput.

millisecond (ms)   A unit of measurement, equal to one-thousandth of a second, commonly used to specify the access time of hard disk drives. See *access time.*

minicomputer   A multiuser computer designed to meet the needs of a small company or a department. A minicomputer is more powerful than a personal computer but not as powerful as a mainframe. Typically, about 4 to 100 people use a minicomputer simultaneously.

minimize   In a graphical user interface, to shrink a window so that it collapses to an icon on the desktop. You minimize a window by clicking the minimize button (the left button in the upper right corner) or by choosing Minimize from the Control menu.

When you minimize an application in Microsoft Windows, the application appears below the Program Manager screen as an icon. If you minimize many applications, the icons may overlap or appear untidy. To tidy up the row of icons, choose Arrange Icons from the Window menu.

MIPS   See *million instructions per second (MIPS).*

MIS   See *management information system (MIS).*

mixed cell reference   In a spreadsheet program, a cell reference in which the column reference is absolute but the row

M N O

reference is relative ($A9) or in which the row reference is absolute but the column reference is relative (A$9). See *absolute cell reference*, *cell reference*, and *relative cell reference*.

mixed column/line chart   See *mixed column/line graph*.

mixed column/line graph   In presentation and analytical graphics, a graph that displays one data series using columns and another data series using lines. You use a line graph to suggest a trend over time; a column graph groups data items so that you can compare one to another. In figure M.3, for example, the trends in manufacturing costs, represented by a line, are compared to expenses, shown as columns.

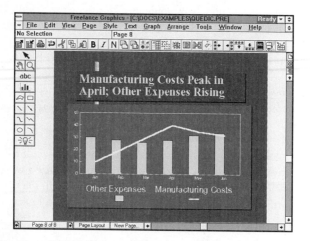

Fig. M.3   *A mixed column/line graph.*

MNP-4   The most popular error-checking protocol (standard), which filters out line noise and eliminates errors that can occur during the transmission and reception of data via computer modem. For error checking to function, both modems—the one sending as well as the one receiving the transmission—must have error-checking capabilities conforming to the same error-checking protocol. See *error-correcting protocol* and *modem*.

MNP-5   The same error-checking protocol as MNP-4, as well as a data-compression protocol for computer modems that speeds transmissions by compressing (encoding, actually) data on the sending end and decompressing the data on the reception end. If the data isn't already compressed, gains in effective transmission speeds of up to 200 percent can be realized. See *data-compression protocol* and *modem*.

mode   The operating state in which you place a program by choosing among a set of exclusive operating options. Within a given mode, certain commands and keystrokes are available, but you may need to change modes to use other commands or keystrokes.

Lotus 1-2-3, for example, has numerous operating modes. Here are several:

Mode	Description
READY	1-2-3 is waiting for you to enter a command or make a cell entry.
VALUE	You're entering a number or formula.
LABEL	You're entering a label.
EDIT	You can edit the cell entry now displayed on the control panel.
POINT	You can use the arrow keys to expand the highlight and define a range.
HELP	1-2-3 is displaying a help screen.
WAIT	1-2-3 is carrying out an operation and can't respond to additional commands or keyboard input.
STAT	1-2-3 is displaying the status of your worksheet.

A key step in learning a program is understanding its modes and how to switch from one mode to another. Beginners may reach a frustrating roadblock when they accidentally choose an unfamiliar mode and don't know how to exit that mode. Find out where the mode indicator is located on-screen and learn what the messages mean. See *mode indicator*.

mode indicator An on-screen message that displays the program's current operating mode. In Lotus 1-2-3, for example, the mode indicator appears in reverse video at the upper right corner of the screen. See *mode*.

model A mathematical or pictorial representation of an object or system that exists in the real world, such as an aircraft fuselage or a business's cash flow.

The purpose of constructing a model is to gain a better understanding of the prototype. By examining or changing the characteristics of the model, you can draw inferences about the prototype's behavior. In a spreadsheet model of a business enterprise, for example, you can explore the impact of increasing advertising expenditures on market share.

CAUTION: *A model is only as good as its underlying assumptions. If these assumptions are incorrect, or if any information is missing from the model, it may not reflect the prototype's behavior accurately.*

modem A device that converts the digital signals generated by the computer's serial port to the modulated analog signals required for transmission over a telephone line and, likewise, transforms incoming analog signals to their digital equivalents. In personal computing, people frequently use modems to exchange programs and data with other computers, and to access on-line information services such as the Dow Jones News/Retrieval Service.

Modem is short for *modulator/demodulator*. The modulation is necessary because telephone lines are designed to handle the human voice, which warbles between 300 and 3,000 Hz in ordinary telephone conversations (from a growl to a shriek). The speed at which a modem transmits data is measured in units called *bits per second*, or *bps* (technically not the same as *baud*, although the terms are often used interchangeably).

Choosing a modem used to be a simple process: you got a slow one (300 or 1200 bps) or a fast one (2400 bps). Now, however, more modem options are available.

Modulation protocols govern the speed of data transmission and reception. Within the United States, almost all 2400 bps modems use the CCITT V.22bis protocol. However, the first high-speed modems (9600 bps and faster) used proprietary modulation protocols so that you had to have the same brand of modem on each end. Now, 9600 bps modems use the CCITT V.32 protocol, and 14,400 bps modems the CCITT V.32bis standard. Both are downward compatible with any other modem, even if it was made by a different manufacturer.

Two common standards for error-checking protocols eliminate errors attributable to noise and other glitches in the telephone system: the MNP-4 and CCITT V.42. For data-compression protocols, two standards predominate: V.42bis and MNP-5. Because data-compression requires error-checking, modems that offer data compression always offer error-control standards as well; in general, a modem offers all four error-control and data-compression protocols (MNP-4, MNP-5, V. 42, and V.42bis) or none. See *acoustic coupler, auto-dial/auto-answer modem, baud rate, Bell 103A, Bell 212A, bits per second (bps), CCITT protocol, direct-connect modem, dirty, echoplex, external modem, full duplex, half duplex, Hayes command set, Hayes-compatible modem, internal modem, MNP-4, MNP-5, reliable link,* and *Universal Asynchronous Receiver/Transmitter (UART).*

M N O

moderated newsgroup   In a distributed bulletin board system such as USENET or Echo Mail, a topical conference in which contributions are screened by one or more moderators before the post appears. The moderator's job, often mistaken for censorship, is to assure that postings adhere to the group's stated topic. A moderator also may rule out discussion on certain subtopics if postings on such subjects turn out to be *flame bait* (postings likely to cause an unproductive and bitter debate with low information content). See *distributed bulletin board, Fidonet, flame, flame bait, newsgroup, unmoderated newsgroup,* and *USENET.*

Modified Frequency Modulation (MFM)   A method of recording digital information on magnetic media such as tapes and disks by eliminating redundant or blank areas. Because the MFM data-encoding scheme doubles the storage attained under the earlier frequency-modulation (FM) recording technique, MFM recording usually is referred to as *double density*.

MFM often is wrongly used to describe ordinary hard disk controllers, those conforming to the ST-506/ST-412 standard. MFM actually refers to the method used to pack data on the disk and isn't synonymous with disk drive interface standards such as ST-506, SCSI, or ESDI. See *data-encoding scheme*, *double density*, *interface standard*, and *Run-Length Limited (RLL)*.

Modula-2   A high-level programming language that extends Pascal so that the language can execute program modules independently.

Developed in 1980 by the European computer wizard and Pascal creator Niklaus Wirth, Modula-2 is an enhanced version of Pascal that supports the separate compilation of program modules and overcomes many other shortcomings of Pascal. A programmer working on a team can write and compile the module he or she has been assigned, and then test the module extensively to make sure that it functions correctly.

Although Modula-2 is increasingly popular as a teaching language at colleges and universities, the C language dominates professional software development. See *C*, *modular programming*, *Pascal*, and *structured programming*.

modular accounting package   A collection of accounting programs—one for each chief accounting function (general ledger, accounts payable, accounts receivable, payroll, and inventory, for example)—designed to work together, even though they aren't integrated into one program.

Modular accounting programs are computerized versions of traditional accounting practices, in which a firm keeps several ledgers: one for accounts receivable, another for accounts payable, and a general ledger. You update the general ledger in batches at periodic intervals after carefully proofing the hard copy for errors. Modular packages generally are sold with several separate programs for each of these functions, and you must follow special procedures to make sure that all the transactions are correctly updated.

These programs haven't found a large market in personal computing for two reasons: they often don't reflect the way people in small businesses keep their books, and they're far from easy to use.

Some, however, are available with automatic links to point-of-sale terminals—for example, Flexware (Microfinancial Corporation) for Macintosh computers and Excalibur (Armour Systems, Inc.) for IBM PC-compatible computers.

modular programming   A programming style that breaks down program functions into modules, each of which accomplishes one function and contains all the codes and variables needed to accomplish that function.

Modular programming is a solution to the problem of very large programs that are difficult to debug and maintain. By segmenting the program into modules that perform clearly defined functions, you can determine the source of program errors more easily.

Modular programming principles have clearly influenced the design of object-oriented programming languages such as SmallTalk and HyperTalk, both of which allow you to create fully functional program objects (such as the buttons in HyperCard) that function so independently that you can copy them from one program to another.

modulation   The conversion of a digital signal to its analog equivalent, especially for the purposes of transmitting signals using telephone lines. See *demodulation* and *modem.*

M N O

modulation protocol   In computer modems, the standards used to govern the speed by which the modem sends and receives information over the telephone lines. See *Bell 103A, Bell 212A,* and *CCITT protocol.*

module   In a computer program, a unit or section that can function on its own. In an integrated program, for instance, you can use the word processing module as though it were a separate, stand-alone program.

moiré effect   *mwah-ray*   An optical illusion, perceived as flickering, that sometimes occurs when you place high-contrast line patterns (such as cross-hatching in pie graphs) too close to one another.

!

CAUTION: *Many business graphics programs produce charts and graphs with undesirable moiré effects. You can avoid this problem by using no more than two or three cross-hatching patterns and separating them with solid white, gray, or black colors. See* cross-hatching.

monitor   The complete device that produces an on-screen display, including all necessary internal support circuitry. A monitor also is called a *video display unit* (VDU) or *cathode-ray tube* (CRT). See *analog monitor, digital monitor, Enhanced Graphics Display, monochrome monitor,* and *multiscanning monitor.*

monochrome display adapter (MDA)   A single-color display adapter for IBM PC-compatible computers that displays text (but not graphics) with a resolution of 720 pixels horizontally and 350 lines vertically, placing characters in a matrix of 7 by 9. See *Hercules Graphics Adapter.*

monochrome monitor   A monitor that displays one color against a black or white background. Examples include the IBM monochrome monitor that displays green text against a black background, and paper-white VGA monitors that display black text on a white background. See *paper-white monitor.*

monospace   A typeface such as Courier in which the width of each character is the same, producing output that looks like typed characters. The following is an example of monospace type:

```
The width of each character in this typeface is exactly
the same.
```

See *proportional spacing.*

morphing   Short for *metamorphosing,* a revolutionary computer animation technique used to "fill in the blanks" between dissimilar figures so that one seems to melt into another, such as changing a man to a werewolf, a bat to a vampire, or a rock singer to a panther.

Morphing, a common film industry special-effects technique, is related closely to another, more prosaic animation technique called *tweening* (short for *in-betweening*), which refers to the computer's capability to calculate and draw frames that are intermediate between the "key" frames hand-drawn by the artist. Morphing is the process of tweening to a *different* object.

Mosaic   A more friendly interface for the Internet created by the National Center for Supercomputing Applications and placed in the public domain. Although it allows you to avoid having to learn unfamiliar UNIX commands, it requires that your computer become a node on the Internet, which is not only technically demanding, but is pricy. See *front end* and *Internet*.

motherboard   A large circuit board that contains the computer's central processing unit (CPU), microprocessor support chips, random-access memory, and expansion slots. Synonymous with *logic board*.

Motorola 68000   A microprocessor that processes 32 bits internally, although it uses a 16-bit data bus to communicate with the rest of the computer. The 68000 can address up to 32 gigabytes of random-access memory (RAM). Running at 8 MHz, the 68000 powers the entry-level Macintosh Classic.

CAUTION: *Avoid purchasing Macs powered by 68000 chips. Today's software designers assume that you're using a peppier machine.*

M N O

Motorola 68020   A microprocessor electronically similar to the Motorola 68000, except that this microprocessor uses a full 32-bit architecture and runs at a clock speed of 16 MHz. The 68020 powers the original Macintosh II, displaced by newer models using the Motorola 68030 chip. Macintosh system software limits the amount of usable RAM to 8M (Apple's System 7 boosts this amount to 4 gigabytes).

Motorola 68030   A full 32-bit microprocessor that can run at substantially higher clock speeds (16 to 50 MHz) than the Motorola 68000 and 68020. The 68030 includes special features for virtual memory management.

The 68030 incorporates a chip that controls page-mode RAM, so any 68030-equipped Macintosh can implement the advanced memory management features of System 7. See *clock speed*, *page-mode RAM*, and *System 7*.

> **TIP:** *If you're buying a Mac, buy a machine based on the 68030. The chip includes circuits that you need to take full advantage of System 7.*

Motorola 68040   A 32-bit microprocessor in Motorola's 680x0 family that represents an evolutionary advance over its immediate predecessor, the 68030. Analogous to the Intel 80486DX microprocessor, the 68040 packs more circuitry into its tiny confines, reducing the need for support chips and improving performance. For example, the 68040 includes a numeric (floating-point) coprocessor, eliminating the need for a coprocessor chip. The 68040 powers the high-end Quadra models of Apple's Macintosh computers.

Motorola 68881   The numeric coprocessor used with the Motorola 68000 and 68020 microprocessors. See *numeric coprocessor*.

mount   To insert a disk into a disk drive. Installing hardware, such as a motherboard, disk drive, and adapters, is also referred to as mounting.

mousable interface   A user interface that responds to mouse input for such functions as selecting text, choosing commands from menus, and scrolling the screen.

mouse   An input device, equipped with one or more control buttons, that's housed in a palm-sized case and designed so that you can roll it about on the table, next to your keyboard. As the mouse moves, its circuits relay signals that correspondingly move a pointer on-screen.

The simplest of all mouse functions is repositioning the cursor: You point to the cursor's new location and click the left mouse button. You also can use the mouse to choose commands from menus, select text for editing purposes, move objects, and draw

m

pictures on-screen. Many typists don't like to take their fingers away from the keyboard, so programs that use the mouse often include keyboard equivalents.

A mouse is distinguished by the internal mechanism it uses to generate its signal and by its means of connection with the computer. Two types of internal mechanisms are popular:

- *Mechanical mouse.* This mouse has a rubber-coated ball on the underside of the case. As you move the mouse, the ball rotates and optical sensors detect the motion. You can use a mechanical mouse on virtually any surface, although a mouse pad made of special fabric gives the best results. A trackball mouse has the ball in the top of the case, and you use your thumb to move the ball.

- *Optical mouse.* This mouse registers its position by detecting reflections from a light-emitting diode that directs a beam downward. You must have a special metal pad to reflect the beam properly, and you can't move the mouse beyond the pad.

See *built-in pointing device, clin-on pointing device, freestanding pointing device, snap-on pointing device,* and *trackball.*

M N O

➡ **TIP:** *Mechanical mice are prone to collect finger grease and dirt within their internal mechanisms. As this mixture hardens, the pointer may behave erratically. Remove the ball-retainer ring, freeing the ball, and clean the ball and the ball rollers with a cotton swab moistened in rubbing alcohol. Blow dust out of the ball chamber and reassemble the mouse.*

mouse elbow   A painful repetitive strain injury (RSI), similar to tennis elbow, that's produced by lifting one's hand repeatedly to manipulate a computer mouse. Ostensibly ergonomic, the mouse turns out to be as severe a threat to one's health as the keyboard, which can cause carpal tunnel syndrome (another repetitive strain injury).

If you develop mouse elbow, learn to use the mouse with your other hand—or learn the keyboard shortcuts for mouse maneuvers. The latter isn't easy with Macintosh systems; Windows and Windows applications, however, tend to offer excellent keyboard shortcuts for frequently used mouse techniques. See *repetitive strain injury (RSI)*.

MPC   See *Multimedia Personal Computer (MPC)*.

MPR II   A standard for computer monitor radiation developed by Sweden's National Board for Industrial and Technical Development in 1987 and updated in 1990. To meet MPR II standards, a monitor can't emit more than 250 nanoteslas of electromagnetic radiation at a distance of a half meter.

Scientists aren't sure whether extremely low-frequency electromagnetic radiation is hazardous to your health, but you can stay on the safe side by selecting a monitor that conforms to MPR II standards. See *extremely low-frequency (ELF) emission*.

ms   See *millisecond (ms)*.

MS-DOS   The standard, single-user operating system of IBM and IBM-compatible computers.

Introduced in 1981, MS-DOS (Microsoft Disk Operating System) is marketed by IBM as PC DOS; the two systems are almost indistinguishable.

MS-DOS's origins lie in CP/M—the operating system for 8-bit computers popular in the late 1970s. The original version of what was to become MS-DOS was created for experimental purposes by a small Seattle firm. Because Microsoft had landed an IBM contract to create an operating system for the IBM Personal Computer, Microsoft bought and developed the program.

MS-DOS is a command-line operating system that requires you to enter commands, arguments, and syntax to use MS-DOS successfully. After mastering MS-DOS commands, however, you can achieve a high degree of control over the operating system's capabilities—including setting file attributes, creating automatically executed batch files, and developing semi-automated backup procedures. Alternatively, excellent utility programs are available that let you avoid DOS by incorporating these tasks in a user interface with pull-down menus and dialog boxes.

The most severe limitation of MS-DOS is the 640K RAM barrier that the operating system imposes on IBM PC-compatible computing. Although many users are migrating to Windows to use its memory-management capabilities and easier-to-use interface, millions of older IBM PC and compatible computers exist that can't run Windows well. MS-DOS is unquestionably the world's most widely used operating system and is likely to remain so for years to come. See *application program interface (API), CP/M (Control Program for Microprocessors), Microsoft Windows, Microsoft Windows NT, MS-DOS QBasic, MS-DOS Shell, Operating System/ 2 (OS/2), protected mode, real mode, terminate-and-stay-resident (TSR) program,* and *UNIX.*

> **TIP:** *For maximum performance with Microsoft Windows, upgrade to MS-DOS 6.0-6.2 and run the MEMMAKER utility to take full advantage of all your system's memory.*

MS-DOS QBasic   An improved BASIC programming environment, supplied with MS-DOS 5.0 and later, that includes extensive on-line help.

MS-DOS Shell   An improved, menu-driven user interface for the MS-DOS operating system, supplied with MS-DOS 5.0 and later, that conforms to the industry-standard user interface. MS-DOS Shell provides menu-driven access to most DOS commands, finally providing much of the functionality that has long been missing from MS-DOS. Users may find less need for utility packages such as PC Tools.

MTBF   See *mean time between failures (MTBF).*

MUD   Acronym for *Multiuser Dungeons and Dragons.* A MUD is a highly addictive computer game designed for network use that offers participants an opportunity to interact with others in a fantasy role-playing environment.

On your computer, you—or more accurately, a character you've created and named—can be deep in the recesses of a gigantic role-playing adventure, replete with elves, dragons, wizards, dungeons, magic, and monsters. Unlike Dungeons and Dragons games for stand-alone computers, you're not playing alone. The other characters you play with, or against, were created and are being controlled by *other* remote users just like you.

The combat scenarios of early MUD games led to an unfortunate phenomenon called *berserking*, in which users log on with the sole purpose of slaying as many characters as possible. More recent MUDs have de-emphasized the violence in favor of fantasy, world-building, and relationships among participants (including romance). See *Internet*.

MultiColor Graphics Array (MCGA)   A video display standard of IBM's Personal System/2. MCGA adds 64 gray-scale shades to the CGA standard and provides the EGA standard resolution of 640 pixels by 350 lines with 16 possible colors.

MultiFinder   A utility program, supplied by Apple Computer, that extends the Finder's capabilities so that the Macintosh can run more than one application at a time. System 7 incorporates MultiFinder, which no longer is a separate utility.

With MultiFinder, the Macintosh becomes a multiloading operating system with some limited capabilities to perform tasks in the background, such as downloading information via telecommunications and carrying out background printing. Contrary to common belief, MultiFinder isn't a true multitasking operating system; when you activate one application, the other application freezes. See *context switching*, *multiple program loading*, *multitasking*, *shell*, and *System 7*.

multilaunching   In a local area network, the opening of an application program by more than one user at a time.

multilevel sort   In database management, a sort operation that uses two or more data fields to determine the order in which data records are arranged. To perform a multilevel sort, you identify two or more fields as sort keys—fields used for ordering records.

In a membership database, for example, the primary sort key may be LAST_NAME, so all records are alphabetized by the member's last name. The second sort key, FIRST_NAME, comes into play when two or more records have the same last name. A third sort key, JOIN_DATE, is used when two or more records have the same last name and the same first name. Use a multilevel sort when one sort key can't resolve the order of two or more records in your database.

multimedia A computer-based method of presenting information by using more than one medium of communication, such as text, graphics and sound, and emphasizing interactivity.

In a multimedia presentation called Beethoven's World, for example, you can see portraits of the composer, hear his music, and even print scores (see fig. M.4). Advances in sound and video synchronization allow you to display moving video images within on-screen windows (see fig. M.5). However, because graphics and sound require so much storage space, a minimal configuration for a multimedia system includes a CD-ROM drive.

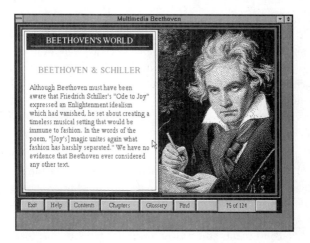

Fig. M.4 *A multimedia application.*

TIP: *Windows users should look for multimedia products (including CD-ROM drives and software) that have the MPC label. This label is your assurance that the product fully conforms to the MPC standards and will function correctly with Microsoft Windows. See* Multimedia Personal Computer (MPC).

6 of 14

Fig. M.5 *A segment of a full-motion video image in a multimedia application.*

multimedia extensions Additions to an operating system that allow multimedia software to synchronize graphics and sound. These extensions—called *hooks* in programmers' slang—allow multimedia software designers to access sound and video capabilities without extensive, non-standard programming. Apple's QuickTime is a multimedia extension to its System 7 software. Windows 3.1 includes the multimedia extensions (called Media Control Interface, or MCI) that were formerly available separately.

Multimedia extensions provide an application program interface (API) for multimedia software developers, who can use multimedia hooks for such tasks as accessing a CD-ROM drive or playing a sound. Early multimedia programs were tied to specific brands and models of CD-ROM drives because no such hooks existed and, in consequence, the programmers had to write code that accessed the drive directly. With multimedia extensions, however, you can use any CD-ROM player (or any other compatible multimedia device) supported by the system software. See *application program interface (API), Microsoft Windows, multimedia, Media Control Interface (MCI),* and *QuickTime.*

m

Multimedia Personal Computer (MPC)   A standard for multimedia hardware and software jointly developed by the MPC Consortium, which includes Microsoft, Philips, Tandy, and Zenith Data Systems. Microsoft Windows 3.1 provides the foundation for MPC. The MPC standard assumes an IBM PS/2 or IBM-compatible hardware platform; Apple Computer, not surprisingly, has offered a competing standard (QuickTime) for its Macintosh computer.

An MPC-capable IBM PC-compatible system includes, minimally, an 80386SX computer running at 20 MHz, 2M of RAM, a VGA graphics display adapter and monitor, a hard disk, a joystick, Microsoft Windows 3.1, a mouse, and an MPC-compatible CD-ROM drive. For high-quality sound, you need a sound adapter. See *CD-ROM*, *multimedia*, and *QuickTime*.

multiple program loading   An operating system that lets you start more than one program at a time; however, only one of the programs is active at any one time. You press a key to switch from one program to another. See *context switching* and *MultiFinder*.

multiple selection   In an electronic spreadsheet program, a selection of two or more non-contiguous ranges. In figure M.6, for example, you see three ranges selected, making it possible for you to format and perform other operations on all three ranges at a time.

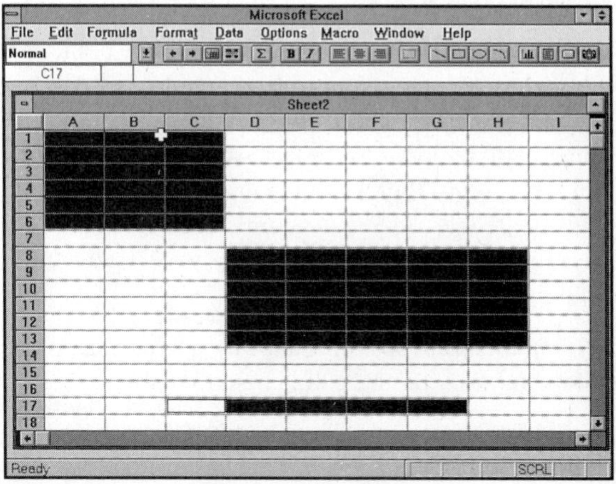

Fig. M.6   *Multiple selection of ranges.*

multiplex   To combine or interleave messages in a communications channel.

multiplexer (mux)   A device that merges lower speed transmissions into one higher speed channel at one end of the link. Another mux reverses the process at the other end of the link.

multiplexing   In local area networks, the simultaneous transmission of multiple messages in one channel.

A network that can multiplex allows more than one computer to access the network simultaneously. Multiplexing increases the cost of a network, however, because multiplexing devices must be included that can mix the signals into a single channel for transmission. See *frequency division multiplexing, local area network (LAN), multiplex,* and *time division multiplexing.*

multiscanning monitor   A color monitor that can adjust to a range of input frequencies so that it can work with a variety of display adapters. Often called a *multisync monitor,* but Multisync is a proprietary name of an NEC multiscanning monitor.

Multisync monitor   See *multiscanning monitor.*

multitasking   The execution of more than one program at a time on a computer system.

Multitasking shouldn't be confused with multiple program loading, in which two or more programs are present in RAM but only one program executes at a time. When multitasking, the active, or foreground, task responds to the keyboard while the background task continues to run (but without your active control). Terminate-and-stay-resident (TSR) programs are unnecessary, because you can run simultaneously any programs you want to, as long as the computer has enough memory.

Critics of multitasking operating systems say that users of stand-alone workstations have little need for multiprogramming

m

operations. Programs that can print or download files in the background, however, hint at the power of multitasking. Imagine being able to write with your word processing program at the same time that your spreadsheet program prints a lengthy report.

Among the operating systems or shells that provide multitasking are OS/2, DESQview, and Microsoft Windows. See *Microsoft Windows*, *multiple program loading,* and *Operating System/2 (OS/2).*

multiuser system   A computer system that can be used by more than one person to access programs and data at the same time.

Each user is equipped with a terminal. If the system has just one central processing unit, a technique called *time-sharing* provides multiple access. A time-sharing system cycles access to the processing unit among users.

Personal computers with advanced microprocessors, such as the Intel 80486, are sufficiently powerful to serve as the nucleus of a multiuser system. Such systems typically are equipped with the UNIX operating system, designed for multiuser systems.

Microprocessors such as the 80486 and Pentium have helped blur the distinction between personal computers and minicomputers. If a minicomputer is a multiuser system designed to meet the needs of 4 to 100 people, multiuser computers based on 80486 and Pentium chips are legitimate minicomputers. Given such advances, the term *personal computer* usually is reserved for computers dedicated to stand-alone applications. See *local area network (LAN), mainframe, minicomputer, time-sharing,* and *UNIX.*

M N O

TIP: *If you're considering installing a system that more than one person will use, familiarize yourself with the pros and cons of the two alternatives: multiuser systems and local area networks.*

Musical Instrument Digital Interface (MIDI)   A standard communications protocol for the exchange of information between computers and musical synthesizers.

MIDI provides tools that many composers and musicians say are becoming almost indispensable. With a synthesizer and a computer equipped with the necessary software and a MIDI port, a musician can transcribe a composition into musical notation by playing the composition at the keyboard. After the music is placed into computer-represented form, virtually every aspect of the digitized sound—pitch, attack, delay time, tempo, and more—can beedited and altered.

m

nano- A prefix indicating one billionth.

nanosecond (ns) A unit of time equal to one billionth of a second. Far beyond the range of human perception, nanoseconds are relevant to computers. An advertisement for 80 ns RAM chips, for example, means that the RAM chips respond within 80 nano-seconds. See *millisecond (ms)*.

National Information Infrastructure (NII) A proposed high-speed, high-bandwidth network that can deliver voice, data, and video services throughout the United States. NII will be developed by private firms, cable television, and telephone companies, with minimal government funding. The major impetus is the delivery of on-demand movies to the home, fueled by good old-fashioned competition.

That NII will be built seems all but inevitable; whether this commercial venture will serve the public good is another matter. It may well end up being a television set with more channels, denying the use of the system for autonomous two-way communication and the construction of virtual communities. See *asynchronous digital subscriber loop (ADSL)*.

National Television Standards Committee (NTSC)
A committee that governs physical standards for television broadcasting in the United States and most of Central and South America (but not Europe or Asia). NTSC television uses 525-line frames and displays full frames at 30 frames per second, using two interlaced fields at about 60 frames per second to correspond to the U.S. alternating-current frequency of 60 Hz. NTSC video connections use standard RCA phonograph plugs and jacks.

Television engineers joke that NTSC really stands for "Never Twice the Same Color," because the NTSC standard provides poor color control. Most European and Asian countries use the PAL standard based on their 50 Hz power-line frequencies.

native code   See *machine language.*

native file format   The default file format a program uses to store data on disk. The format is often a proprietary file format. Many popular programs today can retrieve and save data in several formats. See *ASCII, file format,* and *proprietary file format.*

natural language   A naturally occurring language such as Spanish, French, German, or Tamil, as opposed to an artificial language such as a computer programming language.

Computer scientists are working to improve computers so that they can respond to natural language. Human languages are so complex that no single model of a natural language grammar system has gained widespread acceptance among linguists. The complexity of human languages, coupled with the lack of understanding about what information is needed to decode human sentences, makes it difficult to devise programs that recognize speech. Progress in solving these problems has been slow.

CAUTION: *Computer programs, such as Lotus HAL, occasionally are marketed with the claim that they can accept natural language input, but your input must be phrased so that it conforms to fairly strict syntax guidelines.*

natural language processing   In artificial intelligence, using a computer to decypher or analyze human language.

natural recalculation   In a spreadsheet program, a recalculation order that performs worksheet computations in the manner logically dictated by the formulas you place in cells. If the value of a formula depends on references to other cells that contain formulas, the program calculates the other cells first. See *column-wise recalculation, optimal recalculation,* and *row-wise recalculation.*

near-letter quality (NLQ)   A dot-matrix printing mode that prints almost typewriter-quality characters. As a result, printing when using this mode is slower than other printing modes.

needle drop   In multimedia, using a short excerpt from a recorded musical piece instead of creating an original composition. The term stems from the days of vinyl phonograph needles.

CAUTION: *Don't use recorded music in your multimedia presentations without first seeking permission and paying the required needle drop fee.*

nested structure   A structure in which one control structure is positioned within another. See *control structure* and *DO/WHILE loop*.

NetBIOS   See *Network Basic Input/Output System (NetBIOS)*.

net.god(dess)   A longtime user or founder of a computer newsgroup, who's considered by many users to epitomize the group's preferred moral and ethical stance. If a neophyte threatens to start a *flame war* (an unproductive and angry exchange of ill-considered opinion), a net god or goddess may step in and, like a tribal elder intent on preserving the peace, chide the offender by posting a critical message. The format of the title (including the period) is a humorous take-off on the domain name system of Internet network addresses. See *Internet* and *newsgroup*.

M
N
O

netiquette   Network etiquette; a set of rules that reflect long-standing experience about getting along harmoniously in the electronic environment (electronic mail and computer newsgroups). The basics of netiquette are as follows:

- Keep your messages short and to the point, abbreviate whenever possible, and don't include an extravagant *signature* at the bottom of your message that lists your name and electronic mailing address.

- Don't use ALL UPPERCASE LETTERS. This is considered to be "shouting." To emphasize a word, use asterisks as you would quotation marks.

- If you want to criticize, criticize the idea, not the person. Don't criticize a person's spelling or grammatical errors.

Today's worldwide networks encompass users willing to learn English and trying to participate; they deserve encouragement, not criticism.

- Don't overreact to something you read on-line. If you get angry, don't reply right away. Go take a walk or, better yet, sleep on it. Electronic mail is easily forwarded. Don't say anything that you don't want to wind up on your boss's desk.

- Don't ask members of a newsgroup to censor a particular person's contributions, or disallow discussion of a topic that you find offensive; instead, create a kill file so that those messages don't appear on your screen.

- If you ask a question in a newsgroup, request that replies be sent to you personally, unless you feel that the replies would be of interest to everyone who reads the newsgroup.

- In electronic mail, be cautious in replying to messages that were sent to more than one subscriber. In some systems, your reply will be sent to each person who received the original—which may include every subscriber.

- Don't cross-post a message (send it to more than one newsgroup), or reply to a cross-posted message, unless you're genuinely following the discussion in each newsgroup and believe your message would prove of interest to readers of each of them.

- If you're posting something that gives away the plot of a movie, novel, or television show, put **<SPOILER>** at the top of your message. That way, people can skip reading it if they don't want to know whodunnit.

- If you're posting something that some people may find offensive, such as an erotic story, use the command (available with most networks) that encrypts your text so that it looks like garbage characters. (In USENET, for example, the command *rot13* shifts each letter 13 characters, so that *b* becomes *o*.) To read such a message, use the command that decrypts the text. Any reader who is offended will have to take responsibility for having decrypted the message.

Also, use discretion when "getting personal" with other users. Stalking laws are now being interpreted to encompass e-mail messages. See *cross-post, electronic mail, follow-on post, Internet, kill file, net.police, newsgroup, post, rot-13*, and *spoiler*.

netnews   A collective way of referring to the USENET newsgroups. See *newsgroup* and *USENET*.

NETNORTH   A Canadian wide-area network fully integrated with BITNET that performs the same functions as BITNET. See *BITNET*.

net.police   In a computer newsgroup, participants who believe it's their moral responsibility to chide posters who violate written or unwritten canons of network etiquette. See *netiquette*.

NetWare   A network operating system, manufactured by Novell, for local area networks. NetWare accommodates more than 90 types of network interface cards, 30 network architectures, and several communications protocols. Versions are available for IBM PC compatibles and Macintosh computers. See *network operating system (NOS)*.

network   A computer-based communications and data exchange system created by physically connecting two or more computers.

Personal computer networks differ in their scope. The smallest networks, called *local area networks* (LANs), may connect just two or three computers with an expensive peripheral, such as a laser printer, whereas others connect as many as 75 or more computers. Larger networks, called *wide-area networks* (WANs), use telephone lines or other communications media to link together computers separated by tens to thousands of miles (see fig. N.1).

The basic components of a network are personal computers or workstations that contain a network interface card and are linked by cables to a file server that houses the central mass storage, all of which interact using network operating system (NOS) software. A central file server isn't used in a peer-to-peer network. Unlike a *multiuser system*, in which each user is equipped with a dumb terminal that may lack processing capabilities, each user in a network possesses a workstation containing its own processing circuitry.

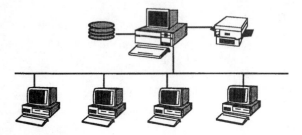

Fig. N.1 *An illustration of a personal computer local area network.*

Personal computer networks also differ in their topology, the geometry of their connections. Common topologies include the star topology, in which machines are linked to a central file server, and the bus topology, in which machines are linked to a single backbone cable. Also, two methods for communicating information via the network's cables exist: baseband and broadband.

Several competing standards govern the communications standard by which data is exchanged in networks. Built into all Macintosh computers is AppleTalk, a low-bandwidth network protocol suitable for small networks. Larger networks can use EtherNet or IBM's token-ring network. See *baseband, broadband, bus network, local area network (LAN), network architecture, network operating system (NOS), network protocol, network topology, star network,* and *token-ring network.*

network administrator   In local area networks, the person responsible for maintaining the network and assisting its users.

network architecture   The complete set of hardware, software, and cabling standards for a local area network design. See *network topology.*

Network Basic Input/Output System (NetBIOS)   A system program included in MS-DOS (Version 3.1 and later) that establishes standard methods for linking personal computers to local area networks.

network drive   In a local area network, a disk drive made available to you through the network, as distinguished from a drive connected directly to the workstation you're using.

network interface card   An adapter that lets you connect a network cable to a microcomputer. The card includes encoding and decoding circuitry and a receptacle for a network cable connection.

Because data is transmitted more rapidly within the computer's internal bus, a network interface card allows the network to operate at higher speeds than it would if delayed by the serial port. Networks such as EtherNet and ARCnet that use interface cards can transmit information much faster than networks such as AppleTalk, which uses serial ports.

network operating system (NOS)   The system software of a local area network that integrates the network's hardware components, usually adequate for connecting up to 50 workstations. Included, typically, are such features as a menu-driven administration interface, tape backup of file-server software, security restrictions, facilities for sharing printers, central storage of applications and databases, remote log-in via modem, and support for diskless workstations.

A network operating system establishes and maintains the connection between the workstations and the file server; the physical connections alone aren't sufficient to support networking. The operating system consists of two parts: the file server software and workstation software. See *file server, LAN memory management program, local area network (LAN), NetWare,* and *workstation.*

CAUTION: *The workstation software can consume enough conventional memory to prevent you from running MS-DOS applications. When considering a network, find out how much workstation memory is required, and whether it's possible to store some or all of it in extended or expanded memory.*

M
N
O

network printer   In a local area network, a printer made available to you through the network, as distinguished from a local printer (a printer connected directly to the workstation you're using).

network protocol   The method used to regulate a workstation's access to a computer network to prevent data collisions. Examples include carrier sense multiple access with collision detection (CSMA/CD) and token passing. See *carrier sense multiple access with collision detection (CSMA/CD)* and *token passing*.

network server   See *file server*.

network topology   The geometric arrangement of nodes and cable links in a local area network.

Network topologies fall into two categories: centralized and decentralized. In a centralized topology such as a star network, a central computer controls access to the network. This design ensures data security and central management control over the network's contents and activities.

In a decentralized topology such as a bus network or ring network, each workstation can access the network independently and establish its own connections with other workstations. See *bus network*, *ring network*, and *star network*.

newsgroup   In a computer bulletin board system (BBS) such as The WELL or a distributed bulletin board system such as EchoMail or USENET, a discussion group that's devoted to a single topic, such as *Star Trek*, model aviation, the books of Ayn Rand, or the music of the Grateful Dead. Users post messages to the group, and those reading the discussion send reply messages to the author individually or post replies that can be read by the group as a whole.

The term *newsgroup* is a misnomer in that the discussions rarely involve "news"; *discussion group* would be more accurate, but the term *newsgroup* has taken root. Synonymous with *forum*. See *FAQ*, *follow-on post*, *moderated newsgroup*, *net.god(dess)*, *netiquette*, *post*, *thread*, *unmoderated newsgroup*, and *USENET*.

> **TIP:** *Need information that's hard to find? Post a question on a newsgroup. Newsgroups offer an astonishingly rich information resource—much richer, according to some users, than the so-called "information databanks" that charge big bucks.*

newspaper columns   A page format in which two or more columns of text are printed vertically on the page so that the text flows down one column and continues at the top of the next (see fig. N.2).

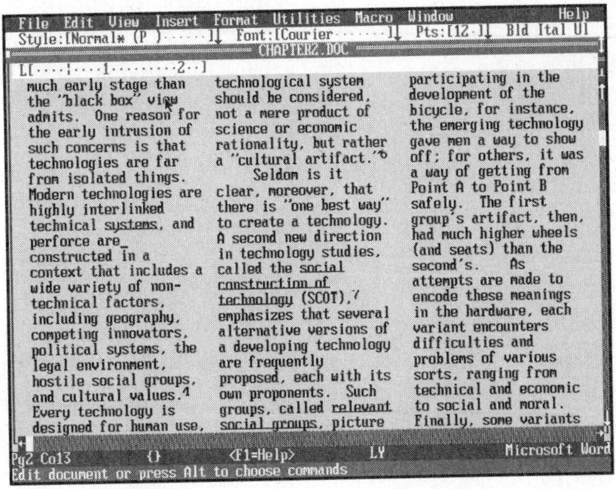

Fig. N.2   *Newspaper columns.*

Sometimes called *snaking columns* to suggest the flow of text, newspaper columns differ from side-by-side columns, which don't divide automatically. High-end word processing programs such as Microsoft Word and WordPerfect do a good job of producing newspaper columns and can even balance the bottom margin of columns (called *balanced newspaper columns*) for a professional-looking effect.

> **TIP:** *Research on legibility demonstrates that a line should have approximately 55 to 60 characters (about 9 or 10 words) for optimum readability. If line lengths exceed this amount, break the text into two or more columns.*

Newton   A personal digital assistant, driven by a 32-bit, 20Mhz RISC processor with 640K of RAM, manufactured by Apple Corporation.

The Newton includes a date book, address book, and freeform notebook in which you enter data using a stylus or using a keyboard you can display on the small screen. The handwriting recognition engine can learn your writing, improving over time, although recognition is slow. Thirty built-in command words can be written directly on-screen, such as PRINT or SEND FAX.

The address book can be used to emit tones to dial a phone number if you hold the phone receiver close to the device. An infrared port sends files at 9600 bps to another personal data assistant, a printer, or your desktop personal computer. With the optional fax/modem you can send mail on NewtonMail, communicate with your office, and fax memos. It's pricy at more than $700; however, if the anticipated paging feature is delivered, it can bring the features more in line with the price. See *NewtonMail, personal digital assistant, reduced instruction set computer (RISC)*, and *stylus*.

NewtonMail   An on-line computer service providing the e-mail features of eWorld to Newton users with a modem. Regular eWorld users who have a Newton and NewtonMail can access NewtonMail from their desktop personal computer. See *eWorld* and *Newton*.

neural networks   An artificial intelligence technique that mimics the way nerve cells are connected in the human brain. Information is supplied to the neural network to train it to recognize patterns. The result is a program that can make predictions, useful in weather forecasting and stock market software.

NLQ   See *near-letter quality*.

node   In a local area network, a connection point that can create, receive, or repeat a message.

In personal computer networks, nodes include repeaters, file servers, and shared peripherals. In common usage, however, the term *node* is synonymous with *workstation*. See *network topology*, *repeater*, and *workstation*.

noise   Unwanted or random electrical signals on a communications channel, unlike the signal that carries the information you want. All communications channels have noise, but if the noise is excessive, data loss can occur.

Telephone lines are particularly noisy, requiring the use of communications programs that can perform error-checking operations to make sure that the data being received isn't corrupted.

non-impact printer   A printer that forms a text or graphic image by spraying or fusing ink to the page. Non-impact printers include inkjet printers, laser printers, and thermal printers.

All non-impact printers are considerably quieter than impact printers, but non-impact printers can't print multiple copies by using carbon paper. See *impact printer*, *inkjet printer*, *laser printer*, and *thermal printer*.

non-interlaced monitor   A computer monitor that doesn't use the screen refresh technique called *interlacing* and, as a result, can display high-resolution images without flickering or streaking. See *interlacing*.

non-procedural language   See *declarative language*.

non-transactional application   In a local area network, a program that produces data that you don't need to keep in a shared database for all users to access. Most of the work done with word processing programs, for example, is non-transactional.

**M
N
O**

non-volatile memory   The memory specially designed to hold information, even when the power is switched off. Read-only memory (ROM) is non-volatile, as are all secondary storage units such as disk drives. See *random-access memory (RAM)* and *volatility*.

non-Windows application   A DOS application program that doesn't require Microsoft Windows to run.

DOS applications can also be run under Windows. Using Standard or 386 Enhanced modes, you can switch from one non-Windows application to another without closing either program. In 386 Enhanced mode, you can multitask two or more DOS applications—if each is running in a window and isn't maximized. Compared to running a DOS application under DOS, you may find that the mouse and the cursor aren't as responsive when running DOS applications in Windows. See *386 Enhanced mode, application program interface (API), maximize, Microsoft Windows*, and *Standard mode*.

no parity   In asynchronous communications, a communications protocol that disables parity checking and leaves no space for the parity bit. See *asynchronous communication, communications protocol, parity bit*, and *parity checking*.

Norton SI   In IBM PC-compatible computing, a widely used benchmark measurement of a computer's throughput.

Short for *Norton System Information*, Norton SI is a program included in Norton Utilities. The program's composite performance index provides a balanced picture of a computer system's throughput, including its internal processing speed and the speed of peripherals such as disk drives. See *benchmark, million instructions per second (MIPS)*, and *throughput*.

NOS   See *network operating system (NOS)*.

notebook computer   A portable computer that typically weighs less than 7 pounds and measures about 8×11×1$\frac{1}{2}$ inches, easily fitting inside a briefcase. See *auxiliary battery* and *battery pack*.

NSFNet   A wide area network developed by the Office of Advanced Scientific Computing at the National Science Foundation (NSF). NSFNet was developed to take over the civilian functions of the U.S. Defense Department's ARPAnet, which, for security reasons, has been closed to public access. NSFNet provided the communications hardware for the Internet, which is fast emerging as the world's electronic mail system. See *ARPAnet* and *Internet.*

NTSC   See *National Television Standards Committee (NTSC).*

NuBus   The high-speed expansion bus of Macintosh II computers. NuBus requires adapters specifically designed for its 96-pin receptacles. See *expansion bus.*

nuke   To erase an entire directory or disk.

null modem cable   A specially configured serial cable that allows you to connect two computers directly, without mediation by a modem.

null value   In an accounting or database management program, a blank field in which you've never typed a value, as distinguished from a value of zero that you enter deliberately. In some applications, you need to distinguish between a null value and a deliberately entered zero; a null value doesn't affect computations, but a zero does.

M N O

number crunching   A slang term for calculating, especially large amounts of data.

numeric coprocessor   A microprocessor support chip that performs mathematical computations at speeds up to 100 times faster than a microprocessor alone.

The Intel numeric coprocessors—8087, 80287, and 80387— are designed to work with their microprocessor counterparts. They work with 80 bits at a time, so a programmer can express a number of sufficient length to ensure accurate calculations. An innovative feature of the Intel 80486DX chip is the inclusion of the numeric coprocessor circuitry on the microprocessor chip. See *binary coded decimal (BCD), floating-point calculation,* and *microprocessor.*

> **TIP:** *If you work with spreadsheets or any other application that performs calculations intensively, a numeric coprocessor will give you substantial gains in the apparent speed of your system without any changes to your software.*

numeric coprocessor socket   A push-down socket on the motherboard of many personal computers into which you or a dealer can mount a numeric coprocessor, such as the Intel 80387. See *numeric coprocessor.*

numeric format   In a spreadsheet program, the way in which the program displays numbers in a cell. With most spreadsheet programs, you can choose among the following numeric formatting options:

- *Fixed.* Displays values with a fixed number of decimal places, ranging from 0 to 15.

- *Scientific.* Displays very large or small numbers using scientific notation; for example, 12,460,000,000 appears as 1.25E+11.

- *Currency.* Displays values with commas and dollar signs and the number of decimal places you specify (0 to 15).

- *Comma.* Displays numbers larger than 999 with commas separating thousands.

- *General.* Displays numbers without commas and without trailing zeroes to the right of the decimal point. If the number of digits to the left of the decimal point exceeds the column width, scientific notation is used. If the number of digits to the right of the decimal point exceeds the column width, the number is rounded.

- *+/–.* Converts the number to a simple bar graph in the cell, with the number of plus or minus signs equaling the positive or negative whole number value of the entry; for example, 5 appears as +++++.

- *Percent.* Multiplies the value by 100 and adds a percent sign; for example, 0.485 appears as 48.5%. You specify the number of decimal places (0 to 15).

n

- *Date.* Converts a number to a date. The number 32734, for example, converts to the date August 14, 1989.

- *Text.* Displays the formula rather than the value computed by the formula.

- *Hidden.* Makes the cell entry invisible on-screen. Use the cell definition to see the contents.

See *cell.*

numeric keypad   A group of keys arranged like the keys on an adding machine, usually located to the right of the typing area on a keyboard. The keypad is designed for the rapid touch-typing entry of numerical data.

Num Lock key   A toggle key that locks the numeric keypad into a mode in which you can enter numbers. When the Num Lock key is on, the cursor-movement keys are disabled.

On IBM PC-compatible keyboards, the keys on the numeric keypad are labeled with arrows and numbers. You can use these keys to move the cursor or to enter numbers. The Num Lock key toggles the keypad back and forth between these two modes.

**M
N
O**

object   In object linking and embedding (OLE), a document or portion of a document that has been pasted into another document using the Paste Link, Paste Special, or Embed Object command. See *applet*, *dynamic object*, *object linking and embedding (OLE)*, and *static object*.

object code   In computer programming, the machine-readable instructions created by a compiler or interpreter from source code. See *source code*.

object linking and embedding (OLE)   *oh-lay*   A set of standards, developed by Microsoft Corporation and incorporated into Microsoft Windows and Apple's Macintosh system software, that you use to create dynamic, automatically updated links between documents, and also to embed a document created by one application into a document created by another.

When you use the Clipboard to copy a Microsoft Excel chart into a Microsoft Word document and later change the Excel chart, your changes aren't reflected in the copy you placed in the Word document. With OLE, however, you can create a *dynamic* link between a source and a destination document so that the changes you make to the source document are reflected in the destination document.

To create a link, copy the source data and choose Paste Link or Paste Special to insert the copy in the destination document, creating a dynamic link. If you make a change to the source document and the source and destination documents are both open, the changes are automatically reflected in the destination document. To easily edit the linked object, just double-click it to launch the application used to create the object. Edit the source document, and the linked copy is updated.

Linking is useful when you want one authoritative version of a file, which you can include in many other documents and applications. This source file can be edited as often as you want, but the location of the file must not be changed.

OLE also supports embedding. When you embed an object, you actually place a fully editable, independent copy of the source document (or a portion of the source document) into the destination file, resulting in a compound file.

Embedding is useful when you want to place a copy of an object in a file, and you don't want any changes you make to this object to be reflected in the original file and vice versa. After embedding the object, you double-click it to use its source application to edit the object. The original file can be edited or removed from its location without affecting the embedded object.

To use OLE, you must be running applications that can serve as client and server applications for OLE purposes. To tell quickly whether an application supports OLE, pull down the Edit menu and look for a command such as Paste Link or Paste Special, which is used for linking. If the Edit menu includes an Insert Object command, the program can function as a destination application for embedding purposes. See *applet, client application, embedded object, linked object,* and *server application.*

object-oriented graphic   A graphic image composed of distinct objects—such as lines, circles, ellipses, and boxes—that you can move independently.

Object-oriented graphics often are called *vector graphics* because the program stores them as mathematical formulas for the vectors, or directional lines, that compose the image. Unlike bit-mapped graphics, which distort when resized, you can resize object-oriented graphics without introducing distortions (see fig. O.1). See *bit-mapped graphic.*

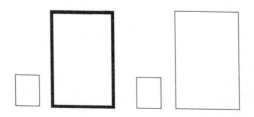

Fig. O.1   *A rectangle enlarged by a bit-mapped graphics program (left) and by an object-oriented graphics program (right).*

object-oriented programming language   A non-procedural programming language in which program elements are conceptualized as objects that can pass messages to each other. Object-oriented programming is the ultimate extension of the concept of modular programming.

In object-oriented programming, the modules are independent enough to stand on their own, so you can copy them into other programs. Rather than create an object again and again, you can copy it, add some new features, and then move the new object to another program. You can move objects around in chunks to compose new programs.

Object-oriented programming languages also have natural affinities with graphical user interfaces. You can display a completed object as an icon and drag the icon around with a mouse to reposition or copy the object. In HyperCard, for example, when you select and copy a button and paste it on another card, you also copy the script. This technique is extremely powerful and easy to learn.

Whether object-oriented programming will ever replace conventional programming techniques is far from clear. Object-oriented programs require a great deal of memory and execute slowly compared to assembly language and C. In the future, as computers improve, programming language speed will be less of an issue, and object-oriented programming may find professional applications. See *declarative language, extensible, modular programming,* and *script.*

Object Packager   In Microsoft Windows, an accessory that transforms an object into a package, which you can then insert in a destination document as a linked or embedded object. The reader of this document sees an icon, which he can double-click to start the application that created the object. Using Object Packager, you can embed a spreadsheet as an icon in a word processing document with a note such as, "Jan, just double-click this icon to see our Excel worksheet showing the Fall Quarter figures I told you about."

Windows 3.1 users can make use of Object Packager for many purposes. Figure O.2 shows five packaged objects created by a variety of applications. This dynamic and interactive document plays a recording, displays text, runs through a worksheet "what-if" scenario, displays a chart, and displays a bit-mapped graphic image. See *annotation* and *object linking and embedding (OLE).*

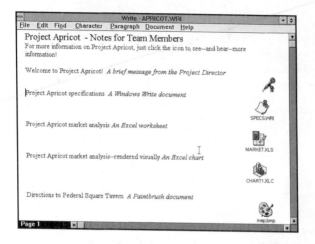

Fig. O.2 *An interactive document combining packages created by several server applications.*

oblique   *oh-bleek*   The italic form of a sans serif typeface. See *sans serif.*

odd parity   In asynchronous communications, an error-checking protocol in which the parity bit is set to 1 if the number of 1 digits in a one-byte data item adds up to an odd number. For example, the following byte has five 1s: 01011011. The parity bit therefore would be set to 1 in an odd parity-checking scheme. If the parity bit indicates *odd* but the data transmitted actually contains an even number of 1s, the system will report that a transmission error has occurred. See *asynchronous communication, communications parameters, communications protocol, even parity,* and *parity checking.*

OEM   See *original equipment manufacturer (OEM).*

office automation   The use of computers and local area networks to integrate traditional office activities such as conferencing, writing, filing, calculating, customer and merchandise tracking, and sending and receiving messages.

M
N
O

Because many tasks such as filing or word processing can be performed much faster on a computer than with manual techniques, many firms hoped to reap huge productivity gains from office automation systems. With some exceptions, these gains haven't materialized, or at best amount to 10–15 percent.

Businesses that are successful in office automation begin by identifying a specific activity that can be done more cheaply or more rapidly on the computer. Then they develop a system of hardware and software for that specific application.

A strategy that has produced significant productivity gains—sometimes over 200 percent—is called re-engineering. In re-engineering, a firm identifies ways to reorganize work so that people can do it more efficiently. Then computers are used to support the altered work roles. In re-engineering, the productivity gains really stem from the redesigned work roles, not from the computer. See *re-engineering*.

> **TIP:** *If you automate a mess, you get an automated mess. Develop ways of working more efficiently, and* then *automate.*

off-line   Not directly connected with a computer; for example, a device that isn't hooked up to your PC is off-line or has been switched to off-line mode. In data communications, not connected with another computer; for example, a workstation you've temporarily or permanently disconnected from a local area network is off-line.

off-screen formatting   See *embedded formatting command*.

offset   In word processing, an amount of space added to leave space for binding. Synonymous with *gutter*.

OK button   A pushbutton you can activate in a dialog box to confirm the current dialog box settings and execute the command. If the OK button is highlighted or surrounded by a thick black line, you can press Enter to choose OK.

OLE client *oh-lay* In object linking and embedding, an application that can serve as the recipient of a linked or embedded object created by a server application. See *object linking and embedding (OLE)*.

OLE server *oh-lay* In object linking and embedding, an application that can provide an object to be linked or embedded into a destination (client) document. See *object linking and embedding (OLE)*.

one hundred percent (100%) column graph A column graph that resembles a pie graph in that each "slice" of the column displays the relative percentage of that data item compared to the total (see fig. O.3). See *stacked column graph*.

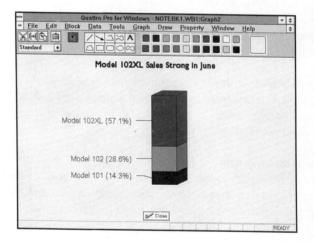

Fig. O.3 *A 100% column graph.*

on-line Directly connected with and accessible to a computer; for example, after you successfully hook it up to your PC and turn it on. In data communications, connected with another, distant computer; for example, the successful connection with a host computer in a client-server network. On a BBS, when a file or application is available to the users.

on-line help A help utility available on-screen while you're using a network or an application program.

on-line information service   A for-profit firm that makes current news, stock quotes, and other information available to its subscribers over standard telephone lines. See *America Online, bibliographic retrieval service, CompuServe, Delphi, Dow Jones News/Retrieval Service, GEnie,* and *Prodigy.*

on-screen formatting   In a word processing program, a formatting technique in which formatting commands directly affect the text that's visible on-screen. See *embedded formatting command* and *what-you-see-is-what-you-get (WYSIWYG).*

OOPS   Acronym for *object-oriented programming system.* See *object-oriented programming language.*

open   Available for modification; not controlled by a single manufacturer.

open architecture   A computer system in which all the system specifications are made public so that other companies will develop add-on products such as adapters for the system. See *open bus system.*

open bus system   A computer design in which the computer's expansion bus contains receptacles that readily accept adapters. An open-architecture system generally has an open bus, but not all systems with open buses have open architectures; the Macintosh is an example of the latter. See *expansion bus.*

Open System Interconnection (OSI) reference model   An international standard for the organization of local area networks (LANs) established by the International Standards Organization (ISO) and the Institute of Electrical and Electronic Engineers (IEEE). Synonymous with *ISO/OSI reference model.*

The OSI reference model separates the communication process into distinct layers insulated from each other, such as the physical hardware (the cabling, etc.), the transport layer (the method by which data is communicated), the presentation layer (the way the transmitted data interacts with programs in each computer), and the application layer (the programs available to all users of the network). Figure O.4 shows the OSI reference model divided into layers.

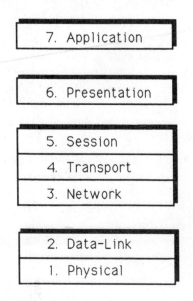

Fig. O.4 *The OSI reference model.*

Because each layer is to some extent independent of the others, you can, in theory, change the cabling (from twisted-pair cable to coaxial cable, for example) without making changes at the other layers. As more manufacturers comply with the OSI model, connectivity will continue to improve. See *local area network (LAN)*.

operating system   A master control program for a computer that manages the computer's internal functions and provides a means to control the computer's operations. The most popular operating systems for personal computers include MS-DOS, OS/2, and the Macintosh System. See *MS-DOS, Operating System/2 (OS/2)*, and *System 7*.

Operating System/2 (OS/2)   A multitasking operating system for IBM PC-compatible computers that breaks the 640K RAM barrier, provides protection for programs running simultaneously, and allows the dynamic exchange of data between applications.

The history of OS/2 has all the drama of 19th-century cutthroat industrial competition. Originally, the operating system was jointly developed by IBM and Microsoft as the heir apparent to MS-DOS. At the time of OS/2's release, there were good reasons to regard OS/2 as the operating system of the future. Yet few users upgraded to OS/2, in part because few software publishers developed OS/2 applications, and early versions of OS/2 ran MS-DOS programs poorly.

Meanwhile, Microsoft Corporation was busily developing Windows, but insisting that Windows was a stopgap measure until the marketplace accepted OS/2. The early versions of Windows were little more than fancy shells. But by 1989, QuarterDeck Office Systems had amply confirmed that its windowing environment, DESQview, running under MS-DOS, could use protected mode without sacrificing full MS-DOS compatibility.

Windows 3.0 was released, stunning the industry by incorporating full protected-mode processing. As millions of copies were sold, the rationale for upgrading to OS/2 was disappearing. Microsoft claimed that the future belonged to Windows: The operating system of the future would be Windows NT (a 32-bit version of Windows), not OS/2. Not surprisingly, these events put a damper on the formerly close and cordial relationship between IBM and Microsoft.

In reply to Microsoft's moves with Windows, IBM seized control of OS/2 development and announced a radical upgrade. The new OS/2, Version 2.0, released in 1992, runs MS-DOS and Windows applications well, and takes full advantage of the 32-bit architecture of 80386 and later microprocessors. It also offers a new graphical user interface similar to that of a NeXT workstation (see fig. O.5). Whether OS/2 can stop Windows' astonishing momentum, however, remains to be seen. Although the most recent release, 2.1, addresses many of the shortcomings of Version 2.0, users still seem reluctant to switch from Windows or DOS. What the operating system of the future will be is still anyone's guess. See *Microsoft Windows*, *protected mode*, and *real mode*.

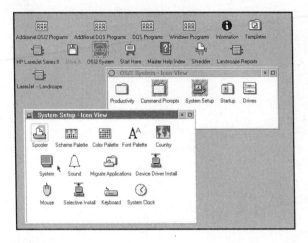

Fig. O.5 *The OS/2 Presentation Manager interface.*

optical character recognition (OCR)   Machine recognition of printed or typed text. Using OCR software with a scanner, a printed page can be scanned and the characters converted into text in a word processing document format.

optical disk   A large-capacity data storage medium for computers on which information is stored at extremely high density in the form of tiny pits. The presence or absence of pits is read by a tightly focused laser beam.

Optical storage technologies are expected to play a significant role in the data storage systems of the 1990s. CD-ROM disks and disk drives offer an increasingly economical medium for read-only data and programs. Write-once, read-many (WORM) drives allow organizations to create their own huge, in-house databases. Erasable optical disk drives offer more storage than hard disks, and the CDs are removable. They are, however, still more expensive and much slower than hard disks. See *CD-ROM, interactive videodisk,* and *write-once, read-many (WORM).*

optical scanner   See *scanner.*

M
N
O

optimal recalculation   In Lotus 1-2-3 and other advanced spreadsheet programs, a method that speeds automatic recalculation by recalculating only those cells that have changed since the last recalculation. See *automatic recalculation.*

option button   See *radio button.*

organization chart   In presentation graphics, a text chart you use to diagram the reporting structure of a organization, such as a corporation or a club (see fig. O.6).

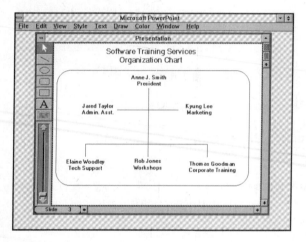

Fig. O.6   *An organization chart.*

orientation   See *landscape orientation* and *portrait orientation.*

original equipment manufacturer (OEM)   The company that actually manufactures a given piece of hardware, unlike the value-added reseller (VAR)—the company that changes, configures, repackages, and sells the hardware.

For example, only a few companies such as Canon, Toshiba, and Ricoh make the print engines used in laser printers. These engines are installed in housings with other components and sold by VARs such as Hewlett-Packard.

orphan   A formatting flaw in which the first line of a paragraph appears alone at the bottom of a page. Most word processing and page-layout programs suppress widows and orphans; the better programs let you switch widow/orphan control on and off and choose the number of lines for which the suppression feature is effective. See *widow*.

OS/2   See *Operating System/2 (OS/2)*.

outline font   A printer or screen font in which a mathematical formula generates each character, producing a graceful and undistorted outline of the character, which the printer then fills in.

Mathematical formulas, rather than bit maps, produce the graceful arcs and lines of outline characters (see fig. O.7). The printer can easily change the type size of an outline font without introducing the distortion common with bit-mapped fonts. (You may need to reduce the weight of small font sizes by using a process called *hinting*, which prevents the loss of fine detail.)

M
N
O

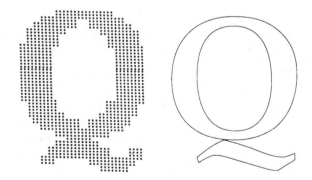

Fig. O.7   *A bit-mapped character (left) and an outline character (right).*

Outline fonts are available as built-in fonts on many laser printers and as downloadable fonts provided on disk. A leading supplier of outline fonts is Adobe Systems, Inc. See *bit-mapped font* and *hinting*.

outline utility　In some full-featured word processing programs, a mode that helps you plan and organize a document by using outline headings as document headings. The program lets you view the document as an outline or as ordinary text.

When you view the document in outline mode, the headings and subheadings appear as they would in an outline (see fig. O.8). The text beneath the headings collapses (disappears) so that only the headings and subheadings are visible.

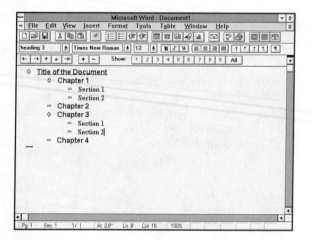

Fig. O.8　*Document headings viewed in outline mode.*

In outline mode, you can move the headings and subheadings vertically; if you move a heading, all the hidden text positioned beneath it also moves. After you switch back to document mode, the outline format disappears, and the document appears normally (see fig. O.9).

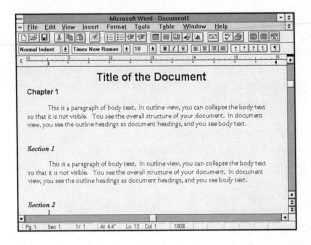

Fig. O.9 *Document headings viewed in document mode.*

output   The process of displaying or printing the results of processing operations. See *input.*

overflow   A condition in which a program tries to put more data in a memory area than the area can accommodate, resulting in an error message.

overlaid windows   In a user interface, a display mode in which windows are allowed to overlap each other. If you maximize the top window to full size, it completely hides the other windows. See *cascading windows* and *tiled windows.*

overlay   See *program overlay.*

overlay chart   In a business graphics program, a second type of chart that's overlaid on the main chart, such as a line chart on top of a bar chart. Synonymous with *combination chart.* See *mixed column/line graph.*

overstrike   Creating a character not found in a printer's character set by placing one character on top of another, such as using O and / to create zeros that can be easily distinguished from an uppercase letter O. Today's graphics-based computer systems eliminate the need for this printing technique; however, users of character-based DOS programs still need it sometimes.

overtype mode   An editing mode in word processing programs and other software that lets you enter and edit text. In overtype mode, the characters you type erase existing characters, if any. In WordPerfect, the overtype mode is called *typeover mode*. See *insert mode*.

overwrite   To write data on a magnetic disk in the same area where other data is stored, thereby destroying the original data.

package   In Microsoft Windows 3.1, an icon, created by Object Packager, that contains a linked or embedded object, file, or part of a file.

packaged software   Application programs commercially marketed, unlike custom programs privately developed for a specific client. Synonymous with *off-the-shelf software*.

packet   A block of information transmitted on a network. A packet contains the address of the sender and recipient, error-checking information, and message data.

packet-switching network   A wide area network that achieves high data transmission speeds with minimal errors by dividing information into packets that are sent by the most efficient route and then reassembled (and checked for accuracy) at their destination.

Individual messages are actually broken down into two or more packets, which may travel alternative routes to their destination. In a packet-switching network, messages (such as electronic mail) are collected by a computer known as a *router*. For any given packet, the router decides which path is, at the moment, the optimum path for sending the packet, and then sends it via a high-speed data transmission system (such as fiber-optic cable or microwave relays). A packet-switching network can optimize line use by sending numerous packets simultaneously.

At the other end, another router receives the message, decodes its address, and routes the message to the appropriate computer destination. The receiving computer rebuilds each individual message by combining the appropriate packets as they arrive. The system then tests each message to make certain it's complete and undamaged. If the message was damaged, the destination computer asks that the message's packets be retransmitted. See *Internet* and *router*.

page   A fixed-size block of random-access memory (RAM). In word processing and desktop publishing, an on-screen representation of a printed page of text or graphics. See *paging memory.*

page break   In word processing, a mark that indicates where the printer will start a new page.

Programs such as WordPerfect insert page breaks automatically (often a line of dots or dashes across the screen) when you've typed a full page of text. The automatic page break is called a *soft page break* because the program may adjust its location if you insert or delete text above the break. You can enter a hard page break, called a *forced page break*, which forces the program to start a new page at the hard page break's location. If you insert or delete above the break, the location of a hard page break moves in direct proportion to the amount of text added or removed.

page description language (PDL)   A programming language that describes printer output in device-independent commands.

Normally, a program's printer output includes printer control codes that vary from printer to printer. A program that generates output in a PDL, however, can drive any printer containing an interpreter for the PDL. PDLs also transfer the burden of processing the printer output to the printer. See *PostScript.*

page layout program   In desktop publishing, an application program that assembles text and graphics from various files. You can determine the precise placement, sizing, scaling, and cropping of material in accordance with the page design represented on-screen.

Page layout programs such as PageMaker and Ventura Publisher display a graphic representation of the page, including non-printing guides that define areas into which you can insert text and graphics.

page orientation   See *landscape orientation* and *portrait orientation.*

Page Up/Page Down keys   On IBM PC-compatible computer keyboards, the keys you press to move the cursor to the preceding screen (Page Up) or the next screen (Page Down). Because the precise implementation of these keys is up to the programmer, some word processing programs use Page Up and Page Down keys to move to the top of the preceding page, rather than to the preceding screen of text.

page-mode RAM   High-performance dynamic random-access memory (DRAM) chips that include a buffer, called a *column buffer*, that stores data likely to be needed next by the central processing unit (CPU).

DRAM chips store data in a matrix of rows and columns. When data is requested from page-mode RAM, the entire row, or page, of data is read into the buffer. Since data tends to be stored sequentially in computers, the next data requested likely will be in the same row. If so, the data is read from the buffer, which is faster than accessing the matrix again.

When requested data is found in the buffer, the result is called a *page mode cycle*. A page mode cycle can be completed in 40 to 60 nanoseconds (ns), instead of the normal 120 ns to 240 ns DRAM cycle time. Page-mode RAM, found in high-end computer systems, should be distinguished from paging memory systems. See *dynamic random-access memory (DRAM), nanosecond (ns), paging memory, random-access memory (RAM), virtual memory,* and *wait state.*

paged memory   See *paging memory.*

paged memory management unit (PMMU)   In computer hardware, a chip or circuit that enables virtual memory. Virtual memory allows your computer to use space on your hard disk to expand the apparent amount of random-access memory (RAM) in your system. With virtual memory, a computer with only 4M of RAM can function as though it were equipped with 16M or more of RAM, enabling you to run several programs simultaneously. See *Microsoft Windows, System 7,* and *virtual memory.*

P
Q
R
S

TIP: *If you're shopping for a computer, avoid IBM PCs or PC-compatibles based on the 8088 or 80286 microprocessors, which don't include PMMU circuitry. For Windows computing, a minimal system is based on the Intel 80386SX microprocessor, which lets Windows implement virtual memory.*

pagination   In word processing, the process of dividing a document into pages for printing. Today's advanced word processing
programs use background pagination, in which pagination occurs
after you stop typing or editing and the microprocessor has nothing
else to do. See *page break*.

paging memory   A memory system in which the location of data
is specified by the intersection of a column and row on the memory
page, rather than by the actual physical location of the data. This
makes it possible to store memory pages wherever memory space of
any type becomes available, including disk drives.

Paging memory is used to implement virtual memory, in which
your computer's hard drive functions as an extension of random-
access memory (RAM). A chip or circuit called a *paged memory
management unit* manages the movement of pages of data in and
out of the memory devices. See *page, paged memory management
unit (PMMU), random-access memory (RAM)*, and *virtual memory*.

paint file format   A bit-mapped graphics file format found in
programs such as MacPaint and PC Paintbrush. See *file format*
and *paint program*.

paint program   A program that allows you to paint the screen
by switching on or off the individual dots or pixels that make up a
bit-mapped screen display.

The first paint program (and the first program for the Macintosh)
was MacPaint. Paint applications also exist for IBM PC-compatible
computers; a leading program is PC Paintbrush. Windows includes
an accessory called Paintbrush.

pair kerning   See *kerning*.

paired bar graph   A bar graph with two different x-axes
(categories axes). A paired bar graph is an excellent way to
demonstrate the relationship between two data series that share
the same y-axis values but require two different x-axis categories.
Because the bars mirror each other, variations become obvious
(see fig. P.1). See *dual y-axis graph*.

p

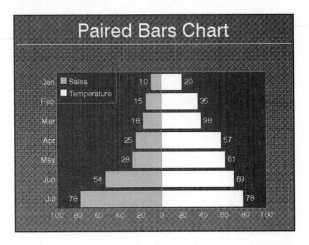

Fig. P.1 *A paired bar graph.*

palette In computer video displays, the colors that the system can display. VGA color displays offer a palette of 262,144 colors, although each screen can display a maximum of 256 colors simultaneously. In paint and draw programs, an on-screen display of options such as colors and drawing tools. See *draw program, paint program,* and *Video Graphics Array (VGA).*

pan In multimedia, the capability of a synthesizer or sound board to alter the left and right channel volumes to create the illusion of movement of the source of the sound.

Pantone Matching System (PMS) A standard color-selection system for professional color printing supported by high-end illustration programs, such as Adobe Illustrator and PageMaker 5.0, that includes about 500 colors, each of which is assigned a PMS number.

paper-white monitor A monochrome monitor that displays black text and graphics on a white background. Paper-white monitors are preferred for word processing and desktop publishing because the display closely resembles the appearance of the printed page. However, some users don't like the glare of a large expanse of white background.

TIP: *When shopping for a monitor, remember that color has its advantages. In a color display, you can locate menu names, accelerator keys, data entry fields, and other on-screen areas more easily. Moreover, most programs permit you to configure the on-screen colors, so you can simulate a paper-white monitor (black text on a white background) if you want.*

paperless office   An office in which using paper for traditional purposes—such as sending messages, filling out forms, and maintaining records—has been reduced or eliminated.

Yet paper remains popular for three important reasons. First, a paper message keeps on broadcasting unless you throw it away, file it, or answer it. In contrast, electronic mail systems let you duck your messages by failing to log on to the system. Second, paper documents have legal status; the exchange of first-class letters, for example, has been recognized by the courts to constitute a legal contract. The legal status of computer-based documents is still unclear. Finally, many people fear the storage of important documents on computer systems without hard-copy backup; wiping out a file is easy.

Despite these barriers to the acceptance of the paperless office, many valid reasons exist for businesses to seek the reduction of paper consumption. Filling out forms directly on computer screens, rather than on paper, can save an organization a great deal of money otherwise spent on filing and other clerical tasks.

parallel columns   See *table columns*.

parallel interface   See *parallel port*.

parallel port   A connection for the synchronous, high-speed flow of data along parallel lines to a device, usually a parallel printer.

Essentially an extension of the computer's internal data bus, parallel ports also negotiate with peripheral devices to determine whether they're ready to receive data, and report error messages if a device isn't ready. Unlike the serial port, the parallel port provides an easy way to connect a printer to your computer. As the length of the cable increases, however, so does the risk of *crosstalk* (interference between the parallel wires). Parallel printer cables, therefore, usually are no longer than 10 to 15 feet.

You can configure the systems of IBM PC-compatible computers with three parallel ports. The device names used by DOS are LPT1, LPT2, and LPT3 (*LPT* is an abbreviation for *line printer*). The device named PRN is the same as LPT1.

parallel printer   A printer designed to be connected to the computer's parallel port.

If a printer is available in serial and parallel versions, the parallel version is the better choice unless you must position the printer more than 15 feet away from the computer. Parallel printers usually are easier to install and use than serial printers.

parallel processing   See *multitasking*.

parameter   A value or option that you add or alter when you give a command so that the command accomplishes its task the way you want. If you don't state a parameter, the program uses a default value or option.

For instance, most programs let you type the name of the file you want to work with when you start the program. If you type **WORD report1.doc**, for example, Microsoft Word and the document file REPORT1.DOC load up at the same time. In this case, the file name is the parameter. If you don't type the file name, Word starts and opens a new, blank document file. See *argument*.

parameter RAM   In the Macintosh environment, a small bank of battery-powered memory that stores your configuration choices after you switch off the power.

parent directory   In DOS directories, the directory above the current subdirectory in the tree structure. You can move quickly to the parent directory by typing **CD..** and pressing Enter. See *directory* and *subdirectory*.

parity bit   In asynchronous communications and primary storage, an extra bit added to a data word for parity checking. See *asynchronous communication* and *parity checking*.

➡ **TIP:** *If you're using a communications program, setting the parity bit option to no parity and the data bits option to 8 bits is the most common configuration. If these settings don't work, try even parity with 7 data bits.*

parity checking   A technique used to detect memory or data communication errors. The computer adds up the number of bits in a one-byte data item, and if the parity bit setting disagrees with the sum of the other bits, the computer reports an error.

Parity-checking schemes work by storing a one-bit digit (0 or 1) that indicates whether the sum of the bits in a data item is odd or even. When the data item is read from memory or received by another computer, a parity check occurs. If the parity check reveals that the parity bit is incorrect, the computer displays an error message. See *even parity* and *odd parity*.

parity error   An error that a computer reports when parity checking reveals that one or more parity bits is incorrect, indicating a probable error in data processing or data transmission.

park   To position a hard drive's read/write heads so that the disk isn't damaged by jostling during transport.

parse   To separate imported data into separate columns so that it appears correctly in a spreadsheet.

When you import data using Lotus 1-2-3's /File Import Text command, for example, the program enters each line of the data into a single cell. Because 1-2-3 uses soft-cell boundaries, you can see the entire line if the adjacent cells don't contain data, but you can't use this data for calculations. The /Data Parse command is used to separate data into distinct columns.

partition   A section of the storage area of a hard disk. A partition is created during initial preparation of the hard disk, before the disk is formatted.

In MS-DOS, every hard disk has at least one DOS partition. MS-DOS versions before 4.0 require you to set up more than one partition on a single hard disk to use a disk larger than 32M. You also can create a second partition to run another operating system, such as UNIX. Each partition is treated by DOS as though it were a separate drive.

Macintosh users may partition their drives to separate the Macintosh System and the A/UX version of UNIX, but utility programs, such as MultiDisk, are available that let you create several system partitions. See *directory* and *subdirectory*.

Pascal   *pass-kal*   A high-level programming language that encourages programmers to write well-structured, modular programs. Pascal has gained wide acceptance as a teaching and application-development language. Pascal is available in interpreted and compiled versions.

Pascal resembles BASIC and FORTRAN in that it's a procedural language: Its statements tell the computer what to do. In contrast to these earlier languages, however, Pascal was designed to take full advantage of modern control structures, eliminating spaghetti code and improving program readability.

A major disadvantage of Pascal is that its standard version (Standard Pascal) contains many shortcomings. The language's inventor, Nicklaus Wirth, has offered a new language, Modula-2, as a successor to Pascal, that directly addresses Pascal's shortcomings. Professional programmers prefer C or C++; however, Pascal is still used for teaching purposes at some colleges and universities.

In personal computing, Pascal lives on, largely due to the influence of Turbo Pascal (Borland International), a high-performance compiler for Pascal that recognizes a number of important and useful extensions to the language. See *BASIC, C, C++, FORTRAN,* and *Modula-2*.

P
Q
R
S

passive matrix display   In notebook computers, a liquid-crystal display (LCD) in which a single transistor controls an entire column or row of the display's tiny electrodes. Passive matrix displays are cheaper than active matrix displays but offer lower resolution and contrast. See *active matrix display.*

password   A security tool used to identify authorized users of a computer program or computer network and to define their privileges, such as read-only, reading and writing, or file copying.

TIP: *Computer hackers and saboteurs know that most people choose passwords based on their birthdays, nicknames, children's names, or easily remembered words such as* password, secret, *or even* none. *Choose a password randomly so that no one will associate the password with you. Open a book and run your fingers across a page until you come across a genuinely random word, such as* wolf, porch, *or* capable. *Then write it down somewhere (not under the keyboard or desk blotter) so that you don't forget it. Another suggestion is to misspell your password in an odd way; for example, instead of* garnet, *use* garnit *or* garnete. *Or vary your password from time to time by inserting a number in the middle of the word.*

password protection   A method of limiting access to a program, file, computer, or a network by requiring you to enter a password.

Some programs allow you to password-protect your files so they can't be read by others, but be sure to keep a record of the password. Many users have lost work permanently because they forgot the password and had no means to retrieve it. (If a method for retrieving a password were included in software programs, a clever hacker would quickly discover it, and your data wouldn't be secure.)

paste   In text editing, inserting at the location of the cursor text or graphics you've cut or copied from another location. In Windows and Macintosh systems, a temporary storage area called the Clipboard stores the cut or copied material while you move to the material's new location. When you paste, the material is copied

p

from the Clipboard to its new location. Most DOS programs include cut, copy, and paste commands but don't use a clipboard. See *block move* and *Clipboard*.

> **CAUTION:** *Bear in mind that the Clipboard stores only one unit of copied or cut text at a time. If you're not careful, you could copy or cut something else, accidentally deleting the Clipboard's contents. To avoid this problem, don't interrupt cut-and-paste operations.*

patch   A quick fix, in the form of one or more program statements, added to a program to correct bugs or to enhance the program's capabilities.

path   In DOS, the route the operating system must follow to find an executable program stored in a subdirectory.

Many important reasons exist for dividing a disk into subdirectories. A drawback is that DOS examines only the current subdirectory when you issue a command to start a program. If the program's executable file isn't in the current subdirectory, the message Bad command or file name appears.

Two methods are used to circumvent the problem of starting programs located outside the current subdirectory. First, you can type the full path name when you issue a command, such as **C:\WP51\WP**, so DOS knows where to find the program. Second, and much better, you can add a PATH statement to your hard disk's AUTOEXEC.BAT file, listing all the subdirectories in which programs are stored. DOS will then check in each directory in the path to look for a file that matches the command you entered.

Most of today's programs automatically create or update the PATH statement in AUTOEXEC.BAT at installation. If you need to add the path statement yourself, use any text editor to create or update the PATH command in the AUTOEXEC.BAT file. Add **PATH**, followed by the full path names of all the directories that contain programs, separating the path names with semicolons. For example: **PATH C:\WP51; C:\WINDOWS; C:\NORTON; C:\WINWORD**.

P
Q
R
S

If you enter **PATH** at the command prompt, DOS displays the path now in effect. See *AUTOEXEC.BAT, current directory, directory, path name, path statement,* and *subdirectory.*

path name In DOS, a statement that indicates the name of a file and precisely where it's located on a hard disk. When opening or saving a file with most applications, you must specify the full path name to retrieve or store the file in a directory other than the current directory. Suppose that you're using WordPerfect, and you want to store the file REPORT9.DOC in the directory C:\DOCS. If C:\DOCS isn't the current directory, you must type **C:\DOCS\REPORT9.DOC** to name and store the file in the correct location.

> **TIP:** *Some applications permit you to define a permanent default directory for storing and retrieving the data files created by the application. If the application you're using permits you to define a default data directory, you don't need to type the full path name when retrieving and storing files.*

path statement In DOS, an entry in the AUTOEXEC.BAT file that lists the directories in which executable programs are listed. See *path.*

PC Abbreviation for *personal computer.* In practice, this abbreviation usually refers to IBM or IBM-compatible personal computers, as opposed to Macintoshes. See *personal computer.*

PC DOS The version of the MS-DOS operating system released by IBM. See *MS-DOS.*

PCL See *printer control language (PCL).*

PCM See *pulse code modulation (PCM).*

PCMCIA See *Personal Computer Memory Card International Association (PCMCIA).*

p

PCMCIA slot A receptacle in the back of a notebook computer that's designed to accept plugs conforming to PCMCIA standards. These slots can be used to plug in PCMCIA-compatible hardwares such as modems and memory cards.

.PCX A file extension indicating that the file contains a graphic in the PCX graphics file format, which was originally developed for the PC Paintbrush program but now is widely used by other applications.

PD See *public domain software.*

PDA See *personal digital assistant (PDA).*

PDL See *page description language (PDL).*

PDN See *public data network (PDN).*

peer-to-peer file transfer A file-sharing technique for local area networks in which each user has access to the public files located on the workstation of any other network user. Each user determines which files, if any, he or she wants to make public for network access. See *TOPS.*

peer-to-peer network A local area network without a central file server and in which all computers in the network have access to the public files located on all other workstations. See *client/ server network* and *peer-to-peer file transfer.*

pel Abbreviation for *pixel.*

pen computer A personal computer equipped with pattern recognition circuitry so that it can recognize human handwriting as a form of data input. To use a pen computer, you "write" on a screen using a special stylus that resembles a pen.

Pen-based computers recognize only printing, and neat printing at that. By using pattern recognition technology, the computer interprets your scribbles and enters words, numbers, symbols, and graphics. You also can use the stylus to choose commands from menus.

Recent advances in pen-based computer technology have brought these devices wider acceptance. Pen-based computers are expected to find a large market among the many professional and technical workers who need to jot down notes or data as they work with a convenient, portable notebook computer. Its present use by package delivery services suggests great potential for field workers, such as police officers who must complete accident reports and other forms in the field. Helping the adoption of pen-based computing is the availability of a special version of Microsoft Windows designed for pen-based computing systems.

Pentium   See *Intel Pentium.*

peripheral   A device, such as a printer or disk drive, connected to and controlled by a computer but external to the computer's central processing unit (CPU).

permanent swap file   In Microsoft Windows, a disk file composed of contiguous disk sectors that's set aside for the rapid storage and retrieval of program instructions or data in the program's 386 Enhanced mode. This storage space is used in virtual memory operations, which use disk space as a seamless extension of random-access memory (RAM). Because the storage areas used in a permanent swap file are contiguous, storage and retrieval operations exceed the normal speed of hard disk operations, which usually distribute data here and there on the disk. The permanent swap file, however, consumes a large amount of space on the disk. See *Microsoft Windows, page memory management unit (PMMU), random-access memory (RAM), swap file, temporary swap file,* and *virtual memory.*

personal computer   A stand-alone computer equipped with all the system, utility, and application software, and the input/output devices and other peripherals that an individual needs to perform one or more tasks. The term *personal computer,* or PC, is used today to refer collectively and individually to stand-alone IBM Personal Computers, IBM PC-compatible computers, Macintosh computers, Apple computers, Amiga computers, and others (such as the Commodore) that are no longer manufactured.

The idea of personal computing, at least initially, was to free individuals from dependence on tightly controlled mainframe and mini-computer resources. With the rise of personal computing, people have gained substantially more freedom to choose the applications tailored to their needs. Yet in recent years, reasons have been found to reintegrate PCs into the data communications networks of organizations, and this goal can be achieved without forcing people to give up the autonomy that personal computing implies.

PCs equipped with sufficient memory and Intel 80486 or Pentium microprocessors can serve as professional workstations—powerful, high-performance computers designed to provide professionals such as graphics designers, engineers, and architects with the computing power they need for calculation-intensive applications, such as computer-aided design (CAD). Similarly, today's high-end PCs can handle a few remote terminals if the PCs have UNIX or some other multiuser operating system. See *professional workstation*.

Personal Computer Memory Card International Association (PCMCIA) An international trade association that has developed standards for devices, such as modems and external hard disk drives, that can be easily plugged into notebook computers. See *Plug and Play*.

personal digital assistant (PDA) A small, hand-held computer, capable of accepting input that the user writes on-screen with a stylus, that's designed to provide all the tools an individual would need for day-to-day organization, including an appointment calendar, an address book, a notepad, and a fax modem. See *Newton*, *pen computer*, and *transceiver*.

personal information manager (PIM) A database management program such as Lotus Agenda that stores and retrieves a variety of personal information, including notes, memos, names and addresses, and appointments.

Unlike a database management program, a PIM is optimized for the storage and retrieval of a variety of personal information. You can switch among different views of your notes, such as people, to-do items, and expenses. PIMs have been slow to gain acceptance, however, because they're hard to learn and because users often are away from the computer when they need the information.

PgUp/PgDn keys See *Page Up/Page Down keys*.

phono plug A connector with a short stem used to connect home audio devices. In computers, phono plugs are used for audio and composite monitor output ports. Synonymous with *RCA plug*.

phosphor An electrofluorescent material used to coat the inside face of a cathode ray tube (CRT). After being energized by the electron beam that's directed to the inside face of the tube, the phosphors glow for a fraction of a second. The beam refreshes the phosphor many times per second to produce a consistent illumination. See *cathode ray tube (CRT)* and *raster display*.

phototypesetter See *imagesetter*.

phreaking An illegal form of recreation that involves using one's knowledge of telephone system technology to make long-distance calls for free.

physical drive The disk drive actually performing the current read/write operation.

A hard disk can be formatted into partitions, sections, and directories that have all the characteristics of a separate disk drive, but are *logical drives*. The data, however, is actually encoded either on the surface of a disk in a floppy drive or a hard disk drive, which is referred to as the physical drive. See *floppy disk*, *hard disk*, *logical drives*, and *secondary storage*.

physical format See *low-level format*.

physical memory The actual random-access memory (RAM) circuits in which data is stored, as opposed to virtual memory—the "apparent" RAM that results from using the computer's hard disk as an extension of physical memory. See *random-access memory (RAM)* and *virtual memory*.

.PIC A file extension indicating that the file contains a graphic in the Lotus PIC format, used by Lotus 1-2-3 to save business graphs.

pica In typography, a unit of measure equal to approximately 1/6 inch, or 12 points. Picas are used to describe horizontal and vertical measurements on the page, with the exception of type sizes, which are expressed in points.

p

In formal typography, one pica is 0.166 of an inch, and 1/6 inch is approximately 0.1667 of an inch, so 6 picas equal exactly 1 inch. Many word processing and page layout programs, however, ignore this difference and define one pica as exactly 1/6 inch.

In typewriting and letter-quality printing, a pica is a 12-point monospace font that prints at a pitch of 10 characters per inch (cpi).

pico-   Prefix for one trillionth (10^{-12}). Abbreviated *p*.

picosecond   One trillionth (10^{-12}) of a second.

PICT   A Macintosh graphics file format originally developed for the MacDraw program. An object-oriented format, PICT files consist of separate graphics objects, such as lines, arcs, ovals, or rectangles, each of which you can independently edit, size, move, or color. (PICT files also can store bit-mapped images.) Some Windows graphics applications can read PICT files. See *bit-mapped graphic*, *file format*, and *object-oriented graphic*.

pie graph   In presentation graphics, a graph that displays a data series as a circle to emphasize the relative contribution of each data item to the whole (see fig. P.2).

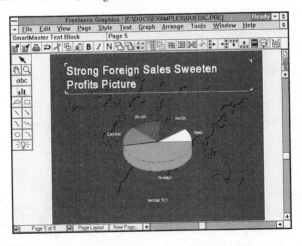

Fig. P.2   *A pie graph.*

Each slice of the pie appears in shades of gray or a distinctive pattern. Patterns can produce moiré distortions if you juxtapose too many patterns. Some programs can produce paired pie graphs that display two data series. For presentations, exploding a slice from the whole is a useful technique to add emphasis. See *exploded pie graph*, *linked pie/column graph*, *moiré effect*, and *proportional pie graph*.

PIF   See *program information file (PIF)*.

PILOT   An authoring language for computer-assisted instruction (CAI), developed by John Starkweather at the University of California-San Francisco in 1968.

PILOT, short for Programmed Inquiry Learning Or Teaching, is exceptionally easy to learn because it has very few commands. Used primarily to develop on-screen instructional materials, PILOT is being displaced by new authoring languages that use graphical user interfaces such as HyperTalk. See *computer-assisted instruction (CAI)*.

PIM   See *personal information manager (PIM)*.

pin feed   See *tractor feed*.

pipe   In DOS and UNIX, a symbol that tells the operating system to send the output of one command to another command, rather than display this output.

In the following example, the pipe (represented by the ¦ symbol) tells DOS to send the output of the TREE command to the MORE command; the MORE command then displays the TREE result page by page on-screen:

```
TREE C:\ ¦ MORE
```

See *filter* and *input/output (I/O) redirection*.

pipeline   In computer design, a hardware assembly line that dramatically speeds the processing of instructions through retrieval, execution, and writing back. Long used in UNIX, the pipeline included in the Intel 80486 allows it to process an instruction every clock cycle. The Intel Pentium microprocessor features two pipelines, one for data and one for instruction, and can therefore process two instructions (one per pipeline) every clock cycle.

piracy   See *software piracy*.

pitch   A horizontal measurement of the number of characters per linear inch in a monospace font, such as those used with type-writers, dot-matrix printers, and daisywheel printers.

By convention, pica pitch (not to be confused with the printer's measurement of approximately 1/6 inch) is equal to 10 characters per inch, and elite pitch is equal to 12 characters per inch. See *monospace*, *pica*, and *point*.

pixel   The smallest element (a picture element) that a device can display and out of which the displayed image is constructed. See *bit-mapped graphic*.

plain text document   A document that contains nothing but standard ASCII text and number characters. See *ASCII*.

TIP: *In many applications, you can save a plain text document in two ways: with or without Enter keystrokes at the end of each line. If you're exporting the document to another word processor, choose the option that saves the document without Enter keystrokes (carriage returns) at the end of each line; after you import the document, paragraphs will word wrap and reformat automatically. Choose the Enter keystroke option only when you need to save plain text for an application, such as uploading a file through telecommunications links.*

plasma display   A display technology used with high-end laptop computers. The display is produced by energizing ionized gas held between two transparent panels. Synonymous with *gas plasma display*.

platen   In dot-matrix and letter-quality impact printers, the cylinder that guides paper through the printer and provides a backing surface for the paper when images are impressed onto the page.

platform   See *hardware platform*.

platform independence   The capability of a local area network to connect computers made by different makers, such as connecting an IBM PC-compatible computer with a Macintosh computer.

platter   Synonymous with *disk*.

plot   To construct an image by drawing lines.

plotter   A printer that produces high-quality graphical output by moving ink pens over the surface of the paper. The printer moves the pens under the direction of the computer, so that printing is automatic. Plotters are commonly used for computer-aided design and presentation graphics.

plotter font   In Microsoft Windows, a vector font designed to be used with a plotter. The font composes characters by generating dots connected by lines.

Plug and Play   An emerging industrywide hardware standard for add-in hardware that requires the hardware be able to identify itself, on demand, in a standard fashion.

Plug and Play requires both hardware and software to do its job. The hardware is a Plug and Play BIOS that senses the system components when you start your computer. This BIOS then remains alert for any significant configuration changes you may make so it can pass this information on to the operating system. The software is an operating system that includes Plug and Play support. With Plug and Play, you don't need to "install" devices; you don't fuss with jumpers and dip switches, sheet feeders and bins, or software-compatible printer drivers for the newest printers.

The enormous installed base of ISA devices aren't compatible with Plug and Play, although the next generation of network adapters, fax modems, and other devices will be. Look for Plug and Play devices to flood the market in 1995, when operating system software support is expected to be available.

PMMU   See *paged memory management unit (PMMU)*.

PMS   See *Pantone Matching System (PMS)*.

p

point   To move the mouse pointer on-screen without clicking the button. In typography, a fundamental unit of measurement (72 points equal approximately one inch). Computer programs usually ignore this slight discrepancy, making a point exactly equal to 1/72 inch. See *pica* and *pitch*.

point-of-sale software   A program that transforms a personal computer into a point-of-sale system for a small business.

For more than a decade, large businesses have used computerized point-of-sale systems that read scanned product bar codes and look up the name and price of the item more quickly and accurately than even the best checker, and also automatically adjust the inventory database as each item is sold.

With the arrival of point-of-sale software and bar code readers for personal computers, even a small retail business can take advantage of this technology. A typical point-of-sale software package such as Retail Store Controller (Microbiz) brings virtually all the functionality of the large business systems to a single-user, PC-based point-of-sale workstation. Included are such features as automatic credit card verification, customer history tracking, bar code label printing, sales tracking by employee, reorder reports, flexible sales analysis and reports, and export links to accounting software. Available accessories include a compatible cash drawer and a receipt printer.

pointer   An on-screen symbol, usually an arrow, that shows the current position of the mouse. In database management programs, a record number in an index that stores the actual physical location of the data record.

The pointer doesn't indicate the position of the cursor. To move the cursor with the mouse, you must click the pointer on the desired cursor position. See *cursor*.

TIP: *If you use Microsoft Windows, learn the meaning of the various pointer shapes. They tell you when the application is ready to select something, jump to related information, or size a graphic object.*

pointing device   An input device such as a mouse, trackball, or stylus graphics tablet used to show a pointer on-screen.

polarity   In electronics, the negative or positive property of a charge.

In computer graphics, the tonal relationship between foreground and background elements. Positive polarity is the printing of black or dark characters on a white or light background; negative polarity is the printing of white or light characters on a black or dark background.

polling   In local area networks, a method for controlling channel access in which the central computer continuously asks or polls the workstations to determine whether they have information to send.

With polling channel access, you can specify how often, and for how long, the central computer polls the workstations. Unlike CSMA/CD and token-ring channel-access methods, the network manager can give some nodes more access to the network than others. See *carrier sense multiple access with collision detection (CSMA/CD)* and *token-ring network.*

polyline   In computer graphics, a drawing tool used to create a multisided, enclosed shape. To use the tool, draw a straight line to a point, and then continue the line in a different direction to a point. By continuing this operation until you return to the starting point, you can create a complex object of your own design. The result is a *graphics primitive*, which the program treats as a single object. Like the more familiar primitives (squares or circles), the polyline object can be independently edited, sized, moved, or colored. Some programs call this tool a *polygon.* See *graphics primitive* and *object-oriented graphic.*

pop-up menu   A menu that appears when you select a certain on-screen item, such as text, a scroll bar, or a dialog box option. The name doesn't truly reflect a direction. If a pop-up menu will appear too close to the top of the screen, it pops down. See *pull-down menu.*

port   An interface that governs and synchronizes the flow of data between the central processing unit and external devices such as printers and modems. Also, reprogramming an application so that it runs on another type of computer. See *central processing unit (CPU)*, *interface*, *parallel port*, and *serial port.*

portable   Capable of working on a variety of hardware platforms.

UNIX is a portable operating system. Most operating systems are designed around the specific electronic capabilities of a given central processing unit (CPU). UNIX, in contrast, is designed with a predetermined, overall structure. Instructions are embedded within the program that allow it to function on a given CPU. See *UNIX*.

portable computer   A computer with a screen and keyboard built in and designed to be transported easily from one location to another.

The first portable personal computers, such as the Osborne I and Compaq II, are best described as "luggables." These computers weighed in at well over 25 pounds and couldn't be carried comfortably for more than a short distance. Today's battery-powered laptop computers are much more portable. See *laptop computer* and *notebook computer*.

portrait monitor   See *full-page display*.

portrait orientation   The default printing orientation for a page of text by which the height of the page is greater than the width (see fig. P.3). See *landscape orientation*.

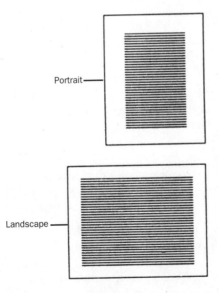

Fig. P.3   *Examples of portrait orientation (top) and landscape orientation (bottom).*

post   In database management, to add data to a data record. In a computer newsgroup, to send a message so that it can be read by everyone who accesses the group. See *distributed bulletin board*, *netiquette*, and *newsgroup*.

CAUTION: *Think twice before posting an international message. In USENET, posting a message worldwide will eventually cost hundreds of dollars in transmission costs, all of which must be paid for by government and organizational subsidies. Is what you have to say important enough to justify such an expenditure?*

POST   See *Power-On Self-Test (POST)*.

postprocessor   A program that performs a final, automatic processing operation after you finish working with a file. Post-processing programs include text formatters that prepare a document for printing, and page description languages that convert an on-screen document into a set of commands that the printer's interpreter can recognize and use to print the document.

PostScript   A sophisticated page description language that's used for high-quality printing on laser printers and other high-resolution printing devices.

PostScript, developed by Adobe Systems, Inc., is a programming language that describes how to print a page that blends text and graphics. Because PostScript is a genuine programming language, you can learn to write PostScript instructions and embed them in documents to be printed. For most users, however, PostScript is invisible and automatic; the program generates the PostScript code that goes to the printer, where a PostScript interpreter follows the coded instructions to generate an image of the page precisely according to these instructions.

A major benefit of PostScript is its device independence; you can print the PostScript code generated by an application on any printer with a PostScript interpreter. Because PostScript printer output uses the printer's maximum resolution, you can take a disk containing a document you've created with an application such as Microsoft Word or WordPerfect to a service bureau, which can print the document using expensive typesetting machines, such as those manufactured by Linotronic, Compugraphic, and Varityper, with resolutions of up to 2,400 dots per inch (dpi). See *page description language (PDL)*, *PostScript font*, and *PostScript printer*.

PostScript font   An outline font that conforms to Adobe Software's specifications for Type 1 printer fonts, which require a PostScript-compatible printer.

Unlike bit-mapped fonts, which often print with crude edges and curves, PostScript's outline font technology produces smooth letters that your printer renders at its maximum possible resolution. A PostScript font comes with a screen font, which simulates the font's appearance on-screen, and a printer font, which you must download to the printer before you print. However, most PostScript laser printers come with several PostScript fonts built into the printer's permanent memory; downloading isn't necessary before using these fonts.

PostScript fonts are scalable, so you can choose any font size you want within a specified range (for example, from 4 to 72 points) and get smooth-looking type at the printer. Note, though, that the type may look jagged on-screen unless you buy Adobe Type Manager, which brings PostScript scalable font technology to the display screen. See *outline font*, *PostScript*, *PostScript printer*, *scalable font*, and *TrueType*.

P
Q
R
S

TIP: *TrueType font technology, jointly developed by Apple Computer and Microsoft Corporation, provides a cost-effective alternative to PostScript fonts and PostScript laser printers. TrueType fonts are scalable outline fonts that don't require a pricy PostScript printer. Moreover, if you're using TrueType with Microsoft Windows 3.1, or with the Mac's System 7, the scaling technology is built in so you also don't need Adobe Type Manager.*

PostScript printer   A printer, generally a laser printer, that includes the processing circuitry needed to decode and interpret printing instructions phrased in PostScript, a page description language (PDL) widely used in desktop publishing.

Because PostScript printers require their own microprocessor circuitry and at least 1M RAM to image each page, they're more expensive than non-PostScript printers. However, they can print text or graphics in subtle gradations of gray. They can also use Encapsulated PostScript (EPS) graphics and outline fonts, both of which you can size and scale without introducing distortions. PostScript printers also can produce special effects, such as rotation and overprinting. See *PostScript*.

posture The slant of the characters in a font. Italic characters slant to the right, but the term *italic* is reserved by conservative typographers for custom-designed (as opposed to electronically produced) serif typefaces.

power down To turn off a device.

power line filter An electrical device that smoothes out the peaks and valleys of the voltage delivered at the wall socket.

Every electrical circuit is subject to voltage fluctuations, and if these are extreme, they may cause computer errors and failures. Flickering lights are a good sign of uneven voltage. If you're using a computer in a circuit shared by heavy appliances, you may need a power line filter to ensure error-free operation. See *surge protector*.

power supply A device that provides the power to electronic equipment. In a computer system, the power supply converts standard AC current to the lower voltage DC current used by the computer.

CAUTION: *The power supply of early IBM PC-compatible computers (63.5 watts) often proved inadequate to power several adapters, a hard disk, and other system upgrades. An overloaded power supply can cause erratic operations, such as read or write errors, parity errors, and unexplained system crashes. For systems with hard disks and several adapters, users should have a power supply of at least 200 watts.*

power surge See *surge*.

p

power up   To turn on a device.

power user   A computer user who has gone beyond the beginning and intermediate stages of computer use. Such a person uses the advanced features of application programs, such as software command languages and macros, and can learn new application programs quickly.

Power-On Self-Test (POST)   Internal testing performed when you start or reset your computer. Part of the BIOS, the POST program first checks the microprocessor by having it perform a few simple operations. Then it reads the CMOS RAM, which stores the amount of memory and type of disk drives in your system. Next, the POST writes, then reads, various data patterns to each byte of memory (you can watch the bytes count off on-screen). Finally, the POST communicates with every device; you see the keyboard and drive lights flash and the printer reset, for example. The BIOS continues with hardware testing, then looks in drive A for DOS; if drive A isn't found, it looks in drive C. See *basic input/output system (BIOS)* and *boot sector.*

PowerPC   A RISC microprocessor developed by Motorola that's competitive with the Intel Pentium chip. The chip is being used by IBM for its RS/6000 line and by Apple Corporation as the next-generation processor for the Macintosh. The PowerPC will support Windows NT, OS/2, and UNIX, based on a promise of industry commitment to PowerOpen, a standard for PowerPC operating systems.

Hailed by the industry as the first real challenger to Intel's market dominance, the PowerPC may have some serious competitors for that title. The Mips R4X00 line of chips are RISC processors that offer a price and performance advantage over Intel, as well as a low-powered chip for portables that Intel hasn't yet delivered. The DEC Alpha, another RISC processor with 150 MHz speed (200 MHz is promised) has also entered the fray. All these processors must overcome the same problems: development of Windows NT, OS/2, and other operating systems to the point of true consumer acceptability; development of applications that can use the advanced technology these designs offer; and acceptance of RISC architecture as the choice for the future. See *reduced instruction set computer (RISC).*

P
Q
R
S

PMJI　In on-line communications, shorthand for *Pardon Me for Jumping In.*

ppm　Abbreviation for *pages per minute*, a crude and often inaccurate measurement of page printers such as inkjet and laser printers. A laser printer that's said to print eight pages per minute may do so only if you choose the built-in Courier font and print a document with no graphics. If you use a different font or include graphics, the document will print more slowly.

PRAM　See *parameter RAM.*

precedence　The order in which a program performs the operations in a formula. Typically, the program performs exponentiation (such as squaring a number) before multiplication and division, and then performs addition and subtraction.

precision　The number of digits past the decimal that are used to express a quantity. See *accuracy.*

presentation graphics　The branch of the graphics profession that's concerned with the preparation of slides, transparencies, and handouts for use in business presentations. Ideally, presentation graphics combines artistry with practical psychology and good taste; color, form, and emphasis are used intelligently to convey the presentation's most significant points to the audience. See *analytical graphics.*

presentation graphics program　An application program designed to create and enhance charts and graphs so that they're visually appealing and easily understood by an audience.

A full-featured presentation graphics package such as Lotus Freelance Graphics for Windows includes facilities for making a wide variety of charts and graphs and for adding titles, legends, and explanatory text anywhere in the chart or graph. A presentation graphics program also includes a library of clip art, so you can enliven charts and graphs by adding a picture related to the subject matter—for example, an airplane for a chart of earnings in the aerospace industry. You can print output, direct output to a film recorder, or display output in a computer slide show.

primary storage   The computer's main memory, which consists of the random-access memory (RAM) and the read-only memory (ROM) that's directly accessible to the central processing unit (CPU).

print engine   Inside a laser printer, the mechanism that uses a laser to create an electrostatic image of a page and fuses that image to a cut sheet of paper. You can distinguish print engines by their resolution, print quality, longevity, paper-handling features, and speed:

- *Resolution.* The print engine used in most laser printers generally produces resolutions of 300 and 600 dots per inch (dpi). Professional typesetting machines called *imagesetters* use chemical photo-reproduction techniques to produce resolutions of up to 2,400 dpi.

- *Print quality.* Write-white engines expose the portion of the page that doesn't receive ink (so that toner is attracted to the areas that print black) and generally produce deeper blacks than write-black engines, but this quality varies from engine to engine. Although dozens of retail brands of laser printers are on the market, the print engines are made by a few original equipment manufacturers (OEM) such as Canon, Ricoh, Toshiba, and Casio. Canon engines are highly regarded within the desktop publishing industry.

- *Longevity.* Most print engines have a life of 300,000 copies, but the life span ratings among brands vary from 180,000 to 600,000 copies. Because printer longevity is estimated from heavy use over a short period of time, you should consider a printer's longevity rating only if the printer will be used in heavy-demand network applications.

- *Paper-handling features.* Early laser printers vexed users with thin paper trays that could hold only 50 or 60 sheets of paper. For convenient use, you should consider a paper tray capacity of at least 200 to 250 sheets.

- *Speed.* Print engines often are rated (optimistically) at speeds of up to 10 pages per minute. Such speeds, however, are attained only under ideal conditions; the same sparse page of text is printed over and over again. When printing a real manuscript with different text on each page, the printer must pause to construct the image. If the printer encounters a graphic, printing may halt for as long as a minute. What really determines a print engine's speed is the controller's microprocessor. The speed demons of laser printing use third-generation microprocessors (such as the Motorola 68020) running at clock speeds of up to 16.7 MHz.

print queue   A list of files that a print spooler prints in the background while the computer performs other tasks in the foreground.

Print Screen (PrtSc)   On IBM PC-compatible keyboards, a key you can use to print an image of the screen display.

> **TIP:** *If the screen display is now in graphics mode, you must run the MS-DOS program GRAPHICS.COM before the screen prints properly.*

print server   In a local area network, a PC that has been dedicated to receiving and temporarily storing files to be printed, which are then doled out one by one to a printer. The print server, accessible to all the workstations in the network, runs print spooler software to manage a print queue. See *local area network (LAN)*, *print queue*, and *print spooler*.

print spooler   A utility program that temporarily stores files to be printed in a print queue and doles them out one by one to the printer. See *background printing*, *print queue*, and *print server*.

printer   A computer peripheral designed to print computer-generated text or graphics on paper.

Printers vary significantly in their quality, speed, noise, graphics capabilities, built-in fonts, and paper usage. The ideal printer would cost much less than $1,000, print text and graphics at resolutions approaching those produced by professional typesetting machinery (such as 300 or 400 dpi), churn out several printed pages per minute, operate quietly, blend text and graphics seamlessly, offer a variety of built-in fonts and font sizes, and use standard, office-quality xerographic bond paper (or your company's printed letterhead).

p

The following list provides a brief overview of the types of printers available today:

- *Letter-quality printers* (also called *daisywheel printers*) form an image the same way office typewriters do—by hammering a fully formed image of a character against a ribbon, thus producing an inked image on the paper. Letter-quality printers can't print graphics.

- *Dot-matrix printers* form an image by extruding a pattern (or matrix) of wires against a ribbon, producing an inked image on paper. Dot-matrix printers print rapidly (100 or more characters per second), but printing speeds degrade considerably when you choose high-resolution modes. Some dot-matrix printers come with several fonts and font sizes, and all can print graphics.

- *Inkjet printers* form an image by spraying ink directly on the paper's surface, producing what appears to be a fully formed image. Inkjet printers, which often are rated at 4 to 6 ppm, are slower than laser printers, but they produce text and graphics output that seems comparable to laser printer quality, are less expensive than laser printers, and produce little noise. Like laser printers, most inkjet printers come with a selection of built-in fonts and can use font cartridges or downloadable fonts.

- *Laser printers* use copy-machine technology to fuse powdered ink to paper, producing high-quality output at relatively high speeds (most are rated at eight or more pages per minute), use cut sheets or letterhead, and operate quietly. Most come with a selection of built-in fonts and can easily accommodate font cartridges or downloadable fonts. Their major drawback was high cost, but laser printers are now available for less than $700.

- *LED and LCD printers* closely resemble laser printers, except that these printers don't use lasers to form the image. LED printers use an array of light-emitting diodes (LEDs) for this purpose; LCD printers use a halogen light, the illumination of which is distributed by means of liquid crystal shutters.

P
Q
R
S

- *Thermal printers* operate quietly, but that's their only advantage. They operate by pushing a matrix of heated pins against special heat-sensitive paper, which means that you must use the right kind of paper. They produce output that resembles that of a cheap dot-matrix printer, except that the paper's surface is shiny and smells bad; even worse, they print slowly. Thermal printers are relegated to minor applications in calculators, fax machines, and portable computer systems.

TIP: *What's the best printer for you? Because inkjet and laser printers are quiet and well supported by most application programs, one of these is probably your best bet. For a home system or for light office use, an inkjet printer may prove ideal. For a busy office, you'll need a laser printer's faster printing speed.*

See *dot-matrix printer, inkjet printer, laser printer, letter-quality printer, light-emitting diode (LED) printer, liquid crystal display (LCD) printer,* and *thermal printer.*

printer control language (PCL) The command set used to control a printer of a given brand. Common printer control languages include the Epson command set for dot-matrix printers, the Hewlett-Packard Printer Control Language (HPPCL) for IBM-compatible laser printers, and the Diablo command set for letter-quality printers.

Printer control languages are often little more than proprietary implementations of the higher-order ASCII control codes, which programs send to the printer to toggle features such as boldfaced printing on and off. Page description languages such as PostScript, on the other hand, are true programming languages in their own right.

printer driver A file that contains the information a program needs to print your work with a given brand and model of printer.

A major difference between the DOS environment and the Macintosh/Windows environments is the way printer drivers are handled. In IBM PC-compatible computing, printer drivers are the responsibility of application programs; each program must come equipped with its own printer drivers for the many dozens of printers available. If a program doesn't include a driver for your printer, you may be out of luck. Microsoft Windows, on the other hand, provides printer drivers for all Windows applications.

Printer drivers are part of the operating environment in the Macintosh. Individual programs don't have printer drivers; instead, they're designed to take advantage of printer drivers provided at the operating system level and stored in the System Folder.

printer emulation   The capability of a printer to recognize the printer control language of a different printer. Widely emulated are Epson, Hewlett-Packard, and Diablo printers.

printer font   A font that doesn't appear on-screen and is available for use only by the printer. When using a printer font, you see a generic screen font on-screen; you must wait until printing is complete to see your document's fonts.

Ideally, screen and printer fonts should be identical; only then can a computer system claim to offer what-you-see-is-what-you-get (WYSIWYG) text processing. Character-based programs running under DOS can't display typefaces other than those built into the computer's ROM. In WordPerfect for DOS, for example, you can choose many different printer fonts in a document, but you can't see the font changes on-screen. Many users are quite satisfied with this technology and get excellent results. For others, seeing the fonts on-screen is necessary to avoid printing errors.

With Microsoft Windows and Macintosh systems, you can use TrueType or Adobe Type Manager (ATM) outline (scalable) fonts, which appear on-screen the way they appear when printed. See *outline font* and *TrueType*.

printer port   See *parallel port* and *serial port*.

procedural language   A language such as BASIC or Pascal that requires the programmer to specify the procedure the computer has to follow to accomplish the task. See *declarative language*.

processing   The execution of program instructions by the computer's central processing unit (CPU) that in some way transforms data, such as sorting it, selecting some of it according to specified criteria, or performing mathematical computations on it.

**P
Q
R
S**

Prodigy An on-line information service jointly developed by Sears and IBM that offers (via modem) personal computer users home shopping, news, stock quotes, hobbyist conferences, and so on.

Innovative features of Prodigy include the use of a bit-mapped graphical user interface and unlimited use of the system for a flat fee. (An exception is electronic mail usage, for which a surcharge may be added based on the number of messages sent.) Prodigy recently added e-mail access to the Internet and has made on-line photos available.

Prodigy, however, has no provisions for software uploading and has limited downloading. Also, part of the screen is occupied by commercial advertisements. See *on-line information service*.

professional workstation A high-performance personal computer optimized for professional applications in fields such as digital circuit design, architecture, and technical drawing.

Professional workstations typically offer excellent screen resolution, fast and powerful processing circuits, and ample memory. Examples include the workstations made by Sun Microsystems and NeXT, Inc. Professional workstations are more expensive than personal computers and typically use the UNIX operating system. The boundary between high-end personal computers and professional workstations, however, is eroding as personal computers become more powerful.

program A list of instructions, written in a programming language, that a computer can execute so that the machine acts in a predetermined way. Synonymous with *software*.

The world of computer programs can be divided into system programs, utility programs, and application programs:

- *System programs* include all the programs the computer requires to function effectively, including the operating system, memory management software, and command-line interpreters. The MS-DOS operating system is an example of system software.

- *Utility programs* include all the programs you can use to maintain the computer system. MS-DOS includes several utility programs, such as CHKDSK. Most users equip their systems with utility packages (such as Norton Utilities or PC Tools) that go beyond the basics that MS-DOS provides.

- *Application programs* transform the computer into a tool for performing a specific kind of work, such as word processing, financial analysis (with an electronic spreadsheet), or desktop publishing.

Additional software categories include programming languages, games, educational programs, and a variety of vertical market programs. See *executable program, high-level programming language, machine language, programming language,* and *vertical market program.*

program generator   A program that creates the program code automatically from a description of the application. In database management programs, for example, you can use simple program generation techniques to describe the format you want graphically. The program generator then uses your input as a set of parameters by which to build the output program code.

program information file (PIF)   A file available for non-Windows application programs that tells Windows how to run them. Windows can still run DOS applications, even without a PIF file. See *Microsoft Windows* and *non-Windows application.*

program item   In Microsoft Windows, an icon that represents an application.

program overlay   A portion of a program kept on disk and called into memory only as required.

programmable   Capable of being controlled through instructions that can be varied to suit the user's needs.

programmable read-only memory (PROM)   A read-only memory (ROM) chip programmed at the factory for use with a given computer.

P
Q
R
S

Standard ROM chips have their programming included in the internal design of the chip circuits, making the chip difficult to modify. If the programming has a bug or the firm decides to add a feature to the computer, redesigning and manufacturing the chip is expensive and time-consuming.

A programmable ROM chip gets around this problem by enabling a chip to be programmed just once, after which the programming becomes permanent. The process of programming the chip is called *burning the PROM*. If changing the programming becomes necessary, making the alterations and burning the new PROMs with the modified information is simple. See *erasable programmable read-only memory (EPROM)*.

programmer   A person who designs, codes, tests, debugs, and documents a computer program.

Professional programmers often hold B.S. or M.S. degrees in computer science, but a great deal of programming (professional and otherwise) is done by individuals with little or no formal training. More than half the readers of a popular personal computer magazine, for example, stated in a survey that they regularly programmed their personal computers using languages such as BASIC, Pascal, and assembly language.

programmer/analyst   A person who performs system analysis and design functions as well as programming activities. See *programmer* and *programming*.

programmer's switch   A plastic accessory included with pre-1991 Macintosh computers that, when installed on the side of the computer, allows you to perform a hardware reset and access the computer's built-in debugger.

TIP: *If you use the MacPlus, SE, or SE/30, you should install the programmer's switch so you can restart the computer after a system crash without flipping the power switch on and off, thus*

p

subjecting your system to the stress of a startup power surge. You can perform a soft boot by choosing Restart from the Finder menu, but only if you can get to the Finder. More recent Macs allow you to restart the system from the keyboard.

programming   The process of providing instructions to the computer that tell the microprocessor what to do.

Stages in programming include design, or making decisions about what the program should accomplish; coding, or using a programming language to express the program's logic in computer-readable form and entering internal documentation for the commands; testing and debugging, in which the program's flaws are discovered and corrected; and documentation, in which an instructional manual for the program is created.

If you would like to give programming a try, begin with an event-driven language such as HyperTalk (Macintosh systems) or Visual BASIC (Windows systems), where you can embed a few lines of programming code in an on-screen object, such as a window or button. Using an event-driven language, you can produce impressive results in short order.

Then, having learned many basic concepts of programming, including variables and control structures, you can tackle a well-structured, high-level language such as QuickBASIC or Pascal. A well-structured language includes a full set of control structures that'll help you learn more about creating a complete, ready-to-run program that performs a task flawlessly.

If you're interested in developing professional programming expertise, you'll also need to learn the details of specific hardware environments, including the capabilities of specific microprocessors. The best way to do so is to learn some assembly language programming or C, a high-level language in which you can embed assembly language instructions. Many professional programming houses are making the transition to object-oriented programming languages, such as C++, so gaining expertise in this area is also desirable. See *C, C++, event-driven environment, HyperTalk, QuickBASIC, object-oriented programming language, Pascal, spaghetti code, Visual Basic,* and *well-structured programming language.*

P
Q
R
S

programming environment   A set of tools for programming that's commonly provided with a computer's operating system. Minimally, the tools include a line editor, a debugger, and an assembler to compile assembly language programs. These tools may not be sufficient for professional program development, however, and often are replaced by an application development system. See *application development system.*

programming language   An artificial language, consisting of a fixed vocabulary and a set of rules (called *syntax*), that you can use to create instructions for a computer to follow. Most programs are written using a text editor or word processing program to create source code, which is then interpreted or compiled into the machine language that the computer can actually execute.

Programming languages are numerous, and most computer scientists agree that no single language will ever suffice to serve the needs of all programmers. Programming languages are divided into high-level languages and low-level languages:

- *High-level programming languages,* such as BASIC, C, or Pascal, allow the programmer to express the program using keywords and syntax that crudely resemble natural human language. These languages are called "high level" because they free the programmer from detailed concerns about just how the computer will physically carry out each instruction. Each statement in a high-level language corresponds to several machine language instructions, so you can write programs more quickly than in lower-level languages, such as assembly language. However, the translation is inefficient, so programs written in high-level languages run more slowly than programs written in low-level languages.

- *Low-level programming languages,* such as assembly language, allow the programmer to code instructions with the maximum possible efficiency. But using low-level languages requires detailed expertise in the exact capabilities of a given computer system and its microprocessor. Also, assembly language programming requires far more time.

Another way of differentiating programming languages is to distinguish between procedural and declarative languages. In a procedural language, such as assembly language, BASIC, C, FORTRAN, and

Pascal, the programmer spells out the procedure the computer will follow to accomplish a given goal. In a declarative language (also called a *non-procedural language*), the language defines a set of facts and relationships and allows you to query for specific results. Examples of declarative languages include PROLOG and Structured Query Language (SQL). The use of declarative languages is restricted, in practice, to expert systems and database query applications. See *BASIC, C, C++, COBOL, compiler, declarative language, expert system, FORTRAN, high-level programming language, interpreter, Modula-2, modular programming, object code, object-oriented programming language, Pascal, procedural language, PROLOG,* and *source code.*

project management program   Software that tracks individual tasks that make up an entire job.

Managing a big project, such as building a submarine or rebuilding the World Trade Center in New York, is far from easy. Thousands of little jobs must be finished at the same time that thousands of other little jobs are finished, because both groups are needed for the next phase of the project. Project management techniques called CPM (critical path method) and PERT (Program Evaluation and Review Technique) were created to help managers find the critical path—that is, the jobs that *must* be completed on time if the whole project is to be finished as scheduled. When the critical path becomes clear, the manager can allocate the resources necessary to complete these tasks in a timely fashion.

Project management software brings to PCs the analytical tools of CPM and PERT, but whether many personal computer users will benefit from this software is doubtful. CPM and PERT are cost-effective only for large projects, something that few PC users likely will encounter.

PROLOG   A high-level programming language used in artificial intelligence research and applications, particularly expert systems.

PROLOG, short for PROgramming in LOGic, was developed by French computer scientist Alain Colmerauer and logician Philippe Roussel in the early 1970s. Like LISP, PROLOG is a declarative language; rather than tell the computer what procedure to follow to solve a problem, the programmer describes the problem to be solved.

The language resembles the query language of a database management system such as SQL in that you can use PROLOG to ask a question such as, "Is Foster City in California?" But an important difference exists between PROLOG and a database management system (DBMS). A database contains information you can retrieve; a PROLOG program, in contrast, contains knowledge, from which the program can draw inferences about what is true or false.

Programmers often use PROLOG to develop expert systems at the research system level. A great deal of effort and time is involved in developing a PROLOG expert system, particularly user interfaces, input/output operations, and other procedures tedious to program in PROLOG.

PROM   See *programmable read-only memory (PROM)*.

prompt   A symbol or phrase that appears on-screen to inform you that the computer is ready to accept input.

property   In Microsoft Windows and MS-DOS Shell, an item of information associated with a program. Properties include the program's startup directory, the application shortcut key, and a password, if any. See *application shortcut key*, *Microsoft Windows*, and *MS-DOS Shell*.

proportional pie graph   In presentation graphics, a paired pie graph in which the size of each pie is in proportion to the amount of data the pie represents. Proportional pie graphs are useful for comparing two pies when one is significantly larger than the other.

proportional spacing   In typefaces, setting the width of a character in proportion to the character shape, so that a narrow character such as *i* receives less space than a wide character such as *m*. The text you're reading now uses proportional spacing. See *kerning* and *monospace*.

proprietary   Privately owned; based on trade secrets, privately developed technology, or specifications that the owner refuses to divulge, thus preventing others from duplicating a product or program unless an explicit license is purchased. The opposite of proprietary is *open* (privately developed but publicly published and available for emulation by others).

In personal computing, the Macintosh uses a proprietary architecture; no other company may produce a Macintosh clone without a license from Apple Computer. In contrast, the IBM Personal Computer's architecture wasn't proprietary, with the exception of the code stored in the computer's read-only memory (ROM). Other companies were able to emulate this code without actually copying IBM's code, enabling many companies, such as Compaq, to make computers that were functionally identical to IBM's offerings.

Exactly who will end up benefiting from proprietary technology is difficult to predict. Adobe Systems, for example, regarded its PostScript font technology as proprietary until 1990, when Apple Computer and Microsoft, averse to Adobe's licensing fees, announced the development of TrueType. In reply, Adobe published the information other firms would need to create PostScript-compatible fonts.

From the user's perspective, proprietary designs or formats entail risk. If the company prospers and the design or format is widely emulated or accepted, the user benefits. But if the company doesn't prosper or fails, the user could be stuck with a computer system or with data that can't be upgraded or exchanged with others. See *clone* and *proprietary file format*.

proprietary file format   A file format developed by a firm for storing data created by its products. A proprietary file format usually is unreadable by other firms' application programs. The popular programs all include the capability to convert the files of several other file formats.

P Q R S

protected mode   In 80286 and later microprocessors, an operating mode that supports virtual memory (which uses space on your hard drive to simulate memory and accesses other memory using techniques such as paging) and enables multitasking, in which two or more programs can run and use the computer's memory simultaneously without conflict.

In protected mode, the computer can use memory beyond the 640K conventional memory barrier. To run MS-DOS programs in this extended memory, 80386 and higher microprocessors can simulate two or more 640K DOS computers, up to the limits of the available extended memory. These simulated "machines," called *virtual machines*, give each DOS application what amounts to its own 640K computer in which to run, and each 640K "machine" is protected from interference by the others.

This mode isn't available unless your system is equipped with memory-management software to switch it on and manage the programs. By far the most popular software for this purpose is Microsoft Windows, running in 386 Enhanced mode. See *386 Enhanced mode, extended memory, memory-management program, Microsoft Windows, Microsoft Windows NT, paging memory, real mode,* and *terminate-and-stay-resident (TSR) program.*

protocol   A set of standards for exchanging information between two computer systems or two computer devices. See *communications protocol, file transfer protocol (FTP),* and *Internet.*

PrtSc   See *Print Screen (PrtSc).*

pseudocode   An algorithm expressed in English to conceptualize the algorithm before coding it in a programming language. See *algorithm.*

public data network (PDN)   An on-line service such as Sprintnet that's used to access a nationwide data network through a local phone call.

public domain software   Software not copyrighted that can be freely distributed without obtaining permission from or paying a fee to the programmer. See *freeware* and *shareware.*

pull quote   In desktop publishing, a quotation extracted from the copy of a newsletter or magazine article and printed in larger type in the column, often blocked off with ruled lines and sometimes shaded.

pull-down menu An on-screen menu of command options that appears after you select the command name on the menu bar (see fig. P.4).

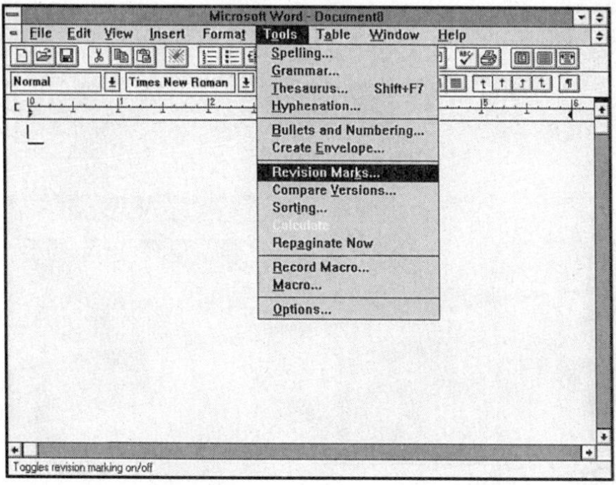

Fig. P.4 *A pull-down menu.*

The term *pull-down* comes from the Macintosh implementation of this idea, in which the menu doesn't stay on-screen unless you hold down the mouse button as you drag the pointer down the menu. In MS-DOS and Windows programs, however, the menu stays on-screen after you click the menu name.

pulse code modulation (PCM) A technique used to transform an incoming analog signal into a noise-free, digital equivalent. In multimedia, PCM is used to sample sounds digitally.

purge To remove unwanted or outdated information, usually from the hard drive, in a systematic—and ideally automatic—manner. Also, in systems using a form of delete protection, purge refers to deleting protected files so that they no longer can be undeleted. See *undelete utility.*

pushbutton In industry-standard and graphical user interfaces, a large button in a dialog box that initiates actions after you choose an option. Most dialog boxes contain an OK button, which confirms your choices and carries out the command, and a Cancel button, which cancels your choices and closes the dialog box (see fig. P.5). The button representing the option you're most likely to choose, called the *default button*, is highlighted.

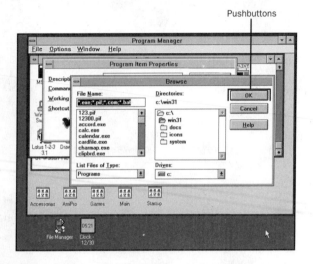

Fig. P.5 *Pushbuttons in a Microsoft Windows dialog box.*

TIP: *In many applications, you can press Enter to choose the default button, usually the OK button. You can press Esc to choose the Cancel button.*

p

QBasic   See *MS-DOS QBasic*.

QEMM 386   A memory-management program by Quarterdeck Office Systems that moves network drivers, disk cache programs, device drivers, and terminate-and-stay-resident (TSR) programs to the upper memory area, thus freeing conventional memory for DOS programs. See *conventional memory*, *memory-management program*, and *upper memory area*.

QIC   See *quarter-inch cartridge*.

quad density   See *high density*.

quarter-inch cartridge (QIC)   A tape cartridge using quarter-inch magnetic tape widely used for tape backup operations.

query   In database management, a search question that tells the program what kind of data should be retrieved from the database. An effective database management system lets you retrieve only the information you need for a specific purpose. A query specifies the characteristics (criteria) used to guide the computer to the required information, ignoring information not required. See *data independence*, *declarative language*, *query language*, and *Structured Query Language (SQL)*.

query by example (QBE)   In database management programs, a query technique, developed by IBM for use in the QBE program, that prompts you to type the search criteria into a template resembling the data record.

The advantage of query-by-example retrieval is that you don't need to learn a query language to frame a query. When you start the search, the program presents a screen that lists all the data fields that appear on every data record; you enter information that restricts the search to just the specified criteria. The fields left blank, however, will match anything.

Suppose that you are searching for the titles of all the Western video-tapes rated PG or PG-13 that you have in stock. Using QBE techniques, you can type the following query:

CATEGORY	RATING	TITLE
Western	PG or PG-13	

This query says, "Find all records in which the CATEGORY field contains *Western* and the RATING field contains *PG* or *PG-13*." See *database management program*, *data record*, and *query language*.

query language   In database management programs, a retrieval and data-editing language you use to specify what information to retrieve and how to arrange the retrieved information on-screen or when printing.

The ideal query language is a natural language, such as English, where you could tell the computer, "Using the database called VIDEOS, show me all the records in which the CATEGORY field contains *Western* and the RATING field contains *PG* or *PG-13*." A good query language, although rigid in syntax, approximates English, as the following example suggests:

```
SELECT title
FROM videos
WHERE CATEGORY = Western
AND RATING = PG
OR RATING = PG-13
```

The dot-prompt language of dBASE is a full-fledged query language, although it has quirks and odd nomenclature that make it difficult to use. Structured Query Language (SQL), already widely used for minicomputer and mainframe databases, is growing in popularity in the world of personal computers. See *database management program*, *natural language*, *query*, *query by example (QBE)*, and *Structured Query Language (SQL)*.

question mark   The wild-card symbol (?) that stands for a single character at a specific location, unlike the asterisk (*), which can stand for one or several characters. In AB?DE, for example, only file names or character strings that are five characters long with AB as the first two characters and DE as the last two characters are selected. See *asterisk* and *wild card*.

queue   See *job queue* and *print queue*.

QuickBASIC   A high-performance compiler for programs written in Microsoft BASIC. QuickBASIC recognizes modern control structures and allows programmers to create structured programs, complete with indentations and a full set of control structures, and to omit line numbers.

QuickBASIC was designed to compile any program written in BASICA or GW-BASIC, the versions of BASIC supplied with most IBM Personal Computers and compatibles. Programs compiled with QuickBASIC execute much faster, making the compiler suitable for the creation of commercial software. See *BASIC, compiler,* and *control structure.*

QuickDraw   The object-oriented graphics and text-display technology stored in every Macintosh's read-only memory (ROM). When creating Macintosh programs, programmers achieve a common look by drawing on the QuickDraw resources to create on-screen windows, dialog boxes, menus, and shapes.

QuickTime   An extension to the Macintosh system software that allows applications that support QuickTime to display animated or video sequences precisely synchronized with high-quality digital sound. In a training document, for instance, you can click an icon to see a QuickTime video sequence (a "movie") that visually shows a specific technique or procedure.

quit   To exit a program properly so that all your configuration choices and data are properly saved.

TIP: *With many programs, switching the computer off while the program is still open is a bad idea. Not only can you lose configuration choices, but you won't be warned to save your work. Also, programs that create temporary files won't have a chance to delete them, as is usually done when you exit the program.*

Microsoft Windows exercises control over every part of your system. Don't end your Windows session by just switching off the computer; you can cause problems as severe as losing the computer hardware settings stored in CMOS. Press Alt+F4 and return to DOS before you switch off the computer.

P
Q
R
S

QWERTY   *kwer-tee*   The standard typewriter keyboard layout, also used for computer keyboards. The keyboard name comes from the six keys on the left end of the top row of letter keys. Alternative keyboard layouts, such as the Dvorak keyboard, are said to speed typing by placing the most commonly used letters on the home row. See *Dvorak keyboard.*

radio button   In a graphical user interface, the round option buttons that appear in dialog boxes. Unlike check boxes, radio buttons are mutually exclusive; you can pick only one radio button option within a group. See *graphical user interface (GUI)*.

radio frequency interference (RFI)   The radio noise generated by computers and other electronic and electromechanical devices. Excessive RFI generated by computers can disrupt the reception of radio and television signals; likewise, RFI generated by other sources can cause screen flickering and even data loss in poorly shielded computers. See *FCC certification*.

ragged-left alignment   In word processing and desktop publishing, the alignment of text on the right margin so that the left remains ragged. Synonymous with *right justification*. See *justification*.

ragged-right alignment   See *justification*.

RAM   See *random-access memory (RAM)*.

RAM cache   See *cache memory*.

RAM disk   An area of random-access memory (RAM) configured by a software program to emulate a disk drive. Data stored in a RAM disk can be accessed more quickly than data stored on a disk drive, but this data is erased whenever you turn off or reboot the computer.

If you're using a 640K DOS system, the RAM disk is created out of the available RAM, leaving little memory for you to run your programs. If you have extended memory or expanded memory, however, you can place the virtual disk in the RAM above 640K. See *configuration file*, *device driver*, *expanded memory (EMS)*, *extended memory*, *RAMDRIVE.SYS*, and *random-access memory (RAM)*.

CAUTION: *Because virtual disk drives operate much faster than real disk drives, placing programs or data in a virtual disk drive can result in major performance improvements, but the benefits come at a stiff price. When you save work to this disk, you're really writing your work to RAM, and everything in RAM is lost when you switch off the computer. Many computer users have lost hours of important work by failing to copy a document from a virtual disk to a real disk at the end of a session.*

RAMDRIVE.SYS   In MS-DOS, a configuration file provided with the operating system that sets aside part of your computer's memory as a virtual disk, which is treated by DOS as though it were a disk drive. RAMDRIVE.SYS is a driver that must be loaded using a DEVICE or DEVICEHIGH statement in your CONFIG.SYS file.

random access   An information storage and retrieval technique in which the computer can access the information directly, without having to go through a sequence of locations. A better term is *direct access*, but the term *random access* has become enshrined in the acronym RAM, commonly used to describe a PC's internal memory, or random-access memory.

To understand the distinction between random and sequential access, compare a cassette tape (sequential access) with a long-playing record (random access). To get to the song you want on a cassette tape, you must fast-forward through a sequence of songs until you find the one you want. Computer disk drives operate in a similar way to a record, in which you can move the arm above the surface of the record and go to the track you want. See *random-access memory (RAM)* and *sequential access*.

random-access memory (RAM)   The computer's primary working memory in which program instructions and data are stored so that they can be accessed directly by the central processing unit (CPU) via the processor's high-speed data bus.

To execute instructions at high speeds, the computer's processing circuitry must be able to obtain information from the memory directly and quickly. Computer memory, therefore, is designed to give the processor random access to the contents.

RAM is a matrix of rows and columns that can hold data or program instructions at each row/column intersection. Each intersection also has a unique address, so the CPU can access each memory location directly by specifying the address and activating the circuit that leads directly to that address.

RAM often is called *read/write memory* to distinguish it from read-only memory (ROM), the other component of a personal computer's primary storage. In RAM, the CPU can write and read data. Most programs set aside a portion of RAM as a temporary work space for your data, so you can modify (rewrite) as needed until the data is ready for printing or storage on disk.

RAM consists of volatile semiconductor memory, which doesn't retain its contents when the power to the computer is switched off. See *primary storage, random access, read-only memory (ROM),* and *secondary storage.*

> **CAUTION:** *Save your work frequently. In the event of a system failure or power interruption, you lose all work in RAM that you haven't recorded (saved) on a magnetic medium such as a disk drive.*

range In a spreadsheet program, a cell or a rectangular group of adjacent cells.

All spreadsheet programs let you identify ranges of cells. A range can include one cell or thousands, with one restriction: the range must be rectangular in shape and consist of consecutive cells. Valid ranges include a single cell, part of a column, part of a row, and a block spanning several columns and several rows (see fig. R.1).

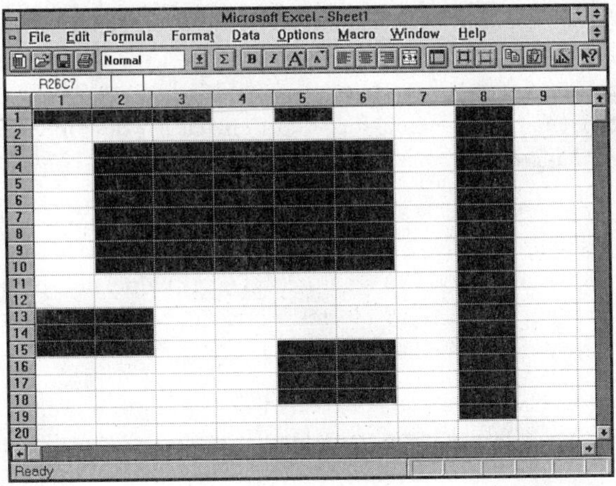

Fig. R.1 *Valid ranges.*

Ranges allow you to perform operations, such as formatting, on groups of cells. For example, you can format one column of numbers with the currency format, even though the rest of the worksheet uses a general format. You can also use range expressions in commands and formulas. See *cell* and *range expression*.

range expression   In a spreadsheet program, an expression that describes a range by defining the cells in opposing corners of a rectangle.

In Lotus 1-2-3, for example, you write a range expression by typing the beginning cell address, two periods, and the ending cell address—**A9..B12**, for example. Excel uses a colon in place of the two periods. See *range name*.

range format   In a spreadsheet program, a numeric format or label alignment format that applies only to a range of cells and overrides the global format. See *global format*, *label alignment*, *numeric format*, and *range*.

P
Q
R
S

range name   In a spreadsheet program, a range of cells to which you attach a distinctive name. A range name is much easier to remember than a range expression. Also, when you refer to the range by entering its name, formulas more clearly describe what's being calculated.

Suppose that you create a worksheet in which range E9..E21 contains your company's sales for the first quarter of 1994. After naming the range FQ1994, you use the range name, not the range expression, in formulas. In a formula that totals the column, for example, you type **@SUM(FQ1994)**.

A second advantage of range naming is that you can move the data in the range to a new location and the range name stays the same. If you type **FQ1994**, the program unfailingly refers to the present location of the data in the range. See *range* and *range expression*.

TIP: *To avoid errors in range references, name your ranges and then use those names in your formulas.*

raster   On a computer or television screen, the horizontal pattern of lines that forms the image. Within each line are dots that can be illuminated individually.

raster display   The display technology used in television sets and computer monitors. The screen is scanned 30 to 60 times each second from top to bottom by a tightly focused electron beam that moves back and forth, line by line, down the screen's raster pattern. See *object-oriented graphic* and *raster*.

raster font   See *bit-mapped font*.

raster graphics   The display of graphic images using a collection of small, separate dots called a *bit map*. The graphic's resolution is limited by the capabilities of the display or printing device. Synonymous with *bit map*.

raster image processor (RIP)   A device that converts vector images into raster images before printing to output devices that require it. See *object-oriented graphic*, *raster graphics*, and *vector-to-raster conversion*.

r

rave   In electronic mail and computer newsgroups, to carry on an argument in support of a position beyond all bounds of reason and sensitivity. Raving is annoying but isn't considered to be a flame unless the argument is couched in offensive terms. See *flame*.

raw data   Unprocessed or unformatted data that hasn't been arranged, edited, or represented in a form for easy retrieval and analysis.

RCA plug   See *phono plug*.

RDBMS   See *relational database management system (RDBMS)*.

read   To retrieve data or program instructions from a device such as a disk drive and place the data into the computer's memory.

README file   A text file, often included on the installation disk of application programs, that contains last-minute information not contained in the program's manuals. Typical README file names are README.1ST, README.TXT, and READ.ME.

> **TIP:** *Be sure to look for README files, and read them; they may contain information that can save you trouble and headaches when installing and using a new program. Chances are that the file was placed on the disk after frustrated users besieged the technical support department with complaints and questions.*

read-only   Capable of being displayed, but not deleted. If a display of read-only data can be edited, formatted, or otherwise modified, it can't be saved as the same file. See *file attribute*, *locked file*, and *read/write*.

read-only attribute   In DOS and OS/2, a file attribute stored with a file's directory entry that indicates whether the file can be changed or deleted. When the read-only attribute is on, you can display the file, but you can't modify or erase it. When the read-only attribute is off, you can modify or delete the file. See *file attribute*.

read-only memory (ROM)   The portion of a computer's primary storage that doesn't lose its contents when you switch off the power. Read-only memory contains essential system programs that neither you nor the computer can erase.

Because the computer's random-access memory (RAM) is volatile (loses information when you switch off the power), the computer's internal memory is blank at powerup, and the computer can perform no functions unless given startup instructions. These instructions are stored in ROM.

A growing trend is toward including substantial portions of the operating system on ROM chips instead of on disk. In the Macintosh, for example, much of the Macintosh System is encoded on ROM chips, including the graphics routines (QuickDraw) that are part of the Mac's application program interface (API). However, upgrading ROM is more difficult and expensive than supplying new disks. See *application program interface (API)*, *erasable programmable read-only memory (EPROM)*, *programmable read-only memory (PROM)*, and *QuickDraw*.

read/write   The capability of an internal memory or secondary storage device to record data (write) and to play back data (read) previously recorded or saved.

read/write file   In DOS, a file whose read-only file attribute is set so that the file can be deleted and modified. See *file attribute*, *locked file*, and *read-only*.

read/write head   In a hard disk or floppy disk drive, the magnetic recording and playback device that travels back and forth across the surface of the disk, storing and retrieving data.

read/write memory   See *random-access memory (RAM)*.

real mode   An operating mode of Intel microprocessors in which a program is given a definite storage location in memory and direct access to peripheral devices.

Real mode, which can directly use up to 1M of RAM, allocates memory space so that programs have direct access to actual memory locations, but has no way of managing more than one program loaded into memory simultaneously; programs can invade each other's memory space or try to access peripheral devices simultaneously. In both situations, a system failure may result. The 80286, 80386, and 80486 microprocessors offer an additional operating mode—protected mode—that supervises the allocation of memory and governs access to peripheral devices. See *Intel 80286*, *Intel 80386DX*, *Intel 80386SX*, *Intel 80486DX*, *Intel 80486SX*, *memory-management program*, and *protected mode*.

real time   The immediate processing of input, such as a point-of-sale transaction or a measurement performed by an analog laboratory device. The computers used in your car are real-time systems.

real-time clock   A battery-powered clock contained in the computer's internal circuitry. The real-time clock keeps track of the current time even when the computer is switched off. This clock should be distinguished from the high-speed clock that governs the microprocessor's cycles.

reboot   To restart the computer. Rebooting is often necessary after a system crash. In most cases, you can restart the system from the keyboard, but especially severe crashes may require you to perform a hardware reset. In a hardware reset, you must push the reset button, or if no such button exists, turn off the computer and turn it back on again. See *programmer's switch*.

recalculation method   In a spreadsheet program, the way the program recalculates cell values after you change the contents of a cell. See *automatic recalculation* and *manual recalculation*.

recalculation order   In a spreadsheet program, the direction in which calculations are performed when you enter new values, labels, or formulas.

Early spreadsheet programs offered two recalculation modes: column-wise recalculation and row-wise recalculation. In column-wise mode, the program recalculates all the cells in column A before moving to column B, and so on. In row-wise recalculation, the program recalculates all the cells in row 1 before moving to the beginning of row 2, and so on.

TIP: *Programs that offer only these two options can produce serious errors. If data is entered in columns that are totaled at the bottom, and the results are summarized to the right of the columns, row-wise recalculation order will recalculate the summary equations before retotaling the columns. In most cases, you obtain the correct answer only by changing the recalculation order to column-wise recalculation.*

Today's advanced spreadsheet programs, such as Lotus 1-2-3, improve recalculation by offering natural recalculation as the default order. In natural recalculation, a formula isn't calculated until all the formulas to which it refers are calculated. The program scans the entire worksheet to determine the logical order of recalculation. See *column-wise recalculation, natural recalculation, optimal recalculation,* and *row-wise recalculation.*

record See *data record.*

record-oriented database management program A database management program that displays data records as the result of query operations, unlike a table-oriented program, in which the result of all data query operations is a table. Purists argue that a true relational database management program always treats data in tabular form and that any program that displays records as the result of queries, such as dBASE, doesn't deserve to call itself relational, even if the program can work simultaneously with two or more databases.

A table-oriented program, in contrast, succinctly summarizes data in tables on-screen, eliminating all extraneous data not specifically called for in the search query. See *data retrieval, relational database management, Structured Query Language (SQL),* and *table-oriented database management program.*

record pointer In a database management program, an on-screen status message that states the number of the data record now on-screen (or in which the cursor is positioned).

r

recover To bring the computer system back to a previous stable operating state or to restore erased or misdirected data. Recovery, which may require user intervention, is needed after a system or user error occurs, such as telling the system to write data to a drive that doesn't contain a disk. See *undelete utility*.

CAUTION: *The DOS RECOVER command is used to recover files from a disk that can't be read because of a few bad sectors. However, RECOVER has proved to be unreliable and sometimes destructive. RECOVER isn't included in MS-DOS 6.0.*

recoverable error An error that doesn't cause the program or system to crash or to erase data irretrievably.

recto The right-hand (odd-numbered) page in facing pages. See *verso*.

recursion In computer programming, a program instruction that causes a module or subroutine to call itself. A recursive function may be used to implement search strategies and perform internal sorting, for example, where the number of recursions is unpredictable.

redirection See *input/output (I/O) redirection*.

redirection operator In DOS, a symbol that routes the results of a command from or to a device other than the keyboard and video display (console). You can use the following redirection operators in a DOS command:

- *Output redirection.* Sends the output of a command to a file or device. The following command, for example, sends the contents of LETTER.DOC to the printer:

    ```
    LETTER.DOC>PRN
    ```

- *Append redirection.* Sends the result of a command to an existing file and adds the output to the existing file's contents. The following command, for example, saves a directory listing in a file named DIR.DOC and adds the information to the end of the file if DIR.DOC exists:

    ```
    DIR B: >> DIR.DOC
    ```

- *Input redirection.* Sets up a file as the input for a command rather than the console, so that the contents of the file are used instead of data input at the keyboard. The following command, for example, runs the SORT command using the file TERMS.DOC as the input to be sorted:

```
SORT < TERMS.DOC
```

See *input/output (I/O) redirection.*

redlining In word processing, a display attribute, such as a distinctive color or double underlining, that marks the text co-authors have added to a document. The redlined text is highlighted so that other authors or editors know exactly what has been added to or deleted from the document. When the document is printed, the text is usually printed with a lightly shaded background.

reduced instruction set computer (RISC) *risk*
A central processing unit (CPU) in which the number of instructions the processor can execute is reduced to a minimum to increase processing speed.

Microprocessors such as the Intel 80386 recognize well over 100 instructions for performing various computations, but the more instructions a chip can handle, the more slowly it runs for all instructions.

The idea of a RISC architecture is to reduce the instruction set to the bare minimum, emphasizing the instructions used most of the time and optimizing them for the fastest possible execution. The instructions left out of the chip must be carried out by combining the ones that remain, but because these instructions are needed far less frequently, a RISC processor usually runs 50 to 75 percent faster than its CISC counterpart.

RISC processors also are cheaper to design, debug, and manufacture because they are less complex. However, simplifying the microprocessor places the burden on programmers, who must restore the complexity by writing lengthier programs. In general, software development doesn't show the same impressive trend of increased efficiency that's evident in the hardware industry—quite the opposite, in fact. The cost of developing a major new application program

r

is so astronomical that all but the biggest companies are being pushed out of the business. For this reason, some argue that it makes much more sense to put the complexity in the hardware, giving programmers a much-needed break. The issue may become moot because today's "ordinary" microprocessors (now called *complex instruction set computers, or CISC* for short) rival the performance of the fastest RISC processors of just two or three years ago. RISC processors may find a niche, however, in special-purpose applications, such as graphics accelerator circuits, in which their speed provides a critical advantage. See *central processing unit (CPU)* and *complex instruction set computer (CISC)*.

re-engineering   A method of computer-based automation that begins by radically redesigning the way work is done and then choosing computer tools that enhance the redesigned work process.

It's no secret that computer technology hasn't delivered on its promise of higher productivity. One reason has to do with old attitudes rather than poor system design. In many firms, after the credit department grants credit, the receiving department receives goods and the accounting department writes checks. The re-engineering strategy for this kind of setting may be to put computers in the receiving department, so that the receiving staff can confirm what's received and write the checks on the spot.

Re-engineering is the latest business buzzword, but the underlying concept is really very simple. You can apply some of the principles of re-engineering to your own computer work just by remembering a few simple rules:

- *Avoid reinventing the wheel.* Develop and refine template versions of important letters, memos, reports, worksheets, newsletters, business forms, and data management forms.

- *Capture information at the source.* A sales manager in the field records sales in a notebook, and then later pecks the information into a Lotus worksheet. The cure? A portable computer running Lotus 1-2-3.

- *Avoid typing the same information twice.* Develop macros, forms, and boilerplate text to automate the creation of documents, including an addressed envelope.

reformat   In operating systems, to repeat a formatting operation on a floppy or hard disk. In word processing or page layout programs, to change the arrangement of text elements on the page.

refresh   To repeat the display or storage of data to keep it from fading or becoming lost. The video display and random-access memory (RAM) must be refreshed constantly. In some older DOS-based programs, a refresh command is used to update the display after you edit a graphic or text (if the screen isn't refreshed automatically).

relational database management   An approach to database management in which data that's stored in two-dimensional data tables of columns and rows can be related if the tables have a common column or field.

The term *relational* as applied to database management refers to the storage and retrieval of data in tables.

Introduced in 1970 by Edgar Codd, the design was founded on a mathematical theory. A true *relational* database, one in which the table defines the relation between the items listed in rows (data records) and columns (data fields), treats all data as tables, and the result of any query is a new table.

Suppose that a video store database lists customer phone numbers and names in a table as follows:

PHONE_NO	NAME
555-4321	Smith, Ted
555-4411	Jones, Jane

Another table contains the titles of rented videotapes, the phone numbers of the customers who rented those tapes, and the due dates:

TITLE	PHONE_NO	DUE_DATE
Blues	555-4321	07/16/94
Danger	555-4411	07/19/94

A query may ask, "Show me the names and phone numbers of customers with tapes due on or before July 19, 1994, and print those film titles." Such a query results in the following table:

NAME	PHONE_NO	TITLE
Smith, Ted	555-4321	Blues
Jones, Jane	555-4411	Danger

Not all database management programs marketed as relational are true table-oriented programs. Most are record-oriented programs relational only to the extent that they can link data in two databases through a common field. dBASE is such a program; data is stored in records, not tables. However, you can use dBASE as though it were a true relational program.

relational database management system (RDBMS)

A relational database management program, especially one that comes with all the necessary support programs, programming tools, and documentation needed to create, install, and maintain custom database applications.

relational operator   A symbol used to specify the relationship between two numeric values. The result of a calculation using a relational operator is either *true* or *false*.

In query languages, relational operators often are used in specifying search criteria. For example, a video store manager may want to tell the computer, "Show me all the telephone numbers of customers with overdue tapes that are due on a date less than or equal to May 7, 1994."

In electronic spreadsheets, relational operators are used, for example, in @IF formulas to perform tests on data so that different values are displayed, depending on whether the result of the test is true or false.

To permit the expression of logical operators in the character-based world of computing, many programs use the following conventions:

= Equal to

< Less than

> Greater than

<= Less than or equal to

>= Greater than or equal to

<> Not equal to

relative addressing   In a program, specifying a memory location using an expression so that the address can be calculated instead of using a specific address. See *absolute address*.

relative cell reference   In a formula in a spreadsheet program, a reference to the contents of a cell that's adjusted by the program when you copy the formula to another cell or range of cells.

To understand what happens when you copy a relative cell reference, you need to know how a spreadsheet program actually records a cell reference. Suppose that you type the formula **@SUM(C6..C8)** in cell C10. The program records a code that means, "Add all the values in the cells positioned in the second, third, and fourth rows up from the current cell." When you copy this formula to the next four cells to the right (D10..G10), it still reads, "Add all the values in the cells positioned in the second, third, and fourth rows up from the current cell," and sums each column correctly (see fig. R.2). See *absolute cell reference* and *mixed cell reference*.

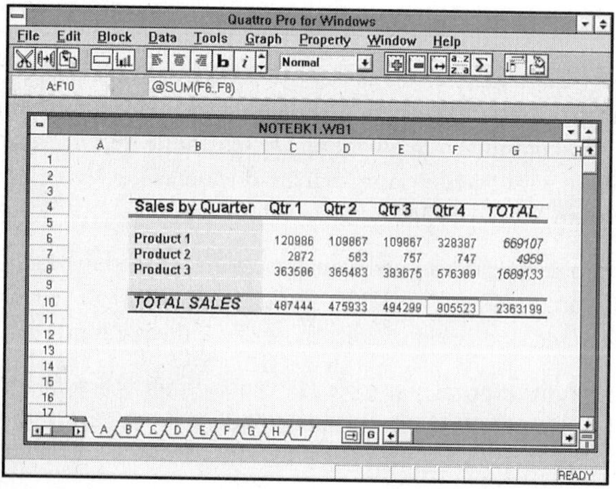

Fig. R.2   *The formulas in cells D10..G10 contain a relative cell reference copied from the first column.*

release number   The number, usually a decimal number, that identifies an improved version of a program rather than a major revision, which is numbered using an integer. A program labeled Version 5.1, for example, is the second release of Version 5 of the program (the first was Version 5.0).

Nothing requires software publishers to use this numbering scheme, and some don't. Further, competitive pressures sometimes encourage publishers to jump to a new version number when the program being released is in fact only an incremental improvement over its predecessor. See *version*.

reliability   The capability of computer hardware or software to perform as the user expects and to do so consistently, without failures or erratic behavior. See *mean time between failures (MTBF)*.

reliable link   An error-free connection established via the telephone system (despite its high line noise and low bandwidth) by two modems that use error correction. See *error-correcting protocol* and *modem*.

remark   In a batch file, macro, or source code, explanatory text that's ignored when the computer executes the commands. See *batch file*.

remote control program   A utility program that lets you link two personal computers so that you can use one to control the operation of the second.

Why would anyone want to control a distant PC? Users of popular remote control programs such as Carbon Copy Plus are using this software to train remote users, to perform tasks at the office while working at home, to install and demonstrate software on clients' computers, and to provide technical support by logging on to the remote computer and determining what went wrong.

remote terminal   See *terminal*.

removable mass storage   A high-capacity data storage device, such as a Bernoulli box or a tape backup system, in which the disk or tape is encased in a plastic cartridge or cassette so it can be removed from the drive for safekeeping. See *Bernoulli box* and *floptical disk*.

P
Q
R
S

removable storage media   A data storage medium, such as a disk or cartridge, that's encased in a plastic cartridge or cassette so that it can be removed from the drive for safekeeping.

rendering   In computer graphics, the conversion of an outline drawing into a fully formed, three-dimensional image.

repagination   In word processing and desktop publishing, a reformatting operation in which pages are renumbered to reflect insertions, deletions, block moves, or other changes to the document's text. Most programs repaginate automatically as you insert and edit text, but some programs require that you repaginate manually before the page numbers are correctly displayed.

repeater   In networks, a hardware device used to extend the length of network cabling by amplifying and passing along the messages traveling through the network. See *bridge*, *local area network (LAN)*, and *router*.

repeating field   In database design, a field in which the user must type the same few data items repeatedly—such as suppliers' names and addresses—thus creating many possibilities for errors due to typos or misspellings. See *database design*, *data integrity*, *data redundancy*, and *relational database management*.

repeating label   In a spreadsheet program, a character preceded by a label prefix that causes the character to be repeated across the cell. For example, Lotus 1-2-3 uses \ to repeat one or more characters across a cell. The entry \= would produce a line of equal signs across the cell.

➡ **TIP:** *You can use repeating labels to create lines across your worksheet. Use repeating hyphens, for example, to create a single line or repeating equal signs to create a double line. See* label *prefix.*

repeat key   A key that continues to enter the same character as long as you hold down that key.

r

repetitive strain injury (RSI) A serious and potentially debilitating occupational illness caused by prolonged repetitive hand and arm movements that can damage, inflame, or kill nerves in the hands, arms, shoulder, or neck.

Also known as *cumulative trauma disorder (CTD)*, RSI occurs when constantly repeated motions strain tendons and ligaments, resulting in scar tissue that squeezes nerves and eventually may kill them. RSI has long been observed among meat packers, musicians, and assembly-line workers, who repeatedly perform the same hand movements. With the proliferation of computer keyboards, RSI is increasingly noted among office workers and poses a genuine threat to personal computer users who work long hours at the keyboard. Specific RSI disorders include *carpal tunnel syndrome (CTS)*, which often afflicts supermarket cashiers, who must drag items over price-code scanners for extended periods.

Symptoms of CTS include burning, tingling, or numbness in the hands, as well as a loss of muscle control and dexterity. Potentially incapacitating to full-time writers, secretaries, and journalists, CTS and other RSI injuries are estimated to cost U.S. corporations an estimated $27 billion per year in medical bills and lost workdays.

> **TIP:** *You can prevent RSI. Adjust your chair height to eliminate any unnecessary extension or flexing of the wrist. Take frequent breaks, use good posture, and vary your daily activities so that you perform a variety of actions with your wrists. Finally, don't rest the heel of your hands on the base of the keyboard and avoid using keyboards, keyboard rests, and laptop computers that provide more than an inch of space below the space bar, inviting you to rest your hands.*

**P
Q
R
S**

replace In word processing programs, a feature that searches for a string and replaces it with another string.

Unless you're absolutely sure that you know what you're doing, use the replace feature only in the mode that requests your confirmation. If you allow the replace to do its work without confirmation throughout the document, it may perform incorrect substitutions. Also, always save your work before performing a replace operation.

With most programs, you can improve the accuracy of the replacement operation by specifying capitalization and whole-word options. If you tell the program to match the capitalization pattern in the search string, such as *Tree* if you want the change only when *tree* begins a sentence, the program replaces only those strings that match the characters and the capitalization pattern (*Tree* is replaced, but not *TREE* or *tree*).

Suppose that you want to delete the word *very* throughout your document. If you perform the replacement, *very* will also be removed from the word *every*. If you select the whole-word option when replacing *very*, the program replaces the string only if it's a whole word—not if it's part of a word. See *string*.

replaceable parameter   In MS-DOS, a symbol used in a batch file that MS-DOS replaces with information you type. The symbol consists of a percent sign and a number from 1 through 9, such as %1.

Suppose that you create a batch file, PRINTNOW.BAT, that contains the statement COPY %1 PRN. If you type the command **PRINTNOW LETTER.DOC**, MS-DOS replaces the %1 symbol with the file name you typed and copies LETTER.DOC to the printer. See *batch file*.

report   In database management, printed output that usually is formatted with page numbers and headings. With most programs, reports can include calculated fields, showing subtotals, totals, averages, and other figures computed from the data. See *band* and *calculated field*.

report generator   A program or program function that allows a non-programmer to request printed output from a computer database.

research network   A wide-area computer network, such as ARPAnet or NSFNet, developed and funded by a governmental agency to improve research productivity in areas of national interest.

r

ResEdit `rez-eh-dit` A Macintosh utility program, available free from Apple Computer dealers, that lets you edit (and copy to other programs) many program features, such as menu text, icons, cursor shapes, and dialog boxes.

reserved memory See *upper memory area.*

reserved word In a programming language or operating system, a word—also called a *keyword*—that has a fixed function and can't be used for any other purpose. In DOS batch files, for example, the word *REM* is reserved to indicate the beginning of a remark (a line of text that DOS will ignore when executing the file). You can use a reserved word only for its intended purpose; you can't use the word for naming files, variables, or other user-named objects. See *keyword.*

reset button A button, usually mounted on the system unit's front panel, that lets you perform a warm boot if the reset key (Ctrl+Alt+Del) doesn't work. On older Macintoshes, the reset button is part of the programmer's switch. Synonymous with *hardware reset.* See *programmer's switch, reset key,* and *warm boot.*

reset key A key combination that, when pressed, restarts the computer. This key combination (Ctrl+Alt+Del on DOS machines) provides an alternative to switching the power off and on after a crash so severe that the keyboard doesn't respond. See *hardware reset, programmer's switch,* and *warm boot.*

resident program See *terminate-and-stay-resident (TSR) program.*

resolution A measurement—usually expressed in linear dots per inch (dpi), horizontally and vertically—of the sharpness of an image generated by an output device such as a monitor or printer.

In monitors, resolution is expressed as the number of pixels horizontally and lines vertically on-screen. For example, a CGA monitor displays fewer lines than a VGA monitor, and therefore, a CGA image appears more jagged than a VGA image. The following table lists the resolutions of common video adapters for IBM PCs and compatibles:

P Q R S

Resolution Adapter	Pixels × Lines
Monochrome Display Adapter (MDA)	720 × 350
Color Graphics Adapter (CGA)	640 × 200
Enhanced Graphics Adapter (EGA)	640 × 350
MultiColor Graphics Array (MCGA)	640 × 480
Video Graphics Array (VGA)	640 × 480
Super VGA (extended VGA)	800 × 600
Super VGA (VGA Plus)	1,024 × 768

Macintoshes with 9-inch screens display 512 pixels by 342 lines, whereas Macs with 12- or 13-inch monitors display 640 by 480.

For printers, resolution is typically measured by the number of dots per inch (dpi) that the printer can print: the higher the number, the sharper the resolution. Low-quality dot-matrix printers print approximately 125 dpi, whereas laser printers typically print 300 or 600 dpi. Professional typesetting machinery prints at resolutions of 1,200 dpi or more.

response time   The time the computer needs to respond and carry out a request. Response time is a better measurement of system performance than access time because it more fairly states the system's throughput. See *access time*.

retrieval   All the procedures involved in finding, summarizing, organizing, displaying, or printing information from a computer system in a form useful for the user.

Return   See *Enter/Return*.

reverse engineering   The process of systematically taking apart a computer chip or application program to discover how it works, with the aim of imitating or duplicating some or all of its functions.

r

Reverse engineering is a common practice in contemporary industry, but it often raises ethical and moral issues that range from clear-cut to murky. In the clear-cut department, microprocessors and other chips have been reverse engineered and copied outright—a clear violation of applicable U.S. and international law—by firms operating outside North America. In a well-publicized example of a murky area of reverse engineering, Advanced Micro Devices (AMD) used reverse engineering to discover how the Intel 80386 microprocessor works. With this information, AMD created a logical simulation of the 80386's performance, and used this simulation to design its own microprocessor (the Am386DX and Am386SX) that approximates the 80386's performance without duplicating its circuitry. The result is 100 percent compatible with the Intel 80386, but it isn't an 80386—or so AMD claims. The chips, for example, operate at 40 MHz and consume substantially less power than Intel's comparable 386 chips. With the entry of Cyrix into the field, offering three 486 chips with interesting design variations, the waters become even more murky. The legal issues raised by reverse engineering will be decided in the courts, but only after years of expensive litigation. See *Advanced Micro Devices (AMD), Cyrix, Intel 80386DX,* and *Intel 80386SX.*

reverse video   In monochrome monitors, a means of high-lighting text on the display screen so that normally dark characters are displayed as bright characters on a dark background, or normally bright characters are displayed as dark characters on a bright background. See *highlighting.*

rewrite   Synonymous with *overwrite.*

RGB monitor   A color digital monitor that accepts separate inputs for red, green, and blue, and produces a much sharper image than composite color monitors.

Although the Enhanced Graphics Display uses RGB techniques, the RGB monitor is synonymous with the Color Graphics Adapter (CGA) standard. See *composite color monitor.*

P
Q
R
S

Rich Text Format (RTF) A text formatting standard developed by Microsoft Corporation that allows a word processing program to create a file encoded with all the document's formatting instructions, but without using any special codes. An RTF-encoded document can be transmitted over telecommunications links or read by another RTF-compatible word processing program, without loss of the formatting.

right justification See *justification*.

ring network In local area networks, a decentralized network topology in which a number of nodes (including workstations, shared peripherals, and file servers) are arranged around a closed loop cable (see fig. R.3).

Fig. R.3 *An illustration of a ring network.*

Like a bus network, a ring network's workstations send messages to all other workstations. Each node in the ring, however, has a unique address, and its reception circuitry constantly monitors the bus to determine whether a message is being sent. For example, a message sent to a node named Laser Printer is ignored by the other nodes on the network.

Each node contains a repeater that amplifies and sends the signal along to the next node. Unlike a bus network, ring networks therefore can extend far beyond the geographic limits of bus networks, which lack repeaters.

The failure of a single node can disrupt the entire network; however, fault-tolerance schemes have been devised that allow ring networks to continue to function even if one or more nodes fail. See *file server, local area network (LAN)*, *network topology*, and *node*.

r

RIP   See *raster image processor (RIP)*.

ripple-through effect   In a spreadsheet program, the sudden appearance of ERR values throughout the cells after you make a change that breaks a link among formulas.

If you introduce into a spreadsheet a change that corrupts a formula so that it evaluates to ERR (error) or NA (unavailable value), all the formulas linked to (dependent on) the corrupted formula also display ERR, and you see the ERR message ripple through the spreadsheet.

If this happens, you may think that you've ruined the entire spreadsheet, but after you locate and repair the problem, all the other formulas are restored.

RISC   See *reduced instruction set computer (RISC)*.

river   In desktop publishing, a formatting flaw that results in the accidental alignment of white space between words in sequential lines of text, encouraging the eye to follow the flow down three or more lines.

Rivers injure what typographers refer to as the *color* of the page, which should be perceived by the eye as an overall shade of gray without interruption from white spaces, bad word breaks, poor character spacing, or uneven line spacing. See *color* and *desktop publishing (DTP)*.

RLL   See *Run-Length Limited (RLL)*.

ROM   See *read-only memory (ROM)*.

Roman   In typography, an upright serif typeface of medium weight. In proofreading, characters without emphasis. See *emphasis*, *serif*, and *weight*.

root directory   On a disk, the top-level directory that MS-DOS creates when you format the disk. See *directory*, *parent directory*, and *subdirectory*.

root name   The first, mandatory part of a DOS file name, using from one to eight characters. See *extension* and *file name*.

rot-13   In USENET newsgroups, a simple encryption technique that offsets each character by 13 places (so that an *e* becomes an *r*). Rot-13 encryption is used for any message that may spoil someone's fun (such as the solution to a game) or offend some readers (such as erotic poetry). If the reader chooses to decrypt the message by issuing the appropriate command, then the reader—not the author of the message—bears the responsibility for any discomfort that may be caused by reading the message. See *netiquette* and *spoiler*.

rotated type   In a graphics or desktop publishing program, text that has been turned vertically from its normal, horizontal position on the page. The best graphics programs, such as CorelDRAW!, allow you to edit the type even after you rotate it.

rotation tool   In a graphics or desktop publishing program, a command option, represented by an icon, that you can use to rotate type from its normal, horizontal position. See *rotated type*.

roughs   In desktop publishing, the preliminary page layouts that the designer creates using rough sketches to represent page design ideas. Synonymous with *thumbnails*. See *desktop publishing (DTP)*.

router   Similar to a bridge, connects only local area networks that use identical protocols. A router passes data only when the data is intended for the other LAN. Routers can also be called on to determine the best route for transmitting data, such as in a packet-switching network. See *bridge, local area network (LAN),* and *packet-switching network*.

row   In a spreadsheet program, a horizontal block of cells running horizontally across the spreadsheet. In most programs, rows are numbered sequentially from the top. In a database, a row is the same as a record or data record.

row-wise recalculation   In spreadsheet programs, a recalculation order that calculates all the values in row 1 before moving to row 2, and so on.

r

CAUTION: *If your spreadsheet program doesn't offer natural recalculation, use row-wise recalculation for worksheets in which rows are summed and the totals are forwarded. Column-wise recalculation may produce erroneous results. See* column-wise recalculation, natural recalculation, optimal recalculation, *and* recalculation order.

RS-232C　A standard recommended by the Electronic Industries Association (EIA) concerning the transmission of data between computers using serial ports. Most personal computers are equipped with an RS-232-compatible serial port, which you can use for external modems, printers, scanners, and other peripheral devices. See *modem, printer, scanner,* and *serial port.*

RS-422　A standard recommended by the Electronic Industries Association (EIA) and used as the serial port standard for Macintosh computers. RS-422 governs the asynchronous transmission of computer data at speeds of up to 920,000 bits per second.

RSI　See *repetitive strain injury (RSI).*

RTFM　In on-line communications, an acronym for *Read the "Fripping" Manual.*

rule　In computer graphics and desktop publishing, a thin, black horizontal or vertical line.

ruler　In many word processing and desktop publishing programs, an on-screen bar that measures the page horizontally, showing the current margins, tab stops, and paragraph indents. Windows and Macintosh programs often let you manipulate margins and indents and to set tabs by manipulating the corresponding on-screen symbols with the mouse.

run　To execute a program.

P
Q
R
S

Run-Length Limited (RLL)   A method of storing and retrieving information on a hard disk that, compared to double-density techniques, increases by at least 50 percent the amount of data a hard disk can store.

The improvement in storage density is achieved by translating the data into a new digital format that can be written more compactly to the disk. The translation is achieved, however, at the cost of adding complex electronics to the storage device. RLL drives therefore are more expensive than their MFM counterparts. See *Advanced Run-Length Limited (ARLL)* and *Modified Frequency Modulation (MFM)*.

running head   See *header*.

run-time version   A limited version of a supporting program that's bundled with a program that can't run without the run-time release.

Early versions of Excel were sold with run-time versions of Microsoft Windows for users who didn't yet own Windows. This version loads each time you use the program, but you can't use it to run other Windows applications. Similarly, programs created using Visual Basic require the file VBRUN300.DLL to run your programs. See *interpreter* and *windowing environment*.

r/w   A common abbreviation for *read/write*, indicating that the file or device has been configured so that you can write data to it as well as read data from it. See *read/write* and *read/write file*.

r

SAA   See *Systems Application Architecture (SAA)*.

safe format   A method for formatting a disk that doesn't destroy the data on the disk if you accidentally format the wrong disk. To format safely with DOS 5.0, use the FORMAT command *without* using the /u switch. Use the UNFORMAT command if you formatted the disk by mistake—as long as you haven't copied more files to the disk. Utility packages such as PC Tools and Norton Utilities also can perform safe formats.

sans serif   *san-sare-if*   A typeface that lacks serifs, the ornamental straight or curved lines across the ends of the main strokes of a character (see fig. S.1). Helvetica and Arial are two readily available sans serif fonts.

A B C D E

Fig. S.1   *Example of a sans serif font.*

Sans serif typefaces are preferred for display type but, when used for body type, are harder to read than serif typefaces, such as Times Roman. See *body type, display type, serif,* and *typeface*.

satellite   In a multiuser computer system, a terminal or workstation linked to a centralized host computer. See *host*.

save   To transfer data from the computer's random-access memory, where it's vulnerable to erasure, to a storage medium such as a disk drive.

By far the most common source of computer-caused grief is work loss resulting from power failures, user errors, or system crashes. Your work is kept in the computer's random-access memory (RAM), which may very well evaporate into nothingness should the power fail or the computer crash. Sooner or later, every user experiences the sense of dismay that comes with the realization that hours and hours of work have just been irretrievably lost.

Do everything you can to protect yourself against lost work. Save repeatedly while you work, every five minutes or so. If you're using a program that has an autosave feature, which saves your work automatically at an interval you specify, by all means activate it! When you quit a program, save all the open documents again. For full protection, perform regular backups, because hard disks fail, too. See *backup procedure, random-access memory (RAM),* and *volatility.*

sawtooth distortion   See *aliasing.*

scalable font   A screen or printer font you can enlarge or reduce to any size, within a specified range, without introducing unattractive distortions. Outline font technology is most commonly used to provide scalable fonts, but other technologies—including stroke fonts, in which a character is formed out of a matrix of lines—are sometimes used. The most popular scalable fonts for Macintosh and Windows systems are PostScript and TrueType fonts. See *bit-mapped font, outline font, PostScript font, printer font, screen font, System 7,* and *TrueType.*

TIP: *Looking for a Mac or Windows system? If you want scalable fonts, choose a Mac that's System 7 capable, or a Windows system with Windows 3.1. Both systems include TrueType capabilities; you will see scalable fonts on-screen and will get good results from a huge variety of printers without having to buy an expensive PostScript-compatible printer.*

scaling   In presentation graphics, the adjustment of the y-axis (values) chosen by the program so that differences in the data are more apparent. Most presentation graphics programs scale the y-axis, but the scaling choice may be unsatisfactory (see fig. S.2). Manually adjusting the scaling produces better results (see fig. S.3). See *presentation graphics* and *y-axis.*

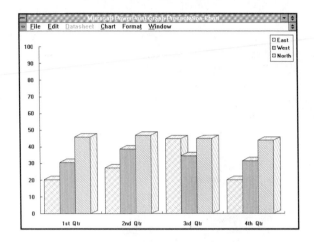

Fig. S.2 *A column graph with unsatisfactory scaling.*

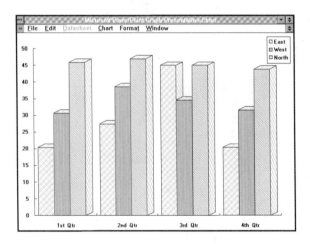

Fig. S.3 *A column graph with manually adjusted scaling.*

scanner   A peripheral device that digitizes artwork or photographs and stores the image as a file you can merge with text in many word processing and page layout programs.

Scanners use two techniques for transforming photographs into digitized images (see fig. S.4). The first technique, *dithering*, simulates a halftone by varying the space between the dots normally used to create a bit-mapped graphic image. Like all bit-mapped images, the digital halftone can't be sized without introducing crude distortions, and the quality may be too crude for professional applications.

A 150 dpi digital-halftone scan, printed on an Apple LaserWriter.

A 150 dpi gray-scale scan with 16 shades of gray, printed on an Apple LaserWriter.

Fig. S.4 *A digital-halftone image (top) and a gray-scale image (bottom).*

The second technique, Tagged Image File Format (TIFF), stores the image using a series of 16 gray values and produces better results, but this technique is still inferior to halftones produced by photographic methods. See *bit-mapped graphic, dithering, halftone,* and *Tagged Image File Format (TIFF)*.

scatter diagram   An analytical graphic in which data items are plotted as points on two numeric axes; also called a *scattergram*.

Scatter diagrams show clustering relationships in numeric data. Computer magazines often use a scatter diagram to compare similarly configured computer systems, with price on one axis and the result of performance testing on the other axis. If this diagram is plotted with the price axis and performance each scaled from low to high, inexpensive high-performance computers and expensive poor performers will clearly stand out from a cluster of average systems.

scatter plot   See *scatter diagram*.

scientific notation   A method for expressing very large or very small numbers as powers of 10, such as 7.24×10^{23}. In spreadsheet programs, scientific notation is usually expressed using the symbol E, which stands for exponent, as follows: 7.24E23.

scissoring   In computer graphics, an editing technique in which an image is cropped to a size determined by a frame that is placed over the image.

Scrapbook   On the Macintosh, a desk accessory that can hold frequently used graphic images, such as a company letterhead, which you can then insert into new documents as required.

screen capture   Saving a copy of a screen display as a text or graphics file on disk.

screen dump   See *Print Screen (PrtSc)*.

screen elements   In Microsoft Windows, the components of the display screen, such as dialog boxes, borders, buttons, check boxes, and scroll bars.

screen flicker   See *flicker*.

screen font   A bit-mapped font designed to mimic the appearance of printer fonts when displayed on medium-resolution monitors. Modern laser printers can print text with a resolution of 300 dpi or more, but video displays, except for the most expensive professional units, lack such high resolution and can't display typefaces with such precision. What you see usually isn't as good as what you get.

P
Q
R
S

In character-based programs running under DOS, no attempt
is made to suggest the printer font's typeface. However, the
more recent versions of DOS applications include a graphics, or
WYSIWYG (what-you-see-is-what-you-get), mode enabling the
display of screen fonts that rivals the display available in programs
with a graphical user interface.

In 1990, Adobe International released Adobe Type Manager (ATM)
for both Macintosh and Windows systems, offering scalable type
technology for screen as well as printer output, even in inexpensive
non-PostScript printers. In 1992, Apple and Microsoft incorporated
their jointly developed TrueType scalable font technology into
Apple's System 7 and Microsoft Windows 3.1, which also produces
excellent on-screen and printer fonts. See *bit-mapped font, laser
printer, outline font, printer font, resolution, TrueType*, and *typeface*.

screen saver   A utility program that prolongs the life of your
monitor by changing the screen display while you are away from
your computer.

Monitors degrade with use, particularly when an image is displayed continuously. Such images "burn" into the screen phosphors, resulting in a ghost image. Prolonged use also decreases
screen sharpness.

Screen-saver utilities blank the screen while you aren't using the
computer. You can set the utility so that the blanking occurs after
a specified amount of time, such as 5 or 10 minutes. To alert you
that the computer hasn't been turned off, screen-saver utilities
display a moving image (such as a clock, stars, or swimming fish)
on a background, although a black screen reduces power consumption by 10 to 15 percent.

Newer VGA monitor screens take much longer to succumb to the
effects of ghosting. However, using a screen saver is still recommended. All monitors should be powered off overnight to prevent
excess wear. See *ghost* and *utility program*.

TIP: *If you're running Microsoft Windows 3.1, don't bother buying a screen-saver utility. One is built into this version of Windows.*

script   A series of instructions that tells a program how to perform a specific procedure, such as logging on to an electronic mail system.

Script capabilities are built into some programs. You must learn how to write the script using what amounts to a mini-programming language. Some programs write the script automatically by recording your keystrokes and command choices as you perform the procedure.

Scripts are similar to macros, except that the term *macro* is reserved for scripts you initiate by pressing a key combination that you define. See *HyperTalk* and *macro*.

scripting   The process of creating a handler—a brief program that traps messages you initiate—for an object in an object-oriented programming language, such as HyperTalk. See *handler* and *inheritance*.

scroll   To move the window horizontally or vertically so that its position over a document or worksheet changes.

In some programs, scrolling is clearly distinguished from cursor movement; when you scroll, the cursor stays put. In other programs, however, scrolling the screen also moves the cursor.

scroll arrow   In a graphical user interface, an arrow (pointing up, down, left, or right) you can click to scroll the screen in the desired direction. The scroll arrows are located at the ends of scroll bars (see fig. S.5).

scroll bar/scroll box   A user interface feature that provides the capability of scrolling horizontally and vertically using rectangular scrolling areas on the right and bottom borders of the window. You scroll the document horizontally or vertically by clicking the scroll bars or scroll arrows or by dragging the scroll boxes (see fig. S.5).

P
Q
R
S

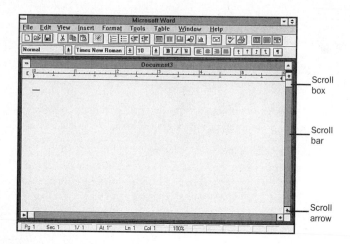

Fig. S.5 *Vertical scroll arrow, bar, and box.*

Scroll Lock key   On IBM PC-compatible keyboards, a toggle key that switches the cursor-movement keys between two different modes with most programs.

The exact function of this key varies from program to program. In some programs, for example, the cursor-movement keys normally move the cursor within the screen. After pressing Scroll Lock, however, the left- and right-arrow keys stop working, and the up- and down-arrow keys scroll the screen without moving the cursor. See *toggle key.*

TIP: *If the cursor-movement keys seem to move the document rather than the cursor, you may have pressed the Scroll Lock key accidentally. Toggle it off and try again.*

SCSI   See *Small Computer System Interface (SCSI).*

search and replace   See *replace.*

secondary storage   A non-volatile storage medium such as a disk drive that stores program instructions and data, even after you switch off the power. Synonymous with *auxiliary storage.* See *primary storage.*

secondary storage medium   The specific data storage technology used to store and retrieve data, such as a magnetic disk, magnetic tape, or optical disk.

second-person virtual reality   A virtual reality (VR) system that doesn't try to immerse the user in a computer-generated world through the use of goggles and gloves, but instead presents the user with a high-definition video screen and a cockpit with navigation controls, such as flight simulator programs.

sector   On a floppy disk or hard disk, a segment of one of the concentric tracks encoded on the disk during a low-level format. In IBM PC-compatible computing, a sector usually contains 512 bytes of information. See *cluster*.

sector interleave factor   See *interleave factor*.

security   The protection of data so that unauthorized persons can't examine or copy it.

As business and professional people have discovered, a reasonably competent hacker can get into almost any computer system, including those that have been protected through such measures as passwords and data encryption. Sensitive data—such as employee performance ratings, customer lists, budget proposals, and confidential memos—can be downloaded on floppy disks that can be carried right out of the office without anyone knowing.

Mainframe computer systems address this problem by keeping the computer and its mass storage media under lock and key; the only way you can use the data is through remote terminals, equipped with a screen but no disk drives. Some experts argue that personal computer local area networks should be set up the same way, forgetting that the excessive centralization of mainframe computer systems was one of the main reasons personal computers were developed.

Concern for security shouldn't prevent a manager from distributing computing power—and computing autonomy—to subordinates. Data encryption and password-protection schemes exist so that even a talented hacker can't penetrate them.

P
Q
R
S

seek   In a disk drive, to locate a specific region of a disk and to position the read/write head so that data or program instructions can be retrieved.

seek time   In a secondary storage device, the time it takes the read/write head to reach the correct location on the disk. See *access time*.

select   To highlight part of a document so that the program can identify the material on which you want the next operation to be performed. In addition to selecting text, you can highlight/select an item from a list box or select a check-box item to toggle it on or off.

selection   Part of a document, ranging from one character to many pages, highlighted for formatting or editing purposes. In programming, a branch or conditional control structure. In data-base management, the retrieval of records by using a query. See *branch control structure*.

semiconductor   A material such as silicon or germanium that lies between excellent electrical conductors, such as copper, and insulating materials in its electrical conductivity. Semiconductor wafers or chips of varying resistance can be assembled to create a variety of electronic devices. In personal computers, semiconduc-tor materials are used for microprocessors, internal storage, and other electronic circuits. See *integrated circuit*.

sensor glove   In virtual reality systems, an interface shaped like a glove that allows the user to manipulate and move virtual objects in a virtual reality environment. See *head-mounted display* and *virtual reality*.

sequence control structure   A control structure that tells the computer to execute program statements in the order in which the statements are written.

One of three fundamental control structures that govern the order in which program statements are executed, the sequence control structure is the default in all programming languages. You can use the branch and loop control structures to alter the sequence. See *control structure*.

sequential access   An information storage and retrieval technique in which the computer must move through a sequence of stored data items to reach the desired one. Sequential access media such as cassette tape recorders are much slower than random-access media. See *random access.*

serial   See *asynchronous communication, multitasking,* and *parallel port.*

serial mouse   A mouse designed to be connected directly to one of the computer's serial ports. See *bus mouse* and *mouse.*

serial port   A port that synchronizes and manages asynchronous communication between the computer and devices such as serial printers, modems, and other computers.

The serial port not only sends and receives asynchronous data in a one-bit-after-the-other stream, it also negotiates with the receiving device to make sure that data is sent and received without the loss of data. The negotiation occurs through hardware or software handshaking. See *asynchronous communication, modem, port, RS-232C,* and *Universal Asynchronous Receiver/Transmitter (UART).*

serial printer   A printer designed to be connected to the computer's serial port.

CAUTION: *If you're using a serial printer with an IBM PC-compatible system, you must give the correct MODE command to configure your system at the start of each operating session—preferably in the AUTOEXEC.BAT file (DOS users) or STARTUP.CMD file (OS/2 users), which the operating system consults when you start up your computer. See your printer's manual for more details.*

P
Q
R
S

serif   The fine, ornamental cross strokes across the ends of the main strokes of a character (see fig. S.6).

A B C D E⌐—Serifs

Fig. S.6 *Example of a serif font.*

Serif fonts are easier to read for body type, but most designers prefer to use sans serif typefaces for display type. See *sans serif.*

server See *file server* and *print server.*

server application In object linking and embedding (OLE), the program that creates the source document. Data from a source document is linked or embedded in one or more destination documents created by client applications. See *client application, destination document, object linking and embedding (OLE),* and *source document.*

server-based application A network version of a program stored on the network's file server and available to more than one user at a time. See *client-based application* and *file server.*

service bureau A business that provides a variety of publication services such as graphics file format conversion, optical scanning of graphics, and typesetting on high-resolution printers such as Linotronics and Varitypes.

set-associative A cache design used in the fastest RAM caches and in the internal caches included on the 486 and Pentium chips. This design divides the cache into two to eight sets, or areas. Data stored in the cache is distributed in bits to each set in sequence. In most instances, when data is later read from the cache, it's read sequentially from each set. This arrangement allows the set just read or written to prepare itself to be read or written again while data is being read from or written to the next set. Set-associative cache design lets the processor complete an instruction in one clock cycle. See *cache* and *internal cache.*

setup string A series of characters that a program conveys to the printer so that the printer operates in a specified mode. In Lotus 1-2-3, for example, the setup string \027\052 turns on an Epson FX printer's italic mode.

shadow RAM   In 80386 and 80486 computers, a portion of the upper memory area between 640K and 1M set aside for programs ordinarily retrieved from read-only memory (ROM). Because RAM is faster than ROM, shadow RAM increases performance. See *random-access memory (RAM), read-only memory (ROM)*, and *upper memory area*.

CAUTION: *Computer manufacturers like to equip their machines with shadow RAM to improve the machines' performance on speed measurement tests. However, using shadow RAM may cause problems with programs that try to use upper memory as extended memory. If you're running Microsoft Windows or any other application requires extended memory, consult your computer manual to determine how to disable shadow RAM.*

shareware   Copyrighted computer programs made available on a trial basis; if you like and decide to use the program, you are expected to pay a fee to the program's author. See *public domain software*.

sheet feeder   See *cut-sheet feeder*.

shell   A utility program designed to provide an improved (and often menu-driven) user interface for a program or operating system generally considered difficult to use. See *front end, user interface*, and *utility program*.

Shift+click   A mouse maneuver accomplished by holding down the Shift key when you click the mouse. Applications implement Shift+clicking differently, but in most, the action extends a selection.

Shift key   The key you press to enter uppercase letters or punctuation marks.

On early IBM keyboards, the Shift key is labeled only with a white arrow. Later keyboards label this key with the word *Shift*. See *Caps Lock key*.

shortcut key   A key combination that provides one-stroke access directly to a command or dialog box, bypassing any intermediate menus. See *hot key*.

side-by-side columns   See *table columns*.

SIG   See *special interest group (SIG)*.

signal   The portion of a transmission that coherently represents information, unlike the random and meaningless noise that occurs in the transmission channel.

signature   In electronic mail and computer newsgroups, a brief file (of approximately three or four lines) that contains the message sender's name, organization, address, e-mail address, and (optionally) telephone numbers. Most systems can be configured to add this file automatically at the end of each message you send.

In virus-protection utilities, a signature is program code identifiable as belonging to a known virus. See *ASCII art, electronic mail, netiquette, newsgroup*, and *virus*.

silicon chip   See *chip*.

Silicon Valley   An area in California's Santa Clara Valley with one of the largest concentrations of high-technology businesses in the world. The word *Silicon* suggests the area's prominence in silicon chip design and manufacturing.

SIMM   See *single in-line memory module (SIMM)*.

simple list text chart   In presentation graphics, a text chart used to display items in no particular order, with each item given equal emphasis (see fig. S.7). See *presentation graphics*.

simulation   In computer applications, an analytical technique in which an analyst investigates an item's properties by creating a model of the item and exploring the model's behavior.

S

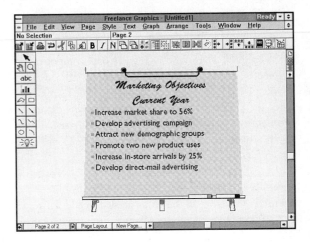

Fig. S.7 *A simple list text chart.*

One of the most important contributions of the computer lies in its new, useful tools for simulation. In aeronautical engineering, for example, the aerodynamic properties of a proposed aircraft could be simulated only through construction of a series of models, which were subjected to wind-tunnel tests. Now, computer simulation techniques are used to design and test thousands of alternative models quickly, pushing the wind tunnel toward obsolescence in modern aerospace firms.

In education, simulation techniques are enabling schools with limited funds to offer students a chance to engage in simulated, on-screen versions of classic laboratory experiments. Simulation is found in computer games, such as Microsoft Flight Simulator. Using simulation in spreadsheet programs, a manager can ask what-if questions such as, "What is the effect on market share if we spend 20 percent more on advertising?"

As with any model, however, a simulation is only as good as its underlying assumptions. If these assumptions aren't correct, the model doesn't accurately mimic the behavior of the real-world system being simulated.

P
Q
R
S

single density   A magnetic recording scheme for digital data that uses a technique called *frequency modulation (FM)*.

Single-density disks, common in early personal computing, use large-grained magnetic particles resulting in low storage capacity, such as 90K per disk, and are rarely used today. They have been superseded by double-density disks with finer grained partitions, and high-density disks with even finer partitions. See *double density, frequency modulation (FM) recording*, and *Modified Frequency Modulation (MFM)*.

single in-line memory module (SIMM)   A plug-in memory unit containing all the chips needed to add 256K, 1M, or 2M of random-access memory to your computer.

single in-line package (SIP)   A plastic package, designed to house and protect an electronic circuit, with a row of pins extending from one side of the package. See *dual in-line package (DIP)*.

single-sided disk   A floppy disk designed so that only one side of the disk can be used for read/write operations. See *single density*.

SIP   See *single in-line package (SIP)*.

site license   An agreement between a software publisher and a buyer that allows the buyer to make copies of specific software for internal use. Often a company using a local area network buys a site license for a program so that all the users on the LAN can access the program. Most site licenses stipulate a numeric limit on the number of copies the organization can make. The cost per copy is much less than buying individual copies.

sixteen-bit   See *16-bit computer*.

skip factor   In a graphics program, an increment that specifies how many data items the program should skip when it labels a chart or graph. Use a skip factor when the categories axis is too crowded with headings. Using months as an example, a skip factor of 3 displays the name of every third month.

slide show   In presentation graphics, a predetermined list of charts and graphs displayed one after the other.

Some programs can produce interesting effects, such as fading out one screen before displaying another. You can add buttons that allow the viewer to alter the sequence in which the slides are displayed, jump to a specific slide, or exit the slide show. See *presentation graphics.*

slot   See *expansion slot.*

slow mail   "Polite" term for the postal service. See *snail mail.*

slug   In word processing and desktop publishing, a code inserted in headers or footers that generates page numbers when the document is printed.

Small Computer System Interface (SCSI)   *scuh-zee*

An interface amounting to a complete expansion bus in which you can plug devices such as hard disk drives, CD-ROM drives, scanners, and laser printers.

The most common SCSI device in use is the SCSI hard disk, which contains most of the controller circuitry, leaving the SCSI interface free to communicate with other peripherals. Up to seven SCSI devices can be daisy chained to a single SCSI port. See *daisy chain, Enhanced System Device Interface (ESDI),* and *ST-506/ST-412.*

SmallTalk   A high-level programming language and programming environment that treats computations as objects that send messages to one another.

Developed by Alan Kay and others at Xerox Corporation's Palo Alto Research Center (PARC), SmallTalk is a declarative language that encourages the programmer to define objects in terms relevant to the intended application. The language is highly extensible because objects can be created quite easily.

Because the language requires a great deal of memory to produce efficient, fast-running programs, professional programmers continue to prefer languages such as assembly language and C. But SmallTalk inspired HyperTalk, the software command language of HyperCard,

P
Q
R
S

an application provided with every Macintosh sold since 1987. In this new guise, SmallTalk has fulfilled its goal of making computer programming more accessible; tens of thousands of Macintosh users have learned how to program in HyperTalk. See *declarative language*, *high-level programming language*, *HyperCard*, and *object-oriented programming language*.

smart machine   Any device containing microprocessor-based electronics that allows the device either to branch to alternative operating sequences depending on external conditions, to repeat operations until a condition is fulfilled, or to execute a series of instructions repetitively.

Microprocessors are so inexpensive that they can be embedded in even the most prosaic of everyday devices, such as toasters, coffee makers, and ovens. At the University of Virginia, an undergraduate engineering student created a microprocessor-controlled barbecue oven that slow-roasts a side of beef at the optimum temperature. A temperature sensor tells the microprocessor whether the beef is too hot or cool, and adjusts the electric heating element. An analysis program calculates the optimum cooking time. Taste testers agreed that the results were indeed impressive.

smart terminal   In a multiuser system, a terminal containing its own processing circuitry so that it not only retrieves data from the host computer, but also carries out additional processing operations and runs host-delivered programs.

smiley   In electronic mail and computer newsgroups, a sideways face made of standard ASCII characters that serves to put a message into context. Synonymous with *emoticon*.

A smiley is intended to substitute for the lack of non-verbal cues and verbal inflections that play so strong a role in effective interpersonal communication. You can send only what you can type, restricted by the letters, numbers, and punctuation marks on the computer keyboard. That can spell trouble, say communications researchers. A comment made as a joke can be misinterpreted, resulting in a flame (a reply that is filled with obscenities and personal attacks), which can set off a flame war (a series of invective-ridden exchanges).

To avoid finding yourself the object of a flame (or worse, a flame war), learn all you can about *netiquette*. In particular, experienced users say, use smileys. Some commonly used smileys are as follows:

:-)	I'm smiling while I make this joke.
:-D	I'm overjoyed about the last thing I typed.
:-*	Here's a kiss.
: 0	I'm yawning; this thing is *so* boring.
;-)	I'm winking or flirting about this joke.
:-7	I say this tongue-in-cheek.
:-(	I'm sad about the thing I just typed.
:-<	I'm *really* sad—frowning at this.
>:-(	I'm angry or annoyed about this.
:'-(	I'm crying—this is *really* sad to me.
:-9	I am licking my lips.
X-(	I'm dead; this has killed me.

See *ASCII art, electronic mail, flame, flame war,* and *netiquette*.

snaf   The messy strips of waste paper that litter the office after the perforated edge is removed from continuous, tractor-fed computer paper.

The term *snaf* was the winning entry in a contest sponsored by National Public Radio's *All Things Considered*. The runner-up, *perfory,* is worthy of mention.

snail mail   A derogatory term for the postal service. In an electronic mail message, one says, "I'm sending the article to you via snail mail."

snaking columns   See *newspaper columns*.

snap-on pointing device   In notebook computers, a pointing device that snaps onto the side of the computer's case via a special port. No serial or mouse port cable is required. Snap-on pointing devices are convenient because you don't have to connect the serial or mouse port cable every time you want to use the computer; you just snap the trackball into its receptacle. See *built-in pointing device, clip-on pointing device, mouse,* and *trackball.*

snapshot   See *Print Screen (PrtSc).*

SNOBOL   A high-level programming language designed for text-processing applications.

Developed at AT&T's Bell Laboratories in 1962, SNOBOL (StriNg-Oriented symBOlic Language) arose from the frustration of its creators with numerically oriented programming languages. They sought to create a programming language that could manipulate text, and they hoped to create a language that would interest people who were not mathematicians.

The language they created is especially strong in its text pattern-matching capabilities and has been used for research work in fields such as language translation, the generation of indexes or concordances to literary works, and text reformatting.

SNOBOL shares with BASIC and FORTRAN a lack of structure and heavy reliance on GOTO statements and, therefore, is little more than a curiosity. SNOBOL4 is available for IBM PC-compatible computers. See *BASIC* and *FORTRAN.*

soft   Temporary or changeable, as opposed to hard (permanently wired, physically fixed, or inflexible). Compare *software,* a *soft return,* and a page break inserted by a word processing program and subject to change if you add or delete text, to *hardware,* a *hard return,* and a page break you insert manually and which remains fixed in place despite further editing.

soft cell boundaries   In a spreadsheet program, a feature of cells that lets you enter labels longer than the cell's width (unless the adjacent cells are occupied).

soft font   See *downloadable font.*

soft hyphen   A hyphen formatted so that it doesn't take effect unless the word containing the hyphen would otherwise word wrap to the next line. In that event, the word is hyphenated to improve the spacing of the line. Synonymous with *optional hyphen*. See *hard hyphen*.

soft page break   In a word processing program, a page break inserted by the program, based on the current format of the text; the page break may move up or down if you make insertions, deletions, or change margins, page size, or fonts. See *forced page break*.

soft return   In a word processing program, a line break inserted by the program to maintain the margins. The location of soft returns changes automatically if you change the margins or insert or delete text. See *hard page* and *word wrap*.

soft-sectored disk   A disk that, when new, contains no fixed magnetic patterns of tracks or sectors. The positions of sectors is set up using software in a process called *formatting*. See *formatting*.

soft start   See *warm boot*.

software   System, utility, or application programs expressed in a computer-readable language. See *firmware*.

software cache   A large area of random-access memory (RAM) set aside by a program such as SMARTDRV.EXE to store frequently accessed data and program instructions. A 1M to 2M hardware cache can improve the speed of disk-intensive applications such as database management programs.

A hardware cache speeds up your computer in two ways. First, a copy of data retrieved from a disk is saved in the cache in case it's needed again. Second, when the system reads data from a disk, it does so one sector at a time. After the sector of data is delivered, the software cache reads the data in the next few disk sectors and saves it in the cache. When the CPU wants the data in the next sector, the cache delivers the data from the cache. Depending on the design of the caching software you use, the speed improvement ranges from great to extraordinary. See *cache controller, cache memory, central processing unit (CPU)*, and *random-access memory (RAM)*.

P
Q
R
S

CAUTION: *Using a cache to avoid the slowdowns caused by hard disk seeking has resulted in a plethora of caches. If you have a hardware cache, a cache on your hard drive, and an external cache, duplicate data and instructions can accumulate so as to actually bog your system down. In general, a single user obtains the maximum improvement with a disk cache. File servers benefit from a very large cache on the hard disk.*

software command language   A high-level programming language developed to work with a program, such as a spreadsheet or database management program.

Software command languages range from the macro capabilities of word processing and spreadsheet programs to full-fledged programming languages, such as the dBASE command language. Like stand-alone programming languages, most include control structures that perform iteration, logical branching, and conditional execution of operations.

The application program already handles all details for saving and retrieving information, the user interface, data structures, error handling, and so on; as a result, you can write a relatively simple program and yet produce an extremely powerful custom application. See *control structure*, *HyperTalk*, and *macro*.

software compatibility   The capability of a computer system to run a specific type of software. The Commodore 64, for example, isn't software-compatible with software written for the Apple II, even though both computers use the MOS Technology 6502 microprocessor.

software engineering   An applied science devoted to improving and optimizing the production of computer software.

software license   A legal agreement included with commercial programs. The software license specifies the rights and obligations of the individual who bought the program and limits the liability of the software publisher. See *site license*.

software package   A computer program delivered to the user in a complete and ready-to-run form, including all necessary utility programs and documentation. See *application software.*

software piracy   The unauthorized and illegal duplication of copyrighted software without the permission of the software publisher.

Software can be duplicated in a matter of seconds. To the consternation of software publishers, software piracy is extremely common and seems to be an endemic problem of personal computing.

As early as 1976, Bill Gates, a co-founder of Microsoft Corporation, complained that he couldn't remain in the business of selling a BASIC interpreter for the Altair computer if people kept on making illegal copies of his program. (Although this sounds like the pitiful whines of a notorious billionaire, the price we pay for our copies of software would probably be much lower if all copies were purchased.) Worse, people who seldom break other moral or legal rules engage in software piracy without hesitation. The computer revolution appears to have happened so quickly that cultural norms and moral values haven't had time to adjust accordingly. Attempts to stop software piracy through copy-protection schemes backfired on the companies that tried them when legitimate users avoided buying the copy-protected programs.

Those who defend software piracy, however, present arguments that seem to amount to little more than thinly veiled excuses for self interest. With today's pricing competition, the proliferation of discount houses, and the availability of inexpensive integrated packages such as Microsoft Works, affordable software is within the reach of any user. See *copy protection.*

P
Q
R
S

CAUTION: *Software piracy is illegal when it occurs at home, but prosecution is far from likely. This isn't the case at the workplace. Companies have been sued for damages attributable to unauthorized software duplication, and an industry consortium has established a toll-free hotline through which whistle-blowers (or disgruntled employees) can report this violation of federal law that carries a penalty of $100,000 per occurrence. A wise manager establishes a policy that absolutely no unauthorized copies of software are to be kept near, or used with, company computers.*

software program   An application program. Despite its redundancy, this term is used frequently, especially in advertisements, articles, books, and manuals written for a computer-illiterate audience. See *application software* and *software*.

software protection   See *copy protection*.

sort   An operation that rearranges data so that it's in alphabetical or numerical order.

Most programs can perform sorts. Full-featured word processing programs, such as WordPerfect, provide commands that sort lists, and electronic spreadsheets provide commands that sort the cells in a range.

In database management programs, sorts are distinguished from index operations. A sort physically rearranges data records, resulting in a new, permanently sorted file—consuming much disk space in the process. You can use the permanently re-sorted records later without repeating the sort operation, but you now have two copies of your database. If you forget to erase the first one, you can easily update the wrong file. However, an index operation creates an index to the records and sorts the index rather than the records. The index file consumes less disk space than a new copy of the whole database. See *data integrity* and *sort order*.

sort key   In sort operations, the data that determines the order in which data records are arranged.

A database sort key is the data field to sort by; in a spreadsheet, the sort key is the column or row used to arrange the data in alphabetical or numerical order. In a word processing program, the sort key is a word, but the word can be in any position. In WordPerfect, the position can be counted from left or right. To sort a mailing list by ZIP code, for example, the sort key is the first word from the right in the last line of the address. See *multilevel sort*.

sort order   The order in which a program arranges data when performing a sort, such as ascending order and descending order. Most programs also sort data in the standard order of ASCII characters. Synonymous with *collating sequence*. See *ASCII sort order*, *dictionary sort*, and *sort*.

sound board   An adapter that adds digital sound reproduction capabilities to an IBM-compatible personal computer.

A major drawback of IBM-format computing is that the tinny, 3-inch speaker can reproduce only a limited range of beeps, honks, and squawks. One advantage of the Macintosh LC II is that it comes equipped with a microphone and software that lets you record your own brief sounds and voice messages.

DOS and Microsoft Windows programs, with the exception of games, rarely include many sounds. Some, however, detect the presence of a sound board automatically and switch to a richer sound palette if one is found. See *adapter* and *multimedia*.

TIP: *Windows users should look for a sound board that's fully supported by Windows' multimedia extensions. These sound boards include Ad Lib Gold Card, Soundblaster, Soundblaster Pro, and Thunderboard.*

Sound Recorder   A Microsoft Windows 3.1 accessory you use to record and play back sounds (see fig. S.8). To operate Sound Recorder, your system must be equipped with an MPC-compatible sound board with recording capabilities, including a microphone. Sound Recorder serves as a control device, turning your computer into a digital tape recorder and placing the recording into a file with the extension .WAV, a file that other MPC-compatible programs can access. See *Multimedia Personal Computer (MPC)* and *sound board*.

Fig. S.8   *The Sound Recorder window in Microsoft Windows 3.1.*

source   The record, file, document, or disk from which information is taken or moved, as opposed to the destination. See *destination*.

source code   In a high-level programming language, the typed program instructions that people write, before the program has been compiled or interpreted into machine instructions that the computer can execute.

source document   In dynamic data exchange (DDE), the document containing data that has been linked to copies of that data in other documents, called *destination documents*. See *destination document* and *dynamic data exchange (DDE)*.

source file   In many DOS commands, the file from which data or program instructions are copied. See *destination file*.

source worksheet   In Microsoft Excel, a worksheet containing a cell or range that has been linked to one or more dependent worksheets. The changes you make to the source worksheet are reflected in the dependent worksheets. See *dependent worksheet*.

spaghetti code   A poorly organized program that results from excessive use of GOTO statements, making the program almost impossible to read and debug. The cure is to use a well-structured programming language, such as QuickBASIC, C, or Pascal, that offers a full set of control structures. See *C, Pascal, QuickBASIC*, and *structured programming*.

special interest group (SIG)   A subgroup of an organization or computer networking system, consisting of members who share a common interest. Common SIG topics include software, hobbies, sports, literary genres such as mystery or science fiction, and artifact collecting of every kind. See *user group*.

speech synthesis   Computer production of audio output that resembles human speech.

Unlike computer voice recognition, speech synthesis technology is quite well developed. Existing and inexpensive speech synthesis boards can do an impressive job of reading virtually any file containing English sentences in ASCII script—although, to some listeners, the English sounds as though it's being spoken with a Czech accent.

Speech synthesis is improving the lives of blind people by making written material more accessible to them; blind writers can proof and edit their own written work by having the computer read their work to them.

spell checker   A program, often a feature of word processing programs, that checks for the correct spelling of words in a document by comparing each word against a file of correctly spelled words.

A good spell checker displays suggestions for the correct spelling of a word and allows you to replace the misspelled word with the correct one. You usually can add words to the spell checker's dictionary.

> **TIP:** *Because of the way they work, spell checkers can't tell when you have committed a common error, such as using a correctly spelled word in the wrong place. Another common error is to separate* can *and* not *in* cannot. *Since both* can *and* not *are correctly spelled, spell checkers don't flag this error. There's no substitute for a final, human proofreading of an important document.*

spike   See *surge.*

split bar   In a graphical user interface such as Microsoft Windows or the Macintosh Finder, a bar you can drag to split the window horizontally or vertically.

split screen   A display technique in which the screen is divided into two or more windows. In word processing programs that have split-screen capabilities, independently displaying two parts of the same document is usually possible, as is displaying more than one document. Splitting the screen is useful when you want to refer to one document, or part of a document, while writing in another. It also facilitates cut-and-paste editing.

In figure S.9, for example, Document3 is displayed in two windows: Document3:1 and Document3:2. To split a window into two panes, you drag the split bar—a thick black line—down the vertical scroll bar. In this example, the Document2 window is split into two panes.

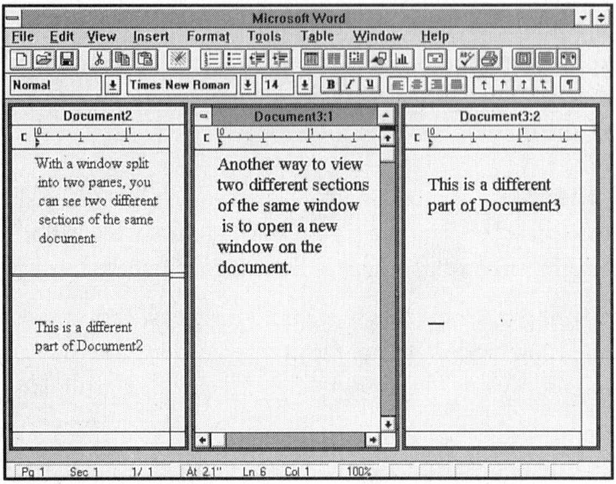

Fig. S.9 *Split screens.*

spoiler   In a computer newsgroup, a message that contains the ending of a novel, movie, or television program, or the solution to a computer or video game. Network etiquette requires that such messages be encrypted so that readers can't read them unless they choose to do so. In USENET newsgroups, the encryption technique is called *rot-13*. See *netiquette* and *rot-13*.

spooler   A program, often included with an operating system's utility programs, that routes printer commands to a file on disk or in RAM instead of to the printer, and then doles out the printer commands when the central processing unit (CPU) is idle.

A print spooler provides background printing; your program thinks it's printing to a super-fast printer, but the printer output actually is being directed to RAM or a disk file. You can continue working with your program, and the spooler guides the printer data to the printer during those moments when the CPU isn't busy handling your work. See *background printing*.

spreadsheet   See *worksheet*.

spreadsheet program   A program that simulates an accountant's worksheet on-screen and lets you embed hidden formulas that perform calculations on the visible data.

In 1978, Harvard Business School student Dan Bricklin got tired of adding up columns of numbers—and adding them up all over again after making a few changes, just to assess the effect of a merger. Bricklin and a programmer friend, Bob Frankston, came up with the idea of a spreadsheet program running on a personal computer. The result was VisiCalc, a program for the Apple II computer.

A spreadsheet is a matrix of rows (usually numbered) and columns (usually assigned alphabetical letters) that form individual cells. Each cell has a distinct cell address, such as B4 or D19. Into each cell, you can place a value, which is a number or a hidden formula that performs a calculation, or a label, which is a heading or explanatory text.

Formulas make a spreadsheet powerful. A formula can contain constants, such as 2+2, but the most useful formulas contain cell references, such as D9+D10. By placing formulas in a spreadsheet's cells, you can create a complex network of links among the parts of a spreadsheet. You don't see the formulas, which are hidden behind the cell, but you see the values they generate.

The point of creating a spreadsheet isn't just to find the answer to a problem. After you complete your spreadsheet, you can enter new values, and the spreadsheet is recalculated in seconds. This form of sensitivity testing—changing values to see how they affect the outcome—is called *what-if analysis* and is one of the main reasons spreadsheet programs have sold so well.

More than 700,000 copies of VisiCalc eventually were sold, providing a major reason for the success of the Apple II personal computer. But VisiCalc met stiff competition from Lotus 1-2-3 in the IBM PC environment and by 1984 had disappeared from the market. VisiCalc may be gone, but its influence lives on; many spreadsheet programs use VisiCalc's slash key (/) command to display the command menu.

Spreadsheets have become integrated programs that combine analytical graphics and database management. Recent trends include the three-dimensional spreadsheet capabilities and the use of high-quality fonts and graphics to enhance the printed result.

P
Q
R
S

As useful as spreadsheets are, remember that they are prone to error. And a spreadsheet is just a model of a business; any model includes only some of the significant determinants of a firm's behavior, and manipulating the model may lead to serious errors. People may be tempted to tweak assumptions so that they get the right answer.

> **CAUTION:** *Don't make business decisions (much less run a country) based on a spreadsheet without carefully thinking through what you are doing.*

SQL   *See Structured Query Language (SQL).*

ST-506/ST-412   A hard disk interface standard widely used in IBM and IBM-compatible computers.

These drives, virtually unavailable today, are slower and cheaper than drives using more recent interface standards, such as ESDI, IDE, and SCSI. MFM and RLL encoding methods are used with the ST-506/ST-412 interface. See *Enhanced System Device Interface (ESDI), Integrated Drive Electronics (IDE), interface standard, Modified Frequency Modulation (MFM), Run-Length Limited (RLL),* and *Small Computer System Interface (SCSI).*

stack   In programming, a data structure in which the first items inserted are the last ones removed. The LIFO (Last In First Out) data structure is used in programs that use control structures; a stack allows the computer to track what it was doing when it branched or jumped to a procedure. In HyperCard, the term *stack* refers to a file containing one or more cards that share a common background. See *control structure* and *HyperCard.*

stacked column chart   *See stacked column graph.*

stacked column graph   A column graph in which two or more data series are displayed on top of one another (see fig. S.10). See *histogram.*

staggered windows   *See cascading windows.*

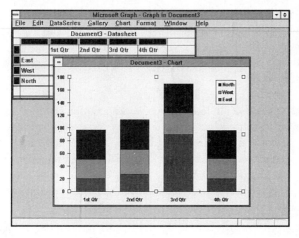

Fig. S.10 *A stacked column graph.*

stand-alone computer   A computer system dedicated to meeting all the computing needs of an individual. The user chooses just the software needed for his or her daily tasks. Links with other computers, if any, are incidental to the system's chief purpose. See *distributed processing system, multiuser system,* and *professional workstation.*

Standard mode   In Microsoft Windows, an operating mode that takes advantage of extended memory in 80286 and higher computers, running programs faster than 386 Enhanced mode. However, Standard mode doesn't provide expanded memory to programs that require it and can run DOS applications only in full-screen mode. Also, virtual memory isn't available. See *386 Enhanced mode, extended memory, Microsoft Windows, multitasking, real mode,* and *virtual memory.*

TIP: *If you have an 80386 or higher microprocessor and at least 2M of RAM, you can run Windows in 386 Enhanced mode, which makes true multitasking and virtual memory available.*

STACKS   In DOS, an area set aside to store information about the current task when an interrupt instruction is issued. After the interrupt is processed, DOS uses the information in the stack to resume the original task. If stacks are required by an application you are running, include a STACKS command in the CONFIG.SYS file to specify the size and number of stacks you want set aside.

star network   In local area networks, a centralized network topology with the physical layout of a star. At the center is a central network processor or wiring concentrator; the nodes are arranged around and connected directly to the central point. Wiring costs are considerably higher because each workstation requires a cable that links the workstation directly to the central processor (see fig. S.11).

start bit   In serial communications, a bit inserted into the data stream to inform the receiving computer that a byte of data is to follow. See *asynchronous communication* and *stop bit.*

startup disk   The disk you normally use to boot your computer. The disk contains portions of the operating system. Synonymous with *boot disk* and *system disk.* See *hard disk.*

startup screen   A text or graphics display at the beginning of a program. Usually, the startup screen includes the program name and version and often contains a distinctive program logo.

statement   In a high-level programming language, an expression that can generate machine language instructions when the program is interpreted or compiled. See *high-level programming language* and *instruction.*

state-of-the-art   A technically sophisticated item that represents the current level of technical achievement.

static object   A document or portion of a document pasted into a destination document using standard copy-and-paste techniques. The object doesn't change if you make changes to the source information. To update the information in the object, you make changes to the source document and copy from the source document again. See *embedded object, linked object,* and *object linking and embedding (OLE).*

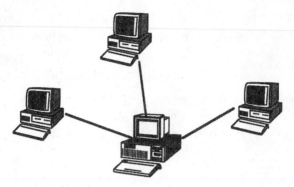

Fig. S.11 *An illustration of a star network.*

static random-access memory (SRAM)   A random-access memory (RAM) chip that holds its contents without constant refreshing from the central processing unit (CPU).

Although as volatile as DRAM chips, SRAM doesn't require the CPU to refresh its contents several hundred times per second. These chips are substantially faster but also are significantly more expensive than DRAM chips and are therefore most often used for RAM caches. See *cache memory, dynamic random-access memory (DRAM), random-access memory (RAM),* and *volatility.*

station   See *workstation.*

statistical software   An application program that makes conducting statistical tests and measurements easier.

status line   A line, usually at the bottom, of an application program's display screen that describes the state of the program. Often included in status lines are the name of the file you are now modifying, the cursor location, and the name of any toggle keys you have pressed, such as Num Lock or Caps Lock.

stem   In typography, the main vertical stroke of a character.

stereoscopy   *ster-ee-`ahs-kah-pee*   A technology that presents two pictures taken from slightly different perspectives that, when viewed together using a stereoscope, creates a profound illusion of three-dimensional space. Stereoscopic viewers were popular in the last

P
Q
R
S

century, and the technology lives on today as one of the foundations of virtual reality. See *head-mounted display (HMD)* and *virtual reality*.

stickup initial See *initial*.

stop bit In serial communications, a bit inserted into the data stream to inform the receiving computer that the transmission of a byte of data is complete. See *asynchronous communication* and *start bit*.

storage The retention of program instructions and data within the computer so that this information is available for processing purposes. See *primary storage* and *secondary storage*.

storage device Any optical or magnetic device capable of information storage functions in a computer system. See *secondary storage*.

stored program concept The idea, which underlies the architecture of all modern computers, that the program should be stored in memory with the data.

An insight of the late physician and scientist John von Neumann as he worked with the hard-wired programs of the ENIAC (North America's first digital electronic computer), this concept suggests a program can jump back and forth through instructions rather than execute them sequentially. With this insight, virtually the entire world of modern computing was launched. See *von Neumann bottleneck*.

streaming tape drive A data storage device that uses continuous tape, contained in a cartridge, for backup purposes.

strikeout A font attribute where text is struck through with a hyphen; for example, ~~this text has strikeout formatting~~. Also called *strikethrough*.

Strikeout often is used to mark text to be deleted from a co-authored document so that the other author can see changes easily. See *overstrike*, *overtype mode*, and *redlining*.

string A series of alphanumeric characters.

string formula   In a spreadsheet program, a formula that performs a string operation such as changing a label to upper- or lowercase.

string operation   A computation performed on alphanumeric characters.

Computers can't understand the meaning of words, and therefore they can't process them like people do; however, computers can perform simple processing operations on textual data, such as comparing two strings to see whether they're the same, calculating the number of characters in a string, and arranging strings in ASCII order.

structured programming   A set of quality standards that make programs more verbose but more readable, more reliable, and more easily maintained.

The essence of structured programming is to avoid spaghetti code caused by overreliance on GOTO statements, a problem found in BASIC and FORTRAN. Structured programming insists that the overall program structure reflect what the program is supposed to do, beginning with the first task and proceeding logically. Indentations help make the logic clear, and the programmer is encouraged to use loop and branch control structures and named procedures instead of GOTO statements. Languages such as C, Pascal, Modula-2, and the dBASE software command language are inherently structured and encourage the programmer to adopt these good habits. See *C, Modula-2, Pascal,* and *spaghetti code.*

Structured Query Language (SQL)   In database management systems, an IBM-developed query language widely used in mainframe and minicomputer systems.

SQL is being implemented in client/server networks as a way to enable personal computers to access the resources of corporate databases. It's data-independent; the user doesn't have to worry about the particulars of how data is accessed physically. In theory, SQL also is device-independent; the same query language can be used to access databases on mainframes, minicomputers, and personal computers. Now, however, several versions of SQL are competing.

P
Q
R
S

SQL is an elegant and concise query language with only 30 commands. The four basic commands (SELECT, UPDATE, DELETE, and INSERT) correspond to the four basic functions of data manipulation (retrieval, modification, deletion, and insertion, respectively). SQL queries approximate the structure of an English natural-language query. The results of a query are displayed in a data table consisting of columns (corresponding to data fields) and rows (corresponding to data records). See *data deletion, data insertion, data manipulation, data modification, data retrieval, natural language,* and *table-oriented database management program.*

style In word processing, a saved definition consisting of formatting commands that you regularly apply to specific kinds of text, such as main headings. Styles can include alignment, font, line spacing and any other text-formatting features. After a style is created and saved, you can quickly apply it to the text by using one or two keystrokes. See *style sheet.*

style sheet In some word processing and page layout programs, a collection of styles frequently used in a specific type of document, such as newsletters, that are saved together. Synonymous with *style library.*

In the old days, professional typists filled out a style sheet listing an author's preferences for all formats (such as titles, footnotes, body text paragraphs, and the like). In word processing software, however, the term describes an on-disk collection of formatting definitions you create. For example, you can have a style sheet entry for normal body text paragraphs that includes the following formats: Palatino, 10-point type size, left justification, single line spacing, and 1/2-inch first line indentation.

When you create a document, you can use a style sheet containing the styles you want available. You can have separate style sheets for annual reports, memos, letters, or any other routine documents.

> **TIP:** *Style sheets can greatly speed reformatting of a document. Suppose that you decide to change to New Century Schoolbook instead of Palatino for the body type. If you don't use styles, you must manually change the font everywhere you originally applied it, carefully skipping over headings and other formats. If you have defined a body paragraph style in an attached style sheet, you make just one change to the style sheet, and the program automatically changes all the text linked to this style.*

stylus   A pen-shaped instrument used to select menu options on a monitor screen or to draw line art on a graphics tablet.

subdirectory   In DOS and UNIX, a directory structure created in another directory. A subdirectory can contain files and additional subdirectories.

When a hard disk is formatted, a fixed-size root directory area is created that's only large enough to contain the information for 512 files. To add more files to the hard drive, you create subdirectories where you can copy the files. Unlike the root directory, subdirectories are a type of file. Like other files, a subdirectory file can be of any size, so there's no limit to the number of files and other subdirectories you can store in a subdirectory structure.

By using subdirectories, you can create a tree-like, hierarchical structure of nested directories so you can group programs and files, and organize your data to suit your needs (see fig. S.12). Directories are linked in a tree structure. The main directory is like the root and trunk, and the subdirectories are like branches.

The main directory created by DOS is therefore called the *root directory*. The entire directory structure of the disk grows from this directory. You can create subdirectories within subdirectories, up to a maximum of nine levels. In this way, you can organize a huge hard disk to make backing up your work and other housekeeping tasks easier. See *root directory*.

P
Q
R
S

submenu A subordinate menu that may appear when you choose a command from a pull-down menu. The submenu lists further choices (see fig. S.13).

Not all menu commands display submenus. Some carry out an action directly; others display dialog boxes.

TIP: *In many programs, you can tell which commands display submenus by the right-pointing triangle (▶) at the right edge of the menu. Command names followed by an ellipsis (...) display dialog boxes.*

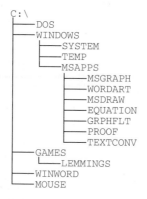

```
C:\
 ├──DOS
 ├──WINDOWS
 │    ├──SYSTEM
 │    ├──TEMP
 │    └──MSAPPS
 │          ├──MSGRAPH
 │          ├──WORDART
 │          ├──MSDRAW
 │          ├──EQUATION
 │          ├──GRPHFLT
 │          ├──PROOF
 │          └──TEXTCONV
 ├──GAMES
 │    └──LEMMINGS
 ├──WINWORD
 └──MOUSE
```

Fig. S.12 *An example of a hierarchical subdirectory structure.*

subroutine A portion of a program that performs a specific function and is set aside so that it can be used by more than one section of the program. A subroutine performs tasks needed frequently, such as writing a file to disk. In BASIC programs, subroutines are referenced by GOSUB statements.

subscript In text processing, a number or letter printed slightly below the typing line, as in this example: n_1. See *superscript*.

suitcase In the Macintosh environment, an icon containing a screen font or desk accessory not yet installed in the System Folder.

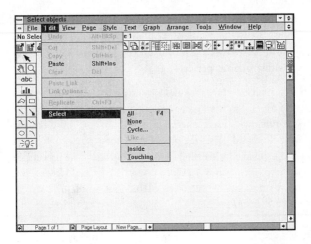

Fig. S.13   *The submenu that appears after choosing the menu option Select.*

supercomputer   A sophisticated, expensive computer designed to execute complex calculations at the maximum speed permitted by state-of-the-art technology. Supercomputers are used for scientific research, especially for modeling complex, dynamic systems, such as the world's weather, the U.S. economy, or the motions of a galaxy's spiral arms. The Cray-1 is an example of a supercomputer.

SuperDrive   An innovative 3 1/2-inch floppy disk drive now standard on Apple Macintosh computers. SuperDrives can read all Macintosh formats (400K, 800K, and 1.4M). With the aid of Apple's Apple File Exchange software, included with all Macintosh system software, the drive also can read and write to 720K and 1.44M DOS disks. It also can format disks in the DOS format.

P
Q
R
S

TIP: *Thanks to SuperDrive, you can move data files easily between IBM PC and Macintosh systems. To achieve a higher level of data compatibility, choose the same applications for both systems. Suppose that you run the Macintosh version of Microsoft Word on your Mac and the Windows version on your PC. The Mac version of Word can read and write to the Windows format without losing any formatting.*

superscalar architecture   A design that lets the microprocessor take a sequential instruction and send several instructions at
a time to separate execution units so the processor can execute
multiple instructions per cycle.

Superscalar architecture includes a built-in scheduler, which looks
ahead in the instruction queue, identifies a group of instructions that
won't conflict with each other or require simultaneous use of a particular service, and passes the group along for execution. The two
pipelines available in the Intel Pentium chip allow the processor to
execute two instructions per clock cycle. The PowerPC, with three
execution units, can handle three instructions simultaneously. See
architecture, Intel Pentium, microprocessor, pipeline, and *PowerPC.*

superscript   A number or letter printed slightly above the
typing line, as in this example: a^2. See *subscript.*

Super VGA   An enhancement of the Video Graphics Array
(VGA) display standard that can display at least 800 pixels horizontally and 600 lines vertically, and up to 1,280 pixels by
1,024768 lines with 16 colors, 256 colors, or 16.7 million colors
simultaneously displayed. The amount of video memory required
for the display of colors is nominal for 16 colors, but as much as
3.9M of video memory is required for 16.7 million colors.

TIP: *Do you really need 1,024 by 768 or higher resolution? With
most Windows application programs, the higher resolution doesn't
show you a sharper version of the same image; instead, you see
more of the image—as much as 50 percent more than an 800-by-
600 resolution display. However, the items on the screen will be
smaller. The higher resolution is most useful for spreadsheet users
who want to see more of their worksheet, writers who want to see
several paragraphs of text at a time, and desktop publishers who
want to lay out an entire page.*

support   Offering assistance with or capable of using or of
working with a device, file format, or program, as in "WordPerfect
supports all the latest PostScript printers and EPS files." See *technical support.*

surge   A momentary and sometimes destructive increase in the amount of voltage delivered through a power line. A surge is caused by a brief and often very large increase in line voltage caused by turning off appliances, by lightning strikes, or by the re-establishment of power after a power outage. See *power line filter* and *surge protector*.

surge protector   An inexpensive electrical device that prevents high-voltage surges from reaching a computer and damaging its circuitry. See *power line filter*.

SVID   See *System V Interface Definition (SVID)*.

swap file   A large, hidden system file created by Microsoft Windows that's used to store program instructions and data that won't fit in the computer's random-access memory (RAM). See *permanent swap file*, *temporary swap file*, and *virtual memory*.

swash   A character that sweeps over or under adjacent characters with a curvilinear flourish.

switch   An addition to a DOS command that modifies the way the command performs its function. The switch symbol is a forward slash (/), which is followed by a letter. For example, the command DIR /p displays a directory listing one page at a time.

symbolic coding   Expressing an algorithm in coded form by using symbols and numbers that people can understand (rather than the binary numbers that computers use). All modern programming languages use symbolic coding.

synchronous communication   Sending data at very high speeds using circuits in which data transfer is synchronized by electronic clock signals. Synchronous communication is used within the computer and in high-speed mainframe computer networks. See *asynchronous communication*.

syntax   The rules that govern the structure of commands, statements, or instructions that are given to the computer.

P
Q
R
S

syntax error   An error resulting from stating a command in a way that violates a program's syntax rules.

SYSOP   *sis-op*   Acronym for *SYStem OPerator*. A person who runs a bulletin board.

system   See *computer system*.

System   The operating system for Apple Macintosh computers, contained in the Macintosh's read-only memory and the System File in the System Folder.

System 7   A 1991 version of the Macintosh operating system software.

Among System 7's benefits are long-overdue improvements to Finder (the program and file-management system), true multitasking (instead of multiple program loading), program launching from menus, true virtual memory (with 68030 micro-processors), peer-to-peer file sharing on networked Macs without the need of a file server, external database access, and hot links across applications that instantaneously update copied data.

System 7 requires a minimum of 2M of RAM, but most users find that 4M is required to get the full benefit of System 7's advanced features. See *file server*, *Finder*, *hot link*, *multiple program loading*, *outline font*, *peer-to-peer network*, and *virtual memory*.

> **TIP:** *Not all existing Mac applications are compatible with System 7. Apple dealers can run a diagnostic program that informs you whether any of your programs are incompatible with System 7.*

system date   The calendar date maintained by the computer system.

Not all personal computers maintain the system date after you switch off the computer. To do so, the system must be equipped with a battery or a clock/calendar board. Otherwise, you can use the DATE command to set the system date manually.

Be sure to keep the system date set correctly. When you create and save files, the operating system records the date and time you saved the file. This information can be important when you are trying to determine which version of a file is the most recent.

system disk A disk containing the operating system files necessary to start the computer. Hard disk users normally configure the hard disk to serve as the system disk.

system file A program or data file that contains information that the operating system needs—distinguished from program or data files that the application programs use.

System Folder A folder in the Macintosh desktop environment that contains the System and Finder files, the two components of the Mac's operating system.

In addition to the System and Finder files, the System Folder also contains all the desk accessories, INITs, CDEVs, screen fonts, downloadable printer fonts, and printer drivers available during an operating session.

Because the System Folder is the only folder that the Finder consults when searching for a file, many applications require you to place configuration files, dictionaries, and other necessary files in this folder so that the Finder can access them. See *blessed folder, control panel device (CDEV), desk accessory (DA), downloadable font, Finder, INIT, printer driver,* and *screen font.*

P
Q
R
S

system prompt In a command-line operating system, the text that indicates the operating system is available for tasks such as copying files, formatting disks, and loading programs. In DOS, the system prompt (a letter designating the disk drive, followed by a greater than symbol) shows the current drive. When you see the prompt C>, for example, drive C is the current drive, and DOS is ready to accept instructions. You can customize the system prompt by using the PROMPT command. See *command-line operating system.*

system resources In Microsoft Windows, a special memory area that's set aside to store information about open windows and objects created by Windows programs. See *free system resources.*

systems analyst   A person who creates specifications, calculates feasibility and costs, and implements a business system.

Systems Application Architecture (SAA)   A set of standards for communication among various types of IBM computers,
from personal computers to mainframes.

Announced in 1987, SAA was IBM's response to criticisms that
its products didn't work well together, and to the competitive
pressure exerted by Digital Electronic Corporation (DEC), which
claimed that its products were optimized for easy interconnection.

Although it's little more than an evolving set of standards for
future development, SAA calls for a consistent user interface and
consistent system terminology across all environments. SAA
influenced the design of Presentation Manager, the windowing
environment jointly developed by Microsoft and IBM for the
OS/2 operating system. See *Operating System/2 (OS/2)*, and
windowing environment.

system software   All the software used to operate and maintain a computer system, including the operating system and utility
program—distinguished from application programs.

system time   The time of day maintained by the computer
system and updated while the system is in operation.

Only computers equipped with a clock/calendar board can keep the
system time when the computer is turned off. If you're using an IBM
PC-compatible computer that lacks this battery-powered system date
circuitry, you can use the TIME command to set the system time
manually.

TIP: *Be sure to set the system time. When you create and save
files, the operating system records the date and time you save
each file. This information can be important when you are
trying to determine which version of a file is the most recent.*

system unit   The case that houses the computer's internal processing circuitry, including the power supply, motherboard, disk drives, plug-in boards, and a speaker. Some personal computer system units also contain a monitor.

The case often is called the *central processing unit* (CPU), but this usage is inaccurate. Properly, the CPU consists of the computer's microprocessor and memory (usually housed on the motherboard) but not peripherals, such as disk drives.

System V Interface Definition (SVID)   A standard for UNIX operating systems, established by AT&T Bell Laboratories and demanded by corporate buyers, based on UNIX Version 5. See *Berkeley UNIX* and *UNIX*.

tab-delimited file   A data file, usually in ASCII file format, in which the data items are separated by tab keystrokes. See *ASCII file* and *comma-delimited file*.

Tab key   A key used to move a fixed number of spaces or to the next tab stop in a document. The Tab key often is used to guide the cursor in on-screen command menus. See *tab stop*.

> **TIP:** *In a word processing program, don't use the space bar to indent the first line of a paragraph. Instead, press Tab or activate the first-line indent command found in most word processing programs. If you change your mind about the amount of the indentation, you can change all the first-line indentations in one keystroke by resetting the amount of the first-line indent or changing the tab settings. If you enter the indentations by pressing the space bar, you must change them all manually.*

table   In a relational database management program, the fundamental structure of data storage and display in which data items are linked by the relations formed by placing them in rows and columns. The rows correspond to the data records of record-oriented database management programs, and the columns correspond to data fields.

In a word processing program, a spreadsheet of columns and rows with mathematical capabilities, usually created using a Table command. In some word processing programs, the data document created when using the mail merge feature organizes the merge data in a table. See *mail merge*, *table-oriented database management program*, and *table utility*.

table of authorities   A table of legal citations generated by a word processing program from references that have been marked in the document.

table columns   Unequally sized blocks of text positioned side by side on a page so that the first block is always positioned next to the second one. Synonymous with *parallel columns with block protect.*

Side-by-side columns, often called *parallel columns,* are used for paragraphs meant to be positioned near one another. Newspaper column formats can't handle this formatting task, because no relationship exists between the paragraphs in one column and the paragraphs in another.

An easy way to create side-by-side paragraphs is to use the table utilities included in some word processing programs (see fig. T.1). See *newspaper columns* and *table utility.*

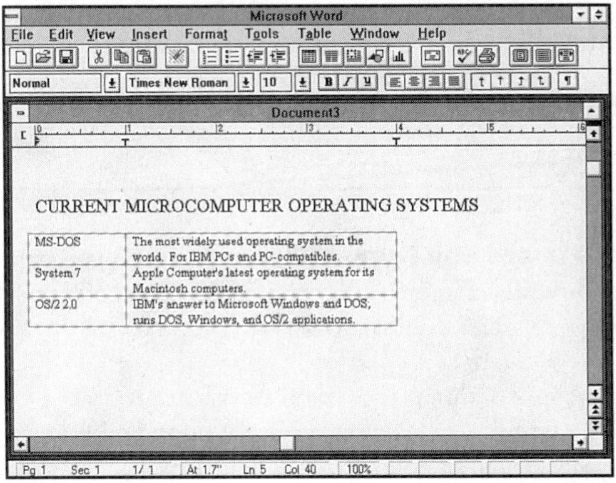

Fig. T.1   *Side-by-side columns created using a table utility.*

table-oriented database management program   A database management program that displays data tables (rather than records) as the result of query operations. See *data retrieval, record-oriented database management program,* and *Structured Query Language (SQL).*

table utility   In a word processing program, a utility that makes the typing of tables easier by creating a spreadsheet-like matrix of rows and columns, into which you can insert text without forcing word wrapping.

When you create a table with tabular columns, you must type the table line by line. If you later want to add a few words to one of the items, the words may not fit, and the rest of the line wraps down to the next line, ruining the column alignment. Table utilities solve this problem by making the *cell*, not the line, the unit of word wrapping (refer to fig. T.1).

tab stop   The place where the cursor stops after you press the Tab key. Most word processing programs set default tab stops every 1/2 inch, but you can set tabs individually anywhere you want, or you can redefine the default tab width. Also, most programs allow you to set flush-right, centered, and decimal tab stops in addition to the default flush-left tab stops, as shown in the following examples:

Flush Right	Centered	Decimal
aligns at right	aligns at center	$2,110.56
		.50986
		54

Tagged Image File Format (TIFF)   A bit-mapped graphics format for scanned images with resolutions of up to 300 dpi. TIFF simulates gray-scale shading. See *bit-mapped graphic*.

tape   A strip of thin plastic, coated with a magnetically sensitive recording medium. In mainframe computing and minicomputing, tape is widely used as a backup medium. Thanks to a dramatic price drop in cartridge tape backup units, tape has become increasingly common in personal computing for backing up entire hard drives. See *backup, backup procedure, backup utility, quarter-inch cartridge (QIC), random access, sequential access*, and *tape drive*.

tape drive   A data storage medium that uses magnetic tape and is commonly used for backup purposes.

In personal computing, by far the most popular drives for backup purposes are quarter-inch cartridge (QIC) drives, which fit in a standard, half-height drive bay. With prices below $180, these drives are fast becoming standard backup equipment for business and professional computing. Also available are the more expensive

8mm VCR cartridge drives, which use VCR tapes, and 4mm digital audio tape (DAT) drives. Widely used in mainframe and minicomputing applications are half-inch tape drives, which use large nine-track tape wheels and cartridges.

TCP/IP   See *Transfer Control Protocol/Internet Protocol (TCP/IP)*.

technical support   Providing technical advice and problem-solving expertise to registered users of a hardware device or program.

technocentrism   An overidentification with computer technology, often associated with a preference for factual thinking, denial of emotions, a lack of empathy for other people, and a low tolerance for human ambiguity. First noted by the psychotherapist Craig Brod, technocentrism stems from the stress individuals encounter as they try to adapt to a computer-driven society.

telecommunications   The transmission of information, whether expressed by voice or computer signals, via the telephone system. See *asynchronous communication* and *modem*.

telecommuting   Performing your work at home while linked to the office by means of a telecommunications-equipped computer system.

The arguments for telecommuting are compelling: It reduces pollution and job stress, reinforces family bonds, saves time, and offers a pleasant work environment. Nevertheless, firms have been slow to adopt telecommuting. Managers distrust the idea, naturally, because telecommuting employees can't be directly supervised; many prefer to use telecommuting for contract-based work rather than risk employees taking time off at the company's expense. Employees, too, have been slow to adopt telecommuting; many workers find that they miss the office, which—despite the harsh realities of a boss, busybody co-workers, and irritable customers—offers social contact. However, as urban transport becomes increasingly difficult and expensive due to crumbling roads, traffic jams, and pollution controls, more and more people probably will work one or more days per week at home. See *remote control program*.

T
U
V

teledildonics   A potential future application of virtual reality and telecommunications technology that could permit two individuals to experience sex with each other, even though they're separated by vast distances.

The technology needed for teledildonics doesn't yet exist, although high-tech labs are working on it. Teledildonics would require communication channels with unbelievable bandwidth. Today's telephone lines can handle up to 14,400 bits of information per second, but teledildonics would require about 3 billion. Still, virtual reality experts believe it's possible. See *bandwidth*, *cybersex*, and *virtual reality*.

telemedicine   The provision of high-quality, up-to-date medical information to community and rural medical practitioners.

In rural areas and community health centers, doctors who are out of touch with the latest knowledge may make faulty diagnoses or prescribe an out-of-date therapy. A telemedicine system that can provide these practitioners with high-quality information could indeed save lives—perhaps thousands of lives. Physicians are already transmitting X-rays and other information to specialists for consultation.

Telenet   A commercial wide-area network with thousands of local dialup numbers. Telenet provides log-on services to various commercial on-line computer services, such as Dialog Information Services and CompuServe.

telepresence   A psychological sensation of being immersed in a virtual reality that's persuasive and convincing enough to pass for the real world.

Riders of the Disneyland attraction Star Tours may have already experienced telepresence. In Star Tours, you board a "ship"—actually, a vehicle that travels on a track at low speeds, simulating turns, spins, acceleration, and braking—and view a high-resolution movie of interstellar travel, which is precisely coordinated with the vehicle's movements. The resulting telepresence convinces you that you're moving at fantastic speeds. See *virtual reality*.

t

teletype (TTY) display   A method of displaying characters on a monitor in which characters are generated and sent, one by one, to the video display; as the characters are received, the screen fills, line by line. When full, the screen scrolls up to accommodate the new lines of characters appearing at the bottom of the screen.

Teletype display mode should be familiar to DOS users. DOS uses a teletype display for accepting commands and displaying messages. See *character-mapped display*.

telnet   In UNIX-based machines linked to the Internet, a program that allows the user to access distant computers via TCP/IP connections. See *Internet, Transfer Control Protocol/Internet Protocol (TCP/IP)*, and *UNIX*.

template   In a program, a document or worksheet that includes the text or formulas needed to create standardized documents. The template can be used to automate the creation of these documents in the future.

In word processing, templates frequently are used for letterheads; the template version of the file contains the corporate logo, the company's address, and all the formats necessary to write the letter, but no text. You use the template by running the template, adding the text, and printing. In spreadsheet programs, templates are available for repetitive tasks such as calculating and printing a mortgage amortization schedule.

temporary swap file   In Microsoft Windows, a disk file that's created only while Windows is running and used for the storage and retrieval of program instructions or data in the program's 386 Enhanced mode. This storage space is used for virtual memory, which uses disk space as a seamless extension of random-access memory (RAM).

T
U
V

A temporary swap file consumes less disk space than a permanent swap file, but storage and retrieval operations are slower. See *defragmentation, Microsoft Windows, permanent swap file, random-access memory (RAM), swap file*, and *virtual memory*.

➡ **TIP:** *You can improve Windows' performance considerably by creating a permanent swap file. The amount of disk space Windows can assign to this task, however, is limited to the largest area containing contiguous empty sectors. To make the maximum amount of virtual memory available, run a disk defragmentation program before setting up the permanent swap file.*

tera-   Prefix indicating one trillion (10^{12}).

terabyte   A unit of memory measurement equal to approximately 1 trillion bytes (actually, 1,099,511,627,776 bytes). One terabyte is equal to 1,000 gigabytes, or 1 million megabytes. See *byte, gigabyte, kilobyte (K)*, and *megabyte (M)*.

terminal   An input/output device, consisting of a keyboard and video display, commonly used with multiuser systems.

A terminal lacking its own central processing unit (CPU) and disk drives is called a *dumb terminal* and is restricted to interacting with a distant multiuser computer. A smart terminal, on the other hand, has some processing circuitry and, in some cases, a disk drive so that you can download information and display it later.

As a personal computer user, however, you may have many valid reasons for wanting to take advantage of centralized computer resources. To do so, you need to transform your computer into a terminal, which is the function of communications software. See *terminal emulation.*

terminal emulation   The use of a communications program to transform a personal computer into a terminal for the purpose of data communications.

terminate-and-stay-resident (TSR) program   An accessory or utility program designed to remain in random-access memory (RAM) at all times so that you can activate it with a keystroke, even if another program also is in memory.

t

CAUTION: *If you're using DOS, use TSR programs with caution because they may cause conflicts that result in system lockups. When running Microsoft Windows, you usually don't have to run TSRs.*

Texas Instruments Graphics Architecture (TIGA)

tee-gah A high-resolution graphics standard for IBM-compatible personal computers. TIGA boards and monitors display 1,024 pixels horizontally by 786 lines vertically with 256 simultaneous colors. See *Super VGA*.

text Data composed only of standard ASCII characters, without any special formatting codes.

text chart In presentation graphics, a slide, transparency, or handout that contains text, such as a bulleted list. See *bulleted list chart, column text chart, free-form text chart, organization chart,* and *simple list text chart*.

text editor In computer programming, a program designed for creating, editing, and storing object code. A text editor resembles a word processing program but contains only the most primitive facilities for text formatting and printing. Because a text editor is designed for writing computer programs, it has features that make the entry and editing of words and numbers easier.

text file A file consisting of nothing but standard ASCII characters (with no control characters or higher order characters). See *ASCII, control code,* and *extended character set*.

text mode An operating mode of IBM PC-compatible video boards in which the computer displays images constructed using the built-in 256-character standard character set; synonymous with *character mode*. Because the character set includes several graphics characters, text mode can display graphic images such as boxes and lines. Also, text can be displayed in bold and reverse video.

T U V

Text mode is one of two standard modes supported by most IBM PC-compatible video systems; the other is called *graphics mode*. Text mode is significantly faster than graphics mode because the computer can rely on the built-in character set rather than construct the image bit by bit on-screen. Character-based programs such as Lotus 1-2-3 and WordPerfect are designed to function in text mode normally, and to shift into graphics mode only when graphics displays are required. See *graphics mode*.

thermal printer A non-impact printer that forms an image by moving heated styluses over specially treated paper. Although quiet and fast, thermal printers have one disadvantage: most of them require specially treated paper that has an unpleasant, waxy feel.

third-party vendor A firm that markets an accessory hardware product for a given brand of computer equipment.

thirty-two bit computer See *32-bit computer*.

thread In a computer newsgroup, a chain of postings on a single subject. Most newsgroup reader programs include a command that lets you follow the thread (that is, jump to the next message on the topic rather than display each message in sequence). See *distributed bulletin board* and *newsgroup*.

three-dimensional graph A business or scientific chart that depicts information using three axes: width (x-axis), height (y-axis), and depth (z-axis). In Microsoft Excel, the vertical axis—the one that measures the data items—is called the value (y) axis, and the horizontal axis is called the category (x) axis (see fig. T.2). The axis that shows depth—the one that seems to go "back" into the page—is the series (z) axis. 3-D graphs are very useful when you're showing more than one data series.

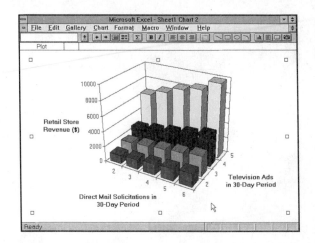

Fig. T.2 *A three-dimensional business graph.*

> **TIP:** *A three-dimensional graph can show the relationship among three values, as shown in figure T.2. This graph reveals the effectiveness of coupling television advertising with direct mail solicitation. In general, the more television advertising, the better the revenue.*

three-dimensional spreadsheet A spreadsheet program that can create a worksheet file made up of multiple stacked pages, each page resembling a separate worksheet.

Suppose that your organization has three divisions, each with its own income statement. You create four spreadsheets, one for each division, and one to summarize the quarterly income amounts. In the summary spreadsheet, you place formulas that use three-dimensional statements. Shown in the formula bar above the spreadsheet window in figure T.3, the statement in cell B4 of spreadsheet Consolidation is

```
@SUM(Northeast..Central:B4)
```

This statement says, "Sum the amounts shown in cell B4 of spreadsheets Northeast, Southeast, and Central, and place the total here."

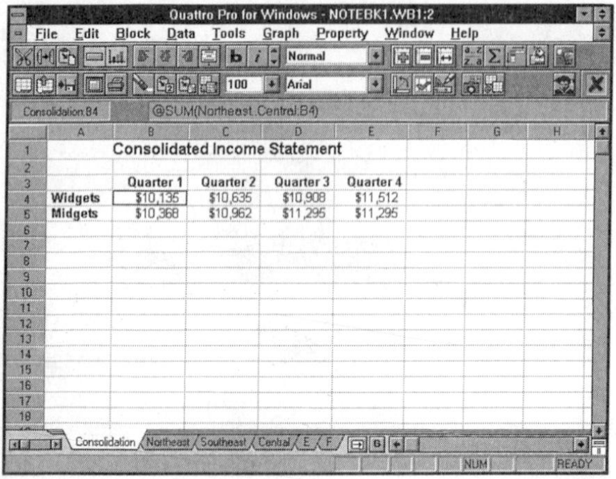

Fig. T.3 *A three-dimensional spreadsheet.*

throughput A computer's overall performance, as measured by its capability to send data through all components of the system, including data storage devices such as disk drives.

Throughput is a much more meaningful indication of system performance than some of the benchmark speeds commonly reported in computer advertising, which involve the execution of computation-intensive algorithms. A computer equipped with slow random-access memory (RAM) chips, no cache memory, or a slow hard disk may not perform as well as its processor speed would indicate. Under Windows, speed may be sluggish unless you install a graphics accelerator to speed screen updating.

TIP: *Before you make a purchasing decision based on benchmarks, find out whether the benchmark includes a full range of computer tasks. PC Magazine, for example, tests CPU instruction mix, floating-point calculation, conventional memory, DOS file access (small and large records), and BIOS disk seek. Look also for benchmarks that measure the system's performance under Windows, for which video speed is critical.*

t

thumbnails See *roughs*.

TIFF See *Tagged Image File Format (TIFF)*.

tiled windows In a user interface, a display mode in which the windows overlap each other (see fig. T.4). If you open additional windows, the others are automatically sized so that you still see all of them. See *cascading windows* and *overlaid windows*.

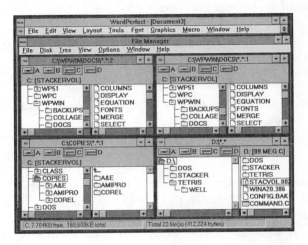

Fig. T.4 *Tiled windows in Microsoft Windows.*

timed backup A desirable application program feature that saves your work at a specified interval, such as every five minutes. Synonymous with *autosave*.

If a power outage or system crash occurs and a timed backup of your work has been performed, you'll be notified when you next start the program that a timed backup is available and asked whether you want to keep it. To prevent the destruction of hours of work, save your work at frequent intervals, and have your software perform automatic saves for you. The best word processing programs include timed backup features that let you specify the interval.

T
U
V

CAUTION: *Using a timed backup feature is no substitute for saving your work to disk at the end of a working session. The files created by timed backup utilities are temporary files that are deleted when you exit the program properly. Use timed backups, but don't forget to save your work. See* backup procedure, save, *and* tape drive.

time division multiplexing   In local area networks, a technique for transmitting two or more signals over the same cable by alternating them, one after the other. Time division multiplexing is used in baseband (digital) networks. See *baseband, frequency division multiplexing, local area network (LAN),* and *multiplexing.*

time out   An interruption, resulting in a frozen keyboard, while the computer tries to access a device (or a remote computer) that isn't responding as it should. The computer keeps trying for a predetermined time and then gives up, returning control to you.

time-sharing   A technique for sharing a multiuser computer's resources in which each user has the illusion that he or she is the only person using the system. In the largest mainframe systems, hundreds or even thousands of people can use the system simultaneously without realizing that others are doing so. At times of peak usage, however, system response time tends to decline noticeably.

title bar   In graphical user interfaces such as Microsoft Windows, a bar that stretches across the top of a window, indicating the name of the document displayed in that window. The color of the title bar indicates whether the window is active. See *graphical user interface (GUI).*

toggle   To switch back and forth between two modes or states. On the IBM PC-compatible keyboard, for example, the Caps Lock key is a toggle key. When you press the key the first time, you switch the keyboard into a caps-entry mode. When you press the key the second time, you switch the keyboard back to the normal mode, in which you must press the Shift key to type capital letters.

t

> **TIP:** *If you're shopping for an IBM PC-compatible system, look for one equipped with a keyboard that has indicator lights for the Caps Lock, Num Lock, and Scroll Lock keys. Without these lights, you may not realize that you've pressed one of these keys accidentally.*

toggle key   A key that switches back and forth between two modes. See *Caps Lock key*, *Num Lock key*, *Scroll Lock key*, and *toggle*.

token passing   In local area networks, a network protocol in which a special bit configuration, called a *token*, is circulated among the workstations. A node gains access to the network only if the node can obtain a free token. The node converts the token into a *data frame* containing a network message.

Every workstation constantly monitors the network to catch a token addressed to that workstation. When a workstation receives a token, it attaches an acknowledgment message to the data frame. When the data frame with an acknowledgment comes back to the source node, the node puts a token into circulation.

Because token passing rules out the data collisions that occur when two devices begin transmitting at the same time, this channel access method is preferred for large, high-volume networks. See *carrier sense multiple access with collision detection (CSMA/CD)*, *contention*, *local area network (LAN)*, and *polling*.

token-ring network   In local area networks, a network architecture that combines token passing with a hybrid star/ring topology.

Developed by IBM and announced in 1986, the IBM Token-Ring Network uses a Multistation Access Unit at its hub. This unit is wired with twisted-pair cable in a star configuration with up to 255 workstations, but the resulting network is actually a decentralized ring network. See *local area network (LAN)* and *token passing*.

T U V

toner   The electrically charged ink used in laser printers and photocopying machines. To form the image, toner is applied to an electrostatically charged drum and fused to the paper by a heating element. See *laser printer* and *toner cartridge*.

toner cartridge   In laser printers, a cartridge containing the electrically charged ink, called *toner*, that the printer fuses to the page. See *toner*.

➜ **TIP:** *You can save up to 50 percent of the retail cost of new toner cartridges by using recycled toner cartridges.*

toolbar   In recent applications, a bar across the top of a window containing buttons, each with a distinctive icon (see fig. T.5). These icons represent frequently accessed commands.

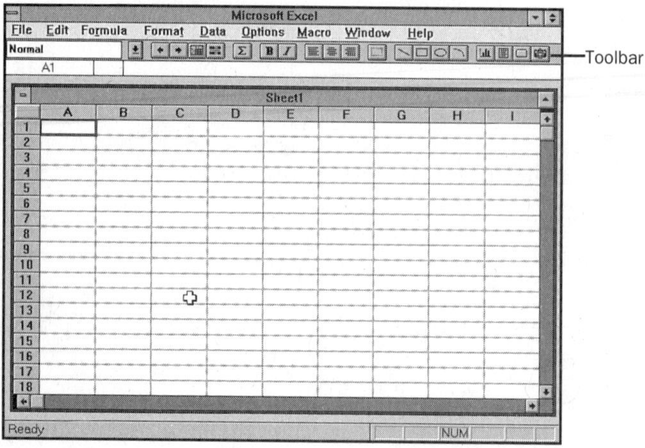

Fig. T.5   *A toolbar.*

Only Microsoft and Macintosh use the term *toolbar*. The bar of buttons with icons found in other applications may be called speedbars, SmartIcons, powerbars, and button bars. See *icon bar*.

toolbox   A set of programs that helps programmers develop software without having to create individual routines from scratch. Some software publishers call these sets developer's *toolkits*.

In programs such as drawing and presentation graphics applications, the on-screen icon bar of drawing tools is called the toolbox.

toolkit   See *toolbox*.

top-down programming   A method of program design and development in which the design process begins with a statement (in English) of the program's fundamental purpose. This purpose is broken into a set of subcategories that describe aspects of the program's anticipated functions. Each subcategory corresponds to a specific program module that can be coded independently. Structured programming languages (such as Pascal, C, and Modula-2) and object-oriented programming languages (such as C++) are especially amenable to the top-down approach. See *C, C++, Pascal,* and *structured programming*.

topology   See *network topology*.

TOPS   A file-serving program for local area networks that allows IBM PC-compatibles and Macintosh computers to be linked in an AppleTalk or EtherNet network.

File-serving software provides peer-to-peer file transfer in which each user has access to the public files located on the workstations of all other users in the network. When a TOPS user decides to make a file public, he or she publishes the file on the network. Every node on the network, therefore, is potentially a file server.

An advantage of TOPS is that, when the user of an IBM PC-compatible computer accesses a file on a Macintosh, TOPS displays the file as though it were in a directory on a DOS disk. When the user of a Macintosh computer accesses a file on an IBM PC-compatible machine, the file appears as it would on the Finder's desktop display: as an on-screen icon. See *file server*.

touch screen   See *touch-sensitive display*.

touch-sensitive display   A display technology designed with a pressure-sensitive panel mounted in front of the screen; synonymous with *touch screen*. You select options by pressing the screen at the appropriate place.

T
U
V

Hewlett-Packard championed the touch-sensitive display concept in the mid 1980s, but users disliked it. The screen quickly becomes smudged and unreadable. Touch-sensitive displays are now used for public-access information purposes in such settings as museums, supermarkets, and airports.

tower case   A computer system unit case designed to stand vertically on the floor rather than sit horizontally on a desk. Tower cases usually have much more room for accessories than desktop cases and permit you to move noisy components, including cooling fans and hard disks, away from the immediate work area. They're inconvenient, however, if you must frequently insert floppy disks into your system.

A major advantage of a tower case is that, with the case on the floor, the monitor is on the desk, at or just below eye level. This location lets you hold your head and neck in a natural position while you work.

tpi   See *tracks per inch (tpi)*.

track   On a floppy or hard disk, one of many concentric rings that are encoded on the disk during the low-level format and that define distinct areas of data storage on the disk. See *cluster* and *sector*.

trackball   An input device, designed to replace the mouse, that moves the mouse pointer on-screen as you use your thumb or fingers to rotate a ball embedded in the keyboard or in a case near the keyboard. Unlike a mouse, a trackball doesn't require a flat, clean surface to operate; as a result, trackballs are often used with portable or notebook computers. See *built-in pointing device, clip-on pointing device, freestanding pointing device, mouse,* and *snap-on pointing device*.

CAUTION: *If you're shopping for a laptop or notebook computer, watch out for keyboard arrangements that place the trackball in an extra-wide area below the space bar. This space provides a convenient and inviting area to rest your hands while you type, a practice that may eventually lead to repetitive stress injury.*

t

tracks per inch (tpi)   A measurement of the data-storage density of magnetic disks, such as floppy disks. The greater the tpi, the more data the disk can hold. In DOS, double-density 5 1/4-inch disks are formatted with 48 tpi, and high-density 5 1/4-inch disks are formatted with 96 tpi. High-density 3 1/2-inch disks are formatted with 135 tpi.

tractor feed   A printer paper-feed mechanism in which continuous (fan-fold) paper is pulled (or pushed) into and through the printer by using a sprocket wheel. The sprockets fit into pre-punched holes on the left and right edges of the paper. Dot-matrix printers normally come with tractor-feed mechanisms.

A disadvantage of tractor-feed mechanisms is that when printing is complete, you must tear off the sides of the paper and separate the sheets. For a long document, this job can become tedious, and you can easily tear a page by accident.

traffic   The volume of messages sent over a communications network.

transactional application   In a local area network, a program that creates and maintains a master record of all the transactions in which network participants engage, such as filling out invoices or time-billing forms. If a system crash results in the loss of data, this record can be used to restore data files to an earlier state. See *non-transactional application.*

transceiver   In wireless wide-area networks, a modem that can send and receive computer data via radio frequencies. See *personal digital assistant (PDA)* and *wireless wide area network.*

Transfer Control Protocol/Internet Protocol (TCP/IP)
The set of standards (protocols) for data transmission and error correction that allows the transfer of data from one Internet-linked computer to another. See *Internet.*

T U V

transfer rate   The number of bytes of data that can be transferred per second from a disk to the microprocessor, after the drive head reaches the place where the data is located.

The maximum transfer rate is limited by how fast the disk rotates and the density of the data on the disk (or how fast data passes under the drive head). These inflexible hardware limitations can be overcome by caching disk information. See *access time, Enhanced System Device Interface (ESDI), hardware cache,* and *Small Computer System Interface (SCSI).*

transient   See *power surge.*

transient command   See *external command.*

translate   To convert a data file from one file format to another, or to convert a program from one programming language or operating system to another. See *file format.*

transparent   In computing, a computer operation or entity that programmers have made invisible so that you don't have to deal with it.

A transparent computer function is present, but you can't see it; a virtual computer function *isn't* present, but you *can* see it. Microsoft Word, for example, inserts formatting codes in your document, but they're transparent—you see only your formatted text. A RAM disk drive, in contrast, isn't a disk drive at all; it's just part of your computer's memory, set aside to act like a disk drive. See *virtual.*

transpose   To change the order in which characters, words, or sentences are displayed. Some word processing programs include commands that transpose text. These commands are useful when characters, words, or sentences are in the wrong order.

trapping   See *error trapping.*

tree structure   A way of organizing information into a hierarchical structure with a root and branches, much like a family tree or genealogy chart. See *directory* and *subdirectory.*

Trojan horse   A computer program that appears to perform a valid function but contains, hidden in its code, instructions that cause damage (sometimes severe) to the systems on which it runs.

A spectacular Trojan horse made headlines in late 1989. More than 10,000 copies of a computer disk purportedly containing information about AIDS were mailed from a prestigious London address to corporations, insurance companies, and health professionals throughout Europe and North America. Recipients who loaded the disks into their computers, however, quickly found that the software was a particularly vicious Trojan horse that completely wiped out the data on hard disks.

Trojan horses, unlike computer viruses, can't replicate themselves, but that may be small consolation indeed to someone who has just lost days or weeks of work. See *virus*.

troubleshooting   The process of determining why a computer system or specific hardware device is malfunctioning.

CAUTION: *If you're using utilities that keep information about your hard disk and CMOS data—such as Mirror, which is available with DOS 5.0 and PC Tools—read the manual's instructions on restoring disk information before you do anything else. Many users automatically reboot the system whenever there is a problem. Rebooting may overwrite the very data you need to solve the problem. Always have a floppy disk formatted as a system disk readily available so that it can be used if you need to reboot the system.*

When a computer fails, most people panic and assume that a huge bill is on the way. Most likely, however, the problem is a minor one, such as a loose connection. Turn off the power and carefully inspect all the cables and connections. Remove the computer's lid and press down on the adapter boards to make sure that they're well seated in the expansion slots. You also should check connections at peripheral devices.

True BASIC   A modern, structured version of the BASIC programming language developed by its originators, John Kemeny and Thomas Kurtz, in response to criticism of earlier versions of BASIC.

With modern control structures and optional line numbers, True BASIC is a well-structured language used to teach the principles of structured programming. The language, which is interpreted rather than compiled, isn't frequently used for professional programming purposes.

TrueType　A font technology, included with Apple Computer's System 7 and Microsoft Windows 3.1, that brings scalable fonts to the screens and printers of Macintosh and Windows systems. Jointly developed by Apple Computer and Microsoft Corporation, TrueType offers a cost-effective alternative to PostScript font technology. TrueType doesn't require an add-on utility program or an expensive, microprocessor-driven interpreter.

The TrueType fonts you see on-screen are exactly the same as the ones you see when you print your document. Furthermore, TrueType fonts are scalable, which means (in brief) that no matter what font size you choose, you'll see that exact font size choice on-screen.

With TrueType, you can print your documents on other systems or printers without going through the hassle of reformatting the fonts. Even programs such as WordPerfect 6.0 for DOS now can use the TrueType fonts stored in the Windows SYSTEM subdirectory. See *Microsoft Windows*, *scalable font*, and *System 7*.

truncate　To cut off part of a number or character string.

truncation error　A rounding error that occurs when part of a number is omitted from storage because it exceeds the capacity of the memory set aside for number storage. See *floating-point calculation*.

TSR　See *terminate-and-stay-resident (TSR) program*.

TTY　See *teletype (TTY) display*.

Turbo Pascal　A high-performance compiler developed by Borland International for Pascal. The compiler comes with a full-screen text editor. Outperforming compilers that cost 10 times as much, Turbo Pascal took the world of DOS programming by storm when released in 1984 and is now one of the most popular compilers ever written.

t

Turbo Pascal creates executable programs (object code). If an error is encountered during program compilation, the editor returns on-screen and the cursor points to the error's location. Turbo Pascal is used in hobby and academic environments, and some professional programmers use Turbo Pascal to prepare short- to medium-sized programs. See *interpreter*.

turnkey system   A computer system developed for a specific application, such as a point-of-sale terminal, and delivered ready to run, with all the necessary application programs and peripherals.

tutorial   A form of instruction in which the student is guided step-by-step through the application of a program to a specific task, such as developing a budget or writing a business letter. Some programs come with on-screen tutorials that use computer-based training techniques.

tweak   To alter an underlying variable slightly so that the computer output is more in line with what is expected.

The first tweak occurred before a national television audience. In 1952, CBS election coverage featured Remington-Rand's UNIVAC computer to predict the outcome of the election based on initial returns. With only 8 percent of the votes tallied, UNIVAC had completed its analysis and made its prediction that Dwight D. Eisenhower would wallop Adlai E. Stevenson in an electoral college landslide, bagging 438 electoral votes to Stevenson's 93.

The problem was that the prediction was too far out of line with the Gallup poll, which showed Eisenhower and Stevenson in a dead heat. To avoid risking UNIVAC's reputation by going public with a wildly inaccurate prediction, UNIVAC programmers tweaked the program to try to make the results "look right." Even after tweaking the numbers, UNIVAC still predicted a big Eisenhower victory, and finally the UNIVAC team became convinced that Eisenhower would win. Eisenhower eventually won 442 votes, very much in line with UNIVAC's original prediction. See *spreadsheet program*.

twisted-pair cable   In local area networks, a low-bandwidth connecting cable used in telephone systems. The cable includes two insulated wires wrapped around each other to minimize interference from other wires.

T U V

Type 1 font A PostScript-compatible font that includes Adobe Systems' proprietary font-scaling technology, which improves type legibility at low resolutions and small type sizes. See *PostScript font*.

typeface The distinctive design of a set of type, distinguished from its weight (such as bold), posture (such as italic), and size.

Today's typefaces stem from the columns of ancient Rome, the workshops of Gutenberg and Garamond, and the ultra-modern design philosophy of the Bauhaus school in 20th-century Germany. Many laser printers come with as many as a dozen or more typefaces available in the printer's ROM, and literally hundreds more can be downloaded.

Notice that professional graphic artists rarely use more than two typefaces in one document. Choose one typeface for display type and a second for body type. See *body type*, *display type*, *font*, and *font family*.

typeover See *overtype mode*.

typeover mode See *overtype mode*.

typesetter See *imagesetter*.

typesetting The production of camera-ready copy on a high-end typesetting machine such as a Linotronic or Varityper.

The current crop of office-quality PostScript laser printers can produce 300-dots-per-inch (dpi) output, which is considered crude by professional typesetting standards, but which may be acceptable for applications such as newsletters, textbooks, instructional manuals, brochures, and proposals. See *resolution*.

type size The size of a font, measured in points (approximately 1/72 inch) from the top of the tallest ascender to the bottom of the lowest descender. See *ascender*, *descender*, and *pitch*.

type style The weight (such as bold) or posture (such as italic) of a font—distinguished from a font's typeface design and type size. See *attribute* and *emphasis*.

typography The science and art of designing aesthetically pleasing and readable typefaces.

UART   See *Universal Asynchronous Receiver/Transmitter (UART)*.

ultra-large scale integration (ULSI)   In integrated circuit technology, the fabrication of a chip containing more than 1 million transistors. The Intel Pentium chip, for example, includes more than 3 million transistors.

undelete utility   A utility program that can restore a file that was accidentally deleted from a disk.

Available from commercial and shareware sources, undelete utilities work because files aren't actually erased from disk drives; DOS changes the first letter of the file's name in the directory list to a non-displaying character. This makes the clusters used by the file available to the operating system for additional write operations. If such operations occur, the file can be erased irretrievably.

CAUTION: *If you've just deleted a file accidentally,* stop! *Use the undelete utility immediately. The UNDELETE command available with DOS beginning with Version 5.0 will do the job for you.*

undo   A program command that restores the program and your data to the stage they were in just before the last command was given or the last action was initiated. Undo commands let you reverse the often catastrophic effects of giving the wrong command.

unformatted text file   See *plain text document*.

unformat utility   A utility program that can restore the data on an inadvertently formatted disk. If the disk has been formatted using a safe-format technique, the data is restored quickly. If the disk hasn't been safe formatted, you can recover the data if you've been using the Mirror utility, provided with DOS beginning with Version 5.0 and with PC Tools. See *safe format*.

uninterruptible power supply (UPS)   A battery that can supply continuous power to a computer system in the event of a power failure. The battery, charged while your computer is switched on, kicks in if the power fails and provides power for 10 minutes or more, during which time you can shut down the computer to preserve the integrity of crucial data.

➡ **TIP:** *An uninterruptible power supply is mandatory equipment if a sudden power outage will result in the loss of crucial data.*

Universal Asynchronous Receiver/Transmitter (UART)
An integrated circuit that transforms the parallel data stream within the computer to the serial, one-after-the-other data stream used in asynchronous communications.

Serial communication requires, in addition to the UART, a serial port and modem. See *asynchronous communication, modem, motherboard,* and *serial port.*

UNIX   `*yoo-nicks*   An operating system used on a wide variety of computers, from mainframes to personal computers, that supports multitasking and is ideally suited to multiuser applications.

UNIX is written in the highly portable programming language C and, like C, was the product of work at AT&T Bell Laboratories. UNIX is a comprehensive programming environment that expresses a unique programming philosophy. With more than 200 commands, inadequate error messages, and a cryptic command syntax, however, UNIX imposes heavy burdens on occasional users and the technically unsophisticated. With the development of UNIX shells, the operating system may play a much wider role in computing.

When the user is insulated from the peculiarities of UNIX, the operating system's other advantages quickly become apparent. UNIX was designed as a multiuser system and, with its multitasking capabilities, UNIX also can perform more than one function at a time. If the future of personal computing lies in linking workstations to corporate minicomputers and mainframes, UNIX operating systems, particularly when equipped with a shell such as NeXTStep, stand a chance of displacing DOS and even OS/2.

u

NeXTStep, a UNIX shell for the NeXT workstation, is as easy to use and as versatile as DOS and OS/2. NeXTStep also includes an application program interface (API) that handles virtually all screen routines, freeing programmers from the tedious programming required to generate screen images from within an application program. NeXTStep is available for IBM PC-compatible computers as NextStep for Intel Processors 3.1. Major computer retailers offer it on selected 486 and Pentium systems. Unfortunately, NeXTStep is expensive ($795 compared to $200 or less for DOS and Windows), has few applications written for it, and isn't gaining much ground yet.

Because Bell Laboratories was prohibited from marketing UNIX by the antitrust regulations then governing AT&T, UNIX was provided without charge to colleges and universities throughout North America, beginning in 1976. In 1979, the University of California at Berkeley developed a version of UNIX for VAX computers. Much preferred in technical and engineering environments, Berkeley UNIX led to other versions that were made available commercially. In the early 1980s, AT&T gained the right to market the system and released System V in 1983.

With System V, AT&T established a set of UNIX standards called System V Interface Definition (SVID), standards toward which most UNIX systems are migrating, and which major corporate purchasers are requiring. IBM adopted the SVID standard for its own versions of UNIX. See *anonymous FTP, archie, Berkeley UNIX, shell, System V Interface Definition (SVID), Wide Area Information Server (WAIS),* and *World-Wide Web (WWW).*

UNIX-to-UNIX Copy Protocol   See *UUCP.*

unmoderated newsgroup   In a distributed computer bulletin board system such as EchoMail (FidoNet) or USENET (Internet), a topical discussion group in which postings aren't subject to review before distribution. Unmoderated newsgroups are characterized by spontaneity, but some postings don't adhere to the group's stated discussion topic, and flame wars may erupt. See *distributed bulletin board, Fidonet, flame war, Internet, moderated newsgroup, newsgroup,* and *USENET.*

T
U
V

unrecoverable application error (UAE)   In Microsoft Windows, a system crash that results from one program invading another program's memory space, thus wiping out part of the other program's code. UAEs were common in Microsoft Windows 3.0. Subsequent versions are more stable, but not crash-free, so remember to save your work frequently.

update   In database management, a fundamental data manipulation that involves adding, modifying, or deleting data records so that data is brought up-to-date.

upgrade   To buy a new release or version of a program, or a more recent or more powerful version of a computer or peripheral.

upload   To send a file by telecommunications to another computer user or a bulletin board.

upper memory area   In an IBM-compatible computer running MS-DOS, the memory between the 640K limit of conventional memory and 1024K. In the original PC system design, some of the memory in this area was reserved for system use, but most was actually unused. Memory management programs, as well as HIMEM.SYS, available with MS-DOS 6.2, can configure the upper memory area so that it's available for system utilities and application programs. See *conventional memory*, *HIMEM.SYS*, and *Microsoft Windows*.

UPS   See *uninterruptible power supply (UPS)*.

upward compatibility   Software that functions, without modification, on later or more powerful versions of a computer system.

USENET   The leading distributed bulletin board system, widely available on UNIX-based computer systems, and linked through the Internet and other computer networks. Offering more than 1,500 newsgroups, USENET is accessed daily by more than 15 million people in more than 100 countries.

u

Within USENET is a discussion group on every conceivable topic—and some you haven't thought of. Each discussion group focuses on a particular subject, such as sports cars, firearms, U.S. history, model aircraft, politics, or jazz. Well-represented subjects are hobbies, politics, scientific disciplines, and topics of current public debate.

Within a group, you read messages from people on the general subject area, such as an opinion of a film the individual has seen. You can reply in two ways: directly to the person (a *reply*), or to the group as a whole (a *follow-on post*). If you want to see additional posts on the same subject, you issue a command that follows the *thread*, which skips to the next message that contains someone else's reply to the message you just read.

USENET generates enough text daily to fill about 18 paperback books. With so much diversity of opinion feeding into this massive system, you can rest assured that reading USENET will be a *very* interesting experience. Another reason for its popularity is its wacky, anything-goes democracy. Most USENET discussion groups are unmoderated, meaning that anyone can post anything. The result? Spontaneity—which sometimes goes over the edge. That's one reason USENET discussions sometimes degenerate into *flame wars*, controversies in which the various parties resort to nasty language to get their points across.

The following is a sample of USENET newsgroups:

- `alt.alien.visitors` Unidentified flying objects, saucer watches, contact of prehistoric civilizations with alien intruders, tales of UFO abductions, secret government UFO files retrieved from top-secret computers by hackers, technical description of an alien warp drive engine under study at a secret Air Force base, disturbing reports of phantom helicopters.

- `alt.rush-limbaugh` Transcriptions of broadcasts, commentary, and debate on points raised by Mr. Limbaugh, such as whether the death of White House aide Vince Foster has anything to do with President and Mrs. Clinton's alleged involvement in the Whitewater affair.

T U V

- `clari.news.disasters` UPI news reports (the same ones the newspapers get) computer-sorted by topic on disasters of all kinds: tornadoes, hurricanes, earthquakes, typhoons, elevators dropping like stones, 50-gallon water heaters exploding and bursting through the roof "like a rocket," plane crashes, Autobahn pile-ups, the works.

- `rec.arts.drwho` Episode titles and summaries, endless discussions of plot loopholes and blunders, parodies, and occasional notes on related subjects, such as Sinbad movies and trivia regarding the sinking of the Titanic.

See *distributed bulletin board, Internet, moderated newsgroup, and newsgroup.*

user   See *end user.*

user default   A user-defined program operating preference, such as the default margins for every new document that a word processing program creates. Also called *preferences, options,* or *setup* in various applications.

user group   A voluntary association of users of a specific computer or program who meet regularly to exchange tips and techniques, hear presentations by computer experts, and obtain public domain software and shareware.

user interface   All the features of a program or computer that govern the way people interact with the computer. See *command-driven program* and *graphical user interface (GUI).*

user-defined   Selected or chosen by the user of the computer system.

user-friendly   A program or computer system designed so that individuals who lack extensive computer experience or training can use the system without becoming confused or frustrated.

A user-friendly program usually includes the following elements: menus are used instead of commands you have to memorize; on-screen help is available at the touch of a key; keyboard program functions are arranged in logical order and follow established conventions; error messages contain an explanation of what went wrong and what to do to solve the problem; intermediate and advanced features are hidden from view so that they don't clutter the screen and confuse beginners; commands that erase or destroy data display confirmation messages that warn you of the command's drastic consequences and provide a way to escape without initiating that operation; and clear, concise documentation that provides tutorials and reference information.

> **TIP:** *Inexperienced users should be assured that user-friendly doesn't guarantee success. Don't give up too soon, learn to read the documentation, and expect to be challenged—even frustrated— from time to time no matter how experienced you become.*

utility program   A program that assists you in maintaining and improving the efficiency of a computer system.

MS-DOS provides many external commands, including utilities such as BACKUP and RESTORE, and utilities to perform tasks such as file compression, defragmentation, shells, undelete, and virus checking. Because DOS can be difficult to use, many users buy utilities more user-friendly than existing DOS utilities. See *shell.*

UUCP   Acronym for *UNIX-to-UNIX Copy Protocol,* an early transfer protocol for UNIX machines that required having one machine call the other one on the phone.

Also, an international, cooperative wide area network that links thousands of UNIX computers. UUCP has electronic mail gateways to BITNET and the Internet. See *BITNET* and *Internet.*

uudecode   *yoo-yoo-dee-code*   A program that converts a file created by the uuencode program into a binary file so you can retrieve the file in the program that was used to create the file. See *binary file* and *uuencode.*

**T
U
V**

V.21, V.22, V.22bis, etc. See *CCITT protocol*.

vaccine A computer program designed to offer protection against computer viruses. By adding a small amount of code to files, an alert sounds when a virus tries to change the file. Vaccines are also called *immunizing programs*. See *antivirus program* and *virus*.

 CAUTION: *The malevolent authors of computer viruses are aware of vaccines and antivirus programs and are busy creating new viruses to thwart them. If you use your computer for vital business or professional applications, protect your data by introducing to your computer only fresh, previously unopened copies of software obtained directly from computer software publishers.*

value In a spreadsheet program, a numeric cell entry.

Two kinds of values exist. The first kind, called a *constant*, is a value you type directly into a cell. The second kind of value looks like a constant but is produced by a formula placed into a cell.

On-screen, the values you enter directly (constants) and the values produced by formulas look alike. Be careful that you don't destroy a spreadsheet by typing a constant on top of a formula. Before changing a number you see on-screen, be sure to check the cell contents in the entry line in the control panel to find out whether a formula is in the cell. See *cell protection* and *label*.

value-added reseller (VAR) A business that repackages and improves hardware manufactured by an original equipment manufacturer (OEM). A value-added reseller typically improves the original equipment by adding superior documentation, packaging, system integration, and exterior finish. Some VARs, however, do little more than put their name on a device. See *original equipment manufacturer (OEM)*.

vanilla   Plain and unadorned, without bells, whistles, or advanced features; "I'm using a plain vanilla 386." See *bells and whistles*.

vaporware   A program that's heavily marketed even though it's still under development, and no one knows whether its development problems will be solved.

The most celebrated vaporware fiasco was Ovation, an integrated program like Symphony and Framework that received a great deal of press attention in 1984. The developer, however, couldn't overcome development problems, and the program was never released.

variable   In computer programming, a named area in memory that stores a value or string assigned to that variable.

VBA   See *Visual Basic for Applications (VBA)*.

VDT   Abbreviation for *video display terminal*. Synonymous with *monitor*. See *cathode ray tube (CRT)* and *monitor*.

VDT radiation   See *cathode ray tube (CRT)* and *extremely low-frequency (ELF) emission*.

VDU   Abbreviation for *video display unit*. Synonymous with *monitor*.

vector font   See *outline font*.

vector graphics   See *object-oriented graphic*.

vector-to-raster conversion   A utility available with many professional illustration programs, such as CorelDRAW!, that transforms object-oriented (vector) graphics into bit-mapped (raster) graphic images. See *bit-mapped graphic* and *object-oriented graphic*.

vendor   A seller or supplier of computers, peripherals, or computer-related services.

Vendor Independent Messaging (VIM)   In electronic mail programs, an application program interface (API) that provides access to messaging services for developers.

may not support the standard. See *Color Graphics Adapter (CGA)*, *Enhanced Graphics Adapter (EGA)*, *Extended Graphics Array (XGA)*, *Hercules Graphics Adapter*, *MultiColor Graphics Array (MCGA)*, *Super VGA*, and *Video Graphics Array (VGA)*.

videotext   The transmission of information—such as news headlines, stock quotes, and current movie reviews—through a cable television system. See *on-line information service*.

view   In database management programs, an on-screen display of the information in a database that meets the criteria specified in a query. With most database management programs, you can save views; the best programs update each view every time you add or edit records.

Also, to display an image on-screen from a different perspective, particularly with 3-D CAD drawings.

VIM   See *Vendor Independent Messaging (VIM)*.

virtual   Not real; a computer representation of something that's real.

virtual community   A group of people who, although they may have never met, share interests and concerns and communicate with each other via electronic mail and newsgroups. The people who see themselves as members of such communities feel a sense of belonging and develop deep emotional ties with other participants, even though the relationships that develop are mediated by the computer and may never involve face-to-face interaction. See *delurk*, *electronic mail*, and *newsgroup*.

virtual device   The simulation of a computer device or peripheral, such as a hard disk drive or printer, that doesn't exist.

In a local area network, a computer may appear to have an enormous hard disk, which actually is made available to the workstation by means of the network links to the file server. See *file server*, *local area network (LAN)*, and *workstation*.

virtual machine   In 80386 and higher processors, a protected memory space created by the processor's hardware capabilities.

T
U
V

Each virtual machine can run its own programs, completely isolated from other machines. The virtual machines can also access the keyboard, printers, and other devices without conflicts.

Virtual machines are made possible by a computer with the necessary processing circuitry and a lot of random-access memory (RAM). The microprocessors, for example, can run two or more virtual DOS machines, each of which can run MS-DOS programs concurrently in their own 640K memory space. Memory management software that supports multitasking, such as Microsoft Windows, is all that's necessary to run more than one standard software package. See *Virtual 8086 mode*.

Virtual 8086 mode   A mode available with 80386 and higher processors, where the chip simulates an almost unlimited number of 8086 machines.

virtual memory   A method of extending the apparent size of a computer's random-access memory (RAM) by using part of the hard disk as an extension of RAM.

Many application programs, such as Microsoft Word for DOS, routinely use the disk instead of memory to store some data or program instructions while you're running the program. Beginning with the Intel 80286 processor, virtual memory is implemented at the operating system level so that it's available to any and all programs. See *virtual memory management*.

virtual memory management   The management of virtual memory operations at the operating system level rather than the application level.

Many personal computer programs use virtual memory. When the computer doesn't have enough memory to store all the program instructions and data, the program automatically creates a *swap file* (a temporary file) and stores the data or instructions on disk.

However, a significant advantage to implementing virtual memory at the operating system level rather than the application level is that any program can take advantage of the virtual memory, with the result that memory extends seamlessly from RAM to the computer's secondary storage. To take advantage of virtual memory at the operating system level, however, the computer must be equipped with a microprocessor that can extend memory addresses into secondary memory in this way. The Intel 8088 and 8086 microprocessors lack this capability, but the 80286, 80386, and 80486 microprocessors have it. In 386 Enhanced mode, Microsoft Windows can take full advantage of the virtual memory capabilities of these microprocessors. In the Macintosh world, Apple's System 7 makes virtual memory management available for users of 68030-based Macintoshes. See *386 Enhanced mode, Microsoft Windows, permanent swap file, swap file,* and *temporary swap file.*

➔ **TIP:** *To implement virtual memory with Microsoft Windows, set up a permanent swap file.*

virtual reality   A computer system that can immerse the user in the illusion of a computer-generated world and of permitting the user to navigate through this world at will. The user wears a head-mounted display (HMD) that displays a stereoscopic image, and wears a sensor glove, which permits the user to manipulate "objects" in the virtual environment.

Virtual reality (VR) systems derive from flight simulators but go far beyond them to immerse the user in a computer-generated world. The range of potential applications includes architecture, for example, where VR systems will allow architects to present clients with three-dimensional VR "walkthroughs" of proposed structures; and physicians will be able to try out new surgical techniques within three-dimensional, simulated "patients."

VR quickly caught the public's imagination, aided by images of the dreadlocked VR researcher Jaron Lanier of VPL Research, Inc.; Grateful Dead guitarist Jerry Garcia's description of VR as "electronic LSD"; and the linkage of VR-generated "worlds" with the popular *cyberspace* genre of science fiction. Lurid depictions of VR-based sex and *teledildonics* (sex with a distant person mediated by modem-linked VR devices) helped fuel public interest. The most promising VR applications, however, are found in unglamorous fields such as firefighting and radiation therapy.

VR's greatest commercial potential undoubtedly lies in the entertainment area. An example: NEC Corporation is demonstrating a "virtual skiing lab," in which virtual skiers don goggles, poles, and virtual

T
U
V

skis. The lab's software simulates slopes worldwide. A virtual skiing salon is slated to open in Tokyo and other cities. A major benefit: the only thing you can break is the credit limit on your MasterCard. See *cyberspace, electrocutaneous feedback, head-mounted display (HMD), second-person virtual reality, sensor glove, stereoscopy, teledildonics,* and *telepresence.*

virus   A computer program, designed as a prank or as sabotage, that replicates itself by attaching to other programs and carrying out unwanted and sometimes damaging operations.

When a virus infects a disk, it replicates itself by attaching to other programs in the system, including system software. Like a human virus, the effects of a computer virus may not be detectable for a period of days or weeks, during which time every disk inserted into the system comes away with a hidden copy of the virus. When they appear, the effects vary, ranging from prank messages to erratic system software performance or catastrophic erasure of all the information on a hard disk. Don't ever assume that a prank message means that's all the virus will do. See *antivirus program, Trojan horse,* and *vaccine.*

TIP: *To protect your system from computer viruses, observe the following rules:*

- *Don't download executable programs from public bulletin boards unless you're certain they're virus free (you actually have seen someone else use the program without problems).*

- *Don't obtain executable programs from mail-order vendors of public domain or shareware programs unless they specifically promise to check each program they sell.*

- *Never download a recently uploaded program on a bulletin board until the sysop has checked it. When you do download the program, download it to a dual-floppy system so that the program can't get near your hard disk.*

- *Don't copy pirated disks of commercial programs, because these disks may contain viruses.*

- *Buy and use virus-checking software.*

V

> • *Install a memory-resident virus-checking program, such as*
> *PC Tools VSafe, which will examine files as you copy them*
> *onto your computer.*

Visual Basic   A high-level programming language for developing applications designed to run in Microsoft Windows.

Using Visual Basic, the programmer uses a screen designer to set up the contents of a window, selecting control objects (buttons, list boxes, etc.) from an on-screen toolbox and placing them in your design. You then write procedures for the objects using a modern version of BASIC.

Visual Basic uses event-driven programming. Procedures are run when you choose a button or other object. If you want to create a custom object, you must do so using C.

Visual Basic 3.0 includes OLE 2.0 support and the Access 1.1 database engine, which makes it easy for you to write a graphical user interface front end for a database. After you create an application, use the Visual Basic Setup Wizard to create installation disks. See *event-driven program.*

Visual Basic for Applications (VBA)   A version of the Visual Basic programming language included with Microsoft Windows applications, such as Excel; also called *Visual Basic Programming System, Applications Edition.*

Visual Basic for Applications is used to create procedures as simple as basic macros and as complex as custom applications, complete with dialog boxes, menus, buttons, and unique commands. See *event-driven program* and *Visual Basic.*

VL-Bus   A standard for the electrical, logical, physical, and mechanical characteristics of a high-speed local bus (an expansion bus that's directly connected to the computer's central processing unit). The standard was created in 1992 by the Video Electronics Standards Association (VESA).

The VL-Bus architecture offers video performance gains of up to 600 percent compared to previous bus designs. This facilitates

T
U
V

rapid screen updating for graphics-intensive programs, such as Microsoft Windows. See *local bus*.

VLSI   See *very large scale integration (VLSI)*.

voice actuation   Computer recognition and acceptance of spoken commands as instructions to be processed. See *voice recognition*.

voice mail   In office automation, a communications system in which voice messages are transformed into digital form and stored on a computer network. When the person to whom the message is directed logs on to the system and discovers that a message is waiting, the system plays the message. Synonymous with *voice store and forward*.

voice recognition   Computer recognition of human speech and transformation of the recognized words into computer-readable digitized text or instructions.

Computers and people share an unfortunate characteristic: they talk much better than they listen. In the most advanced research systems, computers can recognize only about 100 or 200 words, and even this capability is achieved only after the speaker has trained the system to recognize his or her specific voice pattern.

Voice recognition involves some extremely complex pattern-recognition capabilities in the human brain—capabilities that aren't well understood. However, of all the available input options, given the number of people who want to use computers but are unwilling to invest the time to learn how to type, the spoken word is the one that can be used by anyone. Voice recognition is, therefore, seen by many as the input method of the future. See *natural language* and *voice synthesis*.

voice store and forward   See *voice mail*.

voice synthesis   The audible output of computer-based text in the form of synthesized speech that people can recognize and understand.

Voice synthesis is much easier to achieve than voice recognition; you can equip virtually any personal computer to read ASCII text aloud with a minimum of errors. This capability has helped many blind people gain increased access to written works not recorded on cassette tape. See *voice recognition*.

volatility   The susceptibility of a computer's random-access memory (RAM) to the complete loss of stored information if power is interrupted suddenly.

volume label   In DOS, an identifying name assigned to a disk and displayed on the first line of a directory. The name can be no longer than 11 characters and is assigned when you format the disk.

von Neumann bottleneck   *von-`noy-man*   The limitation on processing speed imposed by a computer architecture linking a single processing unit with memory.

This architecture is the product of John von Neumann's discovery of the stored program concept, but its limitations are now apparent. You can create very fast central processing units (CPU) and huge, fast memories, but a seemingly inescapable limitation has emerged: the processor is going to spend more time fetching instructions and data than actually processing the data.

One proposed solution to the von Neumann bottleneck is *parallel processing*, in which a program's tasks are divided among two or more CPUs. Existing programming languages and techniques, however, can't handle parallel processing very well, and new languages that can handle parallel processing involve the programmer in the nitty-gritty procedural details of allocating tasks to the processors.

The design of the Pentium microprocessor helps lessen this limitation. The Pentium chip includes two 8K caches within the chip, one for data and the other for instructions. The instruction cache feeds data to an instruction pipeline that speeds the data on its way to processing. The result is a high probability that the instruction the CPU needs next will be delivered at optimum speed.

VR   See *virtual reality*.

VRAM   See *video RAM (VRAM)*.

Vulcan nerve pinch   A poorly conceived keyboard command that requires the user to contort the hands in an uncomfortable way.

T U V

WAIS   See *Wide Area Information Server (WAIS)*.

wait state   A microprocessor clock cycle in which nothing occurs. A wait state is programmed into a computer system to allow other components, such as random-access memory (RAM), to catch up with the central processing unit (CPU). The number of wait states depends on the speed of the processor in relation to the speed of memory.

Microprocessor speed is expressed in megahertz, and memory chips are rated in nanoseconds (ns). At a processor speed of 1 MHz, a clock cycle is 1,000 ns; at 16 MHz, the clock cycle is 62.5 ns; at 25 MHz, 40 ns. Dynamic random-access memory (DRAM) chips rated at 60 ns are considered fast. A 16-MHz processor is slow by today's standards and isn't even available for 486 systems.

Also, the cycle time for memory chips (how fast two back-to-back accesses can be made) is two to three times the access time, so 60 ns chips are actually performing at 120-180 ns. Wait states, therefore, are programmed into the machine to rule out the serious errors that can occur if DRAM doesn't respond to the microprocessor fast enough.

Wait states can be eliminated—resulting in a "zero wait state" machine—by using fast (but expensive) cache memory, interleaved memory, page-mode RAM, or static RAM chips. See *cache memory, central processing unit (CPU), interleaved memory*, and *random-access memory (RAM)*.

wallpaper   See *desktop pattern*.

warm boot   A system restart performed after the system has been powered and operating; a restart is the electronic equivalent of turning on the system, because it clears the memory and reloads the operating system, but the hard drive doesn't stop and start.

A warm boot is preferable to a cold start because a warm boot places less strain on your system's electrical and electronic components.

With IBM PC-compatible computers, press Ctrl+Alt+Del to restart the system, although this method doesn't always unlock the system. You also can perform a warm boot by pressing the reset button, or on older Macintosh computers by pressing the programmer's switch. Newer Macintoshes have a Restart button on the keyboard. See *cold boot*, *programmer's switch*, and *reset button.*

warm link   In object linking and embedding (OLE) and dynamic data exchange (DDE), a dynamic link that's updated only when you explicitly request the update by choosing an update link command. Warm links have also been available in Lotus 1-2-3 since Release 2.2 and in Quattro Pro since Version 1.0. See *hot link.*

weight   The overall lightness or darkness of a typeface design, or the gradations of lightness to darkness within a font family. A type style can be light or dark, and within a type style, you can see several gradations of weight: extra light, light, semilight, regular, medium, semibold, bold, extra bold, and ultrabold. See *book weight* and *typeface.*

Weitek coprocessors   *why-tek*   Numeric coprocessors created for computers that use the Intel 80386 or 80486 microprocessor.

These coprocessors offer faster performance than the Intel 80387 and 80487SX and are widely used for professional computer-aided design (CAD) applications. (Yes, you read correctly—a coprocessor for a chip that already has a coprocessor.) The Weitek 4167 can perform floating-point math three to five times faster than a 486 alone, if you need that type of processing power.

Unlike the Intel coprocessors, however, Weitek coprocessors can't be used by programs unless you modify the programs to use it. See *computer-aided design (CAD)*, *Intel 80287/Intel 80387/Intel 80487SX*, and *numeric coprocessor.*

well-structured programming language   A programming language that encourages programmers to create logically organized programs that are easy to read, debug, and update.

Modular programming languages encourage clear, logical code by allowing the programmer to break down the program into separate

W
X
Y
Z

modules, each of which accomplishes just one function. More recently, object-oriented programming (OOP) languages, such as SmallTalk and C++, have introduced another approach to modularity. The languages are structured by a hierarchy of objects, such as option buttons, dialog boxes, and windows. A hidden unit of programming code, called a *script*, is linked to each object. The script tells the computer what to do when the object is manipulated.

Well-structured languages are a needed alternative to their predecessors, which allowed programmers to create illogically organized programs that were almost impossible to debug or alter. See *modular programming*, *object-oriented programming language*, *spaghetti code*, and *structured programming*.

what-if analysis   In spreadsheet programs, an important form of data exploration in which you change key variables to see the effect on the results of the computation. What-if analysis provides businesspeople and professionals with an effective vehicle for exploring the effect of alternative strategies, such as "What will my profits look like if I invest another $10,000 in advertising, assuming that past trends hold true?"

what-you-see-is-what-you-get (WYSIWYG)   *whiz-zee-wig*   A design philosophy for word processing programs in which formatting commands directly affect the text on-screen, so the screen shows the appearance of the printed text. See *embedded formatting command*.

white space   The portion of the page not printed. Good page design involves the use of white space to balance the areas that receive text and graphics, and also to improve the readability of the document.

WHOIS   In Novell networks, a command that displays a list of all users now logged on the network. Also, a service that lets you look up information about Internet hosts and users.

Wide Area Information Server (WAIS)   *ways*   A UNIX-based system linked to the Internet; also, a program that permits the user to search worldwide archives for resources based on a series of key words.

Users familiar with personal computer database programs are likely to find WAIS a less-than-satisfactory search tool. You can't use the standard Boolean operators (AND, OR, and NOT) with WAIS; instead, you type a series of search terms, and the program ranks the retrieved documents according to a numerical score that equals the number of times the search words appear in the document. This method generates a list of documents that's sure to contain many "false drops" (irrelevant documents that don't really pertain to the search subject). See *anonymous FTP*, *Internet*, and *UNIX*.

wide area network   A computer network that uses high-speed, long-distance communications networks or satellites to connect computers over distances greater than those traversed by local area networks—about 2 miles. See *ARPAnet*, *Fidonet*, and *Internet*.

widow   A formatting flaw in which the last line of a paragraph appears alone at the top of a new column or page.

Most word processing and page layout programs suppress widows and orphans; better programs let you switch widow/orphan control on and off and to choose the number of lines at the beginning or end of the paragraph that you want kept together. See *orphan*.

wild card   Characters, such as asterisks and question marks, that stand for any other character that may appear in the same place.

DOS uses two wild cards: the asterisk (*), which stands for any character or characters, and the question mark (?), which stands for any single character. Note the following examples:

Wild Card	Stands For
REP*.DOC	REPORT1.DOC
	REPOS.DOC
	REPORT2.DOC
REPORT?.DOC	REPORT1.DOC
	REPORT2.DOC

Winchester drive   See *hard disk*.

W
X
Y
Z

window A rectangular, on-screen frame through which you can view a document, worksheet, database, drawing, or application.

In most programs, only one window is displayed. This window functions as a frame through which you can see your document, database, or worksheet. Some programs can display two or more parts of the same file, or even two or more different files, each in its own window.

A windowing environment carries multiple windowing even further by enabling you to run two or more applications concurrently, each in its own window. See *application program interface (API)*, *graphical user interface (GUI)*, and *Microsoft Windows*.

windowing environment An applications program interface (API) that provides the features commonly associated with a graphical user interface (such as windows, pull-down menus, on-screen fonts, and scroll bars or scroll boxes) and that makes these features available to programmers of application packages. See *application program interface (API)*, *graphical user interface (GUI)*, and *Microsoft Windows*.

Windows See *Microsoft Windows*.

Windows application An application that can run only within the Microsoft Windows windowing environment, taking full advantage of Windows' application program interface (API), its capability to display fonts and graphics on-screen, and its capability to exchange data dynamically between applications. See *non-Windows application*.

Windows Metafile Format (WMF) An object-oriented (vector) graphics file format for Microsoft Windows applications. All Windows applications that support object-oriented graphics can read graphics files saved with the WMF format. See *file format*.

wireless wide area network A radio network for computers equipped with transceivers that are used to receive (or, in two-way systems, to send and receive) electronic mail messages, news broadcasts, and files. Coverage is now limited to a few large metropolitan areas, but future satellite-based systems, which offer saturation coverage, may make wireless data communications more common. See *transceiver*.

.WMF   A file name extension indicating that the file contains a graphic saved in the Windows Metafile Format. See *Windows Metafile Format (WMF).*

word   A unit of information, composed of characters, bits or bytes, that's treated as an entity and can be stored in one location. In word processing programs, a word is defined as including the space, if any, at the end of the characters.

word processing   Using the computer to create, edit, proofread, format, and print documents.

By a wide margin, word processing is the most popular computer application and is probably responsible for the dramatic growth of the personal computer industry. The most popular word processing programs include WordPerfect and Microsoft Word.

What makes word processing so appealing is the ease with which you can change the text before you print it. With typewriters, you must type the document correctly the first time; if you accidentally omit a paragraph, you must manually retype the page on which you made the error, as well as all subsequent pages. With a word processing program, however, you merely insert the missing paragraph. Other editing operations, such as deleting words or sentences or moving text from one location in a document to another, are as easy.

> **TIP:** *A full-page display provides a better view of your document's paragraph-by-paragraph logic. Outlining utilities that are fully embedded within your document's structure can help you see and restructure your document's overall organization. Bear in mind, as you write, that the best cure for a poor sentence or paragraph is to delete the offending passage and rewrite it from scratch. As for wasting time with fonts and formatting, finish all text editing first, and then just remember to keep it simple.*

word processing program   A program that transforms a computer into a tool for creating, editing, proofreading, formatting, and printing documents. Word processing programs top the best-seller lists, and for a simple reason: of all computer applications, people have found word processing the most useful.

W
X
Y
Z

Word processing software was initially developed in two entirely different settings: the corporate word processing pool and the programmer's bench. Beginning in the late 1960s, word processing programs were developed that simulated, as far as possible, the behavior of a fine office typewriter.

Today's most popular programs—WordPerfect and Microsoft Word—stem from a different origin: the programmer's bench. Computer programmers developed totally different kinds of word processors. To write and edit programs, they created text editors that included helpful features, such as search and replace. To print documentation, they developed formatting programs, which produced paginated manuals with automatically generated tables of contents and indexes.

Early formatting programs were completely separate from the text editing program; to print the document, you had to use the text editor to go through the document and embed formatting commands, which in turn told the printer how to print the document.

So that writers could see the results of a formatting mistake on-screen before printing the document, programmers merged text editors and formatters into one program. The result was what-you-see-is-what-you-get (WYSIWYG) software, which displays the results of most formatting commands on-screen. WordStar, the first popular implementation of WYSIWYG technology for personal computers, quickly dominated the CP/M market. After the 1981 debut of the IBM Personal Computer, WordPerfect, another WYSIWYG program, quickly rose to prominence.

During the 1980s, improvements such as spelling checkers, electronic thesauruses, mail merging, and font capabilities were added. By the late 1980s, leading word processing programs were incorporating features such as the capability to wrap text around anchored graphics. With the rise of graphical user interface (GUI) systems such as the Macintosh and PCs running Microsoft Windows, programs acquired the capability to display fonts and font size choices on-screen. Today's word processing software can take on light desktop publishing duties, such as newsletter production, while still offering a writer all the necessary tools for the creation, editing, proofing, formatting, and printing of text.

word wrap   A feature of word processing programs, and other programs that include text-editing features, that wraps words down to the beginning of the next line if they go beyond the right margin.

> **CAUTION:** *If you're just getting started in word processing, remember that you shouldn't press Enter until you're ready to start a new paragraph. If you press Enter at the end of every line, you may find that changing the margins or performing editing operations is difficult after you type the text.*

workgroup   A small group of employees assigned to work together on a specific project.

Much of the work accomplished in large businesses is done in workgroups. If this work is to be done well and in a timely fashion, the workgroup needs to communicate effectively and share resources. Personal computer technology, especially when linked in a local area network (LAN), is thought to enhance workgroup productivity by giving the group additional communication channels (in the form of electronic mail), facilities for the group editing of technical documentation (such as redlining and strikeout), and shared access to a common database. See *redlining* and *strikeout*.

working model   See *crippled version*.

worksheet   In spreadsheet programs, the two-dimensional matrix of rows and columns within which you enter headings, numbers, and formulas. The worksheet resembles the ledger sheet used in accounting. Synonymous with *spreadsheet*.

worksheet window   In spreadsheet programs, the portion of the worksheet visible on-screen (see fig. W.1). With up to 8,192 rows and 256 columns, modern electronic spreadsheets are larger than a two-car garage in size. The worksheet window displays only a small portion of the total area potentially available.

W
X
Y
Z

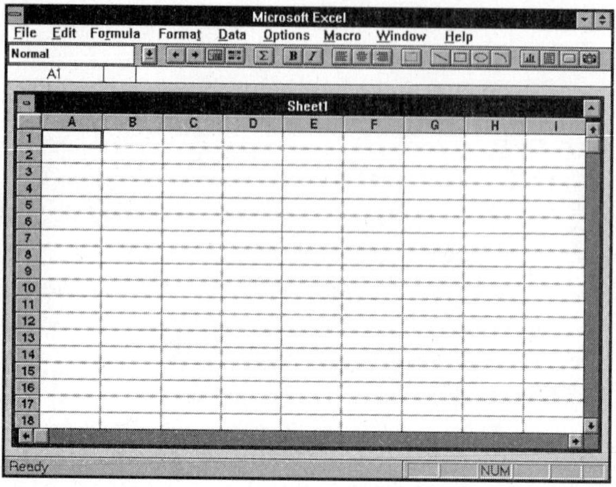

Fig. W.1 *A worksheet window.*

workstation   In a local area network, a desktop computer that
runs application programs and serves as an access point to the network. See *file server*, *personal computer*, and *professional workstation*.

World-Wide Web (WWW)   In UNIX-based machines linked
to the Internet, an experimental hypertext-based document retrieval system. Originally developed at a particle physics laboratory, WWW is constantly gaining additional information as users
contribute more indexed documents.

When you view a Web menu, you see a number of terms that are
underlined (on graphics displays) or numbered (on character displays); these are *links* that, when activated by the appropriate
command, display a related document.

TIP: *Don't expect every resource on the Internet to be accessible
through the Web. To be accessible, a document must have been
coded with links readable by Web servers, and to date, only a very
small portion of the information available on the net is accessible
in this way. You can also use anonymous FTP, Archie, and Gopher to look for Internet resources. See* anonymous FTP, Archie,
file transfer protocol (FTP), Gopher, Internet, *and* UNIX.

W

worm   A computer virus that's designed to find all data in memory or on disk and alter any data it encounters. The alteration may be to change certain characters to numbers or to swap bytes of stored memory. A few programs may still run, but usually data is irretrievably corrupted.

WORM   See *write-once, read-many (WORM)*.

wrap-around type   Type contoured so that it surrounds a graphic (see fig. W.2). Because wrap-around type is harder to read than non-contoured type, use wrap-around type sparingly.

The selected graphic showing its custom text-wrap boundary.

Dragging the graphic into place on the page.

Surrounding text automatically reflows itself around the graphic.

The final page after enlarging and repositioning the graphic.

Fig. W.2   *Text wrapped around a graphic.*

write   A fundamental processing operation in which the central processing unit (CPU) records information in the computer's random-access memory (RAM) or the computer's secondary storage media, such as disk drives. In personal computing, the term most often refers to storing information on disks.

write-back   An aspect of cache design where instructions from the CPU to write changes are held in the cache until time is available to

W
X
Y
Z

write the changes to main memory. Although this design is more complex than a write-through cache, a write-back cache is faster. See *cache* and *write-through*.

write-black engine   See *print engine*.

write head   See *read/write head*.

write-once, read-many (WORM)   An optical disk drive with storage capacities of up to 1 terabyte. After you write data to the disk, it becomes a read-only storage medium.

WORM drives can store huge amounts of information and have been touted as an excellent technology for organizations that need to publish large databases internally (such as collections of engineering drawings or technical documentation). The advent of fully read/write-capable optical disk drives, however, has greatly diminished the appeal of WORM technology. See *CD-ROM*, *erasable optical disk drive*, and *terabyte*.

write-protect   To modify a file or disk so that no one can edit or erase its data.

write-protect notch   On a 5 1/4-inch disk, a small notch cut out of the disk's protective jacket that, when covered by a piece of tape, prevents the disk drive from performing erasures or write operations to the disk.

write-protect tab   On a 3 1/2-inch disk, a tab located in the disk's upper left corner as you hold the disk with the label facing away from you. When you slide the tab up to open the hole, you've write-protected the disk.

write-through   An aspect of cache design where instructions from the CPU to write changes are pushed through the cache immediately, writing to the cache and the main memory at the same time. This design is simpler than a write-back cache, but isn't as fast. See *cache* and *write-back*.

write-white engine   See *print engine*.

WYSIWYG   See *what-you-see-is-what-you-get (WYSIWYG)*.

x-axis   In a business graph, the categories axis, which usually is the horizontal axis. See *bar graph*, *column graph*, *y-axis*, and *z-axis*.

Xbase   A generic term denoting any of the programming environments derived from the original dBASE programming language created by Ashton-Tate, Inc. Because the word dBASE is a registered trademark, the term *Xbase* has come to be used as a description for any programming language based on the dBASE programming language. Examples of the Xbase language would include FoxPro, dBASE, Clipper, Arago, and Force.

XCFN   See *external function (XCFN)*.

XCMD   See *external command (XCMD)*.

XENIX   An operating system developed by Microsoft Corporation that conforms to the UNIX System V Interface Definition (SVID) and runs on IBM PC-compatible computers. See *System V Interface Definition (SVID)* and *UNIX*.

XGA   See *Extended Graphics Array (XGA)*.

x-height   In typography, the height of a font's lowercase letters, measured from the baseline up. Because many fonts have unusually long or short ascenders and descenders, the x-height is a better measurement of the actual size of a font than the type size, measured in points. In figure X.1, for example, notice the variation in x-height in the letter *y*. See *ascender*, *baseline*, and *descender*.

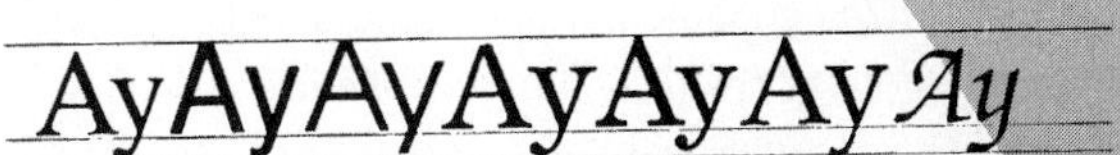

AyAyAyAyAyAy *Ay*

Fig. X.1   *Letters with the same nominal type size that have different x-heights.*

W
X
Y
Z

XMODEM   An asynchronous file-transfer protocol for personal computers that makes the error-free transmission of computer files through the telephone system easier. Developed by Ward Christiansen for 8-bit CP/M computers and placed in the public domain, the XMODEM protocol is included in all personal computer communications programs and commonly is used to download files from computer bulletin boards.

XMS   See *eXtended Memory Specification (XMS)*.

XMS memory   In computers based on the Intel 80286 and higher microprocessors, memory that a memory management program has configured as extended memory. Some DOS programs can use XMS memory to break the 640K RAM barrier. Synonymous with *extended memory*.

XON/XOFF handshaking   See *handshaking*.

X Windows   A network windowing environment commonly used on UNIX-based workstations.

Originally developed at the Massachusetts Institute of Technology and distributed freely to the academic community, X Windows is a device-independent application program interface that can run under operating systems ranging from a disk operating system to a mainframe operating system. However, it's used most frequently on UNIX machines. Unlike Microsoft Windows and other PC-based windowing environments, X Windows is designed for use on a minicomputer-based network.

Many different research labs and computer science departments have adopted and separately developed the freeware version of X Windows, with the unfortunate result that many incompatible versions of X Windows exist. As a result, a consortium of UNIX vendors joined with MIT in 1987 to establish an X Windows standard. However, application development with X Windows is a formidable undertaking. For this reason, several vendors have developed proprietary toolkits for X Windows application development, with inevitable compatibility problems. See *UNIX* and *windowing environment*.

x-y graph   See *scatter diagram*.

X

y-axis   In a business graph, the values axis, which normally is vertical. See *bar graph, column graph, x-axis,* and *z-axis.*

YMCK   Abbreviation for *yellow, magenta, cyan,* and *black.* See *color separation.*

zap   Synonymous with *erase* and *delete.*

Zapf Dingbats   A set of decorative symbols developed by Herman Zapf, a German typeface designer (see fig. Z.1). Dingbats originally were ornamental symbols used between columns or, more commonly, between paragraphs, to provide separation.

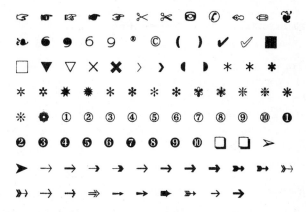

Fig. Z.1   *Zapf Dingbats.*

z-axis   In a three-dimensional graphic image, the third dimension of depth. See *three-dimensional graph, x-axis,* and *y-axis.*

zero-slot LAN   A local area network designed to use a computer's serial port rather than require the user to buy a network interface card.

CAUTION: *Zero-slot LANs are considerably slower than systems that use network interface cards, which take advantage of the computer's high-speed internal bus. Zero-slot LANs are therefore best used for applications in which network applications are limited to occasional access to an infrequently used, shared peripheral (such as a plotter) or electronic mail. See* network interface card *and* serial port.

zero wait state computer   An IBM PC-compatible computer with memory speed optimized by using a scheme such as cache memory, interleaved memory, page-mode random-access memory (RAM), or static RAM chips, so that the microprocessor doesn't have to wait for the memory to catch up with processing operations. See *cache memory, interleaved memory, page-mode RAM, static random-access memory (SRAM),* and *wait state.*

Zero Insertion Force (ZIF) socket   A chip socket design that makes removing and replacing the chip easier and safer.

It's not unusual to bend the pin of a chip when inserting it in socket. On chips such as the Intel DX2 OverDrive chip, it's difficult to straighten out a bent pin so it can be successfully inserted. Using a ZIF socket, you throw a lever and slide out the old chip, slide in the new chip with the pins and pinholes carefully aligned, and push the lever back to its original position. See *Intel DX2 OverDrive* and *Intel Pentium OverDrive.*

ZMODEM   An asynchronous file transfer protocol for personal computers that makes the error-free transmission of computer files through the telephone system easier. ZMODEM is a very fast protocol that lets you use wild-card file names for transfers. It's also well-liked because you can resume the transfer of a file if the first attempt is interrupted before completion. Next to XMODEM, ZMODEM is the most popular file transfer protocol and is included in most communications applications, with the notable exception of the Microsoft Windows Terminal accessory. See *file transfer protocol (FTP), modem,* and *XMODEM.*

zone   In a local area network (LAN), a subgroup of networked computers set aside and named by the network administrator so that these computers can be treated as a group. If an administrator sets up zones called *Marketing, Design,* and *Manufacturing,* for example, someone in manufacturing can address an electronic mail message to everyone in marketing by sending the message to the Marketing zone.

zoom   To enlarge a window or part of a document or image so that it fills the screen.

zoom box   In a graphical user interface, a box—usually positioned on the window border—that you click to zoom the window to full size or restore the window to normal size. Synonymous with *maximize button.* See *graphical user interface (GUI).*

W
X
Y
Z

Add terms to

Que's Computer User's Dictionary

Que's Computer User's Dictionary defines and describes terms of interest to the typical user of personal computers. We have tried to include all terms appropriate to a general audience, but we know that we must have missed some that you think should be in this book. Please help us improve the next edition. Write down the terms you think we should include, and send the list to

> *Que's Computer User's Dictionary*
> Que Corporation
> c/o Julia D. Ward
> 201 West 103rd St.
> Indianapolis, IN 46290

Your feedback is important to us. Thanks for your help!